Purposive Explanation in Psychology

Purposive Explanation in Psychology

Margaret A. Boden

Harvard University Press
Cambridge, Massachusetts
1972

For my mother and father and John

It is usual, among those who wish to show the impossibility of mechanical interpretation of human behaviour, to seek to reduce the assumption to absurdity by pointing to particular instances of its application; to insist, for example, that, if the assumption is accepted, we have to regard the order of sequence of all the letters that make up the text of the Bible, or of a play of Shakespeare, or of any other work of literary genius, as being in principle capable of a purely mechanical explanation, one which makes no reference to the meaning of the words or sentences; or that all the movements by which the artist produces a beautiful painting or sculpture are mechanically determined, and that the appreciation of the beautiful plays no part in the control of them. And this should perhaps be a sufficient *reductio ad absurdum* of the principle.

William McDougall, Body and Mind

But my opponents will say, that from the laws of nature alone, in so far as it is considered to be corporeal merely, it cannot be that the causes of architecture, painting, and things of this sort, which are the results of human art alone, could be deduced, and that the human body, unless it were determined and guided by the mind, would not be able to build a temple. I have already shown, however, that they do not know what the body can do, nor what can be deduced from the consideration of its nature alone, and that they find that many things are done merely by the laws of nature which they would never have believed to be possible without the direction of the mind, as, for example, those things which sleep-walkers do in their sleep, and at which they themselves are astonished when they wake.

Spinoza, Ethic

Acknowledgments

Much of the groundwork for this book was done while I was on a Harkness Fellowship at Harvard University in 1962–1964. Among my teachers and colleagues I should particularly like to thank the late Gordon Allport and Austin Duncan-Jones, as well as Jerome Bruner and Marie Jahoda, for their advice and encouragement over the years. A number of others have read parts of this book at various stages of its development, and their criticisms have improved it considerably. I should like especially to thank Alastair Chalmers, Max Clowes, Ben Gibbs, George Goethals, Richard Herrnstein, William O'Neil and Aaron Sloman. Gay Best and Anne Hardman typed the manuscript efficiently and patiently. Ann Rogers helped to look after my small son, Ruskin, and her kindness is much appreciated. Above all I thank my husband, John Spiers, whose encouragement and understanding have supported me throughout the writing of this book, and whose contribution to it has been inestimable.

I am grateful for permission to quote from the following works: "Matter, Mind, and Models" by M. L. Minsky, in *Proceedings of the International Federation of Information Processing Congress,* vol. I, ed. W. A. Kalenich (Washington, D.C.: Spartan Books, 1965), by permission of IFIP; *Toward a Psychology of Being* by A. H. Maslow, copyright © 1968 by Litton Educational Publishing, Inc., by permission of Van Nostrand Reinhold Co.; *The Nature of Explanation* by K. J. W. Craik (1943), by permission of the Syndics of Cambridge University Press; *The Explanation of Behaviour* by Charles Taylor (1964), by permission of Routledge and Kegan Paul Ltd. and of Humanities Press, Inc., New York; *An Introduction to Social Psychology* (1908; 23rd ed. 1936) and *Body and Mind* (1911) by William McDougall, by permission of Methuen & Co. Ltd.; *Psychology: The Study of Behaviour* by William McDougall, by permission of the Clarendon Press, Oxford; *An Outline of Psychology* by William McDougall, by permission of Methuen & Co. Ltd. and of Charles Scribner's Sons, copyright 1923 by Charles Scribner's Sons, renewal copyright 1951 by Anne A. McDougall; *An Outline of Abnormal Psychology* by William McDougall, by permission of Methuen & Co. Ltd.

and of Charles Scribner's Sons, copyright 1926 by Charles Scribner's Sons, renewal copyright 1954 by Anne A. McDougall; *Modern Materialism and Emergent Evolution* by William McDougall, copyright © 1929 by Litton Educational Publishing, Inc., by permission of Van Nostrand Reinhold, Inc., and of Methuen & Co. Ltd.; *The Energies of Men* by William McDougall, by permission of Methuen & Co. Ltd. and of Charles Scribner's Sons, copyright 1933 by Charles Scribner's Sons, renewal copyright © 1961 by Anne A. McDougall.

MAB

Brighton, England
May 1971

Contents

Purposive Explanation in Psychology

I   Introduction

The basic question of psychology is: Why do men and animals behave as they do? On this point psychologists agree. They do not agree, however, about what type of answer would be most appropriate. That is, they do not agree on what should count as a psychological explanation. As J. A. Deutsch has put it: "There is no concord among psychologists about what the facts they have accumulated are evidence for. This does not mean that they are merely in disagreement about the edifice they wish to erect; they have not decided even what constitutes a building. That is, not only do they disagree about the explanation of their findings, but they are not clear about what it would be to explain them."[1]

Everyday explanations of behavior commonly employ concepts referring to some aspect of the organism's mental life, or mind. Foremost among these concepts is purpose. One often feels that one has explained an action if (perhaps only if) one has shown that it was done for the sake of some purpose or goal which the organism had in mind. And everyday references to purpose normally imply the use of other cognate concepts, such as knowledge, belief, instinct, desire, intention, self, and freedom. For instance, all these concepts are involved when one says that a man intended to get rid of a burglar and deliberately chose to let the burglar hear him coming downstairs because he was naturally too frightened to face him (believing him to be armed), yet could not have faced himself if he had remained upstairs and done nothing to make the intruder go away. Everyone relies on such explanations in daily life. But opinions differ greatly as to their philosophical analysis or interpretation. Consequently, opinions differ also as to whether they are necessary—or even permissible—within a scientific psychology, and what the theoretical implications of their use may be.

To make an explanatory appeal to purpose—or *a fortiori* to mind—is regarded by some psychologists as at best tender-minded, and at worst a capitulation to "the subjective, anthropomorphic hocus-pocus of mentalism."[2] Others allow that "purpose" may be a useful explanatory term at certain levels of psychologizing, but regard it as in principle, and preferably,

1

dispensable. Still others regard purposive categories as essential to psychology and therefore characteristic of any possible psychological explanation. These differing views on the place of purposive terms in theoretical psychology are underlaid by differences of opinion as to the logical relations between purposive and nonpurposive explanations of behavior. Nonpurposive ("mechanistic") explanations—such as those offered by neurophysiologists and stimulus-response theorists, or by physicists, chemists, and computer engineers—are sometimes claimed to be compatible with purposive ("teleological") accounts. Indeed, the two forms are often regarded as in principle intertranslatable. But sometimes they are held to be radically incompatible with one another, so that teleological and mechanistic explanations of behavior must be mutually exclusive. In short, there is widespread disagreement as to the conceptual status of purposive explanation and its usefulness in psychology.

My aim is to account for and to resolve this theoretical disagreement in the terms of my own conceptual analysis of purpose. I wish to show that teleological accounts are complementary to mechanistic accounts, being neither superfluous to nor incompatible with them. My approach is "antireductionist" in holding that there are certain radical differences between the logic of purposive and of mechanistic terms. Consequently, the two terminologies are not intertranslatable, and teleological accounts could not be replaced by mechanistic ones without a real loss of explanatory power. My position is basically "reductionist," however, in holding that purposive phenomena are nevertheless totally dependent on causal (neurophysiological) mechanisms. Far from implying a special type of psychic cause —or any causelessness—teleological phenomena can be exhibited only by physical systems of a certain organizational nature. The behavior of the system must be determined largely by internal models, which represent (and misrepresent) the environment to some extent, and which may be highly idiosyncratic in different members of the same class or species of system. It is this organization which underlies and accounts for the special logical (intensional) features characterizing purposive accounts of behavior. Analogous logical features would characterize descriptions and explanations relating to artificial information-processing systems whose performance is controlled by such internal representations. A psychological being or subject is a physical system organized in this fashion. The mind should be thought of as a set of such representational models, systematically interlinked in certain ways. Only if the concept of mind is interpreted in this sense can one understand how it is possible for the mind to act on the body.

Competing analyses of purpose are to be found in the contemporary and in the historical literature. In describing and comparing a variety of them, I hope to clarify the relevance of teleological explanation to current psychological theory. Some analyses are offered by workers in empirical psychology, and these range from the strictest stimulus-response behaviorism, through increasingly "purposive" theories of a broadly behaviorist type, to the humanist theories favored by the Third Force. Others are drawn from cybernetic sources, for the issues of purpose and mechanism are commonly argued today with cybernetic analogies in mind. Still other conceptual analyses of purpose are developed within the general context of the philosophy of mind.

Traditionally "philosophical" problems are inevitably involved, if only implicitly, in theoretical accounts of purpose. This is so even when the theorist is primarily motivated by practical psychological interests, such as clinical therapy or the empirical study of animal behavior, and even when he believes himself to be entirely avoiding philosophical speculation. Indeed, reductionist or antireductionist approaches to purpose are differentially favored by psychologists primarily because of their supposed implications with regard to questions like the following: is there any real distinction between mental and nonmental aspects of the organism? What is the mind, and does it have a structure? Are there group minds? What is the self, and what is meant by the "unity" or "integration" of the personality? Is each human personality unique? What is human freedom, and is it essential to morality? Are men's actions unpredictable? What is a psychological being, or "subject"? What is the role of ideas mediating between stimulus and response? Are conscious purposes important? Does the mind determine the body?

All these familiar puzzles, in varying formulations, face psy-

3

chological theorists today, and opposing solutions are preferred by different psychological schools. An adequate account of the logical nature of purposive explanation should not only provide acceptable answers to such questions, but should also show why various unacceptable answers, with their corresponding conceptual analyses of teleology, are so tempting. The plausibility of incorrect analyses of purpose rests on their recognition, howsoever confused, of genuine logical features of teleological explanation. These insights should be accepted, though expressed in a less misleading way. Only if it is clear why purpose and mechanism are so commonly assumed to be totally opposed can one hope to convince "antireductionists" of their essential compatibility, and "reductionists" of their necessary complementarity.

A prime example of the way in which wider philosophical implications influence protagonists in psychological debate is provided by the strongly antireductionist stance of the "humanist" Third Force theorists. These psychologists regard the reductionist influence of behaviorist and Freudian psychology alike, and of "objective" science in general, as discouraging and paralyzing to man's freedom of action. For if a man believes purpose, freedom, and moral choice to be philosophically incompatible with mechanism, as most people appear to do, then psychological approaches that stress the basically mechanistic character of the human organism will undermine his view of himself as a freely acting purposive creature. This may have unfortunate practical consequences, since moral and pragmatic choices made without any confidence in their relevance to eventual action are unlikely to be effective—or perhaps even to be made at all. It is significant that most of the professional resistance to reductionist psychology comes from those involved in counseling and therapeutic contexts. Only if mechanism can be shown to be fully compatible with moral-psychological qualities such as purposiveness and freedom will this "dehumanizing" effect of non-purposive science be allayed. If this can be done, the current antipathies between theorists with differing approaches to psychology may also be lessened, for the moral implications of this philosophical question are primarily responsible for the animus that opposing factions in the dispute commonly show toward one another.

4

That the issue of "humanism or reductionism" almost inevitably arouses strong feelings on either side is evident from P. E. Meehl's recent appraisal of the relative merits of "clinical" and "statistical" prediction in psychology. In his opening chapter, Meehl finds it necessary to list a number of adjectives that are commonly employed in comparisons of these two psychological approaches, but which lend less light than heat to discussion. Meehl declares that his list is given for purposes of general "catharsis"; supposedly, the reader who has already encountered these terms will be able to restrain himself from using any of them again in the ensuing argument. Meehl's long list includes such items as dead, pedantic, academic, and blind; rich, sensitive, living, and real; crude, sloppy, primitive, and muddle-headed.[3] He might have added "tough" and "tender-minded." For, as William James remarked when first drawing the distinction, these two intellectual types have a low opinion of each other: "The tough think of the tender as sentimentalists and soft-heads. The tender feel the tough to be unrefined, callous, or brutal."[4] To be regarded as a soft-head is unpleasant, but at least nobody denies that the tender-minded are genuinely concerned with humanity. To be regarded as callous or brutal is much more difficult to bear. It is no wonder when reductionists resent the assumption of moral superiority implied by those who appropriate the term "humanist" to describe their position alone.

A psychologist's philosophical analysis of purpose influences him in his choice of theoretical terminology when formulating a systematic psychology. His primary decision is whether or not to accept "purpose" itself, bearing in mind that it is generally regarded as a distinctly tender-minded term. Assuming the theoretical acceptance of "purpose," comparable decisions remain to be made concerning other psychological words. In one's everyday reliance on teleological explanations, one typically appeals to such concepts as instinct, perception, sentiment, emotion, intention, knowledge, self, freedom, consciousness, and mind. Moreover, one refers unblushingly to phenomena like reproach, reverence, hope, admiration, gratitude, and despair. Psychological theorists who are in any way favorably disposed toward purposive explanation always employ some, if not all, of the terms on the first of these lists and some purposive psychologists

5

readily accept items on the second list also. This universal acceptance of certain terms, on the part of purposive theorists differing from each other in many other ways, requires explanation. The explanation is that these cognate terms are so closely interconnected that all of them are essential to teleological accounts of the most complex purposive phenomena, namely human behavior, and some of them are essential to all teleological accounts of behavior, however primitive. I shall here try to clarify the logical function of these terms within the conceptual structure of purposive explanations.

Since purposive phenomena are so often assumed to be wholly inexplicable in mechanistic terms, one who recommends a basically reductionist analysis of purpose inevitably faces skepticism from those of an antireductionist cast of mind. Even if such skeptics cannot fault his argument concerning the abstract issues of "purpose" and "mechanism," they nevertheless feel that psychological phenomena like knowledge, intention, and self—not to mention hope, reverence, or despair—could not possibly be generated by a mechanistic system. The reductionist should be prepared to meet these doubts in a positive way. In other words, he should supplement his more abstract conceptual analysis by an attempt to suggest how it is in fact possible for mechanistic systems to merit the ascription of the general vocabulary of consciousness.

In default of detailed physiological knowledge of bodily mechanisms, one way of doing this is to show that such vocabulary, or at least some psychological theory closely comparable to it, could be paralleled in a computer simulation. This claim itself requires a rational justification, however, for the relevance of computer analogies to genuinely psychological phenomena is disputed. Despite the fact that contemporary discussions of purpose are often related to a broadly cybernetic context, whether or not cybernetics can properly be quoted in support of the reductionist is a controversial matter. I argue that such support is indeed available for the reductionist's case and that cybernetic concepts illuminate purposive behavior in a number of ways. I also claim that psychological vocabulary may usefully be introduced into purely cybernetic contexts, but it does not follow that it may unexceptionably be applied to any actual or hypothetical machine artifact with no change in its usual meaning.

If this general reductionist claim, that cybernetic analogies are relevant to teleology, is to be supported by reference to the computer simulation of a specific teleological example, the problem arises of how to select the example. A particular systematic psychology must be chosen to function as the theoretical focus for simulation. A mere conceptual eclecticism on the part of the simulator cannot provide the example, for concepts drawn from distinct psychological theories have no theoretical relations established between them, and thus no interrelations that can be represented in the simulation. Even concepts drawn from everyday psychological language, which do have implicit logical connections, are not suitable for simulation unless these relations can first be explicitly stated as a result of careful analysis of the terms involved. It follows that, short of developing his own psychological system, the simulator must take one from the range already available within the theoretical literature. The psychology chosen need not be "exemplary" in the ideal or the optimal sense; it need not be regarded as the best psychology to be found in the texts. However, it should fulfill a number of other criteria if it is to function as a helpful example in elucidating the general relation between purpose and mechanism.

If one is to attempt a computer simulation of a purposive psychology with the specific aim of persuading the skeptic that reductionism need be neither callous nor inhumane, one should meet the skeptic on his own ground as far as possible. In other words, the theoretical psychology selected as the test case for simulation should be one that he can unhesitatingly approve. It should preferably employ a systematic vocabulary that is close to the psychological language of daily life. The psychologist who formulated it should himself be strongly antireductionist in temper. If he offers an explicitly argued philosophical justification of his antireductionist position, so much the better. Insofar as his argument takes account of real features of human psychology and mental life, it must be accommodated within a reductionist analysis and paralleled in the simulation. Insofar as his argument is mistaken or misleading, the properties of purposive explanation that led him to his particular errors should find some analogy in cybernetic terms. Preferably his errors should be common ones, so that criticism of them can be related to comparable mistakes in other writers of a broadly antireductionist type. If all these criteria can be met in selecting a theory for simulation, the exercise as a whole will be relevant to purposive psychologies in general rather than to the selected example in particular.

All these criteria are satisfied by the theoretical psychology of William McDougall, whose writings show a continuing intellectual concern with the place of purpose and cognate terms in psychological explanation. In addition, an examination of the development of his views is a convenient way of exhibiting the changing attitudes to purposive explanation that have arisen since the nineteenth-century beginnings of experimental psychology. McDougall's lifetime spanned a period of marked philosophical and methodological change within psychology. Born in 1871, before the establishment of the first psychological laboratories by William James and Wilhelm Wundt,[5] McDougall in his youth encountered a psychology that was typically mentalist and associationist. The focus was on consciousness rather than on behavior, and strongly realist interpretations of "consciousness," "mind," and other psychological terms were common. By the time of his death in 1938, professional academic psychology had become overwhelmingly behaviorist, positivist, and reductionist. Even the most influential antibehaviorist tradition—Freudian psychodynamics—was markedly reductionist in tone, despite its reliance on purposive vocabulary and explanation. McDougall was not a passive observer of this intellectual ferment: he continually criticized the prevailing psychological fashions and offered his own alternative analysis of the conceptual nature of psychology.

McDougall always insisted on the use of purposive terminology and on its strongly antireductionist interpretation. His tireless championing of teleology was not merely an intellectual obsession; rather, it had the nature of a moral crusade. That McDougall was basically, indeed passionately, concerned with purpose became increasingly evident as his corpus of writings grew. He continually developed, revised, and defended his purposive psychology in numerous articles and books that appeared

8

right up to his death.[6] In an autobiographical paper of 1930 he identified the basis of this single-minded intellectual endeavor as the aim to reconcile science with morals. The theory of morals, he wrote, was his fundamental interest, which had led him to devote his powers to psychology. He regarded belief in the efficacy of moral effort and in the reality of moral choice as an imperative human need: "Without it, we are discouraged, paralyzed, and thrown back, individually and socially, into moral chaos."[7] Mechanistic science, he claimed, denies us this belief. So he spent his life in the search for a teleological science of values and volition that would show the influence of men's choices in seeking their purposes and ideals. Accordingly, his personality theory stressed the autonomous nature of human purposive activity, and its regulation by the moral influences of self-control. McDougall's unrelenting attack on mechanism in psychology (and even in the nonpsychological life sciences) was motivated by his desire to prevent the fatalistic dehumanization of man's self-image, a desire shared by many psychologists today.

The scope of McDougall's system was enormously increased by his methodological habit of taking over everyday psychological terms for use as theoretical concepts. His theory encompassed animal and human, individual and social, normal and abnormal psychology. His physiological training contributed to his interest in psychological phenomena considered in their biological context, and he discussed the indications of purpose and mentality that are evident at various levels throughout the phylogenetic scale. It has been remarked of McDougall: "His *Social Psychology* undoubtedly represents a great advance in the treatment of instinct, emotion and character, inasmuch as the analysis of these factors was at once more systematic, more delicate and more in touch with real life than in any previous attempt in this direction . . . He has given us a systematic treatment of conation and affection that, in completeness and thoroughness, is without a rival, and in penetration is second only to the work of Freud."[8] Clearly, despite his interest in the homing of wasps, the running of rats, and the physiology of neural excitation, there is no question but that McDougall's psychology qualifies as "significant" and "humane."

McDougall constantly reiterated and argued for his philosophical conviction that teleological and mechanistic explanation are mutually exclusive. Notwithstanding his many insights into the nature of purposive behavior, his systematic psychology was flawed by mentalist views and conceptual confusions that have been often associated with the concept of purpose. In particular, his claim that consciousness is causally active and his belief in the incompatibility of purpose and mechanism are each mistaken. These mistakes are common because they rest on a confused recognition of genuine logical features of purposive terminology. For this reason also, they are potentially present in discussions of purpose even when the writers concerned are insufficiently interested in philosophical discussion to raise such matters explicitly. McDougall was more prone to embark on metaphysical speculation than are most psychologists, and more liable to enter into philosophical argument of a continuing and detailed nature.

In developing my account of the nature of purposive explanation, and in comparing the various approaches to it that are to be found in the psychological or philosophical literature, my strategy therefore is to focus rather more closely on McDougall than on any of the other writers I discuss. In the elaboration of a basically reductionist analysis of teleological explanation, he is more helpfully regarded as an intellectual sparring partner than as a revered guru. His treatment of purpose is accepted insofar as it supports the antireductionist element of my own analysis, but rejected insofar as it denies the reductionist element. In criticizing his unacceptable views, I show both how they are mistaken and why he, like many others, came to insist on them. In addition, I suggest how the various theoretical concepts of his systematic psychology might be simulated in a cybernetic context, even though McDougall's strongly antimechanist bias would have made him highly skeptical of any such endeavor.[9] This latter exercise requires a more detailed reference to the theory concerned than may be necessary to illustrate points made in the context of a general conceptual discussion, and so my account of McDougall is relatively full compared with my treatment of other authors. But his system functions throughout my argument as a representative example of purposive psychology, selected according to the criteria mentioned. These criteria preclude choice of the most influential of all such psychologies,

10

namely Freudian theory—aspects of which have already been represented in various programs directed to the computer simulation of personality—since Freud's philosophical views on purpose were emphatically reductionist in temper. Freud is therefore less suitable as an example of a teleological psychologist than is the strongly antireductionist McDougall, given the particular aims of my discussion. This is so irrespective of any comparative judgment that one might make concerning the intrinsic merits of their theories, for my interest is not to recommend one psychological system above others but rather to resolve some of the general conceptual puzzles associated with the philosophical interpretation of purposive terms. Accordingly, McDougall's psychology is not considered here for its own sake, and it should be regarded in the light of its relevance to the general issue of teleology versus mechanism.

Quite apart from its general philosophical base, McDougall's system cannot be uncritically recommended in preference to other psychological theories, whether purposive or not. For example, in any comparative judgment of this type one has to consider the scope or range of a given theory, its potential for detailed application to empirical psychological questions, and also the amount of experimental evidence offered in its support. McDougall's initial training in physiology and medicine led him in 1897 to devote his first publication to the contraction of striped muscle,[10] and his first book, published in 1905, dealt with the general field of physiological psychology. His primer *Physiological Psychology* stimulated some experimental work, earning the description of doing for its generation what Hebb's *Organization of Behavior* (1949) did nearly half a century later.[11] His early work on vision also prompted experimentation,[12] and after his arrival in America he instituted a series of experiments designed to show Lamarckian inheritance in rats.[13] But McDougall was not an experimentalist at heart. After his earliest work he concentrated on wide-ranging theoretical and speculative writings, which were not supported by a systematic program of empirical research, though they were backed up by references to empirical matters. An important reason for McDougall's neglect of strictly controlled experimental techniques was that his theoretical vocabulary was drawn from everyday speech. Thus, it implicitly contained a great deal of psychological knowledge—namely, that common knowledge of the interrelations that are possible between particular psychological variables which is available to all men because it is already codified in the conceptual structure of ordinary language. Accordingly, McDougall's theoretical inferences were primarily "intuitive" rather than deductively explicit, although he did attempt to clarify and redefine the everyday terms he borrowed. Although a strict experimentalist can aim at rigor of a high degree, he cannot reasonably hope to match the range of psychological phenomena that the sensitive layman or clinician can express. Rigor and scope are not essentially incompatible, but to some extent they are unavoidably opposed in practice. These two features of psychological theory are often opposed in polemic also, as Meehl's pejoratives "pedantic" and "sloppy" suggest, and which of them is regarded as the more important depends on one's practical concerns as well as on one's intellectual temper. I make no attempt to single out one level of behavioral inquiry—still less, one particular theory—as the most satisfactory example of "psychology." Had I done so, I would not have chosen McDougall's system. But in view of its theoretical character and its historical context, McDougall's psychology serves as a useful conceptual tool in discussing the nature of purposive explanation.

Anyone who tries to assess the importance of teleological explanation will soon find the philosophical issue of mind and body bearing on his discussion. Indeed, I have already listed a number of questions that seem to share a suspiciously metaphysical air, claiming that they are relevant to psychological theorizing about purpose. McDougall asked all of these, and expressed his answers in a vocabulary that strikes a modern reader as strange, to say the least. For he spoke of the group mind, telepathy, monads, the soul; and he defended animism, dualism, interactionism, psychic energy, and freedom. If such terms are not to raise clouds of dialectical dust obscuring any merit in his views, one must understand why he used them and how one is to interpret them. In particular, acceptable philosophical or empirical content must be distinguished from logically distinct content that one wishes to reject. The prime reason for his use of these terms—as for his insistence on "purpose" itself—was their acknowledged antireductionist overtones. Another was a facet of his personal psychology: he had a self-confessed habit of defending views largely because they were generally unacceptable.[14] A third source of his vocabulary was his nineteenth-century intellectual background, whose terms of philosophical debate he accepted. Discussion of the mind-body problem in general, and of its implications for the definition of psychology in particular, was a prevailing interest among intellectuals of the time. Before the concept of purpose is examined closely, it will be useful to indicate the approaches to this general philosophical problem that were current among psychologists at the turn of the century, sketching McDougall's position in the most detail.

Throughout his life McDougall was fascinated by the puzzle of mind and body, inquiring into the nature of the distinction between them and the relation between mental and physical processes. As early as 1898 he was publishing views on the physiological location of consciousness.[15] In 1911 he devoted an entire book, *Body and Mind*, to the problem. Thereafter he continually returned to the topic in one form or another. In *Body and Mind* he gave a detailed historical and critical account of various views on the mind-body problem, only two years before J. B. Watson was to declare that all such questions are totally irrelevant to psychology. Characteristically, McDougall invited resistance[16] by his defiant choice of language: as though the title itself were not provocative enough, he subtitled the book "A History and a Defense of Animism." The views he expressed in this early book were to remain basically unchanged in his later life. The most important discussions of the problem after *Body and Mind* are his presidential address to the Society for Psychical Research in 1920;[17] the concluding chapters of *An Outline of Abnormal Psychology* in 1926; and *Modern Materialism and Emergent Evolution* in 1929, a book described by McDougall himself as a supplement to *Body and Mind*. The crucial feature of his position was that the distinction between the mental and the physical can be drawn in terms of the different sorts of explanation appropriate to the phenomena concerned. That is, it need not be drawn in terms of a distinction between mental and physical substance, and McDougall accordingly criticized the influential Cartesian tradition.

13

The seventeenth century Cartesian formulation of the mind-body problem had influenced not only philosophers in their speculations, but also physiologists and psychologists in their experiments and theorizing. Descartes' dualist view, propounded in *Passions de l'âme* (1650), implied that the life history of a man is in some sense two life histories, each dealing with an ontologically distinct type of event. Man was described by Descartes as an intimate combination of two substances, mental and physical. The changing states of the mental substance are the individual's psychological processes; they are essentially private and are known directly through introspection. The states of the physical substance are the individual's bodily states; and of these, the brain states are most closely related to his psychological processes. But the nature of this relation presented a difficulty. Descartes posited a reciprocal interaction between the two substances, while at the same time claiming that the physiologist could in principle give a complete and lawful description of all the states of the nervous system. These simultaneous claims generated a methodological optimism but a metaphysical impasse. Experimental physiology—even psychophysiology—was apparently given a philosophical justification. However, Descartes himself admitted that the postulated interactions were totally unintelligible. Purposive, rational, conscious, and voluntary behavior were all said to involve the causal influence of mind on body, while sensation was attributed to the converse influence. But how this could be, Descartes was unable to explain. According to his formulation of the problem, mind and body are so different—and differ in such a way—that no intelligible account of how either might influence the other can possibly be given. Descartes also denied that mental processes are associated with the bodily functioning of animals. This implies that, while the physiologist can study all living things, the psychologist can properly study only man. Comparative psychology must be in principle impossible.

Because of these difficulties, among others, later empirical psychological work inspired by Descartes' vision of an experimental physiology was often justified by a somewhat different theoretical position. The three positions most popular in scientific circles when McDougall was writing *Body and Mind* were

14

all revisions of Descartes' account rather than radical alternatives
to it. These three were Wilhelm Wundt's parallelism; T. H.
Huxley's epiphenomenalism; and the radical materialism derived
from the eighteenth century writings of J. O. de la Mettrie and
Baron d'Holbach and fed by later physiological research on the
nervous system.[18] All these positions were influenced by the
midcentury publication of H. L. F. von Helmholtz's classic paper
on the conservation of energy, which became a theoretical key-
stone of the materialist "Helmholtz school" of medicine.[19] The
wide readership of this paper contributed to the readiness with
which late nineteenth century writers (including Freud and
McDougall) referred to the question of how energy is related to
the mind-body problem. A fourth position, psychical monism,
gained popularity among philosophical thinkers in the last years
of the century, but although it was defended by G. T. Fechner,[20]
it was not so widespread among experimental psychologists as
the three previously mentioned. Psychical monism was a radical
antimaterialism, which denied the reality of matter and allowed
basic ontological status only to mind; by way of the post-Kantian
idealist tradition, it also stemmed from the Cartesian distinction
between mind and body.

Faced with these four alternatives, McDougall carefully examined argument and counterargument: finding the latter generally
more convincing, he declined to accept any one of them. While
criticizing each of these views in their own terms and thus making use of Cartesian terminology, McDougall also made a deliberate attempt to approach the problem anew in terms that would
avoid the metaphysical impasse of the Cartesian position. He did
not fully succeed, for he was led to postulate specifically psychic
energy acting on the physical constituents of the brain. However,
he did shift the emphasis of discussion from mental and physical
substance or content to mental and physical process, and thence
to psychological and physiological explanation. Though he labeled
his own views "animist," "dualist," and "interactionist"—all of
which terms are applicable to Descartes—he suggested somewhat
less strong interpretations of these labels than they were typically given:

We may accept [animism] while remaining wholly on the

plane of physical science . . . The essential notion [of animism] is that all, or some, of·those manifestations of life and mind which distinguish the living man from the corpse and from inorganic bodies are due to the operation within him of something which is of a nature different from that of the body, an animating principle generally, *but not necessarily or always*, conceived as an immaterial and individual being or soul . . . The term "psycho-physical dualism" accurately expresses the essential animistic notion; but it is cumbrous, and the word Dualism is apt to be taken to imply metaphysical Dualism, an implication which I am anxious to avoid; for Animism does not necessarily imply metaphysical Dualism, or indeed any metaphysical or ontological doctrine.[21]

This last point can be clarified by a passage in the later *Outline of Abnormal Psychology.* Here he defined dualism as any view which assumes that "mental and physical processes are distinct in kind and that man is a psychophysical organism in the life of which processes of these two kinds interact." He remarked that "distinct in kind" need not be interpreted "metaphysically," in terms of material and mental substance, but may be interpreted "non-metaphysically," so as to represent "physical and psychical processes as distinguishable in terms of the *general laws* which they seem to obey or manifest," that is, mechanistic or teleological laws.[22]

He postulated psychic energy as the active basis of purposive behavior, but he did not claim that it could act independently of any physical body. His final position on this issue was that, "in speaking of *psycho-physical interaction*, we must recognize that the expression may distort the truth in that it seems to separate the psychical and the physical; whereas these may be but two partial aspects of the concrete reality, two aspects of a system of psycho-physical activity which are distinguishable but inseparable." In the last chapter of *Body and Mind* he endorsed the hypothesis of the soul as an immaterial being, but he explicitly refused to commit himself to regarding it as an immaterial substance, stating it is "a being that possesses, *or is*, the sum of definite capacities for psychical activity and psycho-physical interaction." He admitted that his active interest in psychical research was fed by the hope of finding evidence for

16

a strong version of animism claiming the existence of "some factor or principle which is different from the body and capable of existing independently of it," but he regarded the evidence as in fact ambiguous. He concluded: "Psycho-physical interaction may be, for all we know, a necessary condition of all consciousness. For all the thinking or consciousness of which we have positive knowledge is of embodied minds or souls."[23] McDougall clearly was a typical nineteenth-century thinker in his tendency toward ontological formulations of the mind-body problem: does the soul exist after death, is there such a process as telepathy, does the world contain psychic energy? He was less typical, however, in his firm rejection of Cartesian substance and in his general suspicion of substantival terms in philosophy and psychology.

Psychology in the nineteenth century was commonly defined as "the study of consciousness" or "the science of experience." Wundt himself preferred the German *Erfahrungswissenschaft* (the science of experience). E. B. Titchener's translation of Wundt defined the principal object of psychology as "the investigation of conscious processes," and had the passages: "Psychology . . . seeks to give an account of the interconnection of processes which are evinced by our own consciousness, or which we infer from such manifestations of the bodily life in other creatures as indicate the presence of a consciousness similar to our own"; and "Physiological psychology . . . has for its subject the manifold of conscious processes, whether as directly experienced by ourselves, or as inferred on the analogy of our own experiences from objective observation."[24] For English-speaking readers, the step from "conscious processes" to "consciousness" is a short one; and even "experience" is commonly regarded as synonymous with "consciousness."

The substantival form of the word "consciousness" allows one to forget its implication that someone is being conscious of something, and much nineteenth century psychology reflects this fact. Thus, William James noted the associationist tendency to ignore the mental agent "behind" ideas, referring to the work of Wundt and his followers as "a psychology without a soul."[25] Similarly, McDougall regarded "consciousness" as "a thoroughly bad word" by virtue of its substantival nature, and recommended its replacement by verbs or adverbs. "Experience" he thought to be

17

"much the better term," since it retains the verb form from which it is derived. He complained that the word "consciousness" had "wrought havoc" in psychology, since it encouraged the various forms of idea-psychology that dominated the intellectual life of the time.[26]

McDougall unfailingly attacked idea-psychology for a number of reasons. It indulged man's deep-seated tendency to "reify" experience, to think of experience as a sort of "stuff." Second, it defined the initial task of psychology as the analysis of this stuff into its component parts, into atomistic units having no intrinsic connection with one another. It then defined the subsequent task of psychology as formulating the various associationist laws linking the passive mental atoms together into a sort of compound "mosaic." And fourth, it saw the elemental units as simple in structure, having no inherent organization. All four of these features characterizing idea-psychology were encouraged by use of the word "consciousness," and were wellnigh inseparable from use of the substantival terms "idea" and "sensation."

These four features were also encouraged by the success of atomistic principles of explanation in the physical sciences, and by the writings of Locke and the later associationists, such as Hume, Thomas Reid, David Hartley, James Mill, J. S. Mill, and Ernst Mach. Locke had deliberately adopted Newton as his intellectual model. In *An Essay Concerning Human Understanding* (1690) he described the newborn mind as a featureless *tabula rasa* and represented perception as basically a passive reception of a number of independent units or ideas; these ideas are combined according to simple associative laws, and psychological processes such as memory, reflection, and imagination are dependent on such associations. Experimental psychology developed under the influence of associationism, and nineteenth century accounts of perception and other mental processes overwhelmingly reflected this tradition.

McDougall gave a very different account of perception and of mental life in general. He concentrated on mental process; his basic theoretical concepts were not atomistic; his "psychic" laws involved meaningful activity subject to central control rather than automatic and passive associations; perception was seen as an anticipatory adjunct to action, with a high degree of organization

18

innately present in the perceptual-sensory system; and he held organization to be present as well in anything that could reasonably be termed a "percept." Naturally, then, McDougall was quick to criticize what he called "the atomistic or mosaic psychology."[27] Even in his earliest work on the physiology of the senses, he insisted that the teleological concept of attention was crucial to the explanation of his experimental results.[28] Attention and similar psychological concepts could not be expressed in terms of "ideas." Consequently, McDougall advised his readers to be wary of the words "consciousness," "ideas," and "sensations," even though they could not be avoided altogether.

Idea-psychology was also criticized by McDougall for a fifth reason: its exclusive reliance on introspection as a methodological technique. Wundt had described introspection as "the *sine qua non* of any psychology."[29] Introspection was widely regarded as *the* psychological method, and any knowledge that could not thus be gained was not considered psychological knowledge. This reliance on introspection had intellectual roots in the Cartesian rationalist as well as in the Lockean empiricist tradition. It was not necessarily connected with associationist theoretical assumptions. Indeed, James Ward relied on introspection in his *Encyclopaedia Britannica* article of 1886 on psychology, which was for years the classic anti-associationist text and which is generally considered to have "delivered a blow to associationism from which this doctrine has never yet recovered."[30] The anti-associationist influence of Franz Brentano and of act psychology was evident in the work of Ward, his disciple G. F. Stout, William James, and the Wurzburg School—all of whom were arguing against classical associationism in the first thirty years of McDougall's life. However, the nineteenth century successors of Descartes and of Locke were primarily opposed to each other in what they had to say about consciousness—not in their assumption that consciousness was what psychology was all about, nor in their belief that introspection was the best way to go about it.

McDougall was clearly influenced by Ward and Stout—taking over their neo-Kantian terminology of "cognition," "affection," and "conation," and using them within his own system to distinguish between the three aspects of mind.[31] He did not deny that introspection is an essential part of the method of psychology, but for three reasons he emphasized introspection to a much lesser degree than did the influential figures of his youth. First, by the time of his thirtieth year, the experimental limitations of introspection had become apparent in the seemingly irresolvable wranglings of opposing introspectionist schools.[32] Second, Mc-Dougall claimed that the crucial features even of adult, sane, human mental life were typically not accessible to the introspective method. Many of his theoretical concepts were either purely dispositional and not open at all to introspection—or they sometimes were applicable in spite of apparently conflicting introspective evidence. For instance, sentiments are purely dispositional and nonintrospectable; purposes are sometimes unconscious in the sense that they are not recognizable by the conscious self, even given a degree of introspective effort. Third, McDougall believed that the proper scope of psychology extends beyond the individual adult, sane, human mind. He wished to recognize abnormal and child psychology, animal and social psychology, as genuine examples of psychology. Yet none of these relies purely, if at all, on the introspective method.

Rather, they rely on the observation of behavior. At the turn of the century such observation was grudgingly allowed by psychologists to provide clues to psychological matters. One of Stout's influential texts proclaimed:

> [Psychology] is concerned with what appears to the individual mind . . . There are three sources from which we obtain [psychological facts]; two ultimate and independent, the third secondary and dependent. The first is introspection, or the perception of what takes place within our own mind. The second is the remembrance of past psychological processes, which have taken place within our own mind . . . [The third, if it is really a separate source of knowledge] consists in the observation of phenomena, which betoken the existence of mental processes, quite independently of their being perceived or unperceived by the mind within which they take place . . . [This is] a derivative method which presupposes the other two, although they do not presuppose it . . . All depends on accurate resolution of our own complex consciousness into its constituents [so that we may be able] to explain

the nature and order of the signs which indicate to us the mental processes of others [whether animal or human].[33]

It is clear from this passage that the ultimate aim of "animal psychology" (when this is purely a courtesy title) is to describe the animal's consciousness by analogy to one's own. As Stout himself was not slow to point out, this is a dubious matter at best, and increasingly difficult as one moves down the phylogenetic scale. It is difficult enough to empathize with one's closest personal acquaintance; to try to empathize with dogs, fish, and worms is to overstrain one's faculties. Yet this is precisely what comparative psychologists were trying to do. Even the relatively tough-minded zoological psychologist Conwy Lloyd Morgan insisted that, in the study of animal behavior:

> Inductions reached through the objective study of certain physical manifestations have to be interpreted in terms of inductions reached through the introspective study of mental processes . . . Both inductions, subjective and objective, are necessary. Neither can be omitted without renouncing the scientific method. And then finally the objective manifestations in conduct and activity have to be interpreted in terms of subjective experience. The inductions reached by the one method have to be explained in the light of inductions reached by the other method.[34]

Lloyd Morgan warned against anthropomorphism in his well-known canon, "in no case may we interpret an action as the outcome of the exercise of a higher psychical faculty, if it can be interpreted as the outcome of the exercise of one which stands lower in the psychological scale."[35] But despite this warning, he regarded animal psychology as closely dependent on the introspective method. If difficulties consequently arise in attributing psychological predicates to lower organisms, so much the worse for comparative psychology. Stout noted such difficulties and returned to human psychology in relief, whereas Lloyd Morgan tried to overcome them as best he could. For both these writers, as for most of their contemporaries, it was axiomatic that introspection is the primary psychological method.

Stout had defined psychology as "the positive science of mental process," in which "positive" was contrasted with "moral."[36] Psychology describes what mental process is like, not what it ought to be like. McDougall modified this definition to "the positive science of the conduct of living creatures," and soon afterward to "the positive science of conduct or behaviour."[37] In thus stressing the importance of behavioral data to psychology, McDougall was radically opposed to contemporary definitions of psychology in terms of consciousness, experience, ideas, mental process, or the mind.

The advantages of McDougall's behaviorist definition (which antedated Watson's by some years[38]) over the mentalistic definitions then current were twofold. It allowed observation of behavior and nonintrospectable theoretical concepts in general to count as *psychological*. Moreover, it provided an objective, intersubjectively agreeable definition of the psychological data required to form the observational base of a psychological science, without prejudging the issue of what philosophical analysis to give to the term "mind": " 'Mind' is itself a word whose meaning is extremely vague, one incapable of being clearly defined except in terms of some questionable and speculative hypothesis . . . The conception of behaviour, on the other hand, may be defined in a way which involves no speculative inference or hypothesis . . . by pointing to facts open to the direct observation of all men, and saying—This and this is what we mean by behaviour."[39]

McDougall did not wish to avoid all mention of "the mind," but he regarded it as an expression to be used with care. Occasionally he lapsed into suspiciously Cartesian terminology: in *Body and Mind*, for example, he referred to the mind as an enduring psychic entity which, since it is not a material thing, must be an immaterial thing. But even in his early work such remarks were not characteristic; and in 1929 he stated that in *Body and Mind* he had been "unduly concerned with the question, What are things made of? to the neglect of the more important question, How do events run their course?"[40] In thus emphasizing process rather than substratum, he was echoing his definition of psychology as the study of "behavior" rather than of "consciousness" or "the mind." Although he acknowledged that psychology could be defined as "the science of the human mind,"[41] he preferred to avoid this definition because of the unacceptable ways in which the concept of the mind had been—and was being—used by some psychologists. He explicitly rejected a number of these analyses. For example, mind cannot be identified with the brain or nervous system, for this would tie psychologists down to one type of explanation. Nor can it be regarded as a bundle of faculties, nor as a more or less organized mass of "ideas" regarded as enduring things which pass in and out of "consciousness." Despite the ideomotor theory, he wrote: "Idea-psychology gives us no intelligible theory of action, it cannot relate ideas to the bodily activity in which our mental life expresses itself."[42] He held that while many psychologists recognized the uselessness of all such theories of mind, they took the mistaken step of trying to disregard mind altogether.

In McDougall's view the mind is defined as follows:

[It is] something which expresses its nature, powers and functions in two ways: (1) the modes of individual experience, (2) the modes of bodily activity, the sum of which constitutes the behavior of the individual.

[The] unique mark of mental process [is] a persistent striving towards the natural end of that process.

The *raison d'etre* of mental events seems to be the modification and control of [events within the body and physical events without it].

I believe that the mind has a nature and a structure and a function of its own which cannot be fully and adequately described in terms of structure of the brain and its physical process.

We may define the mind of any organism as *the sum of the enduring conditions of its purposive activities.* And, in order to mark our recognition of the fact that these conditions are not a mere aggregation, but form rather an organized system of which each part is functionally related to the rest in definite fashion, we may usefully speak of the "structure" of the mind.[43]

What McDougall meant by "the structure of the mind," and

how the various purposes of the individual organism are identified and related to each other, is clarified in the following chapters. In particular, the examination of his personality theory
shows that he came to favor a Leibnizian rather than a Cartesian
approach. No mention of this view occurred in *Social Psychology*,
though it was soon to be hinted at in *Body and Mind*; his fullest
statements of it came much later, in an address to the Society
for Psychical Research in 1920 and in *Abnormal Psychology* in
1926. This chronology may perhaps be explained by the fact that,
soon after the publication of *Social Psychology* in 1908, Leibniz's
concept of "monad" was recommended in Ward's second series
of Gifford Lectures, which were so well received that within a
year they ran into a second edition.[44] Ward's use of the concept
was associated with a markedly metaphysical approach seeking
to combine pluralism with idealistic theism, whereas McDougall
referred to monads in an attempt to solve specific difficulties
within personality theory. In *Monadology* (1714) Leibniz had
described the soul as "a colony of monads," each monad being a
psychological individual. McDougall adopted this language to
express his view of the mind as a hierarchically integrated system
of purposes, centering in human beings around the dominant
purposes of the "self." Such an approach is consonant with his
position that one may distinguish between mind and body, mental and physical process, in terms of the suitability of a teleological or a mechanistic explanation respectively.

As McDougall pointed out, any analysis of mind involves questionable and speculative hypotheses. To say that he distinguished
between mind and body by reference to "teleological" and
"mechanistic" explanation is not, at this stage, to say anything
very clearly. It does not put us in a position to question his
speculative hypotheses or to appraise their merits relative to
other philosophical positions. For I have not yet established precisely what McDougall intended by these terms, nor how his use
of them compares with the use of more modern writers. In order
to clarify these matters, I must now turn to an analysis of the
concept of purpose and the distinction between mechanistic and
teleological explanation.

II The Concept of Purpose

If in everyday life one is asked why a certain action or episode of behavior occurred, one frequently attempts to explain it by referring it to a purpose. One says, for instance, that a man's purpose was to alarm the burglar, and it was this which caused him to stamp his feet on his way downstairs. Such an explanation of the foot-stamping would commonly be regarded as perfectly acceptable. But what is a purpose, and how can it affect the course of bodily events?

Definition of Purpose

"Purpose" and "goal" are generally used as synonyms. McDougall himself remarked that in the typical case of purposive action one is said to strive toward a goal, and "the attainment of the goal" is said to be the purpose of one's action or striving.[1] The truth of this remark seems obvious enough. However, were we to rely on it as providing our definition of a purpose, one very natural interpretation of it would lead us into difficulties straight away. Were we to interpret "the attainment of the goal" as the (actual) attainment of the goal, the "perfectly acceptable" explanation given above for the man's foot-stamping would not be acceptable at all. On the contrary, it could only appear highly paradoxical. For the surprise and alarm of the burglar on hearing someone coming downstairs can hardly be said to have "caused" the previous foot-stamping in any sense of the term.

The word "cause" in everyday use has a number of meanings. A causal explanation is most commonly understood to be one that exhibits the determining conditions or energy mechanisms which somehow effect the change. This type of explanation is sometimes distinguished by being said to refer to the efficient causes of change, in contrast with various other types of explanation that are also termed "causal" in everyday usage.[2] The term "efficient cause" is taken from Aristotle, in whose classification of types of cause the efficient cause is the agency that makes a thing move. I shall normally restrict my use of the word "cause" to efficient causes, so as to avoid confusion between its different senses. For

25

the more scientific a person tries to be in his choice of language and in his search for explanation, the more likely he is to use the word in this particular way. This fact reflects the success of scientific explanations that refer natural phenomena to antecedent conditions or to energy mechanisms, such as those typical of physics and chemistry. Consequently, rather different uses of "cause" that are unproblematic in practical everyday contexts may be assimilated to this sense when speculated upon, with very puzzling results. In particular, attempts to illuminate the way in which purposes influence behavior have often been bedeviled by such confusions.

It normally seems harmless to say that a man's purpose of frightening the burglar caused him to tread heavily on the stairs. Indeed, purposes were regarded by Aristotle as a type of cause, and have commonly been referred to in his terminology as final causes ever since. They are termed "final" because it is the end to which the action is directed that is regarded as influencing behavior. Thus, one way of putting the question of how a purpose can *affect* the course of bodily events would be to ask how final causes can do so. But even this way of putting it is apt to be misleading, despite the explicit reminder that the sense of "cause" intended here is not the one appropriate to the physical sciences. This is because the latter sense may exert such a strong influence on the mind that it introduces a subtle change, so that one is understood to ask how final causes *effect* bodily change. This understanding of the question can only lead to paradoxical answers, answers in which final causes are assumed to be a strange subclass of efficient causes.

For instance, it may seem as though the teleologist must believe that "the attainment of the goal" is the cause of action. As the learning theorist C. L. Hull has expressed it: "In its extreme form teleology is the name of the belief that the *terminal* stage of certain environmental-organismic interaction cycles somehow is at the same time one of the *antecedent* determining conditions which bring the behaviour cycle about."[3] Such an interpretation would represent a purpose as a queer sort of event by means of which the future determines the present, a cause working backward in time, which is all the more strange in that an action may be done for a purpose and yet that purpose may

26

never be achieved. With regard to efficient causes, no such hypothetical future cause of present movement can be admitted. By contrast, final causes are tolerant of such circumstances. The sense in which it is acceptable to say that a man's purpose of alarming a burglar "caused" him to stamp his feet is one that is in no way invalidated by the fact that the foot-stamping preceded the burglar's terror. Nor would this sense be undermined if the burglar turned and fought instead of being frightened away, or even if no burglar was there in the first place.

However, even in terms of final (rather than efficient) causation, the fleeing of the burglar cannot be regarded as the cause of the stamping on the stairs. For the man's purpose may be said to cause his actions whether the purpose is actually achieved or not: if for some reason the hoped-for flight of the intruder does not take place, one is not forced to say that the stamping had no cause after all. This suggests that it is inadvisable to define the purpose of an action as "the attainment of the goal," since this form of words is ambiguous. The phrase may be understood to mean the *actual* attainment of the goal, but so interpreted, a purpose cannot reasonably be described as the "cause" of action in any sense of the word. If one is to understand the relation between final causes and efficient causes—in other words, between what I shall call "purposes" and simply "causes"—it is better not to define a "purpose" in this way.

McDougall recognized these points and noted that "it is very difficult to use the substantive 'purpose' without ambiguity."[4] He specifically disclaimed the overliteral interpretation of "purpose" as the actual achievement of the end:

> In discussing teleological causation it is usual to introduce an unnecessary air of mystery by saying that in such cases the end causes or determines or initiates or governs the action . . . The goal may be one we falsely conceive; or it may have been destroyed or removed from the place where we conceive it; but that does not make any essential difference . . . The end or goal of a train of action involves some action not yet obtaining; since then the goal does not exist in the present, it cannot be a causal agency in the events that lead to its realization;
>
> Those of us psychologists who recognize that all action

expressive of Mind is purposive . . . are represented by the mechanists as postulating entities of a peculiar kind which we call "purposes" and to which we ascribe what our critics are pleased to call "a mystic potency." This, of course, is to misread us and to approach the problem of purposive action in a way that is prejudicial to all understanding. We need not pause to try to define exactly how the substantive "purpose" may properly be used.[5]

Paradoxical interpretations of "purpose" are apt to arise because of an unfortunate (substantive) usage of words: "We speak of a purpose as though it were a thing, and then when we ask what sort of a thing it can be, we can find no intelligible answer."[6]

McDougall suggested that it would be preferable to use the nonsubstantive form, "purposive." This term can be used unambiguously because it is based on observable features of behavior. "Purpose" (like "mind," "idea," and "consciousness") is a useful word, but it can lead to ambiguity and misunderstanding. It is better to define "purpose" in terms of "purposive" than vice versa. Purposiveness is shown in a certain pattern or structure of activity and is essential to behavior properly so-called. The observable features that justify calling a process "behavior" are the very features that define purposiveness.

In 1905 McDougall published his first book, *Physiological Psychology*, in which he defined psychology as the positive science of the conduct of living creatures. Three years later he added the term "behavior" to this definition in *An Introduction to Social Psychology*, the first systematic statement of his psychology. In the early editions of *Social Psychology* McDougall characterized behavior as follows: "All instinctive behaviour exhibits that unique mark of mental process, a persistent striving towards the natural end of that process. That is to say, the process, unlike any merely mechanical process, is not to be arrested by any sufficient mechanical obstacle, but is rather intensified by any such obstacle and only comes to an end either when its appropriate goal is achieved, or when some stronger incompatible tendency is excited, or when the creature is exhausted by its persistent efforts."[7] He added a chapter to the fifth edition in 1912, giving a more lengthy description of behavior:

At all levels of complexity behaviour [as distinguished from all merely physical or mechanical movements] presents four peculiar marks: 1. The creature does not merely move in a certain direction, like an inert mass impelled by external force; its movements are quite incapable of being described in the language with which we describe mechanical movements; we can only describe them by saying that the creature strives persistently towards an end. For its movements do not cease when it meets with obstacles, or when it is subjected to forces which tend to deflect it: such obstacles and such opposition rather provoke still more forcible striving, and this striving only terminates upon the attainment of its natural end . . . 2. The striving of the creature is not merely a persistent pushing in a given direction . . . the kind and direction of movement are varied again and again so long as the obstacle is not overcome . . . 3. In behaviour the whole organism is involved . . . All [the] parts and organs are subordinated to and co-ordinated with the organs primarily involved in the activity. 4. . . . There is as a rule some evidence of increased efficiency of action, of better adaptation of the means adopted to the ends sought— the process of gaining the end is shortened, or in some other way exhibits increased efficiency in subserving the life of the individual or of the species.[8]

In the same year his *Psychology* appeared, in which he defined behavior as purposive: "When we say that [living things] exhibit behaviour, we mean that they seem to have an intrinsic power of self-determination, and to pursue actively or with effort their own ends and purposes. The manifestation of purpose or the striving to achieve an end is, then, the mark of behaviour."[9] He listed phenomena demonstrating a scale of purposive behavior, from the amoeba up to man. Further refinements of detail followed in later years, and in 1925 the twentieth edition of *Social Psychology* included the following characterization of purpose:

These [seven] objective marks of purpose may be enumerated as follows: First, a certain spontaneity of movement, a power of initiative. Secondly, a tendency to persistence . . . Thirdly, variation of kind or of direction of the persistent movements. Fourthly, the cessation of the movements when, and not until, they result in the attainment of the goal, in effecting a change of situation of a particular kind. Fifthly, the movements commonly seem to anticipate, or prepare in some manner for, the new situation which they themselves tend to bring about. Sixthly, repetition of the situation that has evoked the train of movements, evokes again a similar train of movements, but the movements so evoked commonly show . . . some degree of improvement in respect of efficiency, *i.e.*, in respect of speed, accuracy, or nicety of adjustment. Seventhly, the purposive action is in a sense a total reaction, that is to say, it is an activity in which the whole organism takes part so far as necessary; the energies of the whole organism seem to be bent towards the one end, all other concurrent processes within it being subordinated to the major or dominant system of hormic activity.[10]

This list of observable characteristics provides a behaviorist definition of purposiveness which is fundamental to McDougall's psychology and which was adopted by many theorists within the behaviorist movement. Whereas all these descriptive criteria are indicative of purpose, McDougall felt the most significant to be the variation of means, the use of many different motor abilities in the effort to reach the goal.

A definition like this one enables us to describe behavior as "purposive" in an entirely objective manner. It also allows us to refer to the observable features that are the marks of purposive behavior in answering our original question, what is a purpose? The "purpose" of a train of action is, typically, the goal or end toward which that action tends, and the achievement of which is observed to terminate the activity. The purpose may often be identified before the action under observation is completed, granted that one is reasonably familiar with the organism concerned. Hull has objected to purposive explanations, complaining that the theorist is helpless in the case of a purposive behavior situation not hitherto known to him.[11] McDougall also noticed this difficulty, but pointed out that continued observation of the animal's behavior would compensate for it: "And, if it be asked —How do we ascertain the nature of the goal? we reply that, though in any particular instance we may be in doubt during observation of the train of action, repeated observation of animals of the same species in similar situations enables us to define the goal . . . And we observe not only that these activities tend to continue, or to be renewed again and again, until that goal is accomplished; but also, we observe, that as soon as that goal is attained, the activities of this general kind cease, to give place to a new cycle, directed towards a different goal."[12]

However, this is not a fully satisfactory definition of purpose, for the possibility of ambiguity and misunderstanding in speaking of the "purpose" of action has not yet been excluded. Typically, the goal or end of action is that state of affairs to which the action in fact leads, or is likely to lead. But this is not always the case. For strictly speaking, the purpose is the goal that the organism *has in mind,* which is desired and is believed by the agent to be, perhaps, attainable by means of the activity in question. If this belief is false, the purpose may not be achieved. Indeed, the very activity which is directed toward that end may preclude the achievement of the goal. For example, offering someone a bribe may be the decisive factor in losing one's chance of promotion, but the bribe was nonetheless offered for the purpose of getting the better job. This essential connection of purpose with the beliefs and desires of the agent is an aspect of the "intensionality" of behavior. It follows that, although purposive concepts are indeed grounded in observable features of behavior, the identification of the particular purpose currently directing behavior may not be a straightforward matter of observation. The extreme variability of human beliefs renders it impossible in principle to formulate a clear empirical, operational definition of any particular human purpose or intention. However confident an observer may be in attributing a goal to another human being, it is always possible that he is wrong because it is always possible that he is mistaken in his assumptions about the background beliefs involved. This type of difficulty has led some personality theorists to reject the everyday term "intention" as unsuited to a scientific psychology, criticizing those self-styled "naive psychologists" such as Fritz Heider who are prepared to assign it a theoretical role.[13] Similar difficulties, in principle, attend the ascription of purposes to animals, but the relative simplicity and nonvariability of animal "beliefs" means that such difficulties may normally be ignored. Rather than defining the "purpose" of an action as the attainment of the goal, therefore,

31

one should define it as the idea of the goal that the organism has in mind. Should the goal be attained, that cycle of purposive behavior will be observed to cease.

Mechanistic Explanation

Granted that we are able to identify purposive behavior—by reference to the descriptive characteristics listed by McDougall —the question remains how it is to be explained. How are we to answer questions asking why a certain behavioral episode occurred? In particular, if we explain it by mentioning the "purpose" of it, what sort of explanation is this, and how does it relate to causal explanations in terms of bodily mechanisms? At this point, it is convenient to regard an "explanation" as any answer to a why question that is accepted by the questioner as making the event in question somehow more intelligible. A "scientific explanation" may be defined as an explanation that is justified by reference to publicly observable facts, and which is rationally linked to other, similar explanations in a reasonably systematic manner. These definitions are deliberately vague. They allow stories of storks to count as nonscientific explanations of the appearance of newborn babies. They do not permit a sharp dividing line between explanation and description. They say nothing of the detailed manner in which scientific explanations must be rationally interlinked, nor precisely how they are "justified" by reference to empirical facts. And they do not specify that the only way in which a phenomenon can be made "more intelligible" is by exhibiting the causal relations or mechanisms involved.

"Scientific explanation" has sometimes been defined in a more restrictive fashion, involving, for instance, universal, exceptionless laws linked in a hypothetico-deductive manner, or being based on observational data and protocol statements of a particular epistemological type.[14] The hypothetico-deductive definition has strongly influenced some psychologists, notably Hull and K. W. Spence. But others, for differing reasons, have criticized this model and its associated research-strategy; psychologists as different as the humanist A. H. Maslow and the behaviorist B. F. Skinner are united in their rejection of this classical positivist model of scientific explanation.[15] This controversy is not crucial for the present argument, and a nonrestrictive characterization of "explanation" in science leaves the issue open. Similarly, it would be inappropriate at this point to adopt a usage of "explanation" that limits the term to accounts of the causal mechanisms underlying the phenomenon to be explained. To do so, while continuing to speak of "purposive explanation," would be to prejudge the issue of whether or not teleological explanations are causal. The term "explanation" should therefore not be understood to cover only causal explanations. Rather, it should be understood in a more general way, to cover all answers to why questions that are commonly classed as "explanatory" in everyday speech. A *fortiori*, this usage will include all answers that are intended and accepted as scientific explanations by practising scientists. Many different types of answers have thus been counted as "explanatory," and the sense in which any given *explanans* makes its *explanandum* "more intelligible" remains to be shown. Our interest lies in explanations of behavior, in psychologists' answers to why questions. Specifically, the points at issue are whether behavior describable as "purposive" is also explicable in terms of "purpose," and what relation purposive explanation bears to nonpurposive accounts.

These are questions to which McDougall repeatedly turned throughout his working life. He insisted that behavior cannot be explained in a nonpurposive fashion, that it is not amenable to stimulus-response explanations or to explanations that are validly employed in the sciences of physics and chemistry. In arguing this position, he distinguished two forms of explanation—"mechanistic" or "mechanical," and "teleological"—which he thought proper to the natural sciences and life sciences respectively. He defined "mechanistic" explanation in several of his works, almost always negatively, and he contrasted it with "teleological" explanation. He also spoke of mechanistic and teleological causation, largely because he assumed that any "explanation" must, by definition, exhibit the causal base or energy mechanism of the phenomenon concerned. This assumption accounts for his tendency to assimilate the terms "explanation" and "causation" and to use them interchangeably. This tendency is evident in the following examples of his definition of "mechanistic" explanation:

> Mechanistic causation [is] the principle of causation that finds the explanation of present events in terms only of the causal influence of antecedent events, without reference of any kind to possible future events.

> [Mechanists explain] solely by reference to physical and chemical causes of movement, without making use of the conception of a goal or of an impulse directed to a goal.[16]

He justified the negativity of his definition in this way:

> When we closely examine this proposition [that in science only mechanistic causation or explanation is admissible], we find it impossible to discover in it any positive meaning. For what is mechanistic causation? In the days when it was possible for men of science to believe in the strictly mechanical theory of the physical world, in the billiard-ball theory . . . the term "mechanistic causation" had a definite and positive meaning: it meant . . . communication of motion, momentum or kinetic energy . . . When, with the progress of physical science, that theory became untenable, very many still clung to the principle—the formula that only mechanistic explanation must be admitted in science—failing to see that, with the passing of the billiard-ball theory, it had lost all positive meaning, and retained only the negative implication that teleological explanation is inadmissible.[17]

This passage shows that, despite his avowedly negative definition, McDougall did allow that one sense of the term "mechanistic" could be distinguished by clearly positive criteria. He himself, in fact, used the term in another positively definable sense, as well as in a purely negative way. In short, McDougall used the term in three different senses. He did not always distinguish clearly between them. Moreover, most writers who use the term do so in a similarly ambiguous fashion, with the result that the crucial issues in the confrontation of teleology with mechanism are often obscured, today as in McDougall's time. If the relation of purpose to "mechanism" is to be clearly understood, it is essential to distinguish between these different senses.

McDougall's admittedly positive sense of "mechanistic explanation" was often marked by his use of the word "mechanical" rather than the word "mechanistic." However, he was not completely consistent in his use of these two terms, tending to employ them interchangeably, particularly in his earlier writings. McDougall's references to the corpuscular "billiard-ball" theory and the "communication of motion, momentum or kinetic energy" suggest that he regarded the explanations of classical mechanics as paradigm cases of mechanical (or mechanistic) explanation in what he called the "positive" sense. Elsewhere, he was more explicit on this point: "So long as Atomic Materialism was accepted the meaning of the word 'mechanistic,' as applied to qualify any description or explanation, any hypothesis or theory or event, was clear and simple; mechanistic was synonymous with mechanical, and the mechanical theory assumed that all changes were changes of position, all processes were movements of matter, and all causation was of the nature of change of momentum by impact of masses."[18] By "Atomic Materialism," McDougall meant the scientific world view crudely formulated by Democritus and stated clearly by Newton, a world view he described as "mechanical materialism in the strictest sense."[19]

If McDougall's use of the expression "mechanistic explanation" in the first sense is compared with Ernest Nagel's more recent usage, it appears to resemble what Nagel has termed "pure mechanical" explanation. According to Nagel, the three least restrictive conditions for a "mechanical" explanation are as follows:

(a) Its ultimate premises assert that the time-rate of change in the momentum of a physical system is a function of the magnitude and direction of the forces acting on it. (b) The direction of the change in momentum of a body is along the direction of the impressed force; and the direction of such a change associated with several forces is along the direction of the vectorial sum of the component forces. (c) The forces are specified exclusively in terms of the spatio-temporal magnitudes and relations of bodies, a universal constant, and a number of constant coefficients (assumed to be listed exhaustively) whose values depend on the individual properties of a given system of bodies.[20]

Explanations that appeal to force functions specifiable in terms of the Newtonian equations and of various factors such as mass, electric charge, magnetic strength, viscosity, elasticity, or friction will be "mechanical" in this sense. Nagel calls theories that provide such explanations "*unrestricted* mechanical theories," since the constant coefficients which may be concerned are unrestricted in type.

By modifying the third condition so that only distinctly mechanical parameters are allowed, Nagel defines a more restrictive class of "*pure* mechanical theories." Such theories demand that "the force-function be specified exclusively in terms of spatio-temporal variables, the universal constant of gravitation, and coefficients of mass." References to electric charge, magnetic strength, or viscosity debar an explanation from being "mechanical" in this sense. The Newtonian theory of gravitation, however, is purely mechanical. An even more restrictive sense of "mechanical" is reached by further limiting the force functions involved, so that only a single prescribed form is allowed: "For example, the force-function may be limited to the form associated with central forces (such as the inverse-square form of Newtonian gravitational theory), or it may be restricted to having the form for contact forces between perfectly elastic bodies."[21] One such *unitary* mechanical theory was Newton's ideal. He regarded his theory of gravitation as unsatisfactory since it appealed to "action at a distance." Its explanations were not "mechanical" in the stringent sense that allows reference to contact forces only. McDougall's "positive" sense of the term "mechanical explanation" was not so restrictive as this third sense of Nagel's. But it did exclude electromagnetic theories, since these are not "billiard-ball" theories expressed purely in terms of "the communication of motion, momentum or kinetic energy." In other words, McDougall's positive sense of mechanistic explanation corresponded most closely to Nagel's definition of "pure mechanical" theories.

McDougall only rarely intended this first sense when using the terms "mechanistic" or "mechanical" explanation. Nor were these terms generally so used by his contemporaries. Although the claim that all natural phenomena have a "mechanistic" or "mechanical" basis was commonly made, by McDougall's time the view that the natural world is explicable in the terms of classical mechanics alone (in terms, that is, of pure mechanical theories) had already passed its heyday. Clearly, the word "mechanistic" was generally being used in a more extended sense. McDougall noted that a number of different forms of explanation were commonly referred to by his contemporaries as "mechanistic." Some of these were typical of various branches of physics itself, others of sciences such as chemistry, biology, physiology, and psychology. The examples he mentioned at various points included explanations typical of classical mechanics, electromagnetic theory, relativity theory, and quantum mechanics; of Mendelian genetics and neo-Darwinian evolutionary theory; of C. S. Sherrington's account of reflex response and neural integrative activity; and of psychologies that viewed behavior in terms of tropisms, drives, conditioned reflexes, and behaviorist stimulus-response connections.

Not all these examples qualify as "mechanical" explanations even in Nagel's "unrestricted" sense, for Nagel's first two conditions provide a distinctly Newtonian flavor. For instance, the first condition stipulates that the *explanans* in the ultimate premises of the theory concerned be "the time-rate of change in the momentum of a physical system." In most of the explanations just listed, the *explanans* is not expressed in such a form. Indeed, there is no one form characterizing all of them, for the conceptual structure of these different types of "mechanistic" explanation varies considerably. Some are explicitly causal; others are not. Some are wholly deterministic, while others are not. Some appeal to exceptionless laws, others to statistical generalizations. Some explain in terms of mathematical field equations and precisely measurable parameters, while others appeal to vaguely specified causes such as Mendelian "factors" or "genes." Still others refer to specific causal mechanisms describable in detail at the biochemical or physiological level, whereas some avoid mention of all mechanisms and rely merely on correlations between observable behavioral units. Some regard the function (in maintaining equilibrium or achieving adaptation) as crucial to the explanation of a particular phenomenon, while others do not. Some are concerned with very small-scale (for instance, subatomic) events, while others deal with whole species and the ecological relationships of vast geographical areas.

There being no formal element or conceptual structure common to all these so-called "mechanistic" explanations, McDougall therefore claimed that mechanistic explanation can only be negatively defined: "With the passing of Atomic Materialism it has become very difficult to define in any positive terms the meaning of 'mechanistic,' and the negative definition . . . remains the only satisfactory and comprehensive one . . . The mechanistic, then, as so defined, includes not only strictly mechanical events (if any such there be) but all that can be adequately described and explained without taking account of prospective reference."[22] This second, negatively defined sense of "mechanistic" may be called the formally mechanistic sense. Formally mechanistic explanations are alike only in that no reference to goals or to possible future events is necessary to their formulation.

McDougall recognized that many of his contemporaries in fact intended more than this by the term "mechanistic," for they believed such explanations to be alike in that the natural phenomena they explain are basically nothing but highly complex physical systems. That is, they held that all the explanations listed above, despite their superficial differences, are reducible to explanations in terms of physicochemical laws. They would doubtless have said the same about more modern types of explanation involving the concepts of molecular biology, information theory, and programming terminology. Some or all of the physicochemical laws concerned may be drawn from a theory of the "unrestricted mechanical" type; but it is not crucial to this general reductionist viewpoint that such Newtonian underpinnings be available. The concepts involved in the laws of physics are different in different historical periods, and one cannot specify a priori just what form physical laws must take. But whatever "the laws of physics and chemistry" may be, the reductionist viewpoint maintains that other scientific explanations are reducible to explanations that are admittedly "physicochemical" in nature. This viewpoint was also labeled "mechanistic" by McDougall, who spoke of "the mechanistic dogma" that "mechanical principles of explanation hold exclusive sway throughout the universe."[23] According to the strongly reductionist view, even those psychological explanations that do refer to goals are reducible to physicochemical explanations. Though not formally mechanistic, such psychological explanations are assumed by the reductionist to be basically mechanistic in that they are reducible to formally mechanistic ones. This third sense of "mechanistic" is not purely negative, for the positive claim is made that the explanations so called are reducible to physicochemical laws. McDougall did not usually make clear the distinction between the second and third senses—largely because he thought that no explanation which was not formally mechanistic could be basically mechanistic. However, since it is this question that is at issue here, the distinction between "formally" and "basically" mechanistic explanations must be stressed.

Teleological Explanation

McDougall held that, in contrast to "mechanistic" explanation, "teleological" explanation can be positively defined. Both in his early and in his later work, he consistently offered three positive criteria of teleological or purposive explanation. A fourth criterion was hinted at or implicit in most of his writings, and was explicitly stated in *The Energies of Men*. These criteria were as follows: first, some prospective reference to possible future events is required. Second, reference is made to purposes or goals that are in some sense ultimate for or fundamental to the organism concerned. Third, a number of subjective psychological categories (such as "consciousness," "foresight," and "desire") are involved. And fourth, purposive explanation entails the postulation of a special form of mental energy.

The last criterion has the form of an empirical hypothesis: it is probably false, and certainly nonessential to purposive accounts of behavior. But the first three are concerned with the logical or conceptual nature of teleological explanation, and they may be accepted. These three have commonly been noted in discussions of purposive explanation, as in the work of certain behavorist psychologists and in the recent philosophical literature. Even when they are not explicitly itemized, they implicitly influence arguments concerning the nature of purpose, because they indicate the general logical form of teleological approaches to behavior. McDougall himself did not enumerate them, and his discussion of them was widely diffused throughout his work, often consisting of very brief passages or unargued assertions, which can be fully understood only in the light of his remarks elsewhere or of his psychology as a whole.

In distinguishing and reformulating these three conceptual criteria, I aim to give a skeleton outline of the logical form of purposive explanation. The explanations provided by a purposive psychology must be of this logical type, whether the background theory is broadly behaviorist, Freudian, or humanist in character. The fuller consideration of McDougall's theoretical psychology will show that his system also was constructed according to this conceptual form. Only in the light of these criteria can one understand why McDougall and many others have believed teleological explanation to be both formally and basically non-mechanistic.

The first logical criterion of teleological explanation is the necessity of prospective reference. In "formally mechanistic" contexts, by definition, no reference to the future need be made in explaining the occurrence of a present phenomenon. But in the psychological explanation of current behavior this is not so, for the very description or identification of the behavior as behavior intrinsically involves reference to a possible future event. This is evident from a consideration of the objective, descriptive criteria of behavior. To regard a series of movements as "behavior" is to identify them as showing a particular type of pattern, namely, as being directed toward a goal, as tending toward a particular change of situation that is the end of the activity concerned. Typically, various means are suitable for a given end. Selection among these depends partly on external circumstances and partly on the individual characteristics of the organism. Thus, the detailed movements of "equivalent" behavioral units may vary considerably. Behavioral subunits are identifiable (and explicable) in terms of the overall goal: a child may move away from his goal object in order to reach it, and will attempt various maneuvers in the process—all of which can be identified as attempts to approach the goal. This is why McDougall insisted that behavior and action must be analyzed in terms of conative units, by reference to the ends sought. Similarly, C. I. Lewis has expressed this insight: "All acts have in common the character of being intended or willed. But one act is distinguishable from another by the content of it, the

40

expected result of it, which is here spoken of as its intent. There is no obvious way in which we can say what act it is which is thought of or which is done except by specifying this intent of it."[24] Movement, by contrast, may be analyzed nonconatively, for example, in terms of muscle twitches or of changes in the spatial co-ordinates of bodily parts. Accordingly, it can be explained in formally mechanistic terms, such as the concepts typical of physiology or physics.

Another way of phrasing this criterion is to state that purposive explanation is not "atomistic." Atomistic explanations connect independently identifiable units. Future units may be predictable from the prior occurrence of other units, granted certain general postulates of correlation. But the future units need not be appealed to in any way for the initial identification of the prior units, and thus are logically isolable from them. Atomistic units may be of many types. In psychology they include mental contents such as the associationist "ideas" and behaviorist units such as pure "stimulus" and "response." In physiology they include units such as muscle twitches and the firing of individual neurons. The ideomotor theory is, at least in intent, an atomistic psychophysiological theory: movements are held to be caused by associationist "ideas." Causal explanations in general—that is, explanations specifying efficient causes—are atomistic, since "causes" must be identifiable independently of their "effects." Thus, all causal explanations are formally mechanistic, though not all formally mechanistic explanations are causal. For instance, explanations of machine performance in programming or "flow-chart" terms are not causal; neither are explanations referring to mere statistical correlations, as in the statement that societies of religion X generally have a higher suicide rate than societies of religion Y.

It follows from McDougall's descriptive list of "objective marks of purpose" that purposive explanation is not atomistic, for some prospective reference is essential to the observational identification of a particular behavioral unit in the first place. As McDougall pointed out, a bird may use its powers of flight in the course of migration, mating, fighting, escaping from danger, building a nest, or pursuing prey; but the identification of its flight movements as an element in one of these activities rather

41

than another requires reference to the whole sequence. Behavior must be analyzed into conative units—but if an element can only be identified as part of a pattern, it is not identifiable as such independently of other elements. A child's movement away from the cupboard cannot be identified as part of an attempt to reach the jam independently of other observed or hypothesized movements, such as prior movements toward the cupboard, subsequent movements toward a stool, and so on. "Means" and "end" are logically complementary terms: it would not make sense to identify a unit of behavior as a means without being prepared to specify a hypothetical goal as its possible end. This does not mean that the specified end must actually occur if the behavioral identification has been correct, for means behavior may occur independently of its end, in the sense that the end may never actually be achieved. Purposive behavior can happen independently of its goal happening. But it cannot be identified as such independently of reference to some possible future unit to which it is supposed to tend. This is the meaning of the statement that purposive explanation does not deal with atomistic units.

According to some philosophies of science, it immediately follows that purposive explanation is not scientific, or is scientific only if it can be translated into atomistic terms.[25] Thus, if one were to accept a basically atomistic account of perception and a correspondingly atomistic epistemology, it would follow that the observational data of science must themselves be expressible in atomistic terms. Similarly, scientific "explanations" would be essentially atomistic, linking independently identifiable units. Such a view is likely to misinterpret the logic of teleological explanations, so that *purposes* are regarded as queer backward-working causes and are rejected on account of their queerness; for instance, Hull criticizes purposive explanation in this way. McDougall rightly objected to this interpretation of teleology. The epistemology of the associationists was atomistic, deriving from the philosophical writings of Locke and Hume. According to this classical empiricist tradition, if purposive explanation is a valid scientific procedure at any level, it must be somehow expressible in atomistic terms. Conative units must be expressible in terms of pure movements, or perhaps, movements plus ideas.

But McDougall recognized that the future reference involved in purposive explanation is neither logically eliminable nor interpretable atomistically as a backward cause. He did not accept the associationists' account of perception; on the contrary, he constantly criticized "the atomistic, mosaic psychology." Accordingly, he was not committed to their epistemological assumptions; he did not interpret knowledge as a set of associationist connections between logically independent ideas. He granted that the data of science must be objective, or publicly observable, and consequently listed "objective marks of purpose" defining a behaviorist rather than an introspectionist psychology. Some "behaviorists" have allowed purposive terms only on the understanding that they could, in principle, be translated into the terms of what Hull has called "mere colorless movements," or pure stimulus and response.[26] Their stimulus-response approach was encouraged by the positivist or operationalist philosophy of science predominant during the development of behaviorism.[27] Operationalism, in turn, was based on the atomistic epistemology of logical positivism, an epistemology that has been increasingly questioned since its initial formulation by the Vienna Circle.[28] A detailed discussion of these epistemological matters would be out of place here. The important point is that it is not self-evident that knowledge should be described in an atomistic fashion, and there are persuasive arguments for rejecting this epistemological approach. McDougall himself did not assume an atomistic epistemology, and in his psychology he stressed organizing cognitive principles as basic features of knowledge and perception; consequently, he was not being inconsistent in claiming that the observational data of psychological science are nonatomistic. Teleological explanation cannot properly be rejected as "unscientific" by virtue of this first criterion unless an atomistic epistemology is taken for granted.

The second criterion of teleology marks a further logical difference between formally mechanistic and purposive explanations. In mechanistic contexts, whatever theoretical level is reached, it is always in principle possible to ask for a further stage of mechanistic explanation at a deeper level. For it is always possible that a future scientific theory might be developed that underlies the theory which is currently regarded as basic in

43

the particular area concerned. For instance, "basic" explanations in terms of the interactions of atoms were eventually underwritten by or reduced to explanations in terms of subatomic particles; and Newtonian mechanics was shown to be explicable in terms of relativity theory. Similarly, use of the mechanistic categories of cause and effect permits one to go on asking for causal explanations ad infinitum. For the question, "What caused that event?" may be asked recursively in a nonterminating progression: however far one goes in the search for causes, one can always sensibly go further still. Admittedly, the notion of a "causal chain" is an abstraction from the flux of physical reality and is to some extent misleading.[29] But granted that this form of explanation is used to account for particular events, one must be prepared, in principle, to go on for ever. In the history of science certain conceptual categories have sometimes been suggested a priori as the only ones truly suitable to an "ultimate" theoretical level of scientific explanation. For example, Newton was dissatisfied with his gravitational theory because it did not analyze physical phenomena in terms of contact forces. But the actual development of science has not vindicated such ideas, and the metaphysical reasons advanced in support of them have not convinced most of the practitioners or philosophers of science. Thus, there are no a priori reasons determining the points at which efforts at mechanistic explanation must cease. The points at which our various mechanistic explanations actually come to a stop will be determined by the pattern of our interests and ignorance at that time, not by any conceptual feature which all these points might have in common.

In contrast, purposive explanations do, in principle, come to a stop. Purposes and goals may be linked together: one may do a thing in order to do something else, and that in order to do a third, and so on. But unlike the concept of cause, the concept of purpose cannot be "chained" indefinitely. All action, actual and intended, cannot be a means to an end. Some action must qualify as an end in itself. There must, therefore, be points where it is senseless to ask why, if what one wants is an answer in terms of some further goal or purpose of the organism concerned. That is, this question is denied application at certain

44

points. These "stopping points" must be represented in the basic theoretical concepts of a purposive psychology.

McDougall's way of expressing this second criterion was to insist that the psychologist must identify certain natural goals or "instincts" of organisms as basic units of theoretical analysis. The organism has these goals naturally, prior to any other purposes it may have. This was a basic claim of McDougall's hormic psychology, which he stated thus: "When, and not until, we can exhibit any particular instance of conduct or behaviour as the expression of conative tendencies which are ultimate constituents of the organism, we can claim to have explained it."[30] As in this passage, McDougall sometimes referred to instincts in the terminology of "natural tendencies." In his last published paper (1938), entitled "Tendencies as Indispensable Postulates of All Psychology," he argued that "tendency" is an irreducibly teleological term.[31] Consequently, he wrote, Newton's laws are better not expressed in terms of "tending," but rather as conditional statements of generalization based on observation, such as: The planet will move in a straight line unless . . . He felt that the use of the expression "tendency" in such a clearly mechanistic, pure mechanical context obscures the differences between living and nonliving things.[32] The term "tendency" is used more commonly in biological contexts than in physics, but McDougall did not object to its use in biology as he did with reference to Newtonian mechanics. For although he commonly used the terms "teleological" and "purposive" as though they were synonyms—as I have also been doing—he did sometimes suggest that biological phenomena are teleological yet not fully purposive. In clearly psychological, purposive contexts he preferred the term "instinct" to "tendency," since it more readily suggests a goal of the organism concerned. According to McDougall, then, purposive explanation characteristically comes to an end with the mention of an inherent tendency or instinct directing behavior toward a natural goal. Given such an "ultimate" explanation, purposive questioning must stop.

McDougall's third criterion of purposive explanation was that it involves various subjective psychological categories, such as consciousness, foresight, striving, and so on:

> For the explanation of [psychophysical events] we have to take into account foresight of the possible future course of events and striving guided by such foresight.

> To say that behaviour is purposive is to imply that it has also an inner side or aspect which is analogous to, and of the same order as, our immediate experience of our own purposive activities.

> One modern authority . . . goes so far as to say that "the idea of consciousness must be rigidly excluded from any definition of instinct which is to be of practical utility." In view of this persistent tendency to ignore the inner or psychical side of instinctive processes, it seems to me important to insist upon it.[33]

In linking purpose with foresight, McDougall acknowledged that the term "purpose" is commonly taken to imply a clearer foresight of the goal than can plausibly be ascribed to animals; but he defended his wider usage by ascribing various levels of consciousness to animals, and ideas of differing degrees of clarity.[34] Similarly, terms such as "intention," "knowledge," and "belief" were ascribed by him to animals in a weaker sense than they are commonly understood in the context of adult human behavior. McDougall recognized both the cognitive aspect of purpose (its implication of foresight, ideas, judgments, and beliefs) and the conative aspect (its close connection with the categories of desire): "Purpose in the fullest sense is desire fixed by self-conscious judgment and resolve."[35] These two aspects of purpose have already been noted in connection with the point that the identification of the purpose of an observable action involves implicit reference to the agent's beliefs and desires.

In claiming that the concepts of *purpose* and *consciousness* are essentially connected, McDougall also insisted that each involves an essential reference to a psychological subject and object, a distinction that is not expressible in nonpsychological, mechanistic terms. His early text *Psychology* contained a chapter on consciousness, in which he wrote:

> We cannot ignore the fact that someone is conscious, the fact that I am conscious, or that some other organism more or less like myself is conscious; that is to say, consciousness does not

exist of itself, but is an activity of some being . . . to which we may conveniently give the general name, *subject*.

A second fundamental fact is that to be conscious is to be conscious of something; which thing is properly called the *object* of my consciousness. Being conscious is, then, an activity of a *subject* in relation to an *object*.[36]

Over twenty years later he was still stressing this feature of purposive concepts: "We frequently use the word *purpose* in an almost purely objective sense; we define a man's purpose in terms of a goal towards which he is set, yet we have to add or imply that this is *his* goal; and this in turn implies the subjective fact that the man inclines . . . towards that goal . . . The word *purpose*, then, denotes a unique relation between a subject and an object, namely, a developed form of the conative relation, the relation of consciously and deliberately seeking or striving for."[37] McDougall allowed, as a theoretical possibility, that consciousness might occasionally involve a psychological subject only, there being no object of thought. But such "anoetic" experience, even if it occurred, would be indescribable and for practical purposes may be ignored:

All experience then is the experience of some subject. Whether all experience takes the form of thinking of an object is a debatable question. It has been pointed out that, while every experience that any one can introspectively observe and report upon is a thinking of an object, yet sometimes we seem to be almost purely passive, to approximate to mere suffering or enjoying without being aware of any object; and it has been argued that we may justifiably postulate a kind of experience that, going yet further in this direction, becomes a pure passivity. Such hypothetical purely passive experience would not be thinking of an object and might be called "anoetic experience."[38]

This third conceptual criterion of purpose may be conveniently expressed by stating that all thought and experience, all psychological and behavioral processes (with the possible exception of passive states of anoetic sentience), are essentially "intensional" in nature. McDougall did not use this term, which is

47

derived from the philosophy of Franz Brentano. As I use it, thought or behavior is "intensional" in that it is directed on a psychological object. A man's intentions—and his intentional behavior—are intensional in this sense; so also are his hopes and fears, his knowledge and beliefs, his perceptions and illusions. Thus, the specific concern here is not with intentional, as opposed to involuntary or "unintentional," phenomena. Rather, the concern is with the general psychological distinction between the thinking subject and the object of thought. The subject-object distinction so stressed by McDougall is thus the basis of the intensionality of thought and of purposive behavior in general. It follows that teleological explanations must necessarily employ intensional sentences.

An "intensional" sentence, according to this use of the term, is a sentence whose meaning involves the notion of the direction of the mind on an object. It may be concerned with inner, sometimes introspectible, psychological processes, or with observable behavior. Recent discussions of intensionality have pointed out that intensional sentences have certain logical peculiarities.[39] Typically, not all of these peculiarities characterize any one intensional sentence, but at least one of them does. In technical terms, these logical peculiarities include indeterminacy, referential opacity, failure of existential generalization, no implication of any embedded clause (or its negation), and non-extensional occurrence of embedded clauses. In plain English, intensional sentences have rather different implications from non-intensional (extensional) sentences, to which they are superficially similar in logical form.

For example, the intensional sentence "It is hoped that the Queen will attend the ceremony" implies neither that she will, nor that she will not, attend; whereas the extensional sentence "It is true that the Queen will attend" implies that she will do so. Similarly, within an intensional sentence the substantive phrase that refers to the object of behavior or of thought may fail to refer to any real thing: one may search for unicorns or pursue a less fanciful goal that is never in fact achieved. In contrast, the extensional "He is near the unicorn" can only be true if a real unicorn is actually in the vicinity. Again, the phrase referring to the object of thought may be essentially indeterminate or incomplete: one may want a pencil, old or new, black or red, blunt or sharp— virtually any pencil will do. But any actual pencil must have quite determinate characteristics in each of these ways, and many others. Further, the phrase in question may occur in such a way that its replacement by another name or description of the same thing would result in a proposition of different truth-value. Hamlet intended to kill the man he heard calling for help behind the arras, but did not intend to kill Polonius; nonetheless, the man behind the arras and Polonius were one and the same person. Hamlet mistook Polonius for the King, and so he was able to *explain* his action by saying, "I took thee for thy better."

As in Hamlet's case, so it is in general; the intensional object (the object of thought) can be described only by reference to the subject's thoughts, such as his purposes, beliefs, expectations, and desires. There may be no actual thing with which the object of thought can be sensibly identified. Even if there is, the identification will seem sensible only on the basis of certain descriptions of the real thing, and the intensional object may be indeterminate in a way that no actual object can be. In his remarks on ascribing an object of thought to a subject of consciousness, McDougall showed his implicit awareness of such logical peculiarities, although he did not express them in detail. These peculiarities underlie the inappropriateness of defining "a purpose" as the actual attainment of the goal. As McDougall realized, the sense in which "a purpose" can be identified with "the attainment of the goal" is the intensional sense, according to which the goal is understood as an object of thought ascribable to the organism considered as a psychological subject.

McDougall, in fact, allowed for a form of explanation satisfying his first two criteria, but not the intensional criterion of consciousness. Such an explanation he regarded as teleological, but not strictly purposive: "[Within the sphere of seemingly purposive activities there may be] a lower type which, though incapable of mechanical explanation and analogous to purposive activity, yet involves no conscious direction, and is therefore not truly purposive."[40] A similar suggestion has recently been made by Charles Taylor, who claims:

It is quite possible that a continuous progression will be found, leading from inanimate non-teleological systems, through animate teleological systems to those which are not only teleological but purposive in character. Thus, it may be that those lower species to which the concept "action" [like other intensional concepts] has no application (as well as those relatively integrated sub-systems in higher organisms which are studied by biologists) are nevertheless such that their behaviour can only be accounted for by teleological, although non-purposive, laws.[41]

Having made the suggestion, Taylor leaves the question open. By contrast, McDougall always held that the nonpsychological life-sciences required a teleological (though nonintensional) type of explanation, and he early argued the point in detail in *Body and Mind*. According to him, neither embryology, morphology, evolutionary theory, nor physiology can rely solely on basically mechanistic principles of explanation: "No single organic function has been found to be wholly explicable on physical and chemical principles . . . in every case there is manifested some power of selection, of regulation, of restitution or of synthesis, which continues completely to elude all attempts at mechanical explanation."[42] For instance:

The physico-chemical doctrine of life must postulate in the germ-cell a physico-chemical mechanism of a complexity beside which that of any tissue-cell of the developed organism . . . seems simplicity itself. For the mechanism of that germ-cell must, if the assumption be true, somehow contain the potentiality of the specific, complex, and widely different mechanisms of all the cells of all the many different tissues of the body; and at the same time it must contain the potentiality of the exact but very complex grouping of these cells within the tissues, and of the ordering of the various tissues in relation to one another, relations which again are of extreme complexity.[43]

McDougall thus raised problems which still await a complete answer. But recent research on the genetic code suggests possibilities of mechanistic explanation that were inconceivable to him. With the present knowledge of the protein-forming systems of the cell, it is possible to counter his vague form of vitalism with specific biochemical facts. It is not necessary to rely solely on an admission of faith in "the mechanistic dogma," without any specific suggestions as to what physicochemical processes are basically involved. Moreover, the biologist G. W. C. Sommerhoff and the philosopher Nagel have given detailed analyses of "teleological" explanations in biology, which show that reliance on such explanations in no way precludes the possibility of regarding living organisms as basically mechanistic physical systems.[44] Their analyses show that these explanations are functional rather than purposive: as McDougall suggested, the biologist's use of "purpose" is less rich than the psychologist's. When the biologist uses the term, he does not imply consciousness of any sort, nor ascribe intensional goals to the organism considered as an agent. His concern is with function rather than purpose in the full sense.[45] The sense in which "teleological" may be applied to biological explanations is, therefore, weaker than McDougall's more usual use of the term. I shall continue to use "teleological" as synonymous with "purposive," as he normally did.

Teleological explanations, then, must satisfy the first three of McDougall's criteria. In the terminology I have introduced, they must be "nonatomistic," they must refer to purposive "stopping points," and they must be "intensional" in character. These criteria distinguish logical or conceptual features of purposive explanations, by virtue of which such explanations differ from formally mechanistic ones.

According to McDougall, purposive explanations also satisfy a fourth criterion, in that they imply a specifically psychic form of energy. He was not always explicit on this issue: for instance, in 1930 he wrote "the hormic theory does not presume to say what form or forms of energy ... are involved."[46] But in his last systematic text, *Energies of Men*, he committed himself to a belief in hormic energy not subject to the laws of physics: "Does mental activity involve some form or forms of energy other than those recognized by the physical sciences? In view of the purposive nature of human activity, the positive answer to this question seems inevitable. We must postulate some energy which conforms to laws not wholly identical with the laws of energy stated by the physical sciences ... We may call it *hormic energy*."[47]

He had already postulated psychic energy in 1905 in his first book, *Physiological Psychology*. There he related consciousness and basic behavioral processes to hypothetical physiological mechanisms. Earlier still, he had suggested a neurophysiological theory of interaction, holding the synapse to be the seat of consciousness.[48] Psychical processes arise from activity at the synapses, and to each primary quality of sensation there corresponds a synaptic process of specific physicochemical nature.[49] In his discussion of "psychophysical interaction" he did not claim that psychical processes can arise in complete independence of the body. His theory of neuronal interaction was stated in terms of the flow of "neurin," or "neurokyme," a form of energy specific to the nervous system. The continuous accumulation and drainage of neurin he supposed to underlie synaptic inhibition and the formation of neural associations, and at the end of his life he was still defending this view against the all-or-none principle of nervous action. In *Abnormal Psychology* (1926) and *Energies of Men* (1932) he appealed again to neurin to account for hypnosis, suggestion, and the phenomena marked by the central working-concepts of the psychoanalytic schools. Much of what McDougall had to say at the neurological level might be given a mechanistic interpretation and compared with other theories of neural action: for instance, his view of such action as continuously graded rather than saltatory. But McDougall himself identified "neurin" with "horme," admitting that the latter word might seem more objectionable to neurophysiologists in view of its "mystical or metaphysical flavour."[50] His final position on horme was that it is energy inherently directed toward specific goals or ends: as such it involves a nonmechanistic form of causation. The validity of this suggested criterion of purpose may conveniently be left undecided at this point.

Strict and Empirical Reduction

Having distinguished between mechanistic and purposive explanations, a problem arises as to the nature of the logical relation between them. It may be that the appropriateness of a purposive explanation excludes the possibility of any mechanistic explanation of the same behavioral episode. If that were the case, then no purposive phenomenon could be explained in terms of a mechanistic physiology or of pure stimulus and response. Or it may be that teleological explanations, while not mechanistic in McDougall's second, "formal" sense, are nevertheless mechanistic in his third, "basic" sense. To clarify this problem, the notion of "reducibility" requires further discussion, for the problem can be restated as the question of whether purposive explanations are reducible to mechanistic ones. Is psychology reducible to stimulus-response behaviorism or physiology?

To ask whether purposive psychology can be reduced to a strict behaviorism or to physiology is to ask a question about the sets of statements constituting these sciences. "Reduction" in general denotes the explanation of one set of statements α by another β, with "explanation" here meaning the logical derivation of all the statements in the set α from the set β. This logical derivation may be effected in various ways, thus effecting various types of reduction. Two senses of "reduction" must be distinguished— strict reduction and empirical reduction.

Strict reduction is a relation that holds between two sets of statements in virtue of logical equivalences between the two sets. That is, α and β must be, at least in part, identical in meaning. They may appear to denote one and the same general domain, to refer to the same aspect of reality, in which case they may be called "totally equivalent." Total equivalence does not necessarily require perfect synonymy, in the sense of a one:one correspondence of symbolic terms. A superficially simple statement in α might be a shorthand expression for a much more complicated symbolic formulation, or for several different formulations, in β. In this case, β would be said to "explain" α rather than vice versa. For instance, machine instructions may be expressed by different levels of language: brief expressions in a computer programming language are shorthand for complex series of detailed expressions in machine code. And it has sometimes been claimed that superficially simple purposive expressions describing behavior are shorthand for disjunctive sets of complex mechanistic expressions using the behaviorist terminology of pure "stimulus" and "response." Thus, "He tried to get the jam" may be shorthand for the many stimulus-response descriptions of the alternative means—behaviors that could satisfy the purposive description. Given a case of total equivalence involving shorthand rather than synonymy, translations from β to α might be said to lose meaning. For they would lose some detailed information: one expression in α may be shorthand for any one of several expressions in β, so α would be ambiguous where β is not. But β would appear to describe in greater detail the same type of domain as α rather than any radically different domain. For example, stimulus-response theory is often thought of as referring to the same general domain, namely behavior, as purposive accounts analyzing behavior at a less detailed level.

Strict reducibility may also cover cases where the two sets of statements are more naturally thought of as describing different domains, referring to different aspects of reality. They are "partially equivalent," in that one domain can be referred to by either α or β, but there is some other domain that can be referred to only by β. Given β alone, therefore, one could express all that could be expressed given α alone, but not vice versa. For example, it is sometimes claimed that purposive accounts of behavior are merely shorthand for physiological ones. But the language of purposive explanation says nothing whatever about brain cells, excitation levels, or neuroanatomy. The ancient Egyptians used purposive language successfully enough, but knew next to nothing about the brain. What is meant, then, by the claim that purposive accounts are "mere shorthand" for physiological ones, is that physiological accounts can express everything that is expressed by purposive accounts—as well as much more. The claim is that psychology and physiology are partially equivalent.

To show that psychology is strictly reducible to physiology would be to show that the meaning of every purposive statement is contained within the meaning of a physiological statement. For example: "He intends to commit suicide" must be expressible in a purely physiological vocabulary, although the "equivalent" physiological statement would also provide extra information about brain states and the like. Once the reduction had been effected, psychological language could be dispensed with. Similarly, were one to effect a strict reduction of purpose to stimulus-response terms, purposive vocabulary would be logically redundant. In either case, its only usefulness would be its shorthand convenience. Only physiological (or stimulus-response) accounts would have any real explanatory power.

Empirical reduction relies on factual, rather than logical, links between the two sets of statements concerned. Statements drawn from α and β are neither totally nor partially equivalent but have clearly different meanings. The explanation of a scientific theory or a set of experimental laws (α) established in one area of inquiry, by a theory (β) formulated for some other, more "basic" domain, would be a case in point. But if the laws and theories of α contain certain terms that are not included among the theoretical terms of β, then α and β may appear to be autonomous sciences dealing with largely different subject matters, and so incapable of reduction one to the other. Clearly, such a reduction cannot be effected given α and β alone, since in a valid logical deduction no term can appear in the conclusion that does not also appear somewhere in the premises. So, in order to derive α from β, one must introduce a class of "bridging" assumptions that state suitable connections between certain theoretical terms in α and others in β. In empirical reduction, the bridging assumptions would be what Nagel has described as "physical hypotheses asserting that the occurrence of the state of affairs signified by a certain theoretical assumption 'B' in the primary science [i.e., the more "basic" β] is a sufficient (or necessary and sufficient) condition for the state of affairs designated by [some theoretical term in α]." Since these bridging statements assert empirical connections between α and β, it is clear that Nagel is right to add that "independent evidence must in principle be obtainable for the occurrence of each of the two states of affairs, so that the expressions designating the two states must have identifiably different meanings."[51]

With the help of such empirical hypotheses to act as bridging statements, all the laws of the less basic science must be logically derivable from the theoretical premises of the more basic science, if the one is to be empirically reduced to the other. For instance, if psychology is empirically reducible to stimulus-response theory, then there must in principle be some stimulus-response statement that is a sufficient (or necessary and sufficient) condition for any particular statement in purposive terms. And if psychology is empirically reducible to physiology, there must be some physiological state of affairs that is a sufficient (or necessary and sufficient) condition of, for example, a man's intention to commit suicide.

There is an important difference between strict and empirical reduction that is often overlooked in discussions of the relation of purpose and mechanism. The strict reduction of science α to science β renders the vocabulary of α logically redundant, or superfluous, in virtue of the total or partial equivalence in meaning of the two theoretical vocabularies. But in the case of empirical reduction, the theoretical terms of α and β have identifiably different meanings. Consequently, the vocabulary of α could not be dispensed with once the reduction had been effected without losing sight of the descriptive properties and explanatory relations expressed by it. For the vocabulary of β would be incapable of expressing these features. In other words, the "real properties" and their relations described by the science α must still be described in the terminology of α. It is therefore particularly important to remember that it is statements, not "properties" or "entities," that are linked by the relation of reduction, when empirical reduction is in question. Otherwise, the inability of β to express the features that are the proper subject matter of α may be taken to imply that those features themselves have somehow been "reduced" out of existence.

For instance, it might be thought that if psychology is empirically reducible to physiology, then psychological properties must be "nothing but" brain states, that there can be no "real" distinction between mental and physical aspects of the organism. On the contrary, the empirical reduction of purposive psychology to a formally mechanistic science would entail neither that purposive language is dispensable in our talk about reality, nor that there is no real distinction between purposive and mechanistic properties. Since our knowledge of "reality" necessarily involves some concept, or theoretical model, that we use to represent reality, logically different models necessarily refer to "different" aspects of reality. So sciences whose vocabularies have distinctly different meanings can be said to refer to quite different aspects of the real world, whether or not there are systematic empirical links between them. To say that purposiveness can be explained by mechanism, given that empirical reduction is in question, is therefore not to say that there is no real distinction between teleological and nonteleological systems. Specifically, even if there is a particular brain state which is a sufficient condition of suicidal intent, it would not follow that the intention to commit suicide is "really" the same thing as that brain state.[52]

Strictly speaking, the only way to prove that one science is reducible to another in either sense is to reduce it. To prove strict reducibility, one should show how expressions in the less basic science may be translated into expressions in the other. ("Translation" is used here in a wide sense to cover cases of total and of partial equivalence.) For instance, one should show how intensional psychological predicates may be expressed in purely physiological terms. One should convey the information that a man intends to commit suicide purely by referring to his brain states, hormones, and so on. Alternatively, one may wish to prove empirical reducibility. One should then state all the theoretical assumptions (and co-ordinating definitions linking these to observables) of α and β, and the experimental laws of α, together with the specific "bridging" statements required to effect the reduction of α to β. This latter exercise obviously requires that α and β each be well-developed disciplines, affording explicit and nonambiguous theoretical assumptions, co-ordinating definitions, and laws. And if the exercise is to be of any practical interest, most of the statements in α and β should be reasonably well-confirmed.

These conditions are satisfied, for example, in the case of thermodynamics and statistical mechanics. The detailed empirical reduction of the former to the latter has already been effected. The bridging statements link α—terms such as "temperature" to β—terms such as "mean kinetic energy of molecules." In fact, the logical status of these bridging statements is somewhat equivocal, for they may be regarded as theoretical conventions created by deliberate fiat, rather than as physical hypotheses. As fiat conventions, they express the decision to assign some α—significance to the β—theoretical terms in question; as physical hypotheses, they record the discovery of empirical correlations between α— and β—terms. Nagel has shown that whether they are regarded one way or the other will depend on the particular theoretical and historical context in which the reduction of thermodynamics to mechanics is being developed.[53] When regarded as fiat conventions, the "reducibility" of thermodynamics to mechanics looks like strict reducibility (with partial equivalence) rather than empirical reducibility. But the fiat conventions linking "temperature" and "mean kinetic energy" were not arbitrarily decided upon. They were suggested by the actual empirical evidence available to underpin an empirical reduction. Analogously, it is arguable that there might come a time when "brain state so-and-so" will be regarded as including "intention to commit suicide" within its meaning. Indeed, this is the most plausible way of stating the claim that psychological statements are strictly reducible to physiological ones, since most people would readily concede that physiological language as it is understood today is incapable of expressing such matters. But there is no practical possibility of establishing a theoretical convention linking "right big toe twitching" with suicidal intentions, since there is no empirical evidence that toe-twitching is in any way connected with suicide. The type of strict reducibility which depends upon bridging statements that are fiat conventions will only be effected between independently established domains of science if there is some possibility of empirical reduction between them. The relation of thermodynamics to statistical mechanics may therefore be cited as an example of one case of empirical reduction which has, in fact, been achieved.

However, neither the formal conditions for reduction nor the requirement that statements be well-confirmed apply in such a degree to psychology and physiology that the one can actually be reduced to the other. The detailed physiological mechanisms explanatory of purposive behavior—if they exist at all—are not known. Still less could such a reduction have been carried out in McDougall's time. Given this situation, the most that can be done by one claiming the possibility of reduction is to suggest the general schematic outlines of the type of reduction he hopes one day will be achieved. If strict reduction is in question, he should offer sample "translations" of equivalent expressions drawn from the two sciences. If he is concerned with empirical reduction, he should try to indicate the nature of the crucial bridging statements involved. Conversely, one who asserts an inherent impossibility of reduction should not only argue *ad hominem* but should also give his "positive" reasons for believing that no such translations or bridging statements are in principle possible. In short, the reductionist must indicate the possible links, logical or empirical, between brain states and suicidal intentions, while the antireductionist must show why it will never be possible to talk about suicide in physiological vocabulary, or to find sufficient conditions of suicide in the states of a man's brain.

McDougall's Attack on Reductionism

McDougall's position on the issue of reductionism has already been indicated. In an early discussion of "the province of psychology," he asked whether purposive and mechanistic explanations are mutually exclusive, and left the question open: "It may be that, in the distant future, science will succeed in establishing the truth of the assumption so widely accepted at the present time by an act of faith ... that all seemingly purposive action is mechanically explicable. If that time comes, psychology will be absorbed in physiology, and physiology in physics." He did not attempt to settle the question here, merely insisting that the psychologist must study the organism as a whole, noting the apparent differences between mechanical processes and behavior, and "must explain and understand in terms of the end or purpose of the activity, rather than in terms only of the antecedent events."[54] However, in later works he made his answer explicit:

> Is human mental activity mechanistic or is it teleological? However these two terms be defined (and as I have said, the only satisfactory way of defining "mechanistic process" is the negative one of defining it as the ateleological), they are by common consent mutually exclusive: if a process is mechanistic, it is not teleological; and if it is teleological, it is not mechanistic.
>
> Active striving towards a goal is a fundamental category of psychology, and is a process of a type that cannot be mechanistically explained or resolved into mechanistic sequences.

Teleological or purposive causation is in no sense a disguised form of the mechanistic causation postulated by the physical sciences.

Wundt seriously asserted that the difference between a teleological series of events and a mechanically determined series lies merely in the point of view, that the same series may be regarded as mechanical when traced from behind forward, and as teleological when traced backward from any given point which we might choose to regard as its end or goal. But the difference between a train of mechanically determined events and a change produced by creative purposive activity is the most radical difference that we can conceive. Here at least we may confidently invoke the logical law of non-contradiction and assert that the psychophysical series cannot be both wholly mechanical and wholly purposive.[55]

These passages make it clear that McDougall denied both types of reducibility. He pointed out that the various concepts of consciousness, and the basic psychological distinction between subject and object, are foreign to physiological explanations mentioning only electrochemical and anatomical properties of the body or nervous system. And he insisted that intensional propositions cannot be restated in any mechanistic terms, whether physiological or behaviorist, where "mechanistic" should be understood in his second, formal sense. In other words, he held that purposive explanations are not strictly reducible to mechanistic ones. A further aspect of McDougall's rejection of strict reducibility was his "dualistic" criticism of the psychical monism that was a popular view in some philosophical circles at the turn of the century. McDougall criticized it as obscuring the differences between living and nonliving things. Despite his assertion that mechanistic process is more probably a subclass of teleological process than vice versa, he did not believe that the natural and life sciences could share a common terminology.[56]

In denying the strict reducibility of psychology to a formally mechanistic science, McDougall was correct. This is because only terms making a distinction between psychological subject and object can give rise to the logical, implicative peculiarities

60

characteristic of intensional sentences. The implicative relations between extensional sentences are quite different. Since no two sentences having different implications can correctly be regarded as identical in meaning, intensional statements cannot be translated into extensional terms. A formally mechanistic science, by definition, is one that makes no intensional reference to goals or to any other object of thought represented in the consciousness of a psychological subject. Hence, a purposive psychology is not strictly reducible to a mechanistic science of behavior.

It might be objected that there are some sentences whose meaning does not involve the notion of the direction of the mind on an object, and which therefore do not qualify as "intensional" according to my definition, but which nevertheless show the logical peculiarities typical of what I term "intensional" sentences. Such sentences, it might be claimed, are logically non-extensional although not psychological. Indeed, the term "intensional" is sometimes defined in a purely logical way, so as to cover all sentences that are not termed "extensional" by logicians.[57] Examples of nonextensional sentences that do not appear to be psychological ones include, "Possibly what caused the power cut was that a swan flew into the wires," "It is necessarily true that if Polonius was the man behind the arras, then Polonius was the man behind the arras," and "The dam is high enough to prevent any future floods." These three sentences respectively satisfy the three nonextensional criteria of no implication of the embedded clause (or its negation), referential opacity, and failure of existential generalization. According to this objection, it is therefore not true that only terms making a distinction between psychological subject and object can give rise to these logical peculiarities.

My answer to this objection is twofold. First, it is clear that sentences that are "intensional" in the psychological sense are also "intensional" in the purely logical sense. The statements of formally mechanistic physiology and pure stimulus-response psychology are not intensional in either sense. Sentences like "It is necessarily true that if hypothalamic activity causes eating then hypothalamic activity causes eating," or like, "The puzzle box is strong enough to prevent the cat destroying it," do not form part of physiological psychology or learning theory. Admittedly, the second of these might occur within the description of the experimental situation in a report of an investigation of operant conditioning. And sentences like, "It is possible that schizophrenia is related to abnormal adrenalin metabolism," might even form part of the theoretical conclusion of an empirical psychophysiological study. But such sentences are not fairly representative of the statements comprising mechanistic sciences of behavior. Consequently, the objection under consideration is not relevant to my argument.

Second, a case could be made for claiming that all "logically intensional" sentences are, in fact, implicitly "psychologically intensional." This is because all logically intensional sentences involve oblique contexts; they all explicitly or implicitly depend on the quotation of thoughts in *oratio obliqua*. For instance, sentences using modal qualifiers such as "necessary," "possible," and "impossible" do not assert or deny the sentential phrases within them directly, but obliquely assert something about them. In each case, what they assert is that if a psychological subject decides to pick one of these sentential phrases as his object of thought, he should regard it in a particular way. Thus, to say that schizophrenia is "possibly" related to adrenalin metabolism is to say that, although there is some evidence for this belief, nobody should unwarily commit himself to it. Even an example like, "The puzzle box is strong enough to prevent the cat destroying it," may be interpreted as meaning that nobody need fear that the cat will destroy the puzzle box, since the logical possibility that the cat might do so is empirically excluded by contingent facts concerning the manufacture of the box. These suggested interpretations treat logically intensional statements as propositions about propositions, not as propositions about the world. And propositions are, roughly, thoughts attributable to thinkers. It follows that if this type of interpretation can be correctly applied in all cases of logical nonextensionality, then the class of sentences denoted by the logical definition of "intensionality" is identical with the class denoted by the psychological definition. However, since nonextensional sentences are uncharacteristic of physiological or strict stimulus-response contexts, this issue is not crucial for my present purposes.

The second type of reducibility appeared to McDougall to be

as chimerical as the first: purposive explanations, he believed, are not empirically reducible to physiological terms either. He argued *ad hominem* that the hypothetical bridging statements offered by his reductionist contemporaries were very vague and not backed up by detailed physiological knowledge. But he also offered "positive" reasons for believing that mechanistic concepts must be inadequate to explain behavior, that the empirical reduction of psychology to physiology is outlawed in principle.

McDougall did provide objective criteria for the theoretical terms of his purposive psychology, as, for example, for the central concept of purposiveness. But the surplus meaning carried by his theoretical terms included a positive element that excluded the possibility of reduction. He believed there could be no reductionist bridging statements because physiological explanations of a mechanistic character state necessary *but not sufficient* conditions of behavior.[58] He made up the insufficiency by hypothesizing a special type of energy producing those changes in the organism that cannot be explained mechanistically. This accounts for his constant use of the expression "teleological causation," and for his protest that "to admit the efficacy of psychical activity in nature is not, as so many seem to imagine, to deny causation."

McDougall's insistence that he did not deny causation may seem strange in view of his attacks on "determinism." He welcomed the development of quantum theory, pointing out in 1930 that "physical science itself is giving up strict determinism and exact predictability." This, he felt, left room for teleological causation, involving "creative" psychic processes not wholly predetermined by past events. But he insisted that these creative processes were neither random nor inexplicable by psychological laws. In the *Social Psychology* he had remarked that "the acceptance of the libertarian doctrine in its more extreme form would be incompatible with any hope that a science of society may be achieved," for a science must be based on lawfulness of some sort. Moreover, he saw that such "extreme" libertarianism is irreconcilable with the concepts of human freedom and moral responsibility: "free will," in the sense of a radical indeterminism, cannot truly reflect the nature of human volition.[59] This is because those who favor the use of the concepts of freedom or volition, as virtually everyone does in daily life, do so largely for their logical connections with the concept of moral responsibility: a man is held morally responsible only for those of his actions that he performed in some sense freely, or of his own volition. If an action is not somehow determined by the man himself but, on the contrary, is random or undetermined, then he can hardly be held responsible for it. It is this that makes "extreme libertarianism" unacceptable as an analysis of the concept of human freedom.

It does not follow, of course, that McDougall's alternative analysis—in terms of causation by irreducibly teleological horme rather than by mechanistic energy—is itself acceptable. The hormic hypothesis that he felt was required for human freedom was closely connected with two more of his "positive" arguments against reductionism. Thus, he claimed that consciousness is something over and above bodily processes, being causally connected with purposive behavior: and the causal connection was supposedly effected by hormic energy. Again, he claimed that purposive explanation terminates with the mention of instincts directing behavior; but these instincts, too, were analyzed by him as involving specifically hormic energy. If he had been right about horme, he would have been right about reducibility.

However, he was not right about horme. McDougall's reasons for postulating horme were grounded in his analysis of conative concepts, wherein he mistook the purely conceptual connection between "desire" and "action toward a goal" for a causal one. In other words, he misinterpreted the concept of an "idea of the goal" so that he assimilated final causes to efficient causes. Accordingly, he interpreted certain logical features of this connection in energetic terms, with the result that he felt bound to speak of a special type of energy, one not constrained by the laws of physics. His claim that horme is inherently directed toward certain ends rested entirely on this conceptual error. As a matter of fact, his hypothesis appears false: so far, no form of energy specific to the nervous system has been identified, still less any form of energy that can be expended only in the pursuit of certain ends. Even to speak of a "hypothesis" here is perhaps incorrect, for it is not clear that the postulation of nonphysical energy is a genuine scientific hypothesis, in principle falsifiable by experimental means. However, the crucial point is that "psychic energy" is not essential to the logic of purposive explanation. This is why McDougall could still use such explanations while avowedly reserving judgment on horme.[60] Many of McDougall's reductionist contemporaries were prepared to use purposive concepts in their accounts of behavior, and McDougall's objective definition of purpose was acceptable to them. But his "mentalist" interpretation of purpose as involving psychic energy was not. McDougall's complaint that mechanists misrepresented his views was justified when he was represented as ascribing causal efficacy to some *future* event. However, his defense of hormic energy is not immune to the criticism that he postulated "entities of a peculiar kind" to which he ascribed "a mystic potency."

Nevertheless, if McDougall was wrong about horme, it does not necessarily follow that his antireductionist position was totally misguided. The question arises whether his arguments rested also on some surer foundation, independent of his hormic hypothesis. In this connection, we must distinguish between his rejection of strict reducibility and his attack on empirical reductionism, for the one may have been justified, while the other was not. His long-drawn-out controversy with the "behaviorist" school concerned both types of reducibility. Some of the early behaviorists claimed that psychology is strictly reducible to mechanistic terms. According to them, the psychologist could dispense entirely with the intensional vocabulary of consciousness, since everything worth saying about behavior could be said in terms of pure stimulus and response. Moreover, the "purer" the stimulus and response, the more physiological in character they appeared to be. For a behaviorist response could be a reflex muscle twitch. And a "muscle twitch" is plausibly represented as one physiologist's shorthand expression for what another physiologist might describe in terms of "action potentials," "neurons," and "muscle fibers." The dividing lines between what are regarded as "psychological" or "physiological" statements are not always clear. In the early years of the century C. S. Sherrington was developing his researches on the reflex activity of the nervous system, and I. P. Pavlov was studying the conditioning of salivary, gastric, and other alimentary secretions.[61] It is not surprising that both of these "physiological" research programs were eagerly welcomed by the early devotees of stimulus and response, although if they had pondered John Dewey's prophetic critique of atomistic interpretations of the reflex arc concept, published in 1896, the initial history of behaviorism might have been different.[62] The view that purposive vocabulary could be eliminated and replaced by the language of stimulus and response was therefore closely associated with the view that psychology is, in principle, strictly reducible to detailed physiological terms.

But well before McDougall's death, and partly owing to his influence, many "behaviorists" had themselves rejected strict reducibility, acknowledging the usefulness of purpose as a basic theoretical category in psychology. In common with present-day behaviorists, however, they all shared a bias toward the empirical reduction of psychology to physiology. K. S. Lashley's discussion of "The Behavioristic Interpretation of Consciousness," published in 1923, typified their general approach.[63] He pointed out that McDougall's objections to empirical reductionism had a long history: the subject-object distinction and the categories of consciousness have commonly been regarded as totally inexplicable in mechanistic terms. He suggested various schematic bridging statements supposed to indicate the physiological mechanisms underlying (and explaining) the phenomena of consciousness. Lashley's suggestions were largely hypothetical, and the general behaviorist bias toward empirical reduction has not yet been justified in detail. Moreover, the question whether the empirical reduction of psychology to physiology is even in principle possible is still controversial. To understand this current controversy, we must first understand how it is that many behaviorist psychologists have come to reject strict reducibility, despite their continuing faith in empirical reductionism.

III   *Behaviorist Interpretations of Purpose*

Psychologists and laymen alike who emphasize the importance of purpose in human life generally regard "behaviorists" as renegades specially deserving of stern reproof. This is not merely a matter of a difference in interests; ethologists and entomologists are not similarly reproved for directing their professional activities to matters of scant human concern. Behaviorism is represented as being worse than irrelevant, for it is seen as having abandoned all hope of a significant psychology, as being radically opposed to any approach that concentrates on the individual's view of the world and his aspirations for personal growth within it. The assumption is that behaviorists are neither practically interested in purpose and intensionality nor even theoretically capable of acknowledging them as genuine psychological phenomena. Behaviorist psychology, according to this view, is limited to discussion of objective truths about the organism, and is essentially inimical to the understanding of subjective phenomena. Consequently, behaviorism is seen by such critics as a real threat to significant human psychology, not merely as an alternative way of spending one's time.

McDougall was no exception to this general rule, though he was more willing to distinguish between different varieties of behaviorism than are many of its critics. His purposivism involved him in constant controversy, and much of his writing is shot through with verbal fireworks directed against contemporaries. He himself described the *Outline of Psychology* as largely a polemic against the currently preponderant mechanical psychology. While he criticized such widely accepted theoretical positions as the Freudian, Adlerian, and Gestalt psychologies, he reserved his choicest sallies for behaviorism. In the *Outline of Psychology* he referred to behaviorism as "a most misshapen and beggarly dwarf," and in 1930 he was still complaining of the "ill-balanced, extravagant, and bizarre dogmas of the behaviorist school."[1] Yet he had been the first to define psychology as the science of behavior, and his last systematic text expressed the opinion that "all psychology is, or should be, behavioristic."[2] It may therefore seem surprising that he clearly regarded behaviorists as his special opponents in psychological matters.

McDougall's attitude to J. B. Watson's behaviorism is least surprising, for Watson rejected purpose, Freud and Adler did not; Watson's psychology was atomistic, Gestalt psychology was not. McDougall's criticism of Watson was thus especially stringent. The popularity of Watson's behaviorism only made him more committed to opposition. In an autobiographical sketch he admitted to "a predilection for unfashionable doctrines" and continued: "Whenever I have found a theory widely accepted in the scientific world, and especially when it has acquired something of the nature of a popular dogma among scientists, I have found myself repelled into skepticism."[3] This attitude led him to question neo-Darwinian evolutionary theory and to champion psychical research; it also contributed to his early rejection of mechanism in psychology and to his related defense of horme.

This latter position was to divide McDougall even from those behaviorists who had a use for "purpose" and who agreed with him in rejecting the strict reducibility of purposive explanation to stimulus-response or physiological terms. For McDougall, purposive action involved the causal efficacy of consciousness, the existence of horme as the motive energy that drives behavior. The behaviorists, by contrast, believed in the empirical reducibility of purposive explanations to a mechanistic physiology. A comparison of various behaviorist interpretations of purpose will show how this issue divided McDougall from his professional colleagues—even from those whose treatment of the concept was generally similar to his own, and whose views he accordingly acknowledged as more acceptable than Watson's.

Watson's Formulation of Behaviorism

In 1913 Watson inaugurated the behaviorist movement with his paper "Psychology as the Behaviorist Views It." Here and in subsequent work Watson repudiated the introspective "idea-psychology." Like McDougall, he rejected the ideomotor theory and complained of the sterile debates on "sensations," "ideas," and the content of "consciousness." Like McDougall also, he noted the introspectionists' neglect of animal psychology. The psychologist should study only behavior; and introspection should be regarded merely as verbal behavior, not as a valid method in itself. Concepts such as imagery, feeling, and thought should be interpreted in behaviorist terms, even if these involve reference to unobserved, implicit movements. "Consciousness" was not to be denied so much as ignored, having no place in a scientific psychology:

> One can assume either the presence or the absence of con-sciousness anywhere in the phylogenetic scale without affecting the problems of behavior one jot or one tittle.
>
> If behaviorism is ever to stand for anything (even a distinct method), it must make a clean break with the concept of con-sciousness.[4]

But although Watson rejected the associationist "way of ideas," he did not reject associationism itself. The basic units to be asso-ciated, according to him, are reflexes analyzable in terms of physi-cal stimulus and physiological response:

> We use the term *stimulus* in psychology as it is used in physi-ology. Only in psychology we have to extend somewhat the usage of the term . . . When the factors leading to reactions are more complex, as, for example, in the social world, we speak of *situations*. A situation is, of course, upon final analysis, resolvable into a complex group of stimuli . . . In a similar way we employ in psychology the physiological term "response," but again we slightly extend its use . . . In psychology our study [is more often concerned] with several complex responses taking place simultaneously.
>
> By response we mean anything the animal does—such as turning toward or away from a light, jumping at a sound, and more highly organized activities such as building a skyscraper, drawing plans, having babies, writing books, and the like.[5]

Pavlov's physiological work on conditioned reflexes provided evidence of new stimulus-response connections and contributed to the influence of psychological behaviorism, being taken up enthusiastically by Watson soon after the publication of the first behaviorist paper. For Watson, to explain behavior is to specify the effective stimulus determining the observed response, and terms such as "purpose," "striving," and "cognition" need never be used: "I believe we can write a psychology, define it as [the science of behavior], and never go back upon our definition: never use the terms consciousness, mental states, mind, content, introspectively verifiable, imagery, and the like . . . It can be done in terms of stimulus and response, in terms of habit formation, habit integrations and the like . . . In a system of psychology completely worked out, given the stimuli the response can be predicted."[6]

In 1915 Watson was elected president of the American Psychological Association, and in 1920 McDougall arrived to take up the Harvard Chair. He was greeted by a hostile review, in the *Journal of Philosophy*, of *The Group Mind*.[7] He also found behaviorism "ascendant and rampant" and the Harvard students very suspicious of his "outlandish theories."[8] The difficulties he experienced in this intellectual climate were no doubt largely responsible for the violence of his attack on behaviorism in the *Outline of Psychology*, published three years later. There, recalling his original definition of psychology, he wrote: "I still regard this definition as a good one, logically perhaps the best. But since my suggestion was made, it has been adopted and carried to an extreme by the 'behaviorists.' In protesting against a too exclusive study of the introspective data, and rightly insisting on the importance of the study of behavior as a psychological method, they have overshot the mark and swung into [an untenable position]. Hence I am disposed to say: 'If you are going to get on, it's time for me to get off.'" He therefore chose to redefine *psychology* as "the science of the human mind" or as "the science which aims to give us better understanding and control of the behavior of the organism as a whole."[9]

In later discussions McDougall continued to insist that for four basic reasons the position that Watson had taken up was "untenable."[10] First, McDougall held introspection to be a valid psychological method, though its importance had been much exaggerated. It provided descriptions of sentient experience that were useful up to a point, and it was particularly useful in giving information about the conscious purposes of the self. It should not be given up entirely. Watson, however, "proposed to effect the needed reform, not by redressing the balance in psychology between the introspective and the objective methods of study, but by the simple expedient of upsetting the balance completely."[11]

A second, related disagreement concerned the significance of consciousness. Watson did not provide a coherent philosophical account of consciousness and on the whole ignored it, stating that he was interested only in behavior. McDougall complained that to ignore a phenomenon is unscientific and indefensible: one has immediate knowledge of consciousness in introspection and cannot ignore or deny it.[12] For McDougall, conscious experience was something over and above both behavior and brain states; thus, he disagreed not only with the philosophically naive Watson but also with the more sophisticated E. B. Holt, who identified consciousness with particular configurations of the nervous system. More important than the ontological status of consciousness was the question of its causal efficacy. While Watson might be willing to admit the existence of conscious states as epiphenomena, he was uninterested in them scientifically, holding them to be causally ineffective. In contrast, McDougall believed that conscious striving is itself causally active, and that purposive behavior is driven by psychic horme rather than by physical energy.

Thirdly, McDougall objected to the atomistic nature of Watson's behaviorism, to its assertion of the strict reducibility of purpose to the language of physical stimulus and physiological response. Despite Watson's claim that his psychology was distinguished from physiology in being concerned with the *whole* organism, McDougall quoted E. C. Tolman with approval in speaking of "that form of the doctrine which Professor Tolman contemptuously refers to as 'a mere Muscle Twitchism of the Watsonian variety.' "[13] Watson did not refer explicitly to purposes or goals in his descriptions of behavior, but nor did he in practice attempt to translate all his terms into the language of stimulus and response. However, a complex human activity such as "building a skyscraper" is essentially goal-directed, or intensional, and cannot be adequately described in atomistic, extensional terms. Similarly, animal behavior such as that described by Wolfgang Kohler in *The Mentality of Apes* is clearly purposive.[14] As McDougall pointed out, the "strict behaviorist" would have to

71

describe it as a series of disconnected movements, movements unconnected by any reference to a goal, and containing several constituents that are meaningless when isolated. Such a description would be not only long-winded and clumsy, but positively misleading.[15] Just as such behavior is not helpfully described as "response," so social "situations" are not helpfully classified as "stimuli," without any reference to complex human purposes and beliefs: "Mechanists fit all behavior to their 'stimulus-response formula,' by means of the simple device of classifying as 'stimuli' everything in heaven and earth, from a flash of light or a simple touch to a religious or political system of beliefs, or an institution such as the Roman Church or the British Empire."[16]

Fourth and last, McDougall disagreed with Watson over the importance of instincts. The disagreement on this issue was partly grounded in confusion over the definition of "instinct." For McDougall, an instinct was an innate propensity for seeking a certain goal, and his examples included a maternal, a self-assertive, and a constructive instinct. Watson defined an instinct as "an hereditary pattern reaction, the separate elements of which are movements principally of the striped muscles," and his examples included the grasping reflex, the blinking reflex, and coition.[17] Defined thus, "instincts" are of little use in explaining adult behavior; and it seems absurd to speak of a "maternal instinct" since this can be taken to imply that a mother does not have to learn how to care for her child. Accordingly, Watson and some other behaviorist writers represented instincts as relatively insignificant in the determination of behavior.[18] They also saw explanations in terms of instincts as being attempts to solve psychological problems by providing convenient verbal labels, in the manner of the discredited faculty-psychology. The popular success of McDougall's *Social Psychology* had indeed led to the proliferation of dubious "instincts" in the writings of armchair psychologists, and by the 1920s McDougall's list of instincts was generally regarded by psychologists with suspicion: "The unit-instinct made prominent by James, and at present exemplified in McDougall's widely read and widely quoted *Social Psychology*, is being questioned by psychologists at the same time that it is being widely and uncritically adopted in sociology and economics."[19] McDougall argued that the evidence showed Watson to be exaggerating the influence of the environment. But Watson's claim that innate motor responses contribute only minimally to behavior is in principle quite compatible with a purposive psychology, which has to postulate natural goals, even though there may be difficulty in drawing limits to the number of instincts so defined.

McDougall's attacks on Watson were largely successful in detail. Watson's lack of conceptual sophistication and his proselytizing fervor provided many tempting targets for his subtler critics. And his exaggerated environmentalism did not do justice to the role of inheritance in behavior, as later ethological and genetic studies would show. But Watson's great achievement was to strengthen immeasurably the psychologist's reliance on an objective experimental methodology, one that could be directed to simple problems and to animal behavior as well as to matters of more obvious human import. Experimental studies of animal behavior and objective methods of mental testing were already developing, alongside the classical introspective "idea psychology," before Watson's epoch-making paper, but they too often had led to endless speculative disputes about the nature of the accompanying mental life, or consciousness. Despite the crudity of his theoretical rationale, Watson's polemic cleared the way for a more fruitful approach to the study of behavior, and his influence was accordingly great. McDougall's criticisms could not detract from this overall achievement; many of these criticisms were echoed by self-styled "behaviorist" workers who readily acknowledged their intellectual debt to Watson.

Perry and Holt: The Irreducibility of Purpose

Watson had discouraged the use of terms associated with "consciousness"; if they were to be used, they should be interpreted strictly in terms of stimulus and response. He did not regard the concept of purpose as either necessary or desirable in psychology. Other behaviorist writers, united in their insistence on objective methods of study, were soon to differ on these points. Such writers included the philosopher R. B. Perry and the psychologists Holt and Tolman, all of whose views McDougall criticized, though admitting them to be more congenial to him than Watson's. Perry defended the use of "purpose" and related terms in a number of philosophical articles appearing about 1920, the time of McDougall's arrival in America.[20] He drew extensively on the psychological writings of Holt, with whom he held many views in common. Perry presented objective criteria of purpose, which he admitted to be much the same as McDougall's, and he stressed the importance of the "margin of modifiability," which covered both variation of means and learning:

> The appetites . . . set the organism to acting until a specific relief is obtained; but just how any individual organism under given circumstances shall satisfy its craving for food or sexual intercourse is ordinarily determined by the results of tentative movements. It is this margin of modifiability, be it great or small, to which we must look for the factor of purpose . . . The variability of purposive action is not an accidental feature. What is required . . . is to be able to say that an act's performance is somehow conditioned by its having or promising a certain result. In order that this shall be possible, it is necessary that acts of the preferred sort shall be actually selected from a larger class of acts. The rejected acts must actually occur so that the preference or selection may be manifested . . . It is necessary that acts of the eligible type and of the ineligible type should occur *tentatively*, and then take on a stable or dispositional character according to the result.[21]

Perry rejected Watson's assumption that purpose and consciousness are strictly reducible to formally mechanistic terms. Thus, he claimed that purposive action cannot be described or predicted in the stimulus-response terms of a strictly peripheralist psychology:

> In proportion as the organism is unified and functions as a whole its behavior is incapable of being translated into simple reactions correlated severally with external events. The observer with his eye on any given set of external conditions finds that he can not predict the organism's behavior. Its behavior is "spontaneous" or internally conditioned . . . In proportion as an organism is an individual its movements are governed by its own internal organization [and by means of

these movements it] determines even its own experiences and fortunes.[22]

Similarly, Perry noted the intensionality of behavior, and the incapacity of a peripheralist behaviorism to express this feature:

> In the case of hunting for a pin, the organism is not, strictly speaking, responding to an object or fact of its environment. The organism is not hunting for any particular pin; and is quite capable of carrying on the hunt, even though there be as a matter of fact no pin in its environment . . . We cannot deal adequately with this matter here, but it evidently requires an epistemological construction that lies beyond the scope of a strictly physiological behaviorism. The recognition of this fact, though it does not, I think, in the least contradict the fundamental thesis of behaviorism, does forbid any hasty or contemptuous dismissal of the traditional association of purpose with non-physical or "ideal" entities.[23]

The "ideas" guiding behavior he regarded as centrally stimulated signs, which may be activated independently of present environmental conditions. The psychologist also needs to use other cognitive terms:

> [Where the appearance of the end result or of some means leading to it] releases in any measure that response which is a part of the consummation . . . we may speak of *conscious* purpose . . . [Tolman writes] "The mere fact that on each single trial [the cat] hits about *until* it gets out seems to me to be sufficient to characterize its activity as purposive" . . . I can not believe that the author is correct in this claim. What the exponents of purposiveness are looking for is an act of which it can be said that its occurrence is due to its promise or forecast. No act . . . can be of the sort required unless it has meaning, that is, arouses anticipatory reactions to its sequel; and unless it is *preferred* because of such anticipation . . . That there is no purpose without cognition may be taken for granted. . . A purpose, then, requires the presence of a supposition, which ordinarily will have assumed the form of a belief . . . It is the practical function of reason . . . to find among the individual's existing propensities the means by which a purpose may be executed . . . What belief does is thus to establish

connecting channels by which the currents of purposive energy are distributed and directed . . . Belief is one of the conditions of action.[24]

Perry distinguished different "propensities" within a purposive action. The higher, selective, or governing propensity may be called the purpose, and it dominates the whole process wherein lower or eligible propensities are selected as means to the main end. For instance, the governing propensity to escape from a puzzle-box selects the eligible propensity to claw at the latch. The governing propensity is the same as the set or determining tendency. "Instincts" and "complexes" are each a special class of determining tendency. The basic instinctive appetites are hereditary, but the means by which they are relieved are not entirely so. In most instinctive animal behavior, responses are concatenated: while each unit may show some degree of purposive variability, the units (purposes) follow one another in an innately determined sequence. But in most human behavior, responses are subordinated: there is a purposive hierarchy of some depth such that there is not merely variability within each component, but variability of components.[25]

Perry's account of instinct and his use of intensional terms such as "purpose" and "belief" were in many ways similar to McDougall's, who admitted that Perry's psychology was largely acceptable to him.[26] But there were two basic differences. First, though granting that the behaviorist cannot ignore introspection, Perry criticised McDougall's speculations about the feelings accompanying instinctive action.[27] Although McDougall abandoned the attempt to define instincts in terms of the accompanying emotional tone, he was always prepared to make remarks about the essentially private conscious data he supposed to accompany action. Second, Perry denied that purposive and mechanistic explanations are mutually exclusive, and interpreted the various types of determining tendency in physiological terms:

It is customary to suppose that the accepted validity of mechanical laws somehow stands in the way of the operation of interest . . . The supposition of an absolute incompatibility between mechanism and interest is, however, contrary both to reason and to fact. There is no reason why an identical process

76

should not obey many laws, and laws of different types . . . A mind is a complex so organized as to act desideratively or interestedly . . . But [biological] processes, interested in their general form, possess characteristic instrumentalities, notably a bodily nervous system . . . A mind embraces certain contents or parts of the environment, with which it deals through its instrumentalities and in behalf of its interests.

The instinct and the complex are . . . organic dispositions, or systematic arrangements in the physical organism which condition specific modes of performance.[28]

In other words, Perry assumed that purposive statements are empirically reducible to formally mechanistic ones. McDougall complained that Perry would not admit "the reality of teleological or purposive causation as a mode distinct in nature from the mechanistic." And he objected that Perry could provide no specification of a physiological mechanism or motor set that would account for the indefinite variability of action.[29] These differences were also to divide McDougall from other behaviorist writers who used purposive terms in psychology.

Holt had cooperated with Perry as early as 1910 on the pro-grammatic article defining "neorealism," a philosophy which interpreted psychological concepts in physicalist terms.[30] Their central aim was to rebut the philosophical idealism rampant at the turn of the century and the Cartesian dualism from which idealism had sprung. The aspect of idealism particularly con-cerned with the mind-body problem was psychical monism, which allowed basic ontological status only to mind. The neo-realists were especially anxious to avoid this ontological claim, without wishing to deny the importance of purpose and values. For the fuller exposition of neorealism, published two years later, Holt wrote a chapter reconciling this basically materialistic philosophy with illusory experiences.[31] Soon afterward he pub-lished an article, "Response and Cognition," and two books, *The Concept of Consciousness* and *The Freudian Wish and Its Place in Ethics*.[32] As these titles suggest, Holt did not wish to outlaw purposive or even moral terms. But he avoided mentalistic interpretations, appealing only to biological and physiological principles in his hypotheses about the mechanisms and energy involved.

Holt welcomed Watson's behaviorism as "valiant and clear-headed," and applauded its materialistic rejection of the view that introspection was a special "inner sense."[33] But like Perry, he regarded its atomistic peripheralist analysis as inadequate in face of the organizational and intensional features of behavior. He attacked the atomistic "bead-theorizing" involved in the identification of behavior with reflex action.[34] He agreed that reflexes are the "least components" of behavior. But behavior is a systematic integration of these components, and as such it cannot be adequately described in terms of reflexes: "The often too materialistically-minded biologist is so fearful of meeting a certain bogy, the 'psyche,' that he hastens to analyse every case of behavior into its component reflexes without venturing first to observe it as a whole . . . Our account has overlooked the most essential thing of all—the *organization* of [behavior].[35]

The cognitive relation between the psychological subject and its object of consciousness can be expressed in behavioral but not in reflex terms: "One could not describe what the animal as a whole is doing in terms of the immediate stimuli; but . . . only in terms of the environing objects toward which the animal's response is directed."[36] Holt emphasized that the "object" is more than mere stimulus, being identified in terms of the specific response relation whereby the organism directs its activities within its environment. The specific response relation is the basis of the psychological features of intensionality, knowing, and meaning. The description of "what the animal is doing" will involve reference to cognition and purpose, but this does not imply the rejection of mechanism: "This thing [purpose] in its essential definition, is *a course of action which the living body executes or is prepared to execute with regard to some object or some fact of its environment* . . . The purpose about to be carried out is already embodied in what we call the 'motor-attitude' of the neuromuscular apparatus."[37]

The organism is physiologically "set" to execute a specific course of action given a specific exciting condition. In his sympathetic discussion of Freud, Holt outlined physiological models for the concepts of complex and instinct, and Perry's discussion of purpose was to draw heavily on this account. Holt's early interest in dynamic psychology endured, and in 1931 he published *Animal Drive and the Learning Process.* Here he described the growth of complex habits from random movements and reflex units, explaining all action in terms of physiological cause and effect: "I have nowhere surreptitiously introduced any 'psychic' principle . . . From the point where we now stand it is but one short step to a definition of awareness and consciousness in terms of physiological process."[38] In a later paper on "Materialism and the Criterion of the Psychic" Holt argued: " 'Immediate awareness by an internal sense' cannot be used by psychology as a criterion of the psychic; that introspection is merely a verbal commentary which supercedes and displaces a state of awareness which it never successfully describes; that awareness is created by motor response; [and] that these motor responses are the only genuine criterion of the psychic."[39]

Predictably, McDougall disagreed with Holt over the status of introspection and criticized Holt's neorealist identification of conscious experience with physical phenomena. The neorealists claimed: "The object or content of consciousness is any entity in so far as it is responded to by another entity in a specific manner exhibited by the reflex nervous system . . . The difference between subject and object of consciousness is not a difference of quality or substance, but a difference of office or place in a configuration."[40] McDougall objected that this seemed to deny both one's immediate knowledge of one's experiences, and the fact that "thinking of a material object is not identical with the existence of that object, but rather a fact of a different order."[41] However, the neorealist definition quoted above does not necessarily identify one's thought of an object with the object itself, but only with some entity or other. Holt took pains to show how his materialist analysis of consciousness could account for the epistemological categories of delusion, and Perry similarly noted that one may search for a pin though there be no pin. According to their explanations, the "entity" in question would then be some neural process representing a pin; a particular motor set may be activated by this cerebral representation even though the environment may prevent the action from achieving its purpose. McDougall also criticized Holt's systematic psychology as expressed in *Animal Drive and the Learning Process,* accusing Holt of "a magnificent contempt for a multitude of facts."[42] The disagreement centered on Holt's appeals to reflexes, habits, motor sets, and drives, rather than to "instincts"; there was dissent not only over the extent of environmental influence but also over the nature of the energy underlying "instincts" or "drives" and energizing purposive behavior. Holt's use of mechanistic physiological models in explaining purposive behavior was unacceptable to McDougall.

Tolman's Purposive Behaviorism

Holt's pupil Tolman was particularly insistent that purpose and the associated cognitive categories are useful psychological concepts. In a series of articles from 1920 onward, he followed Holt and Perry in arguing that Watson's theoretical account of behavior was physiological rather than psychological, and was inappropriate to the behavioral problems which Watson himself discussed. Later, in *Purposive Behavior in Animals and Men,* Tolman summarized his position in distinguishing between the "molecular" and the "molar" approaches to behavior:

> Watson has in reality dallied with two different notions of behavior . . . He has defined behavior in terms of its strict underlying physical and physiological details . . . We shall designate this as the *molecular* definition of behavior. And, on the other hand, he has come to recognize . . . that behavior, as such, is more than and different from the sum of its physiological parts. Behavior, as such, is an "emergent" phenomenon that has descriptive and defining properties of its own. And we shall designate this latter as the *molar* definition of behavior.
>
> Behavior as behavior, that is, as molar, *is* purposive and *is* cognitive. These purposes and cognitions are of its immediate warp and woof. It, no doubt, is strictly dependent upon an underlying manifold of physics and chemistry, but as a matter of first identification, behavior as behavior reeks of purpose and cognition.[43]

The molar definition of behavior is the specifically psychological

80

one. Tolman's choice of the term "emergent" was unfortunate, for it seems to suggest that psychology is not empirically reducible to physiology, a suggestion that Tolman himself repeatedly rebutted. In calling behavior an "emergent" phenomenon, he was merely expressing the view that psychology is not strictly reducible to physiology. The basic theoretical categories of psychology must therefore be defined at the molar level: in short, they must be expressed in purposive terms.

Tolman insisted that Watson's atomistic stimulus and response cannot be the basic psychological concepts because they do not define the properties of behavior at the molar level. In an early article that first appeared in 1922, offering "a new formula for behaviorism," Tolman had suggested that the behavior act should replace the response as a basic concept: "The behavior act is simply the name given to the final bits of behavior as such. The behavior act together with the stimulating agencies constitute the fundamentals upon which the rest of the system is based." Two further concepts, "behavior cue" and "behavior object," were said by him to be analogous to "sense quality" and "meaning" respectively, but: "It is to be emphasized that [neither behavior cue nor behavior object] can be defined in terms of 'immediate conscious feels.' For no one of us ever knows for certain what another organism's 'conscious feels' may be. We know only the behavior implications of those conscious feels."[44] In a discussion of behaviorism and purpose first published in 1925, he pointed out that behavior acts can only be defined (nonatomistically) in terms of goals, and he defended the concept of purpose: "Wherever the purely objective description of either a simple or complex behavior discovers a *persistence until* character there we have what behaviorism defines as purpose. And upon further analysis, we discover that such a description appears whenever in order merely to *identify* the given behavior a reference to some 'end object' or 'situation' is found necessary."[45]

Although here Tolman presented purpose as a purely descriptive concept, in the same year he characterized purpose and cognition as "determiners" of behavior, in a paper analyzing learning in terms of goal-seeking, a set of innate or acquired initial exploratory impulses (initial cognitive "hunches"), and the acquisition of a set of final object adjustments (final cognitions).[46] Here he used these concepts in an explanatory rather than a purely descriptive way, showing how various intensional aspects of behavior are functionally related to one another. He argued that these concepts are fruitful in research, describing some of his maze-running experiments which he claimed could only be satisfactorily understood in purposive and cognitive terms. Much later, in 1948, he defended the ascription of "cognitive maps" to rats and men as an explanation of experiments showing latent learning, vicarious trial and error, searching for the (noxious) stimulus, the use of "hypotheses," and the importance of "spatial orientation."[47]

The sense in which Tolman was using purposive and cognitive terms as explanatory rather than purely descriptive can be clarified by his notion of "intervening variables." In 1935 he wrote that psychology, like physics, depended on a set of logical constructs; and these constructs he classified as independent, intervening and dependent variables.[48] Independent variables are of four types: the environmental stimulus, the heredity and the past training of the organism, and the releasing internal condition of physiological appetite or aversion. The dependent variable is the final resulting behavior. The intervening variables are purposive concepts: demands and cognitions of various types, which show themselves as "behavior readinesses."

The "ultimate demands" of men and rats include demands for food, sex, darkness, and warmth, and in men perhaps also demands for company and social approval. Both species shun electric shocks and hampering barriers, and both tend to seek the shortest route to a goal. "Subordinate demands" concern the particular means-objects that satisfy ultimate ends; they take on special importance for men, and include all the paraphernalia of a society's culture from feather bolsters to Bull Dog Drummond. Tolman remarked that the functions linking ultimate demands to physiological appetite and aversion were probably simple, but that those involving the subordinate demands were no doubt very complex. Tolman's cognitions include "differentiations" (intentions, expectations, and attainments as to quality) and "hypotheses" (intentions, expectations, and attainments as to relations). Human hypotheses can be tried out "mentally" rather than actually, and are sometimes indicated by the reports of "introspection." In his later work Tolman refined his list of intervening variables, adding a new category, the "belief-value matrix," and speaking of "need systems" and "behavior spaces."[49] But the explanatory function of such variables was logically similar to the original cognitions and demands.

Behavior is a function of both independent and intervening variables, and reference to both is required in the explanation or prediction of behavior. The intervening variables are not directly observable but are operationally defined in terms of various systematic ways of behaving. In 1936 Tolman stated they are "all that my operational behaviorism finds in the way of mental processes."[50] In a retrospective account of his work Tolman has admitted that his intervening variables are largely drawn from common-sense psychology and his own phenomenology.[51] The conceptual relations of purposive terms in everyday usage have been suggestive of hypotheses for experimental testing. The purposive terms of Tolman's system categorize and sum up various empirically found relationships, although they do not lead to very precise quantitative predictions.

Tolman defined his intervening variables in behavioral terms, and their explanatory use in his system in no way depended on physiological detail. Although Perry and Holt had previously defended the use of cognitive terms, they had been readier to offer physiological hypotheses in interpretation of such terms. They had similarly spoken of belief as a "condition of action," and of purposes as "governing" action, explaining behavior by reference to purposes and beliefs. But whereas Perry and Holt had identified the purpose with a hypothetical physiological mechanism of a fairly specific sort, Tolman did not. He regarded such physiological speculations as premature, and felt that physiological progress itself might depend on psychological knowledge:

Before studying the laws governing any relatively small group of physiological activities . . . we have to note, first, that such a minor group of physiological processes occurs only within some larger matrix of processes . . . [and this matrix of intervening variables can] often be better identified and controlled in the psychologist's terms of demands, perception and hypotheses than in the parallel physiological ones of widespread (and not easily get-at-able) neural patterns of excitation.[52]

But he acknowledged that physiological concepts would ultimately prove more comprehensive and accurate: "The molecular physiological variables will, of course, underly and may, if you will, be said to explain the molar variables of 'demand,' 'intention,' 'expectation.' But these latter have still to be discovered and schematized at their own level. In other words, the psychologist in the guise of the molar behaviorist, still has, I would assert, his own job to do and can still properly demand his own place in the sun."[53]

Tolman thus agreed with McDougall that behavior qua behavior must be described in purposive terms, and he acknowledged his "very great debt" to McDougall's emphasis on purpose.[54] Description at the physiological level (no matter how detailed) cannot replace purposive description, for it misses the "emergent" intensional or psychological properties of behavior. He remarked in 1925 that he was like McDougall, but unlike Perry, in not considering learning to be conceptually essential to purposive behavior; but later he came to agree with Perry on this issue.[55] He agreed that psychology needs some concept of instincts, "definable in terms of the purely abstract types of success which they predicate, and as so defined necessarily involving a teleological use of language."[56] The later concept of "ultimate demands" was to play a similar part in his system to that played by "instincts" in McDougall's. Including heredity as an intervening variable, Tolman challenged the extreme environmentalism of the early behaviorists. Tolman approved McDougall's list of objective criteria of purpose. But he complained that McDougall mentalistically "inferred" purpose from these criteria, regarding it as something over and above behavior.[57] Tolman, in contrast, held that "purpose" was an intervening variable whose meaning was wholly given by behavioral criteria. And all the terms of his theoretical system, which he defined with care in his *Purposive Behavior* of 1932, were similarly interpreted in a purely behavioral fashion. Some unknown physiological mechanisms presumably underlay purposive behavior, but these were no doubt of a purely mechanistic type: Tolman made no appeal to psychic energy or mental forces.

Not surprisingly, McDougall spoke more favorably of Tolman's "purposive" behaviorism than of the strict, Watsonian variety. But he complained of Tolman's refusal to discuss the subjective consciousness of animals, and of his insistence that even introspective data could not profitably be regarded as reporting the "raw feels" of human subjects. In rebutting Tolman's complaint that he inferred purpose as something over and above behavior, McDougall suggested using the term "purposive" instead.[58] McDougall gave objective criteria for "purpose" and "purposive," and his use of these terms was largely acceptable to Tolman. However, McDougall believed a special type of hormic energy to be involved, although he became fully explicit on this point only in his text of 1932. Tolman, therefore, was not unfair in his complaint that McDougall's use of "purpose" was not consistently objective or purely behavioral.

Later Behaviorists: Hull, Spence, Skinner, and Mowrer

Although he criticized all the contemporary forms of behaviorism, McDougall welcomed the developments that followed Watson's original manifesto. In 1923 he exhorted Watson's students: "If then you must be behaviorists, I beg that you will be purposive behaviorists."[59] In 1925 he distinguished the "strict behaviorism" of Watson from the "purposive behaviorism" of Perry and Tolman, clearly preferring the latter. In 1930 he wrote:

> Fifteen years ago American psychologists displayed almost without exception a complete blindness to the [behavioral feature of] goal-seeking . . . Now, happily, all this is changed; the animal psychologists have begun to realise that any description of animal behaviour which ignores its goal-seeking nature is futile . . . they are busy with the study of "drives," "sets," and "incentives." It is true that their recognition of goal-seeking is in general partial and grudging; they do not explicitly recognize that a "set" is a set toward an end, that a "drive" is an active striving toward a goal, that an "incentive" is something that provokes such active striving . . . Partial, half-

hearted, reluctant as is still the recognition of purposive activity, it may, I think, be fairly said that only the crude behaviourists now ignore it completely; that with that exception, American psychology has become purposive, in the sense that it no longer ignores or denies the goal-seeking nature of human and animal action, but accepts it as a problem to be faced.

It would, then, be otiose in this year of grace to defend or advocate purposive psychology in the vague sense of all psychology that recognises purposiveness, takes account of foresight and of urges, impulses, cravings, desires, as motive of action.

My task is the more difficult one of justifying the far more radically purposive psychology denoted by the adjective "hormic," a psychology which claims to be autonomous; which refuses to be bound to and limited by the principles current in the physical sciences; which asserts that active striving towards a goal is a fundamental category of psychology, and is a process of a type that cannot be mechanistically explained or resolved into mechanistic sequences.[60]

This passage highlights the issue that divided McDougall from his contemporaries: whether psychology is empirically reducible to physiology, irrespective of the strict reducibility of purposive terms.

This issue would have prevented McDougall's acceptance of later behaviorist systems also. Owing to the rapid absorption of behaviorism into the accepted background of American psychology, the number of such systems is large. They include such diverse approaches as the neurophysiological work of K. S. Lashley, with his critique of accounts based purely on simple reflexes; the strict associationism of E. R. Guthrie, which relied on neither the Law of Frequency nor the Law of Effect; Egon Brunswik's probabilism, with its emphasis on the various ways in which the organism may "intend" the perceptual object; and the work of N. E. Miller and John Dollard, who have attempted to account for human behavior and psychopathology in terms of approach-avoidance behaviors that become differentially attached to environmental cues.[61] Because space forbids discussion of all these later behaviorisms, I shall select a sample of three: the hypothetico-deductive approach of C. L. Hull and K. W. Spence; the experimental analysis of behavior offered by B. F. Skinner; and the neobehaviorism of O. H. Mowrer. These represent three disparate approaches to purposive concepts, which illustrate the difference between McDougall's position and the psychological climate already established by the time of his death. The 1930s saw the publication of the first behaviorist papers of Hull and the early work of Skinner, Spence, and Mowrer; after McDougall's death in 1938, behaviorism was further developed and sophisticated by such workers as these. Their detailed accounts of learning and their approaches to systematic theorizing differ, but they all agree in regarding behavior as in principle mechanistically explicable, without recourse to the hypothesis of psychic energy. Behavior is acknowledged to be purposive, in that it fulfils objective criteria of purposiveness such as those suggested by McDougall or Tolman; and teleological language may be appropriate and useful at the molar level. But teleological explanations are not ultimate; they are themselves to be explained by being accounted for in mechanistic terms at the molecular level. The work of these authors was fully developed only after McDougall's death. A brief account should show how naive Watsonian behaviorism has been left far behind by this new generation of behaviorists.

Whereas Tolman had preferred to remain at a clearly molar level, Hull developed an elaborate theoretical system based at the relatively molecular level of simple conditioning. He held that ideally the behavioral features named by molar vocabulary should be explained mechanistically in terms of "colorless movement and mere receptive impulses."[62] In his article "Knowledge and Purpose as Habit Mechanisms," Hull used the concepts of "internal stimulus components" and "pure stimulus acts" to explain how the organism achieves a seeming spontaneity and freedom from its environment.[63] The organism may act in response to the not-here and the not-now, as when it anticipates a future event; and it may be said to "know" the world by building up a representation that to some extent parallels the real world. Purposive behavior involves the elimination of errors and unnecessary acts in behavior sequences, and Hull suggested that a "persisting" stimulus component is an essential mechanism in such elimination. This early analysis of purposive behavior was later refined by the concept of the "habit-family-hierarchy," in terms of which Hull explained the variety of purposive behavior (that which McDougall called the "variation of means").[64] Each goal (and each of its anticipatory subgoals) is associated with a habit-family, a set of responses of differential availability which share a common anticipatory response. This latter mediates the transfer of reinforcement from one family member to others; it is thus one mechanism explaining the "intelligence" or "insight" characteristic of purposive behavior. Hull's fractional anticipatory goal-response serves much the same function as does the idea of expectancy in cognitive theories such as Tolman's.[65] The energizing principles in Hull's system were the basic biological drives, and goal achievement was seen by him as satisfying the needs for food, water, sex, and so on. His list of drives was shorter than McDougall's list of instinctive propensities; but he allowed for the development of a higher order of goals or values, which are only indirectly connected with the basic drives.

In "Mind, Mechanism and Adaptive Behavior," Hull defended the explanation of purposive behavior on purely physical principles.[66] He outlined his hypothetico-deductive system of postulates and theorems, a system in which "consciousness" did not appear. He remarked that unless "consciousness" can be presented as a basic term in postulates from which specific behavioral predictions can be deduced, it cannot be regarded as strictly necessary to the explanation of behavior. But it may be a high-level concept ultimately deducible from such postulates, as molar variables in general are assumed to be, so its use need not be dogmatically banned. In his first systematic text Hull wrote:

> For certain rough practical purposes the custom of naming action sequences by their goals is completely justified by its convenience. It may even be that for very gross molar behavior it can usefully be employed in theory construction . . . [we] do not deny the molar reality of purposive acts (as opposed to movement), of intelligence, of insight, of goals, of intents, of strivings, or of value; on the contrary, we insist upon the genuineness of these forms of behavior. We hope ultimately to show the logical right to the use of such concepts

by deducing them as secondary principles from more elementary objective primary principles.[67]

He went on to criticize Tolman's claim that "emergent" purposive behavior cannot be derived from any conceivable set of
postulates involving mere stimuli and mere movement. He then
recommended the conceptual exercise of imagining self-
maintaining robots whose behavior is complex and adaptive, as
is our own, but to which we should be loath to apply nonme-
chanical principles of explanation. Thus, Hull implies that intensional purposive language can be reduced to extensional,
mechanistic language in the strict sense, for the former is said
to be a deductive consequence of the latter; in this he differs
from both McDougall and Tolman. He also differs from Tolman
in his readiness to suggest specific neurophysiological mechanisms that may underlie the connections he finds at the psychological level.

Hull's general approach is shared by his pupil Spence, although
their views differ in detail. In particular, Spence's account of
motivation differs from Hull's, for he does not commit himself
to the view that drive reduction is the essential mechanism of
reinforcement; nor does he favor the elaboration of physiological
models by psychologists. But their theoretical systems are markedly similar, and Spence has defended Hull's stimulus-response
approach in *Behavior Theory and Conditioning* and in papers
on theory construction in psychology, the postulates and methods of behaviorism, and cognitive vs. stimulus-response theories
of learning.[68] In his view, cognitive and stimulus-response
theories differ in emphasis rather than content, and cognitive
constructs may be fruitful if operationally defined, as Tolman's
were. Since Tolman chose to discuss a wider range of behavior
than Hull, the specification of his theoretical constructs was
necessarily less detailed.[69] Tolman himself has remarked: "Apparently, I have no scientific superego which urges me to be mathematical, deductive, and axiomatic. My intervening variables . . .
do not lead to any then-and-there precise further quantitative
predictions. They do, however (when mixed with a healthy brew
of intuition, common sense, and phenomenology), lead to suggestions for further types of empirical relations to be tested."[70]

89

Although Tolman disagreed with Spence in thinking it "rather silly to be too precise, too quantitative, too deductive and axiomatic, save in very experimentally overcontrolled and over-limited areas," he took pains to provide behavioral definitions of the terms in his elaborate technical vocabulary. Many cognitive concepts have been less carefully defined than Tolman's and as a result have led to insoluble theoretical debates (Spence would have faulted McDougall on this issue, for McDougall's objective criteria of purpose were too vague to satisfy Spence). But to give up all psychological theorizing because of an empiricist impatience with such debates is seen by Spence as a counsel of despair.[71] It is this counsel which is offered by Skinner, a strict behaviorist who avoids systematization of the Hull type.

Skinner, like Hull, represents behavior as based on simple conditioning. But Skinner does not formulate his behavioral analysis in hypothetico-deductive terms. He acknowledges the power of the hypothetico-deductive method in areas of science concerned with variables that cannot be readily manipulated or observed, such as planetary motion, or the interactions of atomic and subatomic particles. But he has argued strongly against philosophies of science which elevate this particular method into the scientific method par excellence, and against psychological studies justified by this theoretical methodology.[72] The method encourages the appeal to intervening variables and the postulation of unobserved processes. For Skinner, behavior is observable; psychology is the study of behavior; and psychology should deal only with correlations between observables.

In his studies of operant and respondent behavior, he regards the "reflex" purely as a correlation between stimulus and response, disowning any neuroanatomical implications about underlying "reflex arcs."[73] He is even suspicious of what he calls the "stimulus-response formula," since it has led theorists such as Hull to postulate unobservable central processes—such as "afferent neural interaction" and "behavioral oscillation"—in order to rescue this formula.[74] In general, he avoids physiological speculation about the neural mechanisms involved in behavior, and similarly avoids appealing to psychological intervening variables such as those employed by Tolman or Hull. Instead of speaking of physiological hunger centers or of hunger itself, for

90

example, he refers to the time elapsed since the rat's last meal. The rat's behavior on finding food is correlated with this independent variable directly rather than with any intervening variable representing the rat's internal state.

Learning depends on reinforcement, and the detailed differences in schedules of reinforcement are very important in the shaping of behavior.[75] But reinforcement is behaviorally defined: "reinforcers" are those stimuli which in fact are correlated with a subsequent change in behavior (a change in the probability of response) when presented with another stimulus or response. Behavior is basically controlled by a small number of primary reinforcers, such as food and water, which may be supplemented by a large number of secondary reinforcers. These are originally neutral stimuli, which after association with primary reinforcement come to control behavior directly. Most human behavior is under the control of secondary reinforcers of various types, which determine the subtleties of human response. As well as a detailed experimental analysis of behavior, Skinner has also produced some nonexperimental writings. *Verbal Behavior* presents a program for the explanation of language in terms of conditioning—an approach that has been criticised by Noam Chomsky, who argues that the basic structural rules of language could not be learned in this way.[76] In the novel *Walden Two* Skinner has outlined a Utopian system of behavioral engineering, some elements of which are already in use, such as teaching machines and the techniques of "behavior therapy."[77] In all his writing, whether experimental or not, Skinner attributes present behavior to the influence of complex contingencies of reinforcement in the past history of the individual.

Since "the purpose" of a behavioral unit has been variously interpreted as the future attainment of the goal or as the present idea of the goal state, it is not surprising that Skinner regards the concept of purpose as superfluous in the study of behavior. In the first book setting out his behaviorist approach, Skinner did not deny that terms such as "purpose" or "trying" could be satisfactorily defined, and even used quantitatively; but he objected to the conceptual schemes associated with such terms wherein attention is focused on intervening variables rather than on the direct description of behavior. He criticised Watson for classifying highly organized activities, such as building a sky-scraper, as "responses," remarking that there is no reason to expect that such activities will obey simple dynamic laws.[78] One may properly speak of "responses" only when the experimental analysis has been pressed to the point where orderly changes occur (that is, changes expressible in terms of stimulus-response correlations). Fifteen years later, in 1953, Skinner repeated his rejection of appeals to purpose, claiming that descriptions or "explanations" of behavior in terms of the organism's purposes are strictly reducible to statements concerning contingencies of reinforcement:

> [There is a] fundamental principle of science which rules out "final causes." But this principle is violated when it is asserted that behavior is under the control of an "incentive" or "goal" which the organism has not yet achieved or a "purpose" which it has not yet fulfilled. Statements which use such words as "incentive" or "purpose" are usually reducible to statements about operant conditioning, and only a slight change is required to bring them within the framework of a natural science. Instead of saying that a man behaves because of the consequences which *are* to follow his behavior, we simply say that he behaves because of the consequences which *have* followed similar behavior in the past . . . [When we describe a man as "looking for his glasses"] what we have added is not a further description of his behavior but an inference about some of the variables responsible for it. There is no *current* goal, incentive, purpose, or meaning to be taken into account. This is so even if we ask him what he is doing and he says, "I am looking for my glasses." This is not a further description of his behavior but of the variables of which his behavior is a function; it is equivalent to "I have lost my glasses," "I shall stop what I am doing when I find my glasses," or "When I have done this in the past, I have found my glasses." These translations may seen unnecessarily roundabout, but only because expressions involving goals and purposes are abbreviations.[79]

These passages clearly claim not merely that purposive statements are empirically reducible to statements in terms of the reinforcements contingent upon past response, but that they are strictly reducible as well: "expressions involving goals and purposes are abbreviations."

More recently, in 1969, Skinner has contrasted "contingency-shaped" and "rule-governed" behavior. One might think that this distinction had been developed largely in response to Chomsky's criticism of Skinner's analysis of language use and language learning, were it not for Skinner's disarming assurance: "I have never been interested in critical reactions, either positive or negative . . . I have never actually read more than half a dozen pages of Chomsky's famous review of *Verbal Behavior*. (A quotation from it which I have used I got from I. A. Richards.)"[80] Be that as it may, Skinner depends on his new distinction to include intensional phenomena such as linguistic and purposive behavior within his system. Primarily, he insists, behavior is directly shaped by contingencies of reinforcement, of which the organism may be totally unaware. But a language-using organism such as man is able to derive verbal rules specifying (or hypothesizing) the contingencies. This derivation is effected by "induction" and "deduction." These rules may then act as reinforced stimuli governing a man's behavior. Rules may be reinforced by their pragmatic success within the physical environment, and by the purely social sanctions associated with them in the person's community. Rules are related, more or less closely, to past contingencies and codify the individual's awareness of the variables controlling his behavior; and "purposes" are a subclass of rules:

> The verbal community generates "awareness" . . . when it teaches an individual to describe his past and present behavior and behavior he is likely to exhibit in the future and to identify the variables of which all three are presumably functions. The description which is thus generated is not yet a rule, but the person may use the same terms to mand [command] his own behavior (as a form of self-control), to make resolutions, to formulate plans, to state purposes, and thus to construct rules . . . A scientific law or a maxim enjoining prudent behavior differs from a resolution, plan, or statement of purpose in the generality of the contingencies which it supplements or replaces. Laws and maxims describe long-lasting contingencies, and once discovered they can be transmitted

to and used by others. A resolution, plan, or statement of purpose is constructed on the spot. It is much more likely to be an incomplete description of contingencies, but it has the same effect as a maxim or law to the extent that it identifies a response and the occasion upon which it may be reinforced. It may also invoke additional reinforcers, positive or negative. A person obeys a law or maxim in part to avoid censure, possibly self-imposed, for failing to do so. He keeps a resolution, carries out a plan, and holds to a purpose in part for similar reasons.[81]

Despite this seeming acceptance of "purposes" as intervening variables (which may be "covert" and "hard to spot"), Skinner insists that purposes are a form or product of behavior, rather than mental precursors determining action.[82] The strict reducibility of purpose to behavioral terms is still implied. Even if we had "a complete account" of a behaving organism, comprising an account of both the observable behavior and the detailed physiological processes occurring at the same time, Skinner claims, we would not regard these two partial accounts as revealing the "double aspect" of the organism: "The organism would be seen to be a unitary system, its behavior clearly part of its physiology."[83] In such a case, the strict reduction of behavioral, including purposive, accounts to physiological terms would have been achieved. According to Skinner, there is no question of "two worlds," nor of irreducibly different mental and physical aspects of reality. The purposive concepts that are unavoidable in everyday discussion of human behavior could ideally be replaced by the atomistic terminology of functional dependence between response and reinforcement. Despite his recent reference to purposes as self-imposed rules, and despite his covertly teleological use of technical terms in the nonexperimental *Verbal Behavior*,[84] Skinner prefers not to use teleological language, even at the descriptive level. In this he differs not only from McDougall but also from many behaviorist colleagues.

Skinner's suspicion of intervening variables is not shared by Mowrer, whose system is built around such concepts as hope, fear, disappointment, relief, and image. Mowrer's interests range from the simplest reflex to the phenomena of language and psychopathology.[85] In his effort to integrate the findings of the many diverse learning theories, he has developed a "two-factor" theory of conditioning, which accounts for both the relaxing (drive-reduction) and the motivating (incentive) functions of reward. Decremental reinforcement reduces drive, and incremental reinforcement induces drive or need. These two types of reinforcement are comparable to reward and punishment respectively, and each may be associated with primary or secondary drives. Primary reinforcers such as food or shock are supplemented by secondary reinforcers such as hope or fear. These emotions become conditioned to the stimuli associated with primary reinforcement; thereafter they are crucial to the sensory feedback that guides ongoing behavior. Cognitive variables such as image are required for the explanation of response selection and initiation, whereby *this* response rather than *that* is selected in the pursuit of some goal. Concepts such as courage, perseverance, and masochism are defined in terms of other intervening variables; but all these variables that mediate between stimulus and response are given operational meaning in terms of observable behavior.

Mowrer describes behaviorism as the strident antithesis to the thesis of introspectionism; his own approach he calls a neobehaviorist synthesis: "The present volume is 'behavioristic' in the sense of approaching the topic of learning in the tradition of Pavlov, Thorndike, Hull, and other objectivists. But it deviates from or transcends this tradition in that it re-admits to consideration various problems which the behaviorists had renounced: hence its qualification as *neo*behavioristic."[86] In particular, neobehaviorism admits the usefulness of the systematic concepts of consciousness:

If we sometimes speak of "consciousness" (a tabued word for the Behaviorists), this is not just a friendly gesture to the past or concession to common sense; it represents instead the growing conviction that the objective study of behavior has now reached the point where some such concept is essential if systematic progress in theory construction is to go forward. Indeed, it is perhaps not too much to say that we have now reached a point at which, if consciousness itself were not experienced, we would have to invent some such equivalent construct to take its place.[87]

But the use of the vocabulary of consciousness does not imply the rejection of mechanism:

> Action which thus appears to be teleological or "purposeful" —and which, in a sense, indeed is—can in this way be accounted for in a purely causal, or consequential, way. We do not have to say that the rat runs "in order to" avoid the shock; we can say instead that the rat runs *because* (or *by-cause*) of fear . . . We assume that behavior *is* governed by its anticipated ends and consequences. But the underlying mechanism which mediates the process is thoroughly cause-and-effect.[88]

Mowrer points out that McDougall made a similar mediational use of the concepts of consciousness. But their interpretations of specific terms differ, and McDougall would not have accepted Mowrer's claim that physicalist principles of conditioning are adequate to the explanation of purposive behavior.

Behaviorism and Empirical Reduction

McDougall rejected the designation "behaviorist" in 1923 because of Watson's use of the term. Yet many of the behaviorist writers who followed and criticised Watson developed views with which McDougall could have felt sympathy. He admitted as much with regard to Perry, Holt, and Tolman, most of whose work appeared within his own lifetime. However, he still refused to classify himself as a behaviorist, and his reluctance to do so was primarily connected with the issue of hormic energy. He distinguished between the systematic description of behavior and its more basic (causal) explanation in terms of specific energy mechanisms; a completely satisfactory account would provide both of these.[89] The description of behavior in terms of his purposive concepts provides more than a mere taxonomy, for these concepts are intervening variables which allow one to predict and to explain behavior on the basis of the functional (intensional) relationships they express. Since these concepts have objective reference, by way of McDougall's behavioral criteria, they can be useful independently of any hypotheses about the type of energy involved. McDougall noted this fact, but he later provided such a hypothesis, which divided him from all the behaviorists. Because of his postulation of horme, he could not accept Tolman's purposive behaviorism; nor would he have accepted Mowrer's neobehaviorism, despite its theoretical use of the vocabulary of consciousness. When he stated that all psychology is, or should be, behavioristic, McDougall meant that the observation of behavior is an important psychological method—even in human psychology, where introspection is also available. He did not mean that we should assume the organism to be a purely physical system.

In other words, McDougall did not share the behaviorist faith in the possibility of an empirical reduction of psychology to physiology. This faith is common to all behaviorists, whether they also believe in the strict reducibility of purpose (like Watson, Skinner, and Hull), or whether they do not (like Perry, Holt, Tolman, and Mowrer). Some behaviorists, such as Holt and Hull, are relatively willing to offer physiological hypotheses indicating the nature of the bridging statements essential for successful reduction. Others, such as Tolman, Spence, and Skinner, prefer to concentrate on behavioral matters, leaving all physiological questions aside. Their caution is largely attributable to their realization that detailed physiological bridging statements are still far distant. McDougall's *ad hominem* argument against Perry and Holt, his complaint that their suggested bridging statements were highly schematic and unsupported by detailed physiological knowledge, has lost little force. There has, of course, been some advance. For instance, recent work on the activating functions of the midbrain reticular system affords a basis for hypothesizing bridging statements linking particular levels of consciousness—and personality traits such as extraversion and neuroticism—with physiological activity in certain fairly grossly specified areas of the brain.[90] And less grossly specified neurophysiological events, such as the firing of individual cells or the activity of small groups of cells, have been correlated with various aspects of visual perception or information-processing, such as the recording of movement in a particular direction or of a particular spatial orientation of a line within the visual field, as well as of rather more abstract visually perceived features.[91] Nevertheless, neurophysiology is in no fit state to prove the feasibility of empirical reduction beyond question, and the issue remains largely speculative.

Hull's suggestion to imagine robots whose behavior is adaptive as is our own is a conceptual exercise intended to minimize the influence of antireductionist assumptions. With the development of cybernetics since McDougall's death, this type of exercise has become increasingly prominent in discussions of the conceptual status of purposive psychology. But the extent and significance of computer analogies of behavior is contested. Moreover, competing philosophical analyses of the concepts involved in purposive explanation throw doubt not only on the admissibility of machine analogies but also on empirical reductionism in general. In short, the question that concerned McDougall so deeply and which divided him from his behaviorist contemporaries is still being debated.

IV Purpose, Reductionism, and Cybernetics

In the contemporary controversy centered on the reducibility of teleological explanation, many reductionists appeal to recent developments in cybernetics to support their case, claiming that there are significant similarities between certain explanations of machine performance and psychological (purposive) explanations of behavior. Such reductionists are typically prepared to use psychological language when describing machine performance, even if in an admittedly analogical sense. The extent of the analogy between behavior and machines—actual or hypothetical—is, however, debatable.

The debate is fed, in part, by doubts about the strength of current types of machine analogy, doubts that may arise even given some sympathy with the reductionist position. But in certain cases it is also fed by an initial bias against machine anologies in general, or even against mechanistic (including behaviorist and physiological) reductionism of any sort. Some writers with an antireductionist position are working psychologists, concerned to defend a particular theoretical system or to provide a rationale for a particular form of psychological therapy. Others are philosophers, primarily concerned with the analysis of purposive explanation as it occurs in everyday life. Many contemporary objections to reductionism are similar to McDougall's doubts on this issue.

The main conceptual outlines of current discussion may be clarified by considering the following questions: how are explanations in programming terms related to explanations in electronic terms? Are explanations in cybernetic contexts ever formally similar to purposive explanations, as characterized by McDougall's first three criteria? If so, does it follow that psychological predicates are ascribable to machines? To what extent can computer simulations support reductionism? Are there any valid a priori arguments showing that it must be impossible to reduce psychology to a mechanistic physiology? Supposing it to be possible in principle, is it likely in practice? In sum, is the reductionist's position philosophically acceptable, and can he draw support from cybernetic research?

99

Antireductionism in Third Force Psychology

Specific criticisms of current cybernetic achievements may be found in the writings of psychologists both with and without an initial reductionist bias. But the most important psychological resistance to machine analogies in general, as also to the reductionist influence of behaviorism, appears in the work of the "Third Force" psychologists. These psychologists are so called because they are united in reaction against the two most comprehensive psychologies now available: behaviorism and classical Freudian theory.

The Third Force includes many different groups, whose philosophical presuppositions differ. Some are existentialists, some phenomenologists, some Gestalt psychologists; others call themselves "organismic," "humanistic," or "self" psychologists, and so on. A. H. Maslow sees all these groups as contributing to an increasingly "total, single, comprehensive system of psychology."[1] The Third Force in general are primarily concerned with personality theory and with the practical problems arising within counseling and therapeutic contexts. They regard personal growth into the future as an important theoretical dimension, and emphasize the significance of purposes, hopes, aspirations, and creativity in the personal life. They insist on regarding each man as a self-determining subject, having his own idiosyncratic experience or view of himself and of the world in which he lives. In all this they echo McDougall; and like him, they stress the importance of regarding the "subjective" (intensional) categories of purpose and consciousness as irreducible to the categories of "objective" mechanistic science. It is not always clear just what type of irreducibility they have in mind. They do not generally discuss this issue in technical philosophical terms; and in any case their background philosophical assumptions differ. Because of their philosophical diversity, it is not possible to detail all their objections to reductionism. But the general flavor of their antireductionist bias may be inferred from a few passages drawn from Maslow and R. D. Laing, who represent "self-actualization" and "existential" psychology respectively.

Maslow has recently reiterated his long-standing objection that the reductive effort "is simply a reflection or implication in science of an atomistic, mechanical world view that we now have good reason to doubt. Attacking such reductive efforts is then not an attack on science in general, but rather on one of the possible attitudes towards science."[2] In an attack on positivist philosophies of science, with their emphasis on the classical rational, objective, and impersonal approach, he has written:

> We are groping . . . toward the phenomenological, the expe-riential, the existential, the idiographic, the unconscious, the private, the acutely personal; but it has become clear to me that we are trying to do this in an inherited intellectual atmosphere or framework which is quite unsuitable and unsympathetic, one which I might even call forbidding. [This intellectual framework is] primarily suitable for the communication and discussion of the rational, the abstract, the logical, the public, the impersonal, the nomothetic, the repeatable, the objective, the unemotional . . . In a word, we keep trying to use the canons and folkways of impersonal science for our personal science, but I am convinced that this won't work.[3]

Maslow is here both arguing for the use of intensional categories within a scientific terminology and pointing out that the psychologist himself is often "involved" in the experimental or therapeutic situation in a way that the natural scientist is not, so that the notion of "objectivity" in human psychology cannot be precisely the same as in the nonpsychological sciences. His first point raises the reductionist question of the relation of intensional categories to the categories of "objective science."

According to one of the "basic propositions" of Maslow's psychology: "The psychologist proceeds on the assumption that for his purposes there are two kinds of world, two kinds of reality, the natural world and the psychic world, the world of unyielding facts and the world of wishes, hopes, fears, emotions, the world which runs by non-psychic rules and the world which runs by psychic laws . . . This assumption does not deny that these worlds are related and may even fuse." However, the precise nature of the "relation" or "fusion" is not made clear. It is even suggested that it cannot be made clear: "I may say that this assumption is acted upon by *many* or *most* psychologists, even though they are perfectly willing to admit that it is an insoluble

101

philosophical problem. Any therapist *must* assume it or give up his functioning. This is typical of the way in which psychologists bypass philosophical difficulties and act 'as if' certain assumptions were true even though unprovable, e.g., the universal assumption of 'responsibility,' 'will power,' etc."[4] More recently, Maslow has insisted: "In dealing with persons, you must make your epistemological peace with the fact that people have purposes and goals of their own even though physical objects do not."[5] But he does not clearly show exactly how this "epistemological peace" is to be made.

A little further on, he hints that the phenomenological and introspective emphasis of his approach might yield to a future methodology more reliant on "public," "measurable" indices of psychological states:

> Today we must study anxiety, depression, or happiness mostly as private experiences and verbal reports. But this is because we can't do any better today. On the day when we discover an externally and publicly observable and measurable correlate of anxiety or of happiness, something like a thermometer or a barometer, on that day a new era in psychology will have begun. Since I think this is not only desirable but possible, I have pressed in this direction. This amounts to seeing data as arranged in a hierarchy of knowledge that parallels an equally necessary idea of "stages or levels of development of science."[6]

This passage might be interpreted as suggesting that there is a publicly observable physiological correlate or sufficient condition of any particular psychological state, and that if it were discovered, then psychological categories could be dispensed with entirely. This would indeed be a "new era" in psychology. But such an interpretation would almost certainly be incorrect. The whole tenor of Maslow's work suggests that one must study phenomena such as anxiety and depression from a strictly psychological viewpoint. To switch to a physiological viewpoint would not be to "do any better" but would rather change the nature of the inquiry so drastically as to destroy it altogether. In the terminology used so far, psychology is not *strictly* reducible to physiology, even if it is *empirically* reducible in principle. Personalistic categories are therefore not replaceable by physiological ones, even though physiological correlates of psychological phenomena may be found and might occasionally prove useful to the personality theorist.

The existential psychologist Laing sometimes seems to suggest that physiological knowledge and machine research are wholly irrelevant to the understanding of behavior, and that personality theory is totally irreducible to mechanism: "The other as person is seen by me as responsible, as capable of choice, in short, as a self-acting agent. Seen as an organism, all that goes on in that organism can be conceptualized at any level of complexity—atomic, molecular, cellular, systemic, or organismic. Whereas behaviour seen as personal is seen in terms of that person's experience and of his intentions, behaviour seen organismically can only be seen as the contraction or relaxation of certain muscles, etc." Strict reducibility is obviously rejected. But empirical reducibility seems also to be rejected, for the "personal" approach is described as not being merely at a different "level of complexity" from cellular or atomic conceptualizations. Whereas organismic or cellular levels of explanation are empirically reducible to atomic ones (our understanding of biological systems thereby being increased), the personal form of explanation is not: "There is a common illusion that one somehow increases one's understanding of a person if one can translate a personal understanding of him into the impersonal terms of [mechanistic processes] ... The theory of man as person loses its way if it falls into an account of man as a machine or man as an organismic system of [physiological] processes."[7]

However, at other times Laing appears content to allow the possibility of empirical reducibility, so long as one acknowledges that psychological language would still be essential to the understanding of behavior as such. One may choose to regard behavior sometimes as behavior and sometimes as physical movement; there is no incompatibility or contradiction involved, just as long as the languages are not mixed:

There is no question here or anywhere of a mind-body dualism. The two accounts [personal and organismic] are each the outcome of one's initial intentional act [i.e., one's initial choice of point of view]; each intentional act leads in its own direction and yields its own results. One chooses the point of view or intentional act within the overall context of what one is "after" with the other. Man as seen as an organism or man as seen as a person discloses different aspects of the human reality to the investigator. Both are quite possible methodologically but one must be alert to the possible occasion for confusion.[8]

This passage is reminiscent of Maslow's picture of the "two worlds," although it more clearly suggests that there are two languages rather than two worlds. Not only Maslow and Laing but all the Third Force would insist that even if empirical reduction is ever effected, the science of psychology will still need concepts germane to "the second kind of world," much as the science of biology today still employs categories foreign to the biochemist. Moreover, these psychological concepts would include "proactive" (future-oriented)[9] terms referring to the conscious purposes of men, and in general would stress the subjective environment, the world as it exists for the experiencing individual. The implication is that, in such a case, the "second world" model or language could not be rejected as being logically superfluous.

According to the Third Force, it is no more false to think of man as a machine than to think of him as a biological system. Laing himself writes: "I am not here objecting to the use of mechanical or biological analogies as such, nor indeed to the intentional act of seeing man as a complex machine or as an animal."[10] But machine analogies may have even more misleading consequences than biological analogies, because machines are *known* to be fully mechanistic, often deterministic systems, which appears incompatible with many of the psychological categories used in describing the personal life. Thus, Rollo May, another existential psychologist, complains: "I take very seriously . . . the dehumanizing dangers in our tendency in modern science to make man over into the image of the machine, into the image of the techniques by which we study him . . . A central core of modern man's "neurosis" is the undermining of his experience of himself as responsible, the sapping of his willing and decision." May insists that he is not arguing "against causality" nor claiming that "free will" disproves "determinism" in bodily processes.[11] Adapting Laing's phrase, one may say that he is rather, "alerting us to the possible occasions for confusion" in the use of machine analogies. The problem is not that the human body cannot be both a physical and a psychological system, but that it cannot be thought of or responded to at one and the same time as specifically human and as merely a body. Since to think of a man as a person is not possible in formally mechanistic terms, machine analogies are particularly prone to "dehumanize" or "depersonalize" psychological theory.

In consequence, the Third Force depreciate machine research, believing that only relatively unimportant behavioral problems can be formulated or approached with such analogies in mind. They would doubtless endorse the following complaint about the type of problems most likely to engage the attention of psychologists with a reductionist bias:

> Too many of today's psychologists take it for granted that a complete mechanical explanation of human behaviour could in principle be achieved. Some of these writers are machine theorists pure and simple—people who think that engineering principles can be directly applied to the explanation of behaviour; others would call themselves "behaviour theorists" and would prefer a neo-Pavlovian terminology. But the upshot is the same. Of course none would dispute that many problems in animal behaviour, and some in human behaviour, can profitably be approached in this way; but these problems are for the most part of slight practical consequence. How unfortunate it will be if all psychologists wholeheartedly embrace a view of their subject-matter which will eventually force them, if they wish for any success at all, to investigate reaction times and rats instead of the social life of aspiring humanity; to do odd jobs for physiologists instead of developing and expounding their own proper study; to frequent, in short, multitudinous back alleys of no moment in preference to the broad highways where all men pass.[12]

Whether or not "behaviour theorists" can profitably approach "the social life of aspiring humanity" is a question about behaviorism in general, not about any behaviorist psychology in particular. Not all behaviorists rely on a strictly atomistic or peripheralist theoretical base, nor do they all confine themselves to theorizing about, or even experimenting on, rats. But they all do assume the empirical reducibility of psychology. Only if it can be shown that the use of purposive and personalistic predicates is essentially incompatible with basically mechanistic assumptions can "behaviorism" in general be so radically faulted as to be pronounced necessarily irrelevant to human concerns. As a way of approaching this question, let us ask to what extent such skepticism as the above about machine research is justified, and whether the psychologist impressed by cybernetic and programming analogies is really bound to be misled into "multitudinous back alleys of no moment."

The Reducibility of Cybernetic Explanations

The reductionist who looks to cybernetic research for support believes that there are significant similarities between cybernetic systems and living organisms. The term "cybernetics" was coined by Norbert Wiener in the 1940s and is derived from the Greek *kybernetes*, "steersman."[13] It is commonly restricted to artifacts and covers all "self-governing" machines, including very simple systems, such as the thermostat, whose equilibrium is maintained purely by some form of negative feedback. However, the homeostasis of biological systems has also been described as "cybernetic," for it is basically similar to the less complex equilibrium of artifacts which is maintained by negative feedback. Wiener himself stressed the analogies between the processes of control and communication in cybernetic machines and living things—including psychological organisms. In an influential discussion of behavior, purpose, and teleology, he used the key terms so that teleological or purposive behavior became synonymous with "behavior controlled by negative feedback," by which he meant behavior that "is controlled by the margin of error at which the [behaving] object stands at a given time with reference to a relatively specific goal . . . The signals from the goal are used to restrict outputs which would otherwise go beyond the goal."[14] A paradigm case of "purposive" behavior suggested by Wiener is a machine designed so as to impinge on a moving luminous "goal."

Negative feedback in the presence of such a "goal" is, no doubt, involved in much purposive activity. Patients with cerebellar disease, for instance, may show a particular type of incapacity to bring a glass of water to their lips which is strikingly like the behavior of an undamped cybernetic system. However, the psychological reductionist requires more than the principle of negative feedback, more than an analogy of biological function or of homeostasis. The sense in which physiological homeostasis and the functional explanations of biologists may be termed "teleological" or "purposive" is weaker than the sense in which behavior and psychological explanations may be so called. The biological sense lacks the crucial psychological feature of intensionality; no reference to the system's subjective idea of the goal is involved. A man's attempt to square the circle, or to frighten away an intruder by making a loud noise on the stairs, can hardly be characterized as "governed by signals from the goal" in the way described by Wiener, for the former goal is unattainable in principle, while the latter (even if it is eventually achieved) provides no signals that can be used to guide the previous stamping on the stairs. Rather, it is the man's idea of the goal that must be conceived of as "governing" the purposive behavior. A psychological system that fails to achieve its goals may sometimes be described as "mistaken" in some of its ideas, but no such intensional category can be properly ascribed to malfunctioning biological or artifactual cybernetic systems whose negative feedback mechanism is set in such a way that they do not achieve their so-called "goal." The psychological reductionist therefore requires a clearly mechanistic analogy of specifically psychological processes, a cybernetic parallel of the mind-body distinction.

For this he looks to information-processing, or symbol-manipulating, machines, and to the associated distinction between the machine's program and the machine itself. The program and the mechanism of a given system are conceptually distinct; to borrow Gilbert Ryle's expression, they fall into quite different "categories."[15] The program is an abstract conceptual system expressed in information-processing language, while the

107

mechanism is a material thing. Moreover, some programmed machines have a particular organizational feature by virtue of which they are more closely analogous to psychological organisms, or intensional "subjects," than are others. The vast majority of information-processing machines are, in fact, digital computers.

Considered purely as a physical thing, the modern high-speed digital computer can be described in the language of electronics. It is a complex arrangement of circuits, a machine made up of resistors, condensers, transistors, and like elements. The operative changes occurring within the machine include such items as momentary electrical pulses in particular wires and alterations of steady voltage levels at certain points in the component circuits.[16] Digital computers are finite-state machines; that is, they must at any moment be in one of a finite number of possible states. This is possible because their basic active components (the "flip-flops") are normally in either of two stable states. The details of the circuitry are arranged so that specific transition rules govern the succession of states in these units: each state is determined by the preceding states according to known rules. Some of these rules may be probabilist, and they may even include a randomizing operator; but in general it is possible to specify the state and the input of such a system and to apply these rules so as to generate the succeeding state. Everything that happens in the machine can be explained mechanistically, for the principles of its physical performance are fully understood by the electronic engineer. Assuming that he has available a complete description of the structure and history of the machine, he can explain every detail of performance at the electronic level. Given a particular output, he can list the various changes in the components that were involved in producing it. In practice, he is usually unable to do this, because of the extraordinary complexity involved. Nor is he able to predict all the states consequent on a given input at a particular time. Nevertheless, in principle such explanations and predictions in the vocabulary of electronics are available. The computer, in other words, is a mechanistic system describable in formally mechanistic terms.

But considered as an information-processing system, the computer must be described in different terms, which specify the

108

information-processing operations it is carrying out, the instructions it is executing. This specification can be made at various levels, for different levels of language are available for this type of description. At the most basic level is the "machine language" or "machine code." This is the only language that can be "read" and followed by the machine itself, without the intervention of any additional translating programs. The machine is constructed so that each instruction written in the machine code elicits a particular operation within the mechanism.[17] Because of this close correspondence between code and mechanism, the machine codes of differently designed machines differ from each other. Sometimes the machine's instructions must be written directly in a purely binary notation; other times they can be expressed with decimal digits and a few verbal symbols like "load," "add," and "store," which are automatically converted to a binary form as they are put into the machine. At the level of the machine language, every single elementary operation that the machine is to carry out must be specified by a separate instruction. The machine's elementary operations are few in number and simple in type; for instance, adding or subtracting numbers, copying an item of information in a specified position in the storage register, shifting an item to another specified position, and counting the instructions executed so far. For even relatively simple information-processing tasks, therefore, the complete sequence or program of instructions required at this level is very long and cumbrous. This remains true even if the programmer uses "shorthand" devices such as subroutines. These are blocks of instructions defining a complex operation—such as computing a sine or a square root—which may be required for many different problems, or many times in the course of a single problem; the programmer can call on a subroutine by means of a special code-name and thus does not need to write out all the individual instructions every time that complex operation is required.

For most people, a program written in machine language is difficult to cope with even at the detailed level, and psychologically quite impossible to understand as a whole. One does not naturally think of information-processing procedures in such small-scale units, and it takes a great deal of effort to do so. Similarly, an accurate spatial "fix" on each grain of sand on a beach would not, in practice, give one much idea of the overall configuration of the beach. To do so one needs a language on a higher level, a language that ignores the constituent details, such as one that expresses the contours and dimensions of the sand dunes.

The higher languages needed in artificial information-processing contexts are the "programming languages," such as IPL-V, ALGOL, FORTRAN, LISP, and COMIT. These are designed to be more readily intelligible to the human programmer than is the machine code, and their greater intelligibility is grounded in two main features. First, the symbolic units or instructions in a programming language correspond to complex series of machine instructions rather than to one instruction only. It is as if the whole program were written in terms of subroutines and other large-scale processing units, all symbolized directly. A corollary is that the programmer using a high-level language can ignore all the operating details of his machine; indeed, he need not even know which machine his program will be run on, because a given program could be run on many differently constructed machines. Second, many programming languages utilize symbols that are already familiar in richer semantic contexts than the programming context itself. For example, ALGOL is markedly similar to algebraic notation; not surprisingly, it is much easier to write sensible mathematical programs in ALGOL than in the binary notation and other parsimonious symbols of the machine code.

Since the machine itself can only read instructions written in machine code, every program written in a programming language has to be translated into the machine's language before it can be run on a specific computer. This translation is effected by special programs (either "compilers" or "interpreters"[18]), which take as input a program in a high-level language and produce as output a program in machine code. As far as the machine is concerned, this translation is absolutely precise: the high-level program is thus strictly reducible and totally equivalent to the machine-code program. But the translation may appear to result in a loss of meaning, in two ways. First, even if the programming language is unlike any familiar notation, it can exhibit structural features of operation that are lost at the level of the machine code. For instance, it can express the fact that a complex sub-routine is a relatively independent functional unit by including a specific name for calling on that routine; no such "bracketing" of the many component instructions involved is possible at the level of the machine code. Second, if the programming language is like a familiar notation, one may be tempted to read too much meaning into it. This extra semantic content may be heuristically or psychologically useful to the programmer working in the high-level language, but it cannot be made available to the machine if it cannot be expressed in the machine code. For these reasons, an instruction which has been compiled or interpreted (that is, translated into machine code) typically does not retain all the meaning that it seems to have when expressed in the uncompiled or uninterpreted form.

In general, the more the programming language superficially resembles a natural language, the more likely that one may read surplus meaning into the program which is not represented by any precise instructions that can be executed by the machine. This semantic impoverishment of programming languages can be illustrated even at the level of the machine instructions. For example, one hypothetical machine-language contains an instruction *Load from 200.*[19] The word "load" might suggest that the relevant operation involves the removal of the item of information from position 200 in the storage register, leaving that position empty. But in fact, this operation merely copies the specified item into another place, leaving it still unchanged at position 200. "*Loading* luggage from a trolley" and "*loading* information from position 200" are therefore quite different, even though as a result of each operation some place that was formerly empty is now occupied. Any confusion arising from such a simple instruction would be quickly and easily dispelled. But the instructions expressed in high-level languages are much more complex and can in principle give rise to more insidious confusions. This is especially so if the analyses of the everyday concepts "borrowed" for the programming language are themselves unclear or controversial—as psychological terms in general are.

No program is strictly reducible to a physical description of any machine. Even a program written in machine code is not synonymous with an electronic account of the consecutive states of the physical mechanism. And since a program written in a programming language can be run on machines of different construction and can be written by someone completely ignorant of electronics, it is clearer still that such a program is not semantically equivalent to any physical account. This is true irrespective of the merely apparent semantic richness of some programming languages.

But descriptions of the machine in programming terms clearly are empirically reducible to descriptions in electronic terms. In the case of programs written in machine code, the bridging statements required list the strict (necessary and sufficient) one:one correspondences that the designer has arranged between the basic linguistic units or instructions of the code and certain electronic operations in the mechanism. In the case of programs written in a programming language, the bridging statements list sufficient, but not necessary, conditions of their physical embodiment or instantiation, for high-level programs can be run on many physically different machines; they can each be converted into a number of programs written in machine code, with the help of the appropriate compilers or interpreters. Even supposing that one knew which particular machine was "running" the high-level program, it would not always be possible to list necessary and sufficient physical conditions for the occurrence of an output specified in the programming language, for outputs classified as "of a certain sort" in programming terms need not be uniquely correlated with any one set of changes in components. Outputs falling under one and the same description may in fact have rather different detailed causal histories. This is even more likely to be true if the output is identified by an expression drawn from everyday psychological language that is used by observers—or by the programmer himself—to describe the overall structure of performance. But even so, the all-seeing engineer could provide a mechanistic explanation, in terms of sufficient causal conditions, for each and every case. Descriptions of machine performance in programming terms are therefore in principle empirically reducible to electronic ones. And all descriptions of machine performance in information-processing or psychological language generally are basically mechanistic in this sense, whether or not they are ever teleological in their superficial form.

According to the reductionist, of course, psychological descriptions and explanations of human and animal behavior are themselves teleological only in form, being basically mechanistic in this sense. Nevertheless, explanations of behavior may be admitted by him to be generally more useful when expressed at the psychological level. Many behaviorists have argued that even if all the physiological details were known, psychological terms would still be needed to express the overall structure and functional dependencies of behavior. Similarly, J. A. Deutsch states that the overall structure of performance, rather than the electronic causes, is crucial to explaining the performance of artifacts—such as his "insightful learning machine":

> The change which occurs in learning in the machine could be engineered in many different ways. Any component which could be made to assume either of two steady states could be used . . . The precise properties of the parts do not matter; it is only their general relationships to each other which give the machine as a whole its behavioral properties. These general relationships can be described in a highly abstract way, for instance, by the use of Boolean algebra. This highly abstract system thus derived can be embodied in a theoretically infinite variety of physical counterparts. Nevertheless, the machines thus made will have the same behavioral properties, given the same sensory and motor side. Therefore, if we wish to explain the behavior of one of these machines, the relevant and enlightening information is about this abstract system and not about its particular embodiment.[20]

The general, programming or "behavioral," descriptions are more commonly relied on by workers in machine research than are their detailed causal counterparts—even if the causal descriptions are known.

But the antireductionist may object that this proves no more than that programming and electronic descriptions differ in the way that "molar" and "molecular" accounts in many formally mechanistic scientific subject-areas differ. For example, descriptions of the stretching and elasticity of copper wires are "reducible" to literal molecular descriptions of the same wires only in the second, empirical sense. And for most practical purposes, they are much more useful, more easily arrived at, and more readily intelligible than the molecular account. What is required, then, is that the reductionist show the particular relevance of cybernetic, as opposed to physical or chemical, analogies to specifically psychological subject-matter. It is here that, according to the antireductionist, all really sound analogies end: in his view, no molar explanation in cybernetic contexts is truly teleological, and thus the empirical reducibility of cybernetic explanations cannot help the reductionist's case. In order to determine whether cybernetic explanations are ever teleological in form, the analogy between programming and psychological contexts must be considered in the light of the three logical criteria of purposive explanation.

Programs and Teleological Explanation

With respect to the first criterion, there is certainly no exact parallel. A prospective reference is not involved in every identification or description of a programming unit as such, whether instruction or subroutine. Nor is such identification necessarily nonatomistic, in the sense of being logically dependent on another, not necessarily prospective, identification within the same category. For instance, an instruction to "add" can be identified at the level of the machine code quite independently of its function in the overall logical operation being carried out; it may be part of a process of multiplication (successive addition) or of subtraction (negative addition), but such facts are not relevant to its identification as an operation of addition. All instructions specified at the level of the machine code have this "atomistic" character, for the machine code is constructed so that consecutive instructions are executed one by one.

However, the reductionist may point out that some complex programs are described by their authors in nonatomistic terms involving a prospective reference. Indeed, Allen Newell, H. A. Simon, and J. C. Shaw describe their General Problem Solver (GPS) in terms of "means-end" relationships, and hierarchies of "goals" and "subgoals."[21] In their words: "GPS, to put it simply, is a

114

program that reasons about ends and means. It is capable of defining ends, seeking means to attain them, and, in the process of so doing, defining new subsidiary ends, or subgoals, to the original end."[22] In this case the programmers claim that a particular operation or routine may be carried out purely because it is judged by the program to be relevant to the achievement of a particular goal-state, and hence the description and explanation of performance should mention this fact.

GPS is a program written to perform relatively varied tasks in problem-solving and learning.[23] It is hierarchical in logical structure; that is, there are "routines" and "subroutines" on many different levels. In principle, it may have an indefinite number of levels, since it involves recursive programming techniques, that is, a routine may operate on itself. The importance of this type of technique is that a relatively simple routine may be written which can then operate on any level; the power of the program is vastly increased in comparison to nonrecursive programs, in which each level has to be independently specified before it can be operated on. Given a certain overall goal, the machine generates a hierarchical means-end analysis of the problem on as many levels as are required. It sets up subgoals as being likely to lead to the overall goal, and selects logical operators according to the calculated probability of their contributing to the goal currently being approached. For example, when proving theorems in the propositional calculus, it applies operators in order to transform one symbolic expression into another and to reduce specific differences between two expressions, where the expressions in question function as the initial state and as the goal state of the problem (or subproblem). The criteria of selection of subgoals and appropriate logical operators are perfectly determinate, although the procedure is heuristic rather than algorithmic. That is, the rules governing the search procedure are not guaranteed to generate the solution but are rather "rules of thumb," like *Protect your queen* in chess. Such heuristics may sometimes prevent consideration of the correct solution—for instance, it may occasionally be necessary to sacrifice the queen—but in general they confine the search within manageable limits and often lead to the solution of the problem.

The overall goal-state may be unattainable in principle. For instance, GPS may be required to show that a certain expression is a theorem of the propositional calculus, but the expression in question may not be a theorem. GPS will attempt a solution employing its normal principles of theorem-proving, and it may or may not reach the conclusion that a solution is impossible. If a particular problem is of a general type that can be coped with by the machine, it may be solved more efficiently or less, for the heuristics employed may or may not be powerful, the selection of criteria and calculation of probabilities may be correct or incorrect, and the subgoals set up may or may not be helpful in generating the required proof. Ultimately, it is the programmer's skill and judgment (particularly in the suggestion and ordering of heuristics) that determines to what extent the program is efficient in dealing with the problems presented.

Performance guided by GPS is constantly described by its authors in terms borrowed from everyday psychology:

> [GPS is] a recursive system that generates a tree of *sub-goals* in *attempting* to *attain* a given *goal*. For every new *difficulty* that is *encountered* a new subgoal is *created* to *overcome* this *difficulty*. GPS has a number of *tests* it *applies* ... GPS contains an ordering of the differences, so that some differences are *considered easier* than others ... GPS will not *try* a *subgoal* if it is *harder* than one of its *supergoals*. It will also not *try* a *goal* if it follows an *easier goal*. That is, GPS *insists* on *working* on the *hard* differences first and *expects* to *find easier* ones as it *goes along*.[24]

Of course, this "purposive" description of GPS is not the only description available, for the program can be expressed atomistically as a series of distinct instructions. GPS is in fact written in IPL-V, a programming language that is interpreted into machine code for execution on a machine. IPL-V is a "list-processing" language, developed largely by the GPS programmers themselves. List-processing languages in general are particularly well suited for writing hierarchical programs involving many different levels of subroutines, for the items on a list may themselves be (names of) lists. The recursive character of programs such as GPS is thus readily allowed for, and the lowest (most detailed) level of all may be logically far removed from the highest level of instructions in the program. IPL-V is a language unlike any natural language or familiar mathematical notation. In it, all instructions must be written entirely as strings of code letters and numbers. For instance, the routine thought of by the programmer as *Find the last symbol on the list* is written as R1. Since this is a routine, "R1" is actually the name of a series of instructions, which specify basic operations, such as locating the next symbol on a list (J60), and refer the machine to the numerically expressed addresses of the particular cells involved.[25] In other words, at the detailed level of the basic subroutines of the IPL-V program—not to mention the level of the machine code itself—the description given in the actual programming language is, in a sense, unintelligible. In a general discussion of programs such as GPS, M. L. Minsky has observed: "Programmers . . . know that there is never any 'heart' in a program. There are high-level routines in each program, but all they do is dictate that 'if such and such; then transfer to such and such a subroutine.' And when we look at the low-level subroutines, which 'actually do the work,' we find senseless loops and sequences of trivial operations."[26] "Senseless" loops and "trivial" operations are all that we find, and the "intelligence" involved in the actual work or performance of the program is no longer apparent. The statement by the GPS programmers with which this paragraph opened was intended by them as a description of the general pattern of logical processes carried out by the machine, as an indication of the machine's "intelligence." And these matters can be made apparent only with the help of this familiar language. Most people would be quite unable to appreciate what was going on, or to predict performance on a different problem, if they were restricted to the stepwise account phrased in IPL-V. Indeed, it is doubtful whether even the programmers themselves would have been able to envisage and compose such a program if they had not allowed themselves to think in these terms at any stage.

To refuse to describe GPS in these terms (that is, to disallow their use even italicized or in quotation marks) would be to relinquish the only way available to express certain significant facts about the structure and operation of the program. And much of what is significant about these facts is their likeness to certain features of human problem-solving. For instance the italicized passage quoted above is enough to suggest that GPS shows certain preliminary analogs of the observable purposive characteristics of "persistence" and "variation of means," both of which McDougall expressly stated could never be exhibited by a machine.[27] GPS (and its predecessor the Logic Theorist)[28] was written by Newell, Simon, and Shaw as an exercise in paralleling human thought processes. It is therefore not surprising that so many anthropomorphic terms appear in their descriptions of machine performance. Nor is it surprising that they overemphasize the similarities involved.[29] But some justification for the use of purposive terms can be gained by observing the operation of the program itself, irrespective of the programmers' theoretical motivation. There is no need to accept the view that GPS is a very close analog (a highly satisfactory theory or model) of human thinking in expressing these likenesses, still less the view that GPS is "really" purposive or that it "thinks" and "tries to attain goals" in the full sense of the words. But to restrict oneself to the level of the IPL-V instructions would be as stultifying as to speak always of "molecules" and never of "elasticity" in wire. More specifically, it would be to lose sight of the ways in which GPS and comparable programs seem to parallel molar (purposive) psychological processes.

If the second criterion of teleology is applied to cybernetic machines, the parallel is even less close. This criterion is the one of "ultimate" purposive explanations; that is, there are certain stopping points in purposive explanation at which no further explanation in purposive terms can possibly be given. In McDougall's terminology, these stopping points characteristically refer to natural tendencies, to instincts directed toward natural goals. Programs could certainly be written so that certain basic goals would be more "fundamental" than others, and explanations in terms of these goals would be somehow "ultimate." The basic goals of the program would be analogous to "natural" or "instinctive" goals in psychology. For instance, McDougall's theory of instincts could be parallelled by a program directing that all goal-seeking performance should be somehow controlled by one or more of these basic goals. Explanations of the machine's performance in terms of the basic goals would be "ultimate" in the sense that no further goal or purpose ascribable to the machine could be mentioned to extend our understanding of its performance. But of course, there would always be some further purpose explaining the performance at a deeper level; namely, one ascribable to the programmer. This point was made by McDougall, although with very much less sophisticated machines in mind, when he stated that machines show "extrinsic" rather than "intrinsic" teleology, being called "purposive" only with reference to the purposes of their designers.[30] The point has also been noted in more recent denials of the propriety of using purposive language in connection with machines.[31]

Moreover, in such cases we know that performance "directed by the basic goals" can always be explained at the mechanistic level. McDougall claimed that instinctive action cannot be mechanistically explained because the behavioral tendencies concerned involve hormic energy, and for this reason he also denied that instinctive behavior can be closely mimicked by any mechanistic artifact. An influential recent conceptual analysis of purpose and the related concept of inherent natural tendencies claims that no cybernetic analogy of behavior, however close, can be truly termed "purposive" because of the basic form of explanation known to be available. That is, since descriptions and explanations of machine performance, however phrased, are always empirically reducible to electronic causal accounts, such descriptions and explanations cannot be regarded as truly purposive. This is the position argued at length by Charles Taylor in *The Explanation of Behaviour*.

Taylor argues that the assumption that behavior is not basically open to mechanistic explanation in terms of causal antecedents is built into the everyday meanings of purposive concepts. On the contrary, the basic explanation is assumed to be in terms of some feature of the organism's intensional world, whether a highly specific intention or some more general purpose which the organism naturally tends to pursue. Consequently, cybernetics could not provide evidence for reductionism, no matter how sophisticated its achievements might be. Defining a "more basic" explanation as one that sets out the regularities on which those cited in a "less basic" explanation depend, Taylor states:

> The claim that the behaviour of a system must be accounted for in terms of purpose or "natural" or "inherent" tendencies concerns the laws which hold at the most basic level of explanation . . . Thus we could construct a mechanical dog, programmed to behave like a real one. In this case the laws descriptive of its external behaviour . . . would be teleological [i.e., expressed in terms of nonatomistically identified units] like those of his real counterpart, they would characterize the behaviour as "goal-directed," but the more basic explanation . . . would not. With systems of this kind we can hardly speak of an account in terms of "natural" or "inherent" tendencies. What we have in effect is the fact of the convergence of events towards a certain result which in turn is accounted for on quite different principles.[32]

In other words, explanations in terms of "tendencies" or "purposes" are not empirically reducible to mechanistic causal accounts.

According to Taylor, accounts in terms of "natural inherent tendencies" explain behavior by referring to essentially noncausal powers of response selection. Both mechanistic and teleological theories of behavior, he claims, aim to express "sufficient conditions" of a behavioral response, B, so that B will, in the given situation, lead to the goal state, G. "Mechanistic" theories attempt to do this in terms of general laws stating correlations between independent variables (representing initial conditions) and dependent (response) variables. The independent variables may be physiological or behavioral, but Taylor concerns himself primarily with theories of the second type. In consort with a critique of various peripheralist, behaviorist psychologies, Taylor argues that mechanistic theories cannot state sufficient causal conditions of behavior because that would require the specification of an infinite set.[33] According to him, organisms respond so as to achieve their goal in an "infinite" number of initial situations. Causal conditions, whether behavioral or physiological, sufficient to generate the physical movements involved in behavior, therefore, cannot be stated. Teleological theories, he asserts, can explain the occurrence of a particular response, by showing that it is the one response required in the situation to lead to the goal state.[34] Its being the one required response is the teleologically sufficient

120

condition of its occurrence since—by virtue of its inherent natural tendencies to seek certain goals—the animal is empowered to select just that response required for the purpose in hand.[35] Of course, the response can be characterized as "required" for the goal state only on the assumption of a set of causal laws linking the class of responses in question to the final state-of-affairs.[36] But the selection of the one appropriate response from the class of potential responses is seen by Taylor as essentially teleological and not explicable in terms of causal generalizations.

Taylor makes some strange remarks about the teleological explanation of instinctive behavior:

> Teleological explanation gives us a notion of "tendency towards" a given condition which involves more than simply the universal and exceptionless movement of events in that direction . . . It holds that a particular result in a given system is privileged, that, in other words, this result will be brought about unless countervailing factors arise. And thus the notion arises not just of an empirically discovered direction of events, but of a bent or pressure of events towards a certain consummation, one which can only be checked by some countervailing force. This, then, is the force of the notion of "power" or "natural tendency," not the *de facto* trend of events, but rather a press of events, which lies behind the view that order exhibited in the behavior of living organisms does not come about by "accident," but is somehow part of their "essential nature."[37]

Being part of their essential nature, the normal behavior of organisms requires no further explanation once it has been exhibited as part of that essential nature; only "abnormal" behavior requires special, nonteleological explanation: "There are no antecedent [mechanistic] conditions for [animals'] normal behavior—unless one wants to count the absence of all lesions, drugs, and any other factors producing abnormality as an antecedent—but any abnormal result has some special factor to which it is traceable." It follows, he suggests, that physiological causes can be necessary "but not sufficient" conditions of "normal" behavior —although they are sufficient conditions of "abnormal" behavior: "The widespread assumption that, because certain physiological states are *necessary* conditions of behavior, behavior must be accounted for by nonteleological physiological laws involves an illegitimate inference."[38]

Taylor never commits himself, as McDougall did, to claiming that there is a special form of energy involved in purposive behavior.[39] However, remarks like these might understandably be taken to suggest that the human body cannot be a purely physical system, in which all changes in its physical state (including the bodily movements involved in goal-directed response) can in principle be explained by other physical changes occurring within or outside the body. He recommends attention to "essential natures" rather than causes, on the assumption that no mechanistic or causal explanation can possibly be given:

> The function of an explanation invoking powers or natural tendencies can be precisely *to shut off further enquiry . . .* This claim to have reached the rock bottom of explanation is not one which is usually made in scientific theory, the possibility always being left open, however unlikely it may seem, that another set of laws will be discovered which are more basic. In this way, therefore, teleological explanation represents a deviation from the modern norm and a throw-back to an earlier type of explanation.[40]

By this Taylor does not mean merely that further inquiry in purposive terms is inappropriate, but that causal explanations of instinctive tendencies are radically misguided. Crucial to the reasoning that leads Taylor to this somewhat mysterious and self-confessedly deviant characterization of natural tendencies, or instinctive powers, is his account of what has been described as the third criterion of teleological explanation. Taylor's remarks on purposive tendencies as "essential natures" which are inherently noncausal must therefore be viewed in the context of this criterion.

The third criterion of purposive explanation concerns the intensionality of behavior, that is, the necessity of distinguishing between subject and object in psychological contexts, and of concentrating on the intensional or subjective environment, rather than the geographical or "pure stimulus" environment, in explaining behavior. The world as it exists for the particular psychological subject concerned must be characterized in terms of the intensional vocabulary of consciousness. According to McDougall, for instance, concepts such as belief, hope, desire, perception, and intention are therefore needed in explaining purposive behavior. A number of recent writers hold views that are closely related to McDougall's, although they differ in detail. The Third Force psychologists stress the importance of the intensional terms just listed and, unlike the neobehaviorist Mowrer, regard them as incompatible with a mechanistic approach in general and with cybernetic contexts in particular.

Taylor, too, regards such concepts as essential to the explanation of most human behavior and incompatible with any mechanistic basis. For him, the explanation of action in general must be in terms of "natural tendencies" to pursue natural goals. The explanation of any particular action must be in terms of some particular desire or intention (whether instinctive or acquired, general or specific) of the psychological subject concerned. If the agent's intention had been different, the action would have been different. Taylor argues that no causal condition can be identified as the "intention" with which an action was performed, since intention is conceptually—not contingently—related to action. Only intentions can qualify as the sufficient conditions of actions, given our current usage of these purposive terms. Were some causal condition to be identified as the explanation (the necessary and sufficient condition) of an action, the "intention" would now be irrelevant, and the term "action" itself would therefore have changed radically in meaning. In Taylor's words, "the account of our behaviour implicit in our ordinary language is teleological in form. And this must be taken in a strong sense. It is not just that such notions as 'action' and 'desire' [and 'intention'] are teleological notions; it is also that their use carries the implication that no nonteleological account is valid."[41] The basic explanation of purposive behavior must be nonmechanistic, if "purposive" is to be used in its everyday sense.

Taylor does not therefore conclude that the reduction of psychology to a mechanistic physiology must be impossible. In this he differs from those contemporary philosophers who argue that a mechanistic explanation of human behavior is utterly inconceivable.[42] Rather, he allows that the everyday assumption that behavior is nonmechanistic may be wrong. It is an empirical question, still to be decided, whether the reduction will ever be effected. But if the reductionist's vision were ever to be realized, our everyday purposive concepts could thereafter be applied only in a radically weakened sense to men, as well as to machines.[43] In ascribing purpose, intensionality, or consciousness to living organisms, we should then be in much the same position as one who now calls someone "sanguine" or "phlegmatic," thereby describing his overt behavior without endorsing the medieval physiology of the humors. Although believing it to be "obviously untrue" that machines can not be devised to show the same observable traits as men, Taylor insists that even strongly humanoid machines can only be called "purposive" metaphorically. Since mechanistic causes are known to be sufficient conditions of machine performance, intensional predicates cannot properly be applied in cybernetic contexts.

A further antireductionist emphasis on the criterion of intensionality has recently been defended by the philosopher R. M. Chisholm.[44] Chisholm has pointed out the various logical peculiarities of intensional sentences. He has also remarked that the use of one psychological (intensional) term tends to involve the use of others; for instance, in ascribing a particular perception to someone on the basis of his observed behavior, one has to make various assumptions about his beliefs or desires. The distinction between the environment as it is "in itself" and the environment as it is "for the psychological subject" underlies the implicative peculiarities to which Chisholm draws attention. He believes that these logical features may provide a distinctive criterion of the psychological. He also claims that they are incompatible with the "unity of science" postulated by reductionists: "Some now believe that . . . the sentences we must use in describing psychological phenomena have certain logical properties that are not shared by any of the sentences we must use in describing nonpsychological phenomena, and that these properties are correctly called intentional. If this view is true, then the basic thesis of physicalism and the unity of science is false."[45] Chisholm clearly believes that no intensional terms can possibly be appropriate to mechanistic phenomena. Either there can be no science of human behavior (a view that even McDougall was reluctant to endorse), or such a science must be nonmechanistic through and through, building on totally irreducible purposive theoretical concepts, rather than on strict stimulus-response concepts or on the explanations offered by a mechanistic physiology. And *a fortiori* no intensional sentences can appropriately describe the performance of clearly mechanistic systems such as digital computers.

The question that must now be asked is whether the reductionist can justify the use of intensional vocabulary in cybernetic contexts, in opposition to these antireductionist views. Many behaviorist psychologists have agreed that a purely peripheralist stimulus-response account of behavior is inadequate. Workers as different as Holt, Tolman, and Hull have all attempted explanations of intensional phenomena in terms of the organism's ideas, or internal representations, of the world—including his desires or purposes with regard to it. But their reductionist hypotheses about the underlying physiological mechanisms were merely schematic and did not make clear how the postulated representations were actually used in the ongoing activity of the animal. Cybernetic research, however, can provide support for the reductionist view of intensionality, for the concept of an internal representation or model has found its way into the recent cybernetic literature, and the physical bases of models in machines are fully understood. Minsky's theoretical discussion of the importance of "models" in cognitive behavior is particularly relevant here.

Of the general relation between "knowledge" and "models," Minsky writes:

> If a creature can answer a question about a hypothetical experiment without actually performing it, then it has demonstrated some knowledge about the world. For, his answer to the question must be an encoded description of the behavior (inside the creature) of some sub-machine or "model" responding to an encoded description of the world situation described by the question.
>
> We use the term "model" in the following sense: To an observer B, an object A* is a model of an object A to the extent that B can use A* to answer questions that interest him about A.[46]

Thus, intelligent creatures must have a model of the outside world. More precisely, they must have something that they can use as a model of the world. They may also have a model of themselves, some parts of which will be particularly useful for controlling different aspects of behavior. "In a creature with high intelligence one can expect to find a well-developed special model concerned with the creature's own problem-solving activity." This model is useful in the planning of behavior, since it enables the creature to represent and analyze its own goals and resources as well as features of the external world. Moreover, the creature's model of itself may include a representation of the fact that it has a representation of itself. This level of representation is required if the system is to answer general questions about itself, such as "What sort of thing am I?" and "What sort of thing am I aiming to become?" Such a model of the self is required for the generation of all purposive behavior that is specifically human. Moreover, specifically human behavior requires the mediation of linguistic models or representations. Minsky makes clear that he sees his "observer B" as being either man, animal, or machine. In all these cases the "model" that underlies any knowledge ascribed to the system, B, cannot be defined independently of B's interests in or relations with the world: "The model relation is inherently ternary. Any attempt to suppress the role of the intentions of the investigator B leads to circular definitions or to ambiguities about 'essential features' and the like."[47]

The model is an information store relating to the environment, which can deal with the questions and answers referred to by Minsky as "encoded descriptions." The structure of the codes making up the model may be crucial in determining the usefulness of the model—particularly as regards its power to generate answers to questions not specifically asked before. Many distinct inputs (stimulus situations) may have one and the same representation at the appropriate level of abstraction, and this may be crucial to efficient response. An illustration of the comparative power of different representations of a given problem situation is provided by Saul Amarel's discussion of the missionary-and-cannibal problem.[48] Amarel shows how successive changes in formulation of "the same" problem each increase the ease of solution for the human problem-solver. Amarel's most powerful representation allows solutions to be generated for an indefinitely large class of new problems of the same general type: for instance, where there is a very large number of cannibals, where they are arbitrarily distributed on either bank of the river at the initial and terminal stages of the problem, where the boat's capacity may vary at different stages in the development of the solution, and where a certain level of missionary "casualties" is allowed.[49] This power of generalization to new cases is of prime importance in assessing the usefulness of the various representations of the problem. In the series of representations suggested by Amarel, elementary actions may be combined into macro-actions, redundant conditions eliminated, symmetries in the problem space exploited, and critical points identified forming a high-level subspace within which the problem may be schematically solved, the detailed solution being generated later. Of course, the choice of appropriate basic elements and attributes and of appropriate representations of action rules and problem states is crucial. This choice will involve decisions on such questions as whether it is necessary to distinguish at all times between each individual missionary, Jo, Jack, or Jim; whether one should consider each and every operation of loading and unloading the boat; whether the direction of the crossing should always be specified; whether the search space is symmetric with respect to time reversal, so that one can safely "work backward" to the solution; and whether the search space should be represented by a graphic diagram or continuous visual array, or by strings of formulae expressed in a symbolic notation. Different decisions on these questions will result in differentially appropriate representations of the problem. Amarel admits that the "appropriateness" of the more powerful representations may be due "solely to certain properties of the perceptual and reasoning processes of humans."[50] It does not follow that these representations are as "appropriate" or fruitful for all, or even any, machine processes of problem solving. Nevertheless, Amarel regards the structure of the models representing the world as crucial determinants of success in problem-solving, whether on the part of man or machine: "An understanding of the relationship between problem formulation and problem solving efficiency is a prerequisite for the design of procedures that can automatically choose the most 'appropriate' representation of a problem (they can find a 'point of view' of the problem that maximally simplifies the process of finding a solution)."[51] Amarel's example illustrates the essential connection, to which Minsky refers, between "knowledge" ("answering questions") and representational "models."

Minsky's notion of "model" provides a basis for the ascription of intensionality to machines. One reason Minsky regards the model relation as "inherently ternary" is that one cannot speak of "items of information" relating to the world without ascribing them to some information-processing system. Similarly, one cannot identify "purposes" or "ideas" or other objects of thought without ascribing them to some psychological subject. These are facts about the logic of information-processing and psychological concepts. One certainly need not infer from them that either man or machine has to have some mysterious quasisubstantial "pure ego" or homunculus to act as the subject term of the relevant epistemological relations. However, this mistaken conclusion has been drawn by some psychologists.[52] Insofar as a machine's performance is guided by its internal, perhaps idiosyncratic model of the environment, the overall performance is describable in intensional terms. That is, the logical features of intensionality mentioned earlier will characterize any statements made about the machine to describe or explain performance guided by the model.[53]

For instance, consider the criterion of referential opacity. If a human observer, or the machine itself, were asked to say what it was doing (for example, what problem it was solving), it would not follow from the truth of "It is trying to find a potato" that "It is trying to find a vegetable of the family *Solonaceae*." If the machine's cognitive structure does not include the information that potatoes are of the family *Solonaceae*, any such statement about its performance must be false. And even if it does have this information somewhere in storage, it will be thoroughly misleading to describe its performance in this way if "membership of the *Solonaceae*" is not one of the criteria actually guiding the search, or potentially capable of influencing the relevant information-processing. This would be the case, for instance, if the problem were defined as, "Find some vegetable that is not orange in color," and the machine had elected to look for a potato as satisfying this description. Analogously, a botanically ignorant chef searching for a potato cannot be described as "seeking a member of the *Solonaceae*," and even a professional botanist collecting vegetables for a stew cannot truly be so described if the potato's taxonomic status is irrelevant to his culinary purposes. In other words, incidental consequences of intentional actions, whether or not they are foreseen by the agent, are "unintentional" because they are not represented in the particular subjective model of the goal that is functioning so as to guide the act. This is why the behaviorist Holt insisted that one cannot identify "what the animal is doing" by reference to extensional properties of the physical environment, but only by reference to the animal's goal objects, considered as intensional variables. Similar restrictions apply to comparable statements about "potato-seeking" machines. In contrast, nonintensional (that is, extensional) terms can be transferred from the potato to its family, independently of the models or information in the machine. If the machine is "near to" a potato, it is necessarily also near to a member of the *Solonaceae* family, near to an object of some determinate size, weight, and biochemical composition. Thus, not how the world is, but how it is represented as being, is crucial to the truth of some statements about the machine, and such statements qualify as intensional.

The machine may have what Minsky calls "a special model concerned with its own problem-solving activity." This model would involve specifications of certain objects as means to par-ticular ends, and certain subgoals as steps to particular goals— as well as a representation of the goal or goals that the machine is actually pursuing. Certain types of performance would suggest to human observers the existence of particular models of the actual nature of the environmental situation and the strategies appropriate for seeking certain goals. For instance, the machine's performance might be explained by an observer in terms of its having an "inappropriate" model of some sort. Thus, if it pushed a pebble into a stewpot, the observer might infer that it had classified or, analogously, perceived the pebble wrongly (as a *potato*). Alternatively, he might infer that it had false information or, analogously, belief about the edibility of pebbles. Third, he might even conclude that it had no model applicable (or mis-applicable) to pebbles at all and was merely acting randomly with regard to the pebble. But a mistaken assumption on the part of the observer about the overall goal being pursued by the machine could lead him to a mistaken hypothesis about the nature of the machine's models (just as one may be misled in ascribing beliefs to a man if misinformed about his general intentions or desires). If the machine's goal in the example had, in fact, been to produce a thoroughly indigestible stew for consumption by one of its programmer's rivals, one would have been wrong to favor any of the three suggested explanations. In such a case the "testimony" of the machine itself, supposing it to be able to print out any subsection of its functioning models, would take precedence over the hypotheses formulated by observers—much as introspective reports often take precedence over third-person descriptions or explanations of behavior. In order to identify the model or representation used, merely on the basis of the system's observed behavior, one has to make some assumptions as to the system's goal. Conversely, in order to identify the system's goals from its observed behavior, one has to refer to its models representing "perceptions" and "beliefs." Even if someone asks the machine's designer what type of representation is being used, the designer cannot tell him what interpretation the model has *for the machine* without telling him how it is used, how it is linked up with sensory input and with motor subroutines. Detailed discussion of this general point must await consideration of the explanatory role of cognitive concepts, but it must be noted here that it underlies Minsky's remark that in the definition of "model" the "intentions" of the system itself cannot be suppressed, and it is a further reason why he characterized the model relation as "inherently ternary."

It may be objected here that I, as well as Minsky, have begged the question in speaking of "intensionality," "knowledge," "question-answering," and representational "models" in machines, for we can agree that if familiar intensional terms are imported into descriptions of machine performance, then they will very likely be used so as to retain their everyday logical characteristics. The basic question is whether their importation is justifiable in the first place. The antireductionist Taylor specifically remarks of some machines that "the laws descriptive of their external behavior would be teleological in form." Elsewhere he claims that "centralist" psychological theories make use of concepts analogous to those involving intensionality, concepts that denote internal states influencing the information-processing within—and therefore the overall behavior of—the organism. But he insists that these concepts are merely "analogous" to genuinely intensional concepts, since the theories in question attempt to account for the properties of these internal states by more basic neurophysiological laws.[54] Taylor does not discuss centralist theories any further, nor does he discuss their "equivalents" in machine terms. Both Chisholm and Taylor would claim that intensional descriptions and explanations are not really appropriate—let alone essential—to cybernetic contexts, since mechanistic alternatives are known to be available.

But the reductionist's case may be that mechanistic (electronic) accounts are not alternative, but rather complementary, to those in the programming or information-processing mode. With reference to Chisholm's antireductionist position, I have tried to show that the information-processing and control features of some (though not all) machines would have to be expressed by terminology having much the same logical (implicative) peculiarities as Chisholm has exhibited in everyday intensional language. The extensional logic that is typical of mechanistic (for instance, electronic) contexts is not adequate to express all aspects of the operation of complex machines such as those Minsky had in mind, where what he called "models" and "encoded descriptions" play a crucial role. The nonextensional terminology needed for describing such machine performance could be invented *de novo*. One could even eschew the basic term "information" itself, because of its suspect intensional origins and its changed meaning when used in specialist contexts.[55] But it is more convenient to carry over familiar terms with their suggestions of inbuilt logical relations rather than try to invent a new technical language appropriate to every stage in the development of "information-processing" machines. It is noteworthy that a worker in machine intelligence, appraising the relative felicity of the roughly equivalent terms "world model," "axiom model," "semantic memory system," and "belief system," has remarked that the "term 'belief system' should perhaps be rather more widely used. It has advantages compared with 'world model' in that it avoids

131

any association with physical 'scale' models, and correctly implies that a robot's 'knowledge' is bound in practice to include approximations to the truth as well as outright errors. It also encourages consideration of the 'conviction' with which a robot should hold a belief."[56] This passage specifies some of the ways in which a technical vocabulary is heuristically inferior to borrowed psychological terminology and implies that nonpsychological terms are less likely to suggest fruitful developments in cybernetic research. Given information-processing systems of the degree of complexity I have discussed, description of the control functions of the system will include reference to its input classifications or "perceptions" (which may sometimes be faulty), to its internal models or "concepts" and "beliefs" (which may be inappropriate), to the tricks and heuristics it employs in situations of difficulty (which may mislead it), and to its goal states or "purposes" (which may be unachievable). All these types of description are required to exhibit the general structure of the information-processing within the system. Analogously, the use of one intensional term necessarily involves the use of others. In arguing that everyday intensional terms may be useful in cybernetic contexts, I do not deny that the convenience of a familiar terminology carries with it the risk of overemphasizing the detailed analogies involved.

With respect to Taylor's antireductionist arguments, it is true that an animal's "inherent tendencies" to pursue certain "goals" cannot be strictly identified with causal mechanisms. Similarly, the sense in which reference to a man's intentions can "explain" his behavior is not a causal one, and intentions cannot sensibly be identified with (efficient) causes. This is because, as Taylor correctly claims, there is a conceptual connection between intention and action. Even to identify a particular behavioral unit in the first place, one has to ascribe some purpose (intention) to the agent. Since actions are conative units, identified in terms of the goals that the agent has in mind, it is necessarily true that the action would have been different if the intention had been different. Indeed, even if the *movements* were the same, the *action* would have been different: McDougall himself pointed out that the very same movements may be involved in a bird's migration or in his escape. Conversely, to identify an "intention," or an "act of will," one must specify the action toward which it (necessarily) tends. Therefore, as Taylor claims, the relation between intention and action cannot be a causal one. "Cause" and "effect" must be contingently, not conceptually, related. Reference to intentions "explains" behavior not by specifying its causes, but by placing the action concerned in the psychological context of the agent's subjective world, by locating it in his mind. Knowing a man's intentions enables one to understand his actions by relating them to his idiosyncratic beliefs and desires. For instance, someone compliments a secretary because he believes that his flattery will help him to get an interview with her boss, which he very much wants. Such explanations make behavior intelligible, and predictable, by exhibiting its intensional structure.

It is this type of "structural" understanding that is provided by explanations of machine performance in information-processing or programming terms. Moreover, the "goal" or "intention" of the machine is not irrelevant, for if it had been different, the performance would have differed or would have had to be described differently. Had the machine in the previous example been attempting a different task, it might not have been manipulating a pebble at this point in time. And even if it had been manipulating a pebble, it would not have been correct to say that it was progressing toward the concoction of an indigestible stew. At most, its activities would as a matter of accidental fact have led to such a stew being produced (although to say it was "accidental" is not to say it was independent of causal laws). To describe the machine in this event as "making an indigestible stew" would be false in a way that it would not have been in the original example. It would mislead one in explaining and predicting the machine's performance. Nor is the machine's "intention" or "goal" conceptually identifiable with any causal condition or physical state of affairs in the machine. Similarly, a single programming instruction is not identifiable with any such state of affairs, although it is only by virtue of specific causal mechanisms that the instruction can ever actually be carried out.

Once a phenomenon has been characterized as "goal-directed" (with or without cautionary quotes), one cannot go on in the same breath to explain units of behavior or performance in causal terms but must continue to use the language of intention. Similarly, a description of performance using programming vocabu-

133

lary will exclude an explanation in electronic terms. These limitations on causal explanation are consequences of the logic (the general conceptual interrelations) of the languages concerned. As Minsky might put it, they follow from the logical structure of the linguistic "models" we use in describing organisms and machines, rather than from the "essential natures" of these systems themselves. Taylor's hypothesis that purposive organisms differ in their essential nature from mechanistic systems blurs this distinction, for it is expressed in the *material* rather than the *formal* mode. Even in the case of "abnormal" behavior or performance, initial description in structural terms demands explanation in structural terms also. Thus, abnormal psychology is largely (though not wholly) the study of purposive or intensional malfunction, as humanist psychiatrists insist. The best "cure" of behavioral abnormality involves purposive and cognitive restructuring of the subjective world-view rather than manipulation of causes. This is not to deny that particular behavioral expressions of abnormal purposes may be eliminated by causal means; for instance, by the conditioning of "behavior therapy" or by drugs. Similarly, if machine performance may be described as continually "running into an infinite loop,"[57] this is because an instruction in the program has been wrongly expressed. The remedy is to debug the program, not to tinker directly with the circuitry. To borrow a phrase from Laing, one's "initial intentional act" of choosing a linguistic level in describing behavior or performance predetermines the type of explanation that one will find appropriate.

Of course, the initial description cannot determine the truth. If, after investigation of the facts, a different type of explanation is found to be appropriate, then the original description must be withdrawn. For instance, one may initially choose the causal level of description and assume that a man's virtually ceaseless "hand movements" are due to some cerebellar malfunction. But a psychological investigation may show that he is really "washing his hands," in symbolic expression of a repressed guilt. (The fact that some form of behavior therapy may successfully eliminate the manual behavior symptom does not show that the purposive description and explanation were inappropriate.) If one does not initially choose the causal level of description, then causal expla-

134

nations will turn out to be the most appropriate only if one finds "a spanner in the works," a mechanical abnormality upsetting the normal functioning of the system (referred to by Taylor as a "countervailing force" checking the normal "press of events"). In such a case the causal condition concerned would be independent of the intentions of the system (or of its designer), and the system's program, goals, or intentions could not explain the particular output concerned. For instance, a schoolboy who does not heed instructions to sit still can no longer be described as "obstinate" or "uncooperative" on this account if he turns out to be deaf. One would have to withdraw the initial purposive description as mistaken, not merely because causally sufficient conditions of the physical movements involved had been found, but because no intention (or instruction) could be found that was also describable as "determining" those changes. In these cases the causal linguistic mode is appropriate while the purposive is not. It is this sort of case to which Taylor refers when he writes: "The normal operation of the system, i.e., the occurrence of events which result in the normal condition is accounted for by teleological laws, while *any* abnormal functioning *must* bring in a set of laws linking interfering factors and non-normal conditions which are not teleological. And this is the basis for the distinction between 'normal' and 'abnormal' itself."[58] But Taylor's "abnormal" behavior would seem to cover only breakdowns of some sort, not the neurotic's expiatory hand-washing or the purposive malfunctions typical of psychopathology.

Taylor's claim that causes are sufficient conditions only of abnormal behavior is connected with his claim that there are no causal conditions sufficient to generate the specific responses selected in purposive behavior.[59] But causal conditions may be sufficient to generate all physical movements, while causal explanations are totally unfitted to express the intensionality of behavior and the purposes determining its general structure. Being able to describe a man as a guilt-ridden murderer provides explanations and predictions of much of his behavior, but it is not a causal description. This is not a mere statement of his past causal involvement in another man's death. Moreover, the distinction between a man who is a murderer and one who merely believes that he is cannot be stated in causal, extensional terms.

This is true whether the man has a "psychopathological" basis for his belief or whether he is just mistaken about the causal effects of his participation in a general shooting-match. Nor can the distinction between two highly complex machines guided by different (and differentially appropriate) models of pebbles and potatoes be stated in causal terms. But of course, their behavior toward pebbles, potatoes, and everything else is generated by a causal mechanism. Both causal and purposive languages or "models" are therefore needed to describe the behavior of all these intensional systems. In this sense, Maslow's insistence that we must keep sight of "both kinds of world" is well-founded.

This duality of available languages also underlies Taylor's strange analysis of purpose and inherent tendency as involving some noncausal "press of events" in the "essential nature" of behaving organisms. For if one is asked to state the general nature of anything, one can only answer by giving a general description of one's model (or models) of the thing. It is impossible to have any psychological commerce with the thing except by means of some model or representation of it; in other words, psychological commerce, or experience, is by common consent intensional. Thus, one cannot convey one's experience or knowledge of a thing independently of one's model of it. One might, of course, speechlessly point to the thing, but this would indicate rather than characterize it. Consequently, a man's general descriptions of his models may be cast in the material or the formal mode, according to his interest in reality or representations respectively. And the shift from formal to material mode is very naturally made.[60] Our descriptions of our models or conceptual schemes may very readily assume an "ontological" air, particularly when they are given in response to a question phrased in the material mode, such as: "Never mind about the language we happen to use about organisms; tell me about the organisms themselves. Are purposive creatures mechanistic in their essential natures, or are they not?" One of the commonest of such questions is: "What sort of thing is a man?" And the commonest answer is that somehow or other he is (or has) a mind and a body. This answer is the natural expression of the fact that we regularly employ at least two different languages in characterizing and conceiving of man: intensional teleological language and extensional mechanistic language. As Minsky has put it:

> [*A man's*] *statement (his belief) that he has a mind as well as a body is the conventional way to express the roughly bipartite appearance of his model of himself.*
>
> Because the separation of the two parts of [his model of himself] is so indistinct and their interconnections are so complicated and difficult to describe, the man's further attempts to elaborate on the nature of this "mind-body" distinction are bound to be confused and unsatisfactory.[61]

With reference to the three logical criteria of teleology, then, the reductionist may argue that some explanations of machine performance are significantly analogous to explanations which are truly teleological in form. The criterion of intensionality can be rather more closely approximated in cybernetic contexts than can the nonatomistic and instinctive criteria, although not all cybernetic machines show any analog of intensionality. Vocabulary drawn from everyday psychological language may be helpful in describing, explaining, and predicting machine performance. Even though the purposive terms involved are used in an analogical sense, nothing would be gained—and much would be lost—by the total prohibition of "teleological" formulations in cybernetic contexts.

Psychological Predicates and Machines

The reductionist allows that teleological formulations are sometimes appropriate in explaining machine performance. Clearly, he cannot regard the empirical reducibility of cybernetic explanations as sufficient in itself to show that such formulations are necessarily and always grossly misleading. The reductionist, that is, must oppose McDougall, Chisholm, and Taylor, for he asserts what they all deny: that purposive terminology is properly applicable to some mechanistic systems, namely, men and animals. He may claim merely that teleological language is appropriate to machines provided that it is understood in an analogical sense. However, he may also be prepared to allow that purposive language is in principle fully applicable to a conceivable machine artifact. Even if the truth of reductionism is assumed, this strong claim may nevertheless be open to objection.

In contemporary philosophical literature there are a number of arguments that would deny psychological predicates to any machine whatever. The denial in these cases is not based on the fact that the hypothesized machine is a mechanistic system. It rests, rather, on features by virtue of which even the reductionist would agree that the machine differs from men. These include "genealogical" features characterizing even hypothetical machines so like men that real men might be fooled by them. Since all these arguments assume a distinction between men and "machines," on which the argument rests, it follows that they can only show the impropriety of ascribing psychological or personal predicates directly to machines. Should any of them be valid, it would not follow that human psychology is irreducible to human physiology.

These arguments are both varied and controversial, and proponents of one do not necessarily defend any others. For example, it has been argued by Paul Ziff, and contested by Keith Gunderson, that psychological language is incompatible with the concept of programmed behavior.[62] It has been said that whether or not one applies a particular psychological predicate will depend largely on the possible basic capacities implied by the nature of the hardware.[63] There might be justification in using *personal* psychological predicates of organic artifacts from the biologist's laboratory, but not of metallic machines, since the categories of *feeling* are only applicable to "soft" organisms moving about in a world of "hard" objects. This view may be held together with the view that some nonpersonal psychological predicates could be applicable to metallic machines—for instance, thinking and conscious.[64] It is sometimes suggested that no psychological term can be correctly ascribed to a machine, since current linguistic usage forbids calling one and the same thing "a machine" and "conscious," "thinking," "purposive," and so on. Alternatively, it is said that if a sufficiently humanoid artifact were ever produced, then current usage would change, so that psychological terms would be applied on the basis of observable behavior traits *irrespective* of whether a thing is called "a machine."[65] This would

138

doubtless involve a shift in the current meaning of "machine," in that certain moral-psychological attitudes now considered appropriate to "machines" would no longer be considered always appropriate. Thus, indifference to gross damage to some machines might be considered in the same light as indifference to animals' injuries is now.[66] Only a detailed philosophical analysis of the concepts involved could possibly settle such hypothetical questions; and even this could not settle them if, as is highly likely, current usage of psychological concepts does not unambiguously determine their use in such hypothetical cases. Any recommendations as to future usage would obviously reflect the initial reductionist or antireductionist philosophical biases underlying the whole inquiry.

Even were it possible to settle these issues with finality now, a detailed discussion of them would be unnecessary here. The "physiological" reductionist need not insist that some conceivable artifact must merit the ascription of all familiar psychological predicates without any qualification or shift in meaning. An apparent exception is the biologist's artifact, functioning according to normal physiological principles. But since it is not unknown for matters of life and death to hang on niceties of genealogy in human beings, even here the reductionist could allow that, in practice, one might choose to regard facts of "genealogy" or history as crucial to the literal application of some psychological terms.[67] Similarly, the physiological psychologist need not commit himself as to whether a cat's pain is "the same as" an ape's or a man's, even though he uses cats and apes as experimental animals in his investigations of pain behavior. The reductionist can afford to admit that machine analogies of behavior are only analogies, while drawing support from such analogies insofar as they are close ones. Certainly, the extent to which they are close analogies can only be decided insofar as the meanings of the psychological terms involved are clear—whether these are drawn from everyday speech or from the technical vocabulary of a professional psychologist. And the philosophical arguments in question all involve conceptual analyses of particular psychological predicates. These could possibly be of use to the reductionist in suggesting how a specific machine "analogy" might be strengthened, as K. M. Sayre's detailed analysis of the everyday concept of *recognition*, in consort with a critique of current "pattern recognition" programs, helps draw attention to conceptual limitations of these programs.[68] But this is not to say that these arguments can undermine the reductionist's general position. He may reasonably be asked to examine critically the claims made by those impressed by current cybernetic "analogies." But he does not have to decide whether or not some hypothetical and purely fanciful artifact could be termed "purposive" or "psychological" in the literal, nonanalogical sense. For the truth of physiological reductionism in the case of naturally produced living organisms does not rest on giving positive answers to such questions.

Still less does the reductionist's case require that any psychological term can be applied in its full sense to present-day machines. When speaking of machines such as those currently available, one cannot use familiar psychological expressions, such as purpose, behavior, perception, knowledge, belief, instinct, emotion, or voluntary action, without notional quotation marks. All these psychological terms are conceptually connected, and for them to be used in their full sense requires at least a degree of purposive (cognitive and motor) complexity. This complexity is not approached by any extant machine. Consequently, no psychological term can be applied directly to current machines, except in a weak analogical sense.

For instance, even a relatively successful "pattern-recognition" program such as that of Leonard Uhr and Charles Vossler cannot truly be said either to *recognize* patterns or to *perceive* the objects it classifies.[69] This program can generate its own criteria, and evaluate and adjust them in response to particular features of the patterns it encounters, so that those operators are retained which are found to be most useful in cases of "difficulty," where two patterns are easily confused. When tested for the ability to classify nonsensical doodles, the program's performance is significantly better than that of any human subject so far tested, although this is not so in the case of familiar letters or designs, where the human's learning experience is already so much the greater. Nonetheless, this is not true recognition, for—as Sayre has shown at length—recognition in fact cannot be correctly conceived of as a form of classification. This is not to say that the ability to classify is uninvolved in recognition. But a program that can merely classify, however efficiently, cannot be said to "recognize" in the full sense in which man can be said to do so. One reason for this (others are suggested by Sayre[70]) is that the concept of recognition is closely connected with that of perception. One cannot speak of the machine's performance as true perception, partly because it is essential to the concept of perceptual discrimination as normally understood that the discriminations be used in the guidance of motor (instrumental) activity. Assuming this point to be correct, it must be noted that the Uhr and Vossler program does not provide for motor activity of any sort.

A recent program intended as an analog of instinctive behavior does provide for movement—but not for active manipulation of objects in the environment. Thus J. E. Doran describes an automaton that combines "insight" and trial-and-error to find its way home, its path tending to improve on successive trials but never becoming stereotyped.[71] Doran's aim is to investigate the relation of the organism to its environment, and to stress the importance of the classification of possible environments from the standpoint of the organism. The "subjective" environment of the automaton (rather than the geographical environment) is crucial in determining its performance and allows for the analog of insight in behavior. Variable parameters determining the relative costs of exploration and exploitation (that is, searching for a better plan or relying on the best plan reached so far) affect the overall pattern of behavior. These parameters include size of memory store, rigor of evaluation standards, depth of lookahead in planning, and the "thinking" time used in planning. Changes in these parameters affect the time-cost of decision-making, with resultant changes in performance. Doran shows that considerations such as these must enter into any machine analog of instinctive behavior, and he sketches an automaton with two basic goals ("warmth" and "food"), which may conflict with one another in certain environments. Clearly, this program is open to considerable development, but in its present form this machine is much too simple to merit the unqualified ascription of psychological vocabulary.[72] The term "percipient" would be more applicable to Doran's machine if it showed some analog of instrumental activity, molding the environment to suit its own purposes. This would require a continuous series of discriminations of and motor adjustments to features of, or objects within, the environment. Such discriminations and adjustments are involved in truly "perceptual" behavior. Moreover, the behavioral repertoire of Doran's machine is small. So· also is the behavioral repertoire of radar-based guided missile systems, which do make continuous adjustments to changing input information from the environment. Even GPS, a program designed to give a comparatively wide range of performance, is at present restricted to a small number of logical operations, by means of which it tackles a limited variety of problems. Consequently, the possible "variation of means" in the performance of all these machines is very restricted. This behavioral criterion of purpose was regarded by McDougall and R. B. Perry, for instance, as the most important of all, and the more limited the variation of means, the more reluctant one should be to regard a system as truly purposive.

Reductionism and Computer Simulation

The reductionist has so far been represented as claiming that certain very general logical features of psychological language find their equivalents in the description and explanation of machine behavior—in particular, the intensionality of psychological predicates; the interconnections of concepts like perception, belief, intention, and goal; and the logical relations between causal and psychological explanations of behavior. Insofar as such features are paralleled in cybernetic contexts, the reductionist can claim support for his case. And he need not be prepared to ascribe psychological predicates in their full everyday sense to any actual or hypothetical machine. However, there is another way in which the reductionist may look to cybernetics for support. He may argue that machine analogies could provide a key to understanding the way in which the corresponding behavior is actually produced—and thus a key to carrying out the empirical reduction. He then directs attention to computer simulations of behavior.

Computer simulations are not attempts at robot-building or mimicry of behavior; they are not the sort of exercise commonly envisaged in science fiction. Instead of being concerned with the problem of ascribing psychological predicates directly to machines, they are concerned with the theoretical problem of explaining certain aspects of behavior.[73] The basic import of the term "simulation" is that some attempt is made to represent certain aspects of a system that is not itself a computer. But simulation "of a guided missile" or "of behavior" is simulation of theories about these phenomena, rather than being an attempt to mimic the missile or the behavior itself. Thus, a computer simulation of problem-solving aims at the representation of a psychological theory of problem-solving. The machine intelligence approach, by contrast, aims to solve the given problem, irrespective of the way in which it may be solved by any living system. The simulator seeks to represent a psychological theory by a precisely definable program in such a way that its consequences can be unambiguously determined, given specific values of the relevant parameters. These consequences can then be checked against their equivalents in real behavior.

Strictly speaking, the embodiment of the program in an actual machine is unnecessary, for it is the logical consequences of the program that are crucial. But the consequences of a complex program or theory can usually only be ascertained, in practice, by actually running the program on a computer; man's unaided powers of computation are not sufficient to show all the detailed implications of the theories he himself has produced. So some aspects of machine performance must be counted as "equivalent" to the behavioral features being simulated. For this it is necessary only that certain features of the simulation be stipulated as logically equivalent to behavioral features, in terms of correspondence rules initially set up by the programmer: what is required is modeling rather than mimicry. If a theory concerns movement (as McDougall's does, for instance, via his theoretical concept of an instinctive action tendency), then movement must be modeled somehow in the simulation. Although it may sometimes be convenient to build a motor automaton, as Doran found in his attempt to program an analog of instinctive behavior, it is usually unnecessary—for these theoretical purposes—for the simulation actually to move. It could, for example, "map" the modeled movement on an inbuilt graph or screen, or it could merely express changes in spatiotemporal co-ordinates in some mathematical notation. Which of these "equivalents" of actual movement the program provides will be determined largely by the usefulness to the human user of the alternative forms of representation. If one were trying to mimic behavior closely so that psychological predicates could properly be applied to the machine itself, one would have to provide for actual movement, for only thus could the ascription of any psychological predicates involving, or essentially connected with, the concept of movement be justified —including predicates as different as "hurrying toward" and "perceiving." But the simulator does not attempt such mimicry. Computer simulations, then, are intended as explanatory models of behavior rather than as replicas of it.

The explanatory power of a machine model of behavior depends on the extent to which the details of the underlying information-processing are functionally equivalent to the psychological processes actually underlying behavior.[74] This is why the pure machine intelligence approach does not necessarily contribute to the psychological explanation of cognitive behavior, for it merely aims to achieve the same results as human intelligence without requiring that they be reached in an essentially similar way.[75] Ideally, for every psychological process involved in the production of behavior there should be some corresponding data process involved in the production of machine performance, and these isomorphic processes should each be functionally related to the system's overall behavior in the same way.[76] In fact, the computer data-processing will, at best, be functionally equivalent to the psychological processes hypothesized by a psychological theory and characterized by means of the relevant theoretical terminology. Because Newell, Simon, and Shaw's cognitive theory postulated heuristic processes as predominant in human thinking, they therefore programmed GPS heuristically rather than algorithmically. The attempted level of detailed equivalence between machine performance and behavior varies with the level of one's theoretical interests and achievements. Thus, if a cognitive theory represents certain heuristics or other strategies as paramount, then the programmed equivalents of these strategies must be correspondingly weighted. Given that detailed machine performance is functionally equivalent to behavior as represented by a psychological theory, the explanatory power of the program will equal that of the theory itself.

144

Unsatisfactory theories make for unsatisfactory programs. For instance, if human thinking is not predominantly heuristic, then no heuristic program can be an adequate simulation of it. A program may therefore be "satisfactory" in representing a particular psychological theory, but "unsatisfactory" in representing behavior itself.

Simulations can help the reductionist in that if a particular theory is simulated satisfactorily (the functional relationships in machine performance paralleling those posited by the theory), then the theory is applicable at least to *some* mechanistic systems. Therefore, to the extent that the theory in question is explanatory of behavior, one may say that it is *possible* for the functional relationships observed in and underlying behavior to be generated by a mechanistic system. Of course, it does not follow that they *must* be so generated. Computer simulations of psychological theories could not prove the reductionist's case, for they do not themselves provide the detailed empirical reduction of psychological theories to neurophysiological terms that would be required for such a proof. But they may provide hints as to the general nature of the neurophysiological mechanisms involved, in the sense that they suggest what functions the brain is executing. They may or may not be helpful in hypothesizing precisely how the brain is doing so. Computer simulations of cell assemblies or of learning in neural networks could be regarded as models of physiological or of very low-scale psychological theories.[77] Simulations on this theoretical level are clearly more likely to suggest specific reductive hypotheses than are those directed to a more markedly "molar" level, such as simulations of personality theories. Nevertheless, the satisfactory simulation of well-confirmed molar psychological theories could support the reductionist's position by showing the functional relationships concerned to be *possible* in mechanistic systems.

The simulation of psychological processes, such as problem-solving, pattern-recognition, game-playing, and translation, has in fact turned out to be more difficult than many expected. The disappointment following the initial optimism is sometimes explained by the claim that purely digital (as opposed to analog) computers are basically incapable of providing functional equivalents of all forms of human information-processing.[78] Digital

145

computers are finite-state machines. As A. M. Turing's alternative term—"discrete state" machines—suggests, such information-processing systems operate by carrying out, in sequence or in parallel, a number of discrete steps.[79] Analog computers, by contrast, are not finite-state machines: the parameters representing the information being processed are continuously variable. For instance, numbers may be represented by voltage levels rather than by arrays of closed or open switches; and mathematical operations such as addition or multiplication are carried out by special electronic circuits, which can be combined in networks to perform more complex operations. Consequently, a high degree of electronic knowledge is required in order to write an analog program, but the digital programmer need know nothing of electronics. Analog computers are, however, mechanistic systems functioning according to the laws of physics and chemistry. It might be said that all mechanistic systems are basically finite-state, since quantum mechanics describes physical change in terms of transitions between discrete states; but the analog-digital distinction is not normally thought of at this theoretical level. All information-processing that proceeds by discrete steps can, in principle, be simulated on a digital computer, for to each step there may correspond a functionally equivalent step in the simulation. So if all information-processing in human brains is discrete in type, then all human thought processes could be simulated by digital techniques. Sometimes it is argued that not all human thought is of this type, and psychologists are advised to concentrate machine research on partially analog rather than purely digital devices.

This advice is given, for example, by H. L. Dreyfus, who rests his case on the continuous-discontinuous distinction between analog and digital systems mentioned above.[80] Some thought processes, he claims, must be based on analog (cerebral) mechanisms, and therefore no functionally equivalent data-processing could be digital in form. Recent neurophysiological evidence shows that—while *axonal* conduction is all-or-none in fashion—*synaptic* events are continuously variable.[81] The brain, then, is not a wholly digital or finite-state system. Although Dreyfus refers to this neurophysiological evidence, he also claims that human psychological processes typically involve essentially inde-

146

terminate information-processing, and that this makes digital simulation impossible. He distinguishes four areas of intelligent behavior, in which the problems are: associationist (such as simple memory games, word-by-word translation, and "trial-and-error" maze problems); non-formal (such as riddles and natural language translation); simple formal (such as tic-tac-toe, checkers, and theorem-proving in decidable mathematics); and complex formal (such as chess, complex combinatory problems, and theorem-proving in undecidable mathematics). He claims that only the associationist and simple formal problems can be adequately dealt with by solely digital techniques.

The complex formal problems may be solved digitally, provided that the search space has been intuitively structured appropriately beforehand. Dreyfus criticizes a number of the more successful programs (including GPS), in that the problems they deal with are often trivial and always formalizable to a high degree. Problems requiring any degree of insight or intelligent judgment would, he claims, involve analog techniques of information-processing. At present, the "insight" or "judgment" seemingly apparent in some programs is in fact specifically provided by the programmer—for instance, in the initial choice and ordering of heuristics, or in the initial structuring of the search space. Indeed, in discussing the possibilities of mechanization relating to representations of the missionary-and-cannibal problem, Amarel has explicitly stated that the critical structuring of the search space is likely to be more difficult to automate than is the recognition of useful properties of the search space, given an "appropriate" representation.[82] The choice of basic elements and operations in terms of which to represent a problem is less straightforward than is the recognition of formal features such as symmetries and redundancies within a given representation. Dreyfus would probably add that Amarel restricts himself to "complex formal" cases, where the end state is specificable in advance, where there is a finite or strictly defined set of feasible actions, and where the set of constraints restricting the applicability of actions are clearly specifiable in advance.

Appealing to behavioral, largely introspective evidence (including the human protocols quoted by the GPS programmers), Dreyfus distinguishes three types of information-processing that he claims are essential to most human thinking. These are reliance on the fringe of consciousness, discrimination between the essential and the accidental, and tolerance of ambiguity. All these he sees as dealing with information that is somehow ambiguous or indeterminate. He infers that the requisite information-processing could not consist of discrete, determinate operations, nonambiguously defined. Since analog processes are not discrete but continuous, Dreyfus concludes that satisfactory simulations of psychological phenomena would have to be largely analog in type.

Insofar as he mentions limitations of specific published programs, Dreyfus' critique has some validity. Critics basically more sympathetic to digital computer research than Dreyfus have pointed out similar limitations. For instance, Newell himself has remarked on the excessive "single-mindedness" and non-distractibility of GPS; W. R. Reitman suggests that the organizational structure of programs such as Argus would be more suitable to the representation of human thought; and Ulric Neisser has expressed strong doubts as to the simulability of thought by means of current programming techniques.[83] Some of these criticisms are relevant to the problem of simulating personality theories. Similarly, Amarel is less optimistic about the mechanization of "insight" than about the automation of formalizable processes. But it is not clear that Dreyfus' depreciation of digital devices in general is well founded, for even if his claim is granted that the information dealt with is typically indeterminate or ambiguous, it may be argued that Dreyfus confuses the information code with the information coded. The former may be discrete, while the latter is in some sense indeterminate. Indeed, Sayre has objected that any symbolic code must be discrete: "It is an essential feature of a usable code that it can be quantized into discriminable and determinate parts at some level of operation."[84] Dreyfus himself uses the twenty-six letters of the alphabet to represent his "ambiguous and indeterminate" information. Hand-written script—unlike typescript—is physically continuous (as the neural parameters involved in the natural "coding" of the environment may be), but it is interpretable by human beings only because they can regard it as if it were physically discontinuous. It is not necessary to claim that all

148

cognitive representations must be symbolic codes, and thus discrete in nature, in order to fault Dreyfus' assumption that indeterminate information can be represented only in a non-discrete form. Indeed, some of Amarel's representations of the "complex formal" missionary-and-cannibal problem are graphic diagrams, and so continuous rather than discrete in character. But since indeterminate information is sometimes represented in a discrete fashion, Dreyfus' critical emphasis on the physical discontinuity of digital machines is misplaced.

However, if Dreyfus' analysis of the analog-digital distinction is misplaced in emphasis, it may be that this distinction is important to the simulator for other reasons. Thus, R. L. Gregory argues that the engineering distinction between continuous and discontinuous systems is psychologically trivial. But he, too, holds that analog-processing would have to be involved in the representation of some behavior. The important distinction between analog and digital systems, for Gregory, is not *how* they represent but *what* they can represent. As he puts it: "The distinction is between representing events *directly* by the states of the system, and representing *symbolic accounts* of real (or hypothetical) events. Real events always occur in a continuum, but symbolic systems are always discontinuous."[85] Both analog and digital systems can represent events by manipulating symbolic systems appropriate to the information being modeled. Because of the discrete nature of symbolic codes, analog machines that manipulate symbols function stepwise, as if they were digital machines (like a slide rule fitted with a click-stepper). But only analog systems can represent the outside world directly by parallel changes in their own internal states. Symbol manipulation is typically slower than "direct" information-processing, since many symbolic steps may be involved. Digital devices, which have to represent information by means of some symbolism, are therefore unsuitable for processing information which is itself changing continuously in time. If one has to deal with the information that there is a tiger nearby preparing to pounce, so as to know which way to jump, one needs to process the changing perceptual information at least as fast as the tiger is changing it. An analog device can do this, for its own internal states may change as fast as the external situation does—at least up to a point, at which one may be eaten by the tiger. Evidently the human brain is a largely analog system, which can both represent changing information directly (and thus function in "real time"), and process information symbolically. And any "perceiving" machine capable of avoiding the attentions of a tiger would have to be at least partially analog in type. But this is not because the perceptual information dealt with is "indeterminate" or "nondiscrete."

Since analog computers are clearly mechanistic systems, arguments that are *anti*-digital but *pro*-analog—such as those offered by Dreyfus and Gregory—cannot properly be directed against reductionism in general. Gregory, indeed, has no such intention in mind in recommending analog systems; his philosophical assumptions are broadly reductionist in type. Even Dreyfus, whose philosophical sympathies are phenomenological, explicitly refuses to question the fundamental assumption that the brain is a mechanistic system, that it is a part of the physical world functioning according to the laws of physics and chemistry. Further, he admits that *in principle* all physical processes can be described in a mathematical formalism (the appropriate physicochemical differential equations), which can in turn be manipulated on a digital computer.[86] In this sense, then, he allows that the brain and all analog computers are in principle simulable on a digital device. But he holds that in practice, even if the relevant neurophysiological equations were known, the extent of time and memory storage required to solve them digitally would be prohibitive. This may be so. And if it is, then digital computer research is limited in its psychological potential, though whether it can therefore be justly described as limited to "multitudinous back alleys of no moment in preference to the broad highways where all men pass" is debatable. But the antireductionist cannot rest his case merely on the probable claim that the brain, like analog computers, is not a finite-state system, for such a position would seem to imply that one cannot give a reductionist (in McDougall's terms, a mechanistic) explanation of the physicochemical processes involved in any analog device. This implication is false. In sum, "antidigital" arguments do not show that human behavior cannot be accounted for in terms of a mechanistic neurophysiology, for they are insufficient to show that the brain is not a physical system.

The Reduction of Psychology to Physiology

A few antireductionist writers have claimed that the brain is not a physical system obeying the laws of physics and chemistry alone, and they have offered hypotheses as to the nature of the nonphysical factors involved. McDougall himself believed some brain processes to be significantly influenced by hormic energy obeying psychic laws. If this were the case, the empirical reduction of psychology to a mechanistic physiology would be impossible. Nor would there be any reason to expect that functional equivalents of psychological processes must be possible, in principle, in a simulation powered by purely physical processes —although they might be possible if nonphysical energy were not necessary to the functional properties exhibited by brains. The hypothesis of specifically mental influences at work within the brain is not entirely dead. It is not usually expressed in terms of "energy," concern with which was a typical nineteenth-century preoccupation, but an occasional defense of it can still be found in contemporary literature.

Neo-Freudian references to "psychological (drive) energy" may be discounted, since these do not imply the postulation of any basically nonmechanistic, nonphysical energy.[87] We may also discount the neurologist R. W. Sperry's recent suggestion that: "the conscious phenomena of subjective experience do interact on the brain process exerting an active causal influence ... [We postulate] the existence of potent mental forces that transcend the material elements in cerebral function." For Sperry's "potent mental forces" are explicitly said to be an integral part of the brain process itself. They are conceived as holistic flow patterns of cerebral excitation, and so as direct (molar, emergent) properties of the biophysical substance of the brain that do not "intervene, interfere, or in any way disrupt the physiology of brain cell activation."[88] But the neurophysiologist J. C. Eccles and the psychologist Cyril Burt have lent their support to the hypothesis of psychic influences well after

151

the year of McDougall's death, and their hypothesis does suggest that such influences intervene in and disrupt the physiology of the brain.[89]

Briefly, they postulate a mental "field" of influence interacting with cerebral neurons. The brain is said to function as a "detector," which has a sensitivity of a different kind and order from that of any physical instrument, picking up mental influences that are too slight to be picked up by such instruments and which are therefore ignored by physics. Certain "critically poised" neurons act as detectors and amplifiers of this mental force or "will". The admittedly obscure Cartesian notion that interaction takes place between an extended brain and a nonspatial mind is rejected. Thus, Eccles notes: "This hypothesis assumes that the 'will' or 'mind influence' has itself a spatio-temporal patterned character in order to allow it this operative effectiveness."[90]

Quite apart from the difficulty of conceiving how a specifically mental influence could thus be spatiotemporal in form, this "hypothesis" has two grave drawbacks as far as the working scientist is concerned. First, it does not lead to any specific research program; and second, it does not appear to be a genuinely testable hypothesis. Indeed, the first drawback is a consequence of the second. The hypothesis is not falsifiable, since no amount of empirical evidence could strictly prove the absence of such ill-defined influences. Nor is it verifiable, for if minute influences were to be picked up by future physical instruments, they could *ipso facto* be regarded as physical—rather than mental—forces. In such a case, the most the experiments would prove is that cerebral neurons are associated with physical influences not associated with other cells. No such experimental results have as yet been obtained. If novel types of influence were detected, these might naturally be termed "mental," but no experiments could force one to settle for a strongly dualist interpretation of this word. As a consequence of these features, the "psychic energy" hypothesis has few adherents today and is not an important element of the current opposition to reductionism.

Even if the brain is assumed to be a physical system, however, it may be that the reduction of psychology to physiology will

152

never be effected in practice. If the reductionist hopes for bridging statements that specify one:one correlations between particular brain-states and teleologically identified behavioral units, he is almost certainly doomed to disappointment. It is not even *in principle* likely that a condition expressible in purely physiological terms is the necessary and sufficient cause of, for example, the expression of the intention to commit suicide, for an Englishman, a Japanese, and a Spaniard may all express this intention, but the linguistic models or representations involved will differ greatly from case to case—and so, presumably, will their cerebral bases. Moreover, the social norms and religious concepts (in McDougall's terms, the sentiments) bound up with the notion of "killing oneself" may also vary considerably, and will have accordingly varied neurophysiological representations. Further ground for skepticism here is provided by the experimental evidence for the equipotentiality of brain tissue. Efforts to establish the cerebral localization of behavior have met with remarkably little success.[91]

Even if the reductionist merely hopes for bridging statements specifying cerebral conditions *sufficient* for this behavior, on the part of an individual member of a particular linguistic and social community, he will probably be disillusioned. This is because, as regards the physical functioning of the brain, investigators are in much the same position as one who encounters an extremely complex computer of unknown design. He has first to discover which programming language the highest-level instructions are written in. He cannot assume that it bears any more similarity to the programming languages he already knows than does the as yet undiscovered supreme psychological theory bear to the psychological theories he accepts in everyday life. When he has discovered the general language involved, he then has to classify specific outputs according to the particular high-level instruction governing performance at any given time. If he manages, by dint of careful experimentation and observation, to do this, he next has to find some way of translating this high-level instruction into electronic terms. Inside the machine, of course, this translation is effected by the compiler or interpreter program (or programs, as there may be a hierarchy of programming languages, each requiring a special "compiler" for

153

translation to the adjacent level). But this engineer does not have the compiler. Nor does he have the machine code, so he has little, if any, notion as to the general principles of the compiler. If he has to rely on experimentation (even ethically uninhibited experimentation) to decode the high-level instruction directing a particular class of outputs, it is clear that he is likely to be disappointed because of the complexity of the task. Should the compiler be so obliging as to print out the instruction in machine code for him, on some immensely long sheet of paper, his job is still not finished, for he has to provide an electronic equivalent for each instruction specified at the level of the machine code, and he has yet to discover how to do this. In short, he is faced with a daunting task, and it would be unrealistic to be surprised at his failure.

Perhaps the most that the investigator can hope for with any degree of confidence is that he will discover the nature of the highest-level program, some general principles of the compiler, and the principles of the computer's mechanism at the physico-chemical (nonprogrammed) level. He could then "reduce" descriptions of the machine's performance in the high-level programming language to descriptions expressed in physico-chemical terms. But these "reductions" would be schematic rather than detailed, and would be useless for precise prediction. Unless and until he has effected a really detailed reduction, he will be unable to specify the sufficient causal conditions of most classes of output. And as a matter of psychological fact, if he did manage—perhaps with the aid of a super-obliging compiler—to specify such conditions, the specification would be useless to him in this form. This "model" of the computer would be unintelligible to him as a whole. The idea that he might be able to rely on it in practice for prediction or explanation of particular outputs that happen to interest him is psychologically absurd.

Analogously, the human neurophysiologist may never be able to offer more than the general principles of brain function. These may perhaps include some differential features of the cerebral mechanisms involved in broadly different types of purposive activity, such as the various instincts and other features marked by key concepts in a personality theory. But the physiologist

154

may never be able to specify sufficient causal conditions of all those classes of human behavior that are interesting enough to cry out for explanation and prediction. One could not then explain a man's threat to commit suicide, in any language, nor predict his wife's behavior should he do so, merely by specifying their physiologically identified brain-states. One would have to rely—as now—on intensional expressions referring to their hopes, beliefs, desires, self-image, and general world-view. One would be able to offer no mechanistic, purely physiological explanations powerful enough to deal with "the social life of aspiring humanity." To be sure, one might appeal to centralist explanations referring to cerebral models, or representations. One might, for instance, say that a man's cerebral model of suicide activated the muscles of his trigger-finger with fatal effect. Such explanations are naturally termed "physiological," because the brain processes involved are generally assumed to be mechanistic in nature. These explanations are nevertheless not formally mechanistic in character, since models, whether cerebral or cybernetic, can only be identified by intensional criteria. The causal mechanisms involved in the cerebral models of different individuals, and directing the actions of those individuals, will probably never be known in detail. But it does not follow that purposive behavior differs in its essential nature from the performance of mechanistic systems. It does not follow, that is, that psychological phenomena are not completely caused by mechanistic neural processes.

Psychology may be empirically reducible to physiology in principle, even though contingent facts (such as cerebral equipotentiality, as well as the differences between natural languages and between social institutions and conventions) make it extremely unlikely that the reduction will ever be effected in anything but a highly schematic form. In other words, psychology may sensibly be said to be "empirically reducible" to physiology in a weak sense that implies the total dependence of teleological phenomena on physical causal mechanisms, the absolute necessity of the mechanistic embodiment of the mind, but which does not imply that bridging statements will actually be found to correlate every psychological statement with a specific neurophysiological statement.

155

In discussing the questions whether the reductionist's position is philosophically acceptable and whether he can draw any support from cybernetic research, I have tried to show that a positive answer can be given to both of them. But it will be clear that "the reductionist" is a label covering a number of rather different positions. To have a reductionist bias toward empirical reduction is to believe behavior to have causally sufficient conditions in physiological states, to regard the brain as a physical system, and to encourage inquiry into the principles of cerebral function. This bias need not be acompanied by a great degree of confidence that psychological descriptions will ever be reduced to physiological ones in detail. And it may consistently be held together with what might be called an "antireductionist bias" (against the strict sense of "reduction"), namely, the conviction that a rich intensional language is essential to the expression— and therefore to the explanation—of psychological phenomena. This particular combination is favored by some behaviorist psychologists. Moreover, it possibly characterizes some members of the Third Force, such as Maslow and perhaps even Laing, but it cannot be attributed to all of them since they hold very diverse philosophical views.

This philosophical approach affords a possibility of reconciliation between "reductionist" and "antireductionist" psychologists. However, the notion that no such reconciliation is possible is widespread, both in everyday discussions of human psychology and in more theoretical contexts. McDougall himself, like Taylor and Chisholm, though for only partly similar reasons, opposed reductionism in both senses of the term. He believed that no system powered by purely physical energy could possibly exhibit the observable features of hormic behavior; it was therefore inconceivable to him that any machine could provide "evidence" in support of reductionism. Anyone who recommends a basically reductionist approach must try to show how it is possible that specifically human behavior, as well as the purposive behavior of animals, might be generated by a mechanistic system. McDougall's personality theory was markedly "molar" in nature, for his theoretical terms included instinct, intention, volition, freedom, and self. The question thus arises whether the behavioral features marked by his theoretical concepts could in fact be exhibited by any purely mechanistic system. One way of dealing with this question is to ask to what extent his theory could be represented in a cybernetic simulation. Another is to ask whether any basically mechanistic interpretation can be given to his concepts, and to the vocabulary of consciousness in general. McDougall's theory is a convenient test case in this context because of, not in spite of, his strongly antireductionist views. If McDougall's insights into the nature of purposive action can be accepted as an integral part of a basically reductionist analysis of behavior, the fear that significant human psychology must give way to "reaction times and rats" can be allayed.

V *Purpose, Instincts, and Natural Goals*

If one asks "Why did John's leg move in that way?" the answer may be, "Because he wants to make a lot of noise," or perhaps, "Because he is practising a new dance with which to impress his girl friend." Both these answers are teleological, but there is an important difference between them. The first seems to require a further why question, namely, "Why does he want to make so much noise?" The answer to this must be in terms of some further purpose or goal of John's, for instance, "To let the burglar know that he is coming downstairs," or "To annoy the visitor trying to sleep in the next room." And these answers themselves would be similarly questioned. However, on being told that John is moving his leg in a certain way so as to be able to impress his girl friend, one would be unlikely to ask why again, for this answer appears to provide a natural stopping-point. It refers to a goal that any man may reasonably be expected to follow. If one does insist on asking why again, the answer will very likely be an impatient shrug, or, just possibly, "Because it gives him pleasure." Should one then inquire, "Why does he want pleasure?" no conceivable answer could be given, except perhaps that he is human.

It is thus characteristic of purposive explanations that there are certain points where the question why is denied application, insofar as it asks for a further goal or purpose of the organism concerned. In a purposive psychology, therefore, some purposes or goal objects must be represented by basic theoretical concepts. That is, explanation of behavior by reference to one of these concepts is ultimate, whereas explanation by reference to other purposes is not. Teleological explanation thus involves purposive stopping points. But there may be disagreement over what count as the stopping points. This disagreement may be centered on the general type of concept required, or it may concern the details of the list once the general type has been agreed.

McDougall's theory of instincts supplied his view of what the acceptable stopping points should be. According to him, the ultimate explanation of all behavior, no matter how sophisticated it may appear, must refer it to the direction of an instinct. In drawing up his list of instincts and arguing against various alternative stopping points suggested by other writers, McDougall exemplified the second criterion of teleological explanation previously distinguished. A consideration of the place of instincts in McDougall's theoretical system should illustrate the importance of this criterion within purposive psychologies generally.

Hedonistic Psychology

Had McDougall been asked why John, an apparently normal young man, should want to impress his girl friend, he might have muttered "Sex!"; he would certainly not have answered, "Because it gives him pleasure." He would have defended his answer against this suggested alternative in terms of his distinction between hormic and hedonistic psychology. McDougall relied on this distinction in the introductory chapter of *An Introduction to Social Psychology* (1908) and on many later occasions, his clearest statement of it being given in 1930 in his paper "The Hormic Psychology."[1] Here he argued that if behavior is explained in terms of psychological factors, as opposed to physiological mechanisms, a choice has still to be made between two types of account: hedonistic and hormic. He differed from many of his contemporaries in preferring the second.

A hedonistic theory of action is one that assigns a crucial motivating role to feelings of pleasure and pain. These are regarded as positive or negative reinforcers, which stamp in or stamp out activity, or which the organism constantly tends to approach or avoid. Purely hedonistic theories view pleasure and pain not merely as "crucial" but as ultimate motivational factors, in that all action is assumed to be explicable by reference to these feelings. Hedonism is psychological rather than physiological in that it stresses intensional factors, for pleasure and pain are attributable only to psychological subjects. Some nineteenth-century psychologies and early varieties of behaviorism were broadly hedonistic in character, although the specific theoretical roles assigned to hedonistic concepts differed. In 1928 L. T. Troland reviewed a number of such theories and distinguished between hedonism of the past, the present, and the future.[2]

McDougall adopted Troland's distinction in his own discussion of hedonism two years later. He explicitly rejected Freud's pleasure principle and the theories of E. L. Thorndike, Troland, and J. S. Mill; and he implied the rejection of reinforcement theories and drive-reduction theories insofar as they appeal to feelings of pleasure, pain, or tension as motivators of action.

Hedonism of the past may be rejected by the purposive psychologist because it is not teleological. That is, despite its intensional character, it does not explain behavior in terms of any prospective reference, but merely in terms of past events. In McDougall's words:

> Not every theory of action that assigns a role to pleasure and pain is teleological. Two prominent American psychologists, Drs. E. L. Thorndike and L. T. Troland, have elaborated a theory which remains strictly mechanistic, though it assigns a role to pleasure and pain. In this theory, pleasure accompanying any form of activity "stamps in" that activity, affects the brain structures in such a way that similar activity is the more likely to recur under similar conditions; and pain has the opposite effect. It is clear that there is nothing teleological in this form of hedonic theory; it is a hedonism of the past. It is a striking evidence of the strength of the prejudice against teleological causation, that Dr. Troland, who believes that all things and events are in reality psychical, should thus choose to elaborate his psychical theory in terms of purely mechanistic causation.[3]

Hedonism of the present may be either teleological or mechanistic, and in the latter case was naturally rejected by McDougall:

> A second form of hedonism may be called "hedonism of the present." It asserts that all action is to be regarded as prompted by the pleasure or the pain of the moment of experience. Its position in relation to mechanism and teleology is ambiguous. It can be held and stated in a mechanistic form: the feeling accompanying present process is a factor of causal efficacy in the total configuration, one that prolongs and modifies the total process. It can be stated in a teleological form: the pleasure of the moment prompts efforts to prolong the plea-

surable activity and secure more pleasure; the pain of the present moment prompts an effort to get rid of the pain and secure ease. In this second form the role assigned to foresight renders the formulation teleological.[4]

Only hedonism of the future is unambiguously teleological: "The traditional psychological hedonism is thoroughly teleological. It asserts that all human action is performed for the sake of attaining a foreseen pleasure or of avoiding foreseen pain."[5]

However, even the teleological forms of hedonism are unacceptable. The reason for this is that insofar as pleasure and pain can be regarded as specific feelings it is untrue that all activity is motivated with reference to these feelings, and to these feelings alone. McDougall recognized this fact:

> We do seek to prolong pleasant activities and to get rid of pain. But it is not true that all, or indeed any large proportion, of our activities can be explained in this way. Our seeking of a goal, our pursuit of an end, is an activity that commonly incurs pleasure or pain; but these are incidental consequences. Our striving after food, or a mate, or power, knowledge, revenge or relief of others' suffering is commonly but little influenced by the hedonic effects incident to our striving. The conation is prior to, and not dependent upon, its hedonic accompaniments, though these may and do modify its course.[6]

Thus, to have said of the young man in the previous example that he was moving his knee, or trying to impress his girl friend, "because impressing her would give him pleasure" would almost certainly be untrue. His "striving after a mate" would, with any luck, afford him pleasure, but that cannot be accepted as the explanation of his striving. This is not to say, however, that pleasure and pain must be mere idle epiphenomena accompanying behavior. McDougall, for instance, believed that they do have some function in its guidance. Pleasurable feeling was defined by him as a sign or indicator of progress toward or achievement of a goal; and pleasure and pain may play a part in the guidance of the detailed tactics involved in action: "Pleasure and pain are not in themselves springs of action, but at the most of undirected movements; they serve rather to modify

161

instinctive processes, pleasure tending to sustain and prolong any mode of action, pain to cut it short; under their prompting and guidance are effected modifications and adaptations of the instinctive bodily movements."[7]

In his remarks about the feelings of pleasure and pain, however, McDougall fell into the same trap of overgeneralization that snared the hedonists: "The continued obstruction of instinctive striving is *always* accompanied by painful feeling, its successful progress towards its end by pleasurable feeling, and the achievement of its end by a pleasurable sense of satisfaction."[8] This trap is laid by the many ambiguities of the word "pleasure," and of related expressions such as, "He is doing it for pleasure" and "He is pleased to do it."

A relatively simple, dual analysis of the concept of pleasure was suggested by Gilbert Ryle:

> "Pleasure" can be used to signify at least two quite different things.
>
> (1) There is the sense in which it is commonly replaced by the verbs "enjoy" and "like." To say that a person has been enjoying digging is not to say that he has been both digging and doing or experiencing something else as a concomitant or effect of the digging; it is to say that he dug with his whole heart in his task, i.e. that he dug, wanting to dig, and not wanting to do anything else (or nothing) instead. His digging was a propensity-fulfilment. His digging was his pleasure, and not a vehicle of his pleasure.
>
> (2) There is a sense of "pleasure" in which it is commonly replaced by such words as "delight," "transport," and "rapture," "exultation" and "joy." These are names of moods . . . Connected with such moods, there exist certain feelings which are commonly described as "thrills of pleasure," "glows of pleasure" and so forth . . .
>
> It should be mentioned that "pain" in the sense in which I have pains in my stomach, is not the opposite of "pleasure." In this sense, a pain is a sensation of a special sort, which we ordinarily dislike having.[9]

According to Ryle's dual analysis, the word "pleasure" *may* name moods or feelings of pleasure, and a man may sometimes aim to experience such feelings. Indeed, implantation of electrodes into the Olds-Milner "pleasure center" of the brain in rats can result in virtually continuous self-stimulation by the rat, if it is provided with a lever that completes the electric circuit when pressed; and if the subject is a man, he may describe his lever-pressing activity as a conscious attempt to elicit the pleasurable or orgasmic feelings thus produced.[10] However, to say that a man does something "for pleasure" may mean no more than to say that it is done deliberately, voluntarily, and purposively, but not (or not primarily) for the sake of any purpose outside itself. The activity seems to be regarded as an end in itself, as when a man digs, wanting to dig and not wanting to do anything else (or nothing) instead. Thus, Ryle holds that in at least one important sense of the word "pleasure"—that in which pleasure is equated with enjoyment—pleasure is not contingently but conceptually connected with purposive behavior. In this sense an organism might be said to pursue its natural goals "for pleasure," since they are ends in themselves.

A more complex analysis of "pleasure" and related expressions has recently been provided by J. C. B. Gosling, who shows that Ryle's account neglects certain important senses of the term altogether and overlooks the fact that experiencing pleasure at the prospect of something is a central criterion of "wanting" that thing.[11] Consequently, to say that a man is enjoying a particular purposive activity—in that he wants to do it rather than anything else—is not, in fact, to eliminate all reference to "pleasure" (in some sense of the term) over and above the activity itself. Nevertheless, Gosling agrees that this sense is not one in which "pleasure" can be regarded as a feeling of an identifiable qualitative nature. Drawing on his subtle analysis of the ambiguities of "pleasure," Gosling distinguishes various different empirical and ethical forms of hedonism, each of which is in some degree implausible or unacceptable. The plausibility of traditional hedonistic doctrines depends on their illegitimate conflation of all these different senses of "pleasure." In particular, psychological (as opposed to ethical) hedonists usually confuse those cases in which the term may be understood as referring to feelings of some sort with cases in which the term serves to point out that the action is indeed purposive and deliberately performed. Gosling's analysis, like Ryle's, allows that "pleasure" is conceptually

163

connected with action done and desired "for its own sake." Consequently, the term may naturally be ascribed to cases of purposive action directed to instinctive goals. But in this particular sense the term does not imply any distinctly pleasurable feelings either accompanying or motivating the action. McDougall's ascription of "pleasurable feeling" to all cases of successful instinctive activity rested on his failure to recognize these points.

The extent to which feelings of pleasure accompany action is a contingent, and sometimes a difficult question. As a matter of fact, they are not usually the prime end of action even when they do occur. This will, perhaps, seem obvious to all but the confirmed cynic in cases such as "John's dancing to impress his girl friend." But even activities that are commonly regarded as "purely pleasurable," such as the gamboling of lambs at play, have been assigned ulterior motives by many psychologists. For instance, play behavior has been explained in terms of a basic motive to refine one's motor skills or to achieve "competence."[12] Interestingly, McDougall rejected such explanations of play: though he held human play to be largely for the purposes of competition, he regarded animal and baby play as purposeless activity accompanied by pleasure: "I suggest that [in play] the animals are merely exercising their various motor mechanisms in turn under the guidance of their sense-organs, and finding pleasure or satisfaction in so doing. Play is activity for its own sake, or, more properly, it is a purposeless activity, striving toward no goal." Rejecting any suggestion of an ulterior motive in play (whether hedonistic or otherwise), he also refused to allow that play is purposive activity *done for its own sake,* because he refused to posit an instinct of play. Whichever analysis of "play" is the most acceptable, the relevant point is that there is often a question as to whether pleasure is the prime end or merely an accompaniment of action. Such issues are particularly difficult to settle in the case of animal behavior. Characteristically, McDougall was not averse to describing the subjective accompaniments of behavior in animals. Speaking of dogs playing at chasing, he observed: "The pursuer is not really hunting him . . . he experiences, we may feel sure, little or none of the emotional excitement proper to the hunt."[13] Possibly, we may agree with Tolman, in preferring to leave such questions unasked.

Ignoring the problems involved in ascribing "excitement" to dogs or "pleasure" to rats, one might allow that men sometimes do something *purely* for pleasure, as when a man activates the electrodes implanted in the Olds-Milner center of his brain, or takes a drug for its euphoric psychological effects. However, the second case in particular might be excepted (and very probably would have been by McDougall) as being in fact an instance of a rather more abstract aim, such as "escape from reality," "increase of self-knowledge," or "gaining the approval of the peer group." Such larger motives might be ascribed to the drug-taker even though he himself insists that he is doing it "purely for pleasure." By virtue of the rarity of solely pleasurable motivation, any purely hedonistic psychological theory must be either false or circular; and its plausibility derives from the complex ambiguity of the word "pleasure."

Similar difficulties attend the behaviorist psychologist's Law of Effect in some of its formulations; for example, in Thorndike's statement of the principle that "pleasure stamps in; pain stamps out," which was the original formulation of the law.[14] Some of the later behaviorist theories of a basically hedonistic type which, unlike Thorndike's, do not mention the word "pleasure"—referring instead to "reinforcement," for example—have also been faulted on grounds of circularity.[15] However, the concept of "reinforcement" may be behaviorally defined and used to formulate noncircular versions of the Law of Effect. P. E. Meehl has discussed this problem at length, and has suggested two formulations of the law: a weak version, in which all stimuli that strengthen any response also strengthen all learnable responses; and a strong version, in which all increments in response strength involve such a trans-situational reinforcer.[16] Hypotheses such as these are not subject to the "circularity" criticism of hedonism, but they are formally mechanistic rather than teleological. Admittedly, the question of what are the trans-situational primary reinforcers for a given species is markedly similar to the question of what are that species' natural goals. The latter form of words, however, implies a context of purposive terminology, whereas the former does not.

The Explanatory Role of Instinct

Hedonism (even when teleological in type) being unacceptable to him, McDougall's preference was for what he termed a "hormic" psychology. He laid the foundations of his hormic theory in the first edition of *An Introduction to Social Psychology.* In 1930 he summarized his position thus: "The essence of [the hormic theory] may be stated very simply. To the question—Why does a certain animal or man seek this or that goal?—it replies: Because it is his nature to do so." This answer implies that for any given species certain goals are naturally followed by the animal, such that mention of them provides a stopping point to a string of why questions. Anyone who is familiar with the species concerned knows that they pursue certain goals, that their purposive behavior is directed in a characteristic manner: "For any one species the kinds of goals sought are characteristic and specific; and all members of the species seek those goals independently of example and of prior experience of attainment of them, though the course of action pursued in the course of striving towards the goal may vary much and may be profoundly modified by experience."[17]

The possibility of listing objective criteria defining the concept of purposive behavior implies that the goals of ongoing behavior are identifiable by observation, given sufficient familiarity with the organism. As McDougall put it, "repeated observation of animals of the same species in similar situations enables us to define the goal."[18] Familiarity with the organism is essential because of the prospective reference involved in a teleological description of current behavior. At the time of observation the hypothetical goal state has not yet occurred, and its nature can only be inferred on the basis of assumptions drawn from past observations of the patterns of activity of the animal concerned. Therefore, as C. L. Hull has pointed out, one could not immediately identify the goals of an unfamiliar animal, or say "what it was doing." To be sure, one might expect to find that certain very general goals were relevant to its behavior. But one could not even expect to find these general purposes in action if the animal being observed were totally unfamiliar, as animals in general might be to Martians. In other words, the reinforcers actually shaping a rat's behavior would become apparent to a Martian psychologist only after careful observation over a length of time. As Meehl has put it:

> [The Martian] notes that when the rat turns to the right he brings about the following states of affairs . . . He ends up nearer to the right-hand wall, which is painted green; he twists his own body to the right in responding; he ends up in a wooden box having knots in the wood; he ends up nearer the North pole; and to a dynamo on the other side of the campus; and he comes into the presence of a cup of sunflower seeds . . . Is it possible that the gradual strengthening of the right turning is dependent upon one, some, or all of these changes following it? Our scientist from Mars would proceed to study a series of standard rats in the situation, altering the above variables systematically by usual inductive procedures. As a matter of empirical fact, he would discover that, within certain very wide limits, alterations in the first five have no effect. The sixth, the sunflower seeds, have a tremendous effect.[19]

The Martian even has to discover that the rat "needs" to eat something more than it "needs" to be close by a wall of a particular color, as well as discovering what the rat is actually prepared to eat. But even for the human observer, an appeal to a general natural goal must be supported by knowledge about more specific regularities in the behavior of the organism. For instance, unlike the Martian, the human psychologist knows that eating is a typical natural goal. But he too has to discover which substances are accepted as foods by the species, and that in learning situations sunflower seeds generally have a greater reinforcing effect on mice than on men. Since hemlock is not accepted as a human food and is in fact known to be a poison, one could hardly explain Socrates' drinking the hemlock in terms of the natural goal of food-gathering.

It would be difficult to find a purposive psychologist who would not admit food-seeking as an instinct, who would not accept "in order to find food" as an *ultimate* purposive explanation of human and animal behavior. However, mere mention of a goal object, which can often be regarded as a crucial means

167

object in the furtherance of striving toward a "natural" goal, is not necessarily enough to bring purposive explanation to a stop, particularly in the case of human behavior. Sometimes human beings seek food for a purpose other than eating, such as making money on the black market, contributing to a harvest festival, or painting a still life. Food is then the man's goal object, but it is not functioning as a means object in his striving for food; food-seeking is not the natural goal directing the activity. Even if the man does eat the food, his behavior may be governed not by his natural food-seeking tendencies but by his competitive urge, for example, to eat more spaghetti than anyone else within a given time.

In such cases McDougall's theoretical distinction between the man's intention and his motive is relevant. McDougall suggested the example of a man observed giving money to a beggar: his intention to give money is clear, but his motive is not.[20] In everyday life, McDougall noted, three possible motives might plausibly be ascribed to the unknown man, *X*, either singly or in combination:

> You might guess that *X* was a timid person and that he gave the coin because he was afraid of the other man, afraid of being assaulted by him if he did not give. Secondly, you might guess that *X* was a pitiful or kindly man, and that he was moved to give by pity. Thirdly, if you were "inclined to be cynical," you might guess that *X* is a man who likes to feel himself superior to others and who enjoys any situation that enhances his feeling of superiority to others and their sense of his power over them.[21]

Closer observation of *X*'s behavior at the time, or the long-term observation available to his acquaintance, could decide; alternatively, if one asked *X* himself, "Why did you do that?" he might reply, "I couldn't help feeling sorry for the poor devil." As McDougall remarked, each of these three explanations is expressed in terms of the felt emotions of the man *X*, whether fear, pity, or pride. That is, "common sense" here seems to make no distinction between *motives* and *emotions*: "Common sense identifies emotions with motives. Common sense, when it has named correctly the emotion dominant during any man's action, holds

168

that it has explained the action, made it intelligible, in general terms."[22] To what extent "common sense" or ordinary language actually does identify motives and emotions is not at issue.[23] The point is that McDougall did not wish to make this identification, since he defined "emotions" as affective feelings, and held that such a feeling could not itself be a causal power moving a person to act. Only the hormic energy of the instincts could provide such a motive power. But he held that a distinct emotion accompanies the action of every instinct, and that common sense is therefore right insofar as it provides a *clue* to the truly "motive" instincts involved in action: "The human emotions [can be] regarded as clues to the instinctive impulses, or indicators of the motives at work in us."[24] In his example, the three felt emotions correspond respectively to three basic motives: the instinct of flight, the parental instinct, and the self-assertive instinct. It is these instinctive motives, singly or in combination, which underlie and ultimately explain the man's intentions.

In the case of a man whose intention is to find food, his motive may or may not be the instinct of food-seeking. If he does not eat the food when he gets it but takes it to the church altar for a harvest festival, then the motivations underlying religious activity in general will be relevant. Whether or not a purposive psychologist postulates a distinctly *religious* instinct, other motives than food seeking must be considered by him in explaining such behavior. McDougall did not posit a specifically religious instinct but would have explained this "paradoxical" food-seeking behavior by reference to the conscious religious intentions of the man and the basic motives contributing to his religious *sentiment*. Yet the fact that one can sometimes give a further purposive explanation of a man's intention to find food does not detract from the claim that "food-seeking" in general is an ultimate conative tendency.

All purposive psychologists are logically committed to the claim that ultimate psychological explanation involves reference to what McDougall called an "instinctive impulse" or "motive." Only this type of theoretical term can function as a final stopping point in explanations of behavior. But in everyday life one is often content with a different type of stopping point. When in day-to-day conversation one asks why a man is doing something, one is often simply asking what is his intention in doing it. In such cases the concern is not with the dynamic, motivational base of the behavior but merely with its intended direction. The questioning therefore stops when the questioner is confident of having discovered the intention. The intention is not always so clear as in McDougall's example of the alms-giving, for human behavior may involve complex contingency planning for the future, as well as the furtherance of several independent purposive series simultaneously. Moreover, a course of action may be intellectually planned but never put into action. The "continued observation" of the goal-seeking behavior that suffices to show an animal's goal is therefore often impracticable where human behavior is concerned, and only verbal inquiry directed to the agent himself can reveal his intention.

This accounts for the fact that an influential philosophical analysis of the everyday concept of "intention" has emphasized the importance of the agent's answer to the question, why did you do that? G. E. M. Anscombe's analysis cites the verbal behavior of giving reasons for doing something as the primary criterion of what it is to do the thing intentionally. Consequently, "intention" can only be ascribed to animals in a secondary, derivative sense, for the behavioral criteria of purpose (exclusive of verbal behavior) are not supposed to be central to this concept. To emphasize the primacy of the agent's speech in identifying human intentions is not to insist that introspective verbal reports should always be taken at face value. Anscombe, like Freud and McDougall, approves the use of nonverbal behavioral criteria for the identification of purposes that are atypical in not being consciously acknowledged by the human agent. Nevertheless, the paradigm case of intentional action is one in which the agent's verbal behavior is of crucial importance. Moreover, only a particular logical type of answer to the question, why did you do that? is appropriate, if the action is to be accepted as intentional. In general, the answer must give a reason for acting, and this reason must mention a "desirability characteristic" of the action. In other words, the intended goal must be represented by the agent as somehow desirable if the concepts of intending or wanting are to be properly employed. To be sure, one may occasionally accept a man's answer that he is doing something "for no particular reason," but this answer could not be accepted in general without destroying the purposive concepts involved.[25]

The relation of this analysis of "intention" to the psychological concept of instinct may be clarified by recalling the previous example of a man who was asked why he had formed the intention of giving money to a beggar. The man might have replied not in terms of emotions or basic motives, but in terms of some further intention, such as "I wanted to palm off my last forged sovereign." This explanation could be carried further by mentioning yet other intentions, "I wanted to appear innocent when searched by the policeman who was tailing me," and so on. But eventually questioning would stop, at the point where the man referred to an apparently self-explanatory intention, one that the questioner could regard as clearly desirable in itself. Since different ideologies classify different goals as "desirable," it might seem that in some cases such a point could never be reached. However, the questioner himself need not desire the goal nor share the intention that he sees as explaining the action. Rather, he must recognize that the intended goal is reasonably called "desirable" given the background beliefs and general purposes of the man being interrogated, together with his basic human nature. In a purposive psychology, the ultimate explanatory role of instincts implies that every explanation in terms of "intention" that would be accepted without further question in the daily life of a particular cultural community should be referred to a basic, instinctual motivation. Using McDougall's theoretical terminology, this can often be done only by way of referring it to a sentiment, a dynamic complex drawing on several instincts. This reflects the fact that the basic motivations involved in cases exemplifying "one and the same intention," or even "one and the same desirability characteristic," may differ greatly. For instance, a well-fed man's purchase of a basketful of loaves and fishes may be grounded in his religious, aesthetic, or commercial sentiments, or even in his sexual desire for a starving wench. There is no general instinctual analysis appropriate to every particular case of a given intention. Nevertheless, any intention, or any goal property accepted as a desirability characteristic in a philosophical analysis of "intention" or in a moral theory, would have to be referred to at least one psychologically plausible instinctual base

171

before it could be accepted as a significant theoretical term within a purposive psychology.

It follows that intentions can play a significant, if not ultimate, explanatory role in teleological accounts of behavior. Despite the impossibility of giving operational definitions of intentions, it is not "naive" in a derogatory sense to assume that a reference to intention may have genuine explanatory power. Neither the psychologist nor the layman need deny that to ascribe an action to an intention (to a typically conscious and perhaps relatively immediate goal) is thus far to explain it. Such ascription does make the action more intelligible. It allows one to distinguish "intentional" from "unintentional" aspects or consequences of behavior, for only the first are represented in the particular inner model of the goal that directs the action. In general, successive statements of the agent's intention serve to locate the purposed action within the cognitive and conative structure of his mind, his idiosyncratic intensional system of knowledge, beliefs, and desires. This system includes his beliefs as to what actions are desirable (qua means), given that other actions are desired (qua ends), and his various sentiments centered on particular objects, so it helps to indicate the motivational basis of his action. But only if the statement of the agent's final intention is as motivationally "transparent" as "John wants to impress his girl friend" could one accept it as expressive of the ultimate explanation of behavior. Because of the complications brought about by language and by the sentiments, human intentions are commonly motivationally "opaque." For instance, a man may intend to find food in order to display it in the harvest festival, to the general end of glorifying the ways of God to man. Unless one is prepared to accept religious behavior as directed by a specifically religious instinct or motive, this statement of intention cannot be regarded as transparently expressive of the basic motives at work.

Although McDougall drew on ordinary language in distinguishing between "intentions" and "motives," it should not be assumed that his use of these terms was identical with common usage. His theoretical distinction is indeed implicit in some examples drawn from everyday speech, as in the almsgiving example he cited. But it would not be correct to analyze all

172

everyday uses of these two words in this particular fashion. For instance, "motive" and "intention" are sometimes used inter-changeably, and sometimes they are not. The overall goal or end of a man's action may be referred to indiscriminately as his "motive" or as his "intention," whereas the subgoals directing the purposive actions comprising his means behavior may be termed "intentions" but not "motives." Thus, a man who intends to paint a still life has the subordinate intention of buying some loaves and fishes; his motive for buying the food is to paint a still life, but his goal of procuring the food would not be termed his motive by anyone who knew of the overall aesthetic goal directing his activity. Further, the word "motive" is commonly used to express still other psychological distinctions. In short, "motive" has a number of different uses in daily conversation, only one of which corresponds to McDougall's use so far de-scribed. These various everyday meanings need not be itemized, but it should be noted that in ordinary usage, as in some sys-tematic psychologies, the word "motive" may be defined in terms of common human goals that are not natural goals. For example, one may speak of the "motive of patriotism" or the "religious motive." McDougall occasionally used the word in this way, in order to refer to the conative aspect of his theoretical construct, "sentiment." The patriotic and religious sentiments were then said by him to be energized by the patriotic and religious motives.[26] However, his primary definition of "motives" specified instincts or natural goals. Consequently, in referring an intention to a motive, he was usually attempting to give its ultimate purposive explanation.

McDougall explicitly stated that purposive explanation appeals to instinctive dispositions as "ultimate constituents" of living organisms. By this he meant partly that instinctive explanations are "irreducible" in the two senses distinguished before:

> We must accept these conative dispositions as ultimate facts, not capable of being analysed or of being explained by being shown to be instances of any wider more fundamental notion . . . The empirical data of psychology must be explained in terms of fundamental conceptions proper to it as an inde-pendent science . . . When, and not until, we can exhibit any

particular instance of conduct or of behaviour as the expression of conative tendencies which are ultimate constituents of the organism, we can claim to have explained it.[27]

Taken by itself, this quotation might suggest that he was merely rejecting what I have called *strict* reducibility, as Tolman did too. But McDougall claimed also that satisfactory behavioral explanation requires "causal explanations in terms of energy and the interplay of energies."[28] According to him, irreducibly psychic horme is the true motive power underlying action. This was the full import of his remark that psychology is an "independent" science with its own "fundamental conceptions." Since horme is associated with the instincts, no explanation of behavior can be fully satisfactory until its instinctive motivational base has been exhibited. McDougall applied this principle in going beyond a man's conscious intention of giving alms to a beggar, to display the motives impelling him to action. In so doing, he believed himself to be exhibiting the hormic energy involved. Because horme is supposed to act nonmechanistically, such basic psychological explanations are "ultimate" in the sense of being totally irreducible to mechanistic ones.

Of course, they are also "ultimate" in the sense that they provide logically final stopping-points, by mentioning ends-in-themselves. This is evident from McDougall's answer to someone who insists on asking why again, even after a natural goal has been mentioned. McDougall characterized the typically hormic answer to the question why an animal pursues a certain goal as, "Because it is his nature to do so."[29] His answer to the further question, "Why is it his nature to do so?" was: "When any creature strives towards an end or goal, it is because it possesses as an ultimate feature of its constitution what we can only call a disposition or latent tendency to strive towards that end . . . Each organism is endowed, according to its species, wth a certain number and variety of such conative dispositions as a part of its hereditary equipment."[30] In other words, an animal inherits his "nature" ready-made. His natural goals are already given from the moment of conception, and the subsequent life process can neither add to nor subtract from their number. McDougall accepted that the mechanism of inheritance is genetic, and he believed that each hormic "conative tendency" or "disposition" directed to a natural goal might be carried by a single Mendelian unit-gene. Although this belief was illusory, and in linking the concept of natural goal so strongly with the traditional concept of instinct McDougall was led into unnecessary confusions, the important point here is that the conceptual character of the question "Why is it his nature to do so?" is quite different—and was seen by McDougall to be different—from that of a question like "Why is John learning to dance?" Only if one is prepared to envisage what McDougall called "the external teleology of the theologians" can these two questions be assimilated, for then each of them could be answered in terms of some further purpose—although one of these would be a purpose not of the organism concerned but of God.[31] Without recourse to such theological underpinnings, no further answer can reasonably be given to questions of the type, "Why is that animal pursuing such and such a natural goal?"

Or more accurately, no answer can be given in purposive terms. It may be possible, however, to give a different sort of answer. According to McDougall, one could, in principle, give a causal answer—though this would involve mention of both physical and hormic energy. According to the reductionist, one could in principle give a mechanistic physiological answer. And both McDougall and the reductionist would agree that one could answer by saying, "The rat is eating now because he's been starved since Saturday," or, "John is trying to impress her because he has an X and a Y chromosome, and she has two X's." All these alternative answers offer different types of explanation as to why the organism is pursuing a particular natural goal; and with the exception of McDougall's hormic explanation, they are all compatible with each other. But none of them offer a purposive answer to the question. And to speak of "inheritance" in general is not to offer a purposive explanation either; it rather fends off further purposive questioning by saying that the animal is just made that way.

A recent philosophical analysis of "powers" clarifies the sense in which such an answer is explanatory, and shows why it may appear that the regress of explanation is "closed" by reference to the nature of the thing concerned. Rom Harré has defended the ascription of "powers" or "tendencies" to things, materials, and persons, arguing that these concepts are neither magical nor occult but have an important explanatory role to play in empirical science. They refer to the intrinsic nature or constitution of a thing, by virtue of which it reacts to external conditions in a characteristic way. Powers may be ascribed to inanimate material things, such as those studied by the physicist and chemist, or to living organisms, such as plants and animals. The analysis of a particular instance of "power" has two aspects: it describes, hypothetically, the characteristic pattern of behavior one may expect to observe in specified conditions, and it states, categorically, that this behavior is largely dependent on the intrinsic nature of the thing. But this intrinsic nature need not be specified: "To ascribe a power to a thing or material is to say something specific about what it *will* or *can do*, but to say something unspecific about what it *is*. That is, to ascribe a power to a thing asserts only that it can do what it does in virtue of its nature, whatever that is. It leaves open the question of the exact specification of the nature or constitution in virtue of which it has the power. Perhaps that can be discovered by empirical investigation later." However, the logical possibility of discovering the constitution responsible for the power has to be allowed in order that the power may properly be ascribed to the thing:

> We do not have to spell out the nature or constitution of the subject in detail, i.e. one is not called upon to perform the analysis of the thing or material to be justified in ascribing a power. In the ascription of powers the categorical component is like a promissory note, we need only believe that it is not logically impossible for it to be cashed. In order for it to be proper to ascribe a power we must believe that it is in principle possible to ascertain the nature of the subject. We are not committed to being able to tell it then and there.[32]

To ascribe powers is thus to offer "schematic explanations," and in the growth of knowledge of the natures and constitutions of things the explanations are filled out.

This analysis of powers casts some doubt on the propriety of uses of this concept that imply the impossibility of any further explanation once the power has been identified. Charles Taylor's use may thus be called into question, since he claims that appeal to powers or natural tendencies in the explanation of purposive behavior shuts off all further inquiry and gives us the absolute rock bottom of explanation. Harré's analysis can, however, afford some justification to the psychologist who explains behavior by reference to inherent tendencies to seek particular goals, provided that the psychologist believes these instinctive powers to be grounded in, and in principle explicable by, the constitution of the organism. He may, like Tolman and Maslow, believe that the causal nature or constitution of the organism is wholly mechanistic, or he may, like McDougall, believe that it is not. But in ascribing instincts to organisms, he is providing schematic explanations rather than mere descriptive labels, explanations that may be filled out by later research into causal mechanisms. The regress of explanation is "closed" by appeal to a sort of natural necessity, for while the animal is what it is, it must behave in this way. Even the ascription of powers to physico-chemical materials, such as gold or DNA, is like the psychologist's ascription of instincts in this respect. But this natural necessity is assumed to be explicable in terms of the causal mechanisms involved, whether or not they have already been discovered. It is perfectly in order for the psychologist to appeal to instincts as basic explanatory concepts in the period before these mechanisms are elucidated. Indeed, it is admissible for him to do this even if he believes that practical difficulties may always prevent discovery of the detailed mechanism or constitution of purposive creatures.

For McDougall, then, explanations in terms of natural goals are "ultimate" in three senses: they provide purposive stopping points; because of their hormic energy content they are irreducibly nonmechanistic; and they appeal to constitutional features that are innately given. For the reductionist psychologist who offers purposive explanations, the second of these senses is unacceptable, but explanation by instinct is ultimate in the first and third senses. This difference distinguishes "hormic" from merely "purposive" psychology.

The Identification of Instincts

Having sketched the general character of natural goals, the question now arises as to how they are to be identified, and how one is to classify behavior directed by them. The basic conative impulses directed to natural goals may be termed "instincts," "natural tendencies," or "innate propensities." McDougall used all these terms, his earliest and enduring preference being for the first. According to McDougall's original definition of "instinct" it was "an inherited or innate psycho-physical disposition which determines its possessor to perceive, and to pay attention to, objects of a certain class, to experience an emotional excitement of a particular quality upon perceiving such an object, and to act in regard to it in a particular manner, or, at least, to experience an impulse to such action." He pointed out that this definition represents an instinct as showing "all three aspects of mental process": the cognitive, the affective, and the conative. He tried to solve the problem of how to identify the instincts by stressing the affective aspect. Each instinct, he claimed, has its own "emotional excitement of a particular quality," which is the only *constant* aspect of the instinct, and by which the instinct is to be recognized.[33] He correlated flight with fear, repulsion with disgust, curiosity with wonder, and pugnacity with anger with some plausibility; but he was hard put to name emotions correlated with the instincts of acquisitiveness or gregariousness. He had to admit that men very rarely experience the "primary" emotions as pure feelings. Also, he admitted that the bodily expressions of emotion in animals close in evolutionary terms—while to some extent similar—may be very faint and overlaid with acquired habits or social inhibitions. In short, his attempt to identify instincts via emotions was not successful. He eventually came to identify them in terms of goals, but because of his view of the teleological function of affect, he still held the signs or expressions of emotion to be clues to the instinct.

Even while claiming to identify instincts via emotions, McDougall referred to the "nucleus" of the instinct as including "a native impulse to some *specific end*," and characterized an instinctive disposition as "a relatively independent functional unit in the constitution of the mind."[34] These remarks fore-

178

shadowed the method of identification that he ultimately accepted. In 1912 he wrote: "When any creature strives towards an end or goal, it is because it possesses as an ultimate feature of its constitution what we can only call a disposition or latent tendency to strive towards that end."[35] In 1925 he clarified his concept of an instinct as a conative disposition directed to a certain end: "An instinct is *not defined by the kind or kinds of bodily activity* to which it impels the animal, *but* rather by the nature of the objects and situations that evoke it, and, more especially, *by the nature of the goal,* the change in the situation, in the object or the animal's relation to it, to which the instinct impels." He quoted Tolman's position that "any instinct is to be defined in terms of the end or goal towards which the instinctive action tends."[36]

A teleological method of defining instincts is logically essential to purposive psychologies. No other type of definition can provide the theoretical stopping points required by purposive explanations. This accounts for the fact that, even while still hoping to identify the instincts by way of their felt emotional tone, McDougall defined the nucleus of an instinct in terms of a specific goal or end. Given a teleological definition of instinct, it follows that "instinctive" behavior is not necessarily fixed or rigid in its motor aspect; it may be very flexible and show intelligent adaptation. For the purposive psychologist, therefore, "instinct" and "intelligence" are complementary rather than opposed. McDougall's teleological definition put him at cross purposes with many behaviorist writers, namely, the disciples of J. B. Watson. Because Watson defined "instincts" in terms of bodily activity or motor patterns, the details of which are *ex hypothesi* relatively rigid and innately determined, Watson's "instincts" were rarely appealed to in explaining human behavior. In contrast, Tolman's purposive behaviorism relied heavily on the concept of instinct.

If one defines "instincts" as very general goals directing all behavior, one has to explain the details of motor activity in terms other than the natural goal defining the instinct concerned. McDougall realized this, and his "other terms" included purposes or goals of a more specific character, such as a child's (or a chimp's) placement of one box on top of another as a means of reaching food. But, like Charles Taylor, he did not clearly see that reliance on teleological explanation alone cannot account for all the detailed features of behavior, since some behavior must be "conatively undecidable." In other words, it is essential to the concept of purposive behavior that there be alternative means available to, or "required for," the end; if there are not, the objective criteria of purpose cannot be satisfied. It follows that if the particular behavioral response actually produced by the animal is to be explained in detail, or to be characterized as "required" for the achievement of the goal in a sense stronger than that in which the other nonselected members of the class of potential responses in question could be characterized as "required," then some *non*teleological factors must be appealed to in its explanation. That is, the detailed selection of means behavior typically depends on factors other than the purposes (at whatever level) currently involved. Explanations referring to such factors are therefore formally mechanistic in nature, unlike explanations referring to inherent natural tendencies or to hormic energy. The nonteleological factors involved may include learnt motor habits controlled by reinforcing stimuli (or "plea-sure" and "pain"), physiological factors such as hormone levels and neuromuscular structure, and inherited response-sets associated with particular classes of releasing stimuli. McDougall appealed to all of these, as well as to the physical mechanisms involved. But he claimed that the underlying physiological processes are not purely mechanistic, that they also involve hormic energy and specifically psychic methods of cognitive representation. This claim was responsible for much of the "endless controversy" attending McDougall's theory of instincts.[37]

A further source of controversy was McDougall's difficulty in drawing up a list of instincts and the apparently limitless proliferation of "instincts" suggested by writers influenced by him.[38] McDougall's list of human instincts varied at different times. His first attempt at enumeration in *An Introduction to Social Psychology* listed seven instincts identified by fairly well-defined emotions (flight, repulsion, curiosity, pugnacity, self-abasement, self-assertion, and the parental instinct); five important instincts not associated with well-defined emotions (reproduction, food-seeking, acquisition, construction, and the gregarious instinct); and "a number of minor instincts, such as those that prompt to

180

crawling and walking."[39] His final catalog of human instincts was as follows:

1. To seek (and perhaps to store) food (food-seeking propensity).

2. To reject and avoid certain noxious substances (disgust propensity).

3. To court and mate (sex propensity).

4. To flee to cover in response to violent impressions that inflict or threaten pain or injury (fear propensity).

5. To explore strange places and things (curiosity propensity).

6. To feed, protect and shelter the young (protective or parental propensity).

7. To remain in company with fellows and, if isolated, to seek that company (gregarious propensity).

8. To domineer, to lead, to assert oneself over, or display oneself before, one's fellows (self-assertive propensity).

9. To defer, to obey, to follow, to submit in the presence of others who display superior powers (submissive propensity).

10. To resent and forcibly to break down any thwarting or resistance offered to the free exercise of any other tendency (anger propensity).

11. To cry aloud for assistance when our efforts are utterly baffled (appeal propensity).

12. To construct shelters and implements (constructive propensity).

13. To acquire, possess, and defend whatever is found useful or otherwise attractive (acquisitive propensity).

14. To laugh at the defects and failures of our fellow-creatures (laughter propensity).

15. To remove, or to remove oneself from, whatever produces discomfort, as by scratching or by change of position and location (comfort propensity).

16. To lie down, rest and sleep when tired (rest or sleep propensity).

17. To wander to new scenes (migratory propensity).

18. A group of very simple propensities subserving bodily needs, such as coughing, sneezing, breathing, evacuation.[40]

Although this list is numbered, McDougall himself admitted that precise enumeration is difficult if not invidious. For instance, he suggested that the acquisitive propensity perhaps comprises two or more propensities, one to take possession, another to store or hoard; the migratory propensity is perhaps not really native to the species; and the comfort propensity may actually include several distinct propensities. Finally, he suggested that perhaps in the human species the native propensities are less uniform (as between individuals or races) than in animal species. This list is clearly a mixed one, with simple propensities such as coughing and sneeezing included along with seemingly much more sophisticated ones, such as the constructive and laughter propensities.

McDougall's critics were not slow to point out his difficulties in drawing up the list, and he had to defend his position repeatedly. Within the four years from 1922 to 1925 he reiterated his defense at length in *An Outline of Psychology*, in two articles, and in a supplementary chapter on instincts published in the twentieth edition of *An Introduction to Social Psychology*.[41] He denied that theories of instinct were "merely the old fallacious faculty psychology served up in a different form," claiming that in no other way could one so easily describe the functional interdependencies observable in behavior, and he quoted Tolman to this effect.[42] Moreover, according to McDougall, theories of instinct explain behavior by exhibiting its dynamic, energetic base —as drive theories are sometimes assumed to do in the mechanistic mode. He acknowledged that there was much disagreement over what should be included in a list of instincts but rather rashly termed this fact "irrelevant." And he agreed that to posit an instinct for every goal that is accepted as a stopping point in everyday life would be to offer a vacuous explanation: "Lightly to postulate an indefinite number and variety of human instincts is a cheap and easy way to solve psychological problems."[43]

Up to a point, of course, the fewer instincts that one postulates the better equipped one is to offer purposive explanations. This follows from the fact that a teleological explanation of a behavioral unit or action refers it to some goal or end state other than itself. Thus, the fewer actions that are regarded as ends in themselves, the more can be explained in purposive terms. A short list of instincts is logically more powerful than a long one. But the specification of the list presents a problem. A teleological classification of instincts can be drawn up only by observing the functional dependencies of behavior, guided by certain general criteria inherent in the concept of "natural goal." Most of the practical difficulty in drawing up the list arises because it is not always clear which ends actually are served (or intended to be served) by a particular activity. This is especially true of human behavior.

McDougall's disagreement with Freud over the primacy of the sexual instinct is germane to this point. McDougall was unconvinced by Freud's representation of the functional dependencies to be observed in human behavior:

> Freud [unduly extended] the sphere of influence of a single instinct, namely the sex instinct. Impressed by the immense strength and influence in human life of the sex instinct, his attention became concentrated upon it; and, as he found it necessary to recognize various other instinctive tendencies, such as curiosity, disgust, self-assertion, submission, and acquisitiveness, he has endeavoured to exhibit them as in some sense derivatives from, or components of, the sex instinct. However, even Freud does not carry this tendency to the extreme of denying all other human instincts; he recognizes, however vaguely and inadequately, a group of instincts which he calls "the ego-instincts" and which he regards as perpetually conflicting with the sex instinct or group of sex instincts.[44]

McDougall disagreed with Freud in regarding self-assertion and submission, for instance, as *relatively independent functional units*. Though they may be elicited in sexual situations, they are not always or typically so elicited, except perhaps in certain pathological conditions, where acts of assertion or submission may even replace the normal sexual act as consummatory behavior for the individual.

In considering the question how the instincts are to be identified, McDougall insisted that it should be possible to identify a fixed number of them:

> It may be, and often is, difficult to mark off a particular action or train of behavior as the expression of one instinct. But the difficulty is not one of principle, but rather one of practice. In principle it is legitimate to ask How many instincts has this

species of animal? and to endeavor to define the objects or situations which will bring each one into play, the kind of behavior which each one will determine, and the kind of goal (or change of situation) which will satisfy the impulse and bring the train of activity to a close.[45]

However, this passage shows that McDougall recognized the practical difficulties involved. It would probably be optimistic to expect general agreement on a list of human, or even animal, instincts if the list were compiled purely on the basis of observing the relatively independent functional units in behavior.

Future psychologists may possibly be able to draw on increased knowledge of causal mechanisms when comparing alternative teleologically classified lists. Assuming that the detailed causal basis of behavior had been discovered, the correlations between teleologically and mechanistically identified phenomena might be sufficiently systematic to justify the inclusion or exclusion of a particular "instinct." For example, it might be found that one part of the brain is causally involved in taking possession of things, that another part is causally responsible for storing or hoarding things, and that these two cerebral locales can function quite independently. It would then be reasonable to endorse McDougall's suggestion that the "acquisitive" propensity should more properly be regarded as two propensities, one to "take possession," another to "store or hoard." It does not follow that instincts could ever be identified with causes, for neither instinct, nor intention, nor any other conative concept is correctly assimilable to the formally mechanistic category of causation. Nevertheless, since instincts can be regarded as causally based powers in the material constitution of the organism, causal information might reasonably be considered relevant to their enumeration. Nor does it follow that causal information must be helpful in the enumeration of instincts, for it may turn out that there is no simple correlation between the behavioral instances of a given teleological tendency and the activation of a particular physiological mechanism. It is illegitimate to assume that the relations between teleologically identified phenomena and underlying energy mechanisms must necessarily be simple ones.

Even if one has little or no physiological knowledge to help in drawing up a list of instincts, one is not confined merely to observing the goals and means-end dependencies evident in behavior. One may also rely on a number of general criteria implicit in the concept of a "natural goal." McDougall himself relied on such criteria in formulating his own list of propensities and in criticizing alternative suggestions made by contemporaries. These criteria include evolutionary considerations and the abstractness of the goal.

McDougall characterized natural goals as "of a nature to contribute to the welfare of the individual, or of the group, or of the species."[46] This characterization is broadly acceptable, because if the basic goals of any species were not largely beneficial, then the species would not have survived—although restrictions on the flexibility with which such goals can be pursued may lead to extinction eventually. In this sense, then, the biological ends of individual and species survival may determine the contents of the list, within certain very wide limits. One may expect to find sexual and food-seeking instincts, for instance. Some theorists, although not McDougall, have gone on to include instincts of self-preservation or race preservation.[47] In this they have been mistaken. Such biological ends are *not* properly ascribed to the individual animal itself, and so cannot properly be included within a psychological classification of instincts. One cannot extend the series of purposes properly attributable to the organism by adding "in order to preserve the species," because this "end" does not involve a state of affairs or a change in situation that an animal can recognize or react to specifically, thereupon ceasing its former activity. The animal's behavior therefore cannot show McDougall's "fourth mark of purpose", the cessation of the movements when, and not until, they result in the attainment of the goal, in effecting a change of situation of a particular kind. Though many of the activities of extant species will in fact tend to the preservation of the species, there are not sufficient grounds for postulating an instinct of species survival, because of the connection between the concepts of purpose and cognition (specifically: recognition of the goal state). Even in the case of man, who can conceive of such a goal, one cannot identify such an instinct, as opposed to the appearance in some individuals of a conscious purpose directed toward the preservation of mankind.

185

Some of McDougall's followers proposed such items as the "instinct of workmanship," the "instinct of make-believe," and the "religious instinct." Not only did McDougall—like Freud—not posit a religious instinct, but he also explicitly refused to include instincts of play, rivalry, or imitation:

> The grounds for rejecting [an instinct of imitation] are similar to, but stronger than, those which lead us to reject instincts of rivalry and of play; namely, (1) the very high generality of the object or situation which must be assumed to evoke such an instinctive impulse; (2) the extreme diversity of its alleged manifestations; (3) the absence of any clear evidence of such an instinct in animals; (4) the possibility of explaining all out-wardly imitative behavior in other ways.[48]

The theory of evolution provided McDougall's justification for applying the third of these criteria: he was unwilling to accept that any new instinct could suddenly emerge in man without having been foreshadowed in an animal species. He appealed to man's evolutionary origins in rejecting many of the more dubious "instincts" postulated by other theorists, and in attempting to curb what Tolman called "the excesses in the matter of instinct-manufacture committed by the sociologists."[49] He even cited evolution in refusing to list a religious instinct, because he saw no justification for ascribing a religious instinct, however primi-tive, to animals. In this he differed from Darwin himself, who had been prepared to ascribe innate animistic tendencies to his pet dog. The dog would growl at unattended parasols blown by the wind on the family lawn, and Darwin anthropomorphically concluded that the dog was growling at some imagined invisible spirit supposed by it to be manipulating the parasols as bodily persons can do.[50]

The fourth criterion mentioned by McDougall requires no special discussion: it is merely Occam's razor, or what McDougall called "the principle of economy of hypothesis."[51] The first, how-ever, needs clarification. McDougall remarked that the principle of defining instincts in terms of the goals they tend to bring about "requires very careful handling in connection with some problems of human instinct." He continued:

186

For example—What degree of generality may be assigned to the goal of an instinct? The majority of the psychologists who recognize any human instincts postulate "an instinct of imitation"; and they continue to do so in spite of the fact that . . . its goal can be defined only as the performing of any action witnessed by the imitator . . . This kind of "instinct psychology" may fairly be likened to the "faculty psychology" which we all profess to repudiate with scorn.[52]

Similarly: "To assume [an instinct of competition] would be to assume a higher degree of generality and abstractness, in respect both of the object and the goal, than any known instinct displays."[53]

McDougall does not specifically say why "a high degree of generality or abstractness" in object or goal debars a hypothetical "instinct" from his list. But his reason may be inferred from his views on the innate perceptual capacities essential to instinctive behavior. He defined an instinct as an innate disposition "to perceive, and to pay attention to, objects of a certain class,"[54] from which it follows that "instinctive activity is normally initiated by an activity of perception, more or less complex, the capacity for this activity is given in the innate constitution of the animal." Any such capacity requires an inborn specification of "objects of a certain class": "Such a specific object, any object that evokes an instinctive response, may be likened more profitably to a key that unlocks a door. The key and the lock are unlike one another, but they are made for one another; each implies the other and is useless without it." The "certain class" concerned cannot be abstract, because truly abstract classes can be defined only by means of language, not by any list of perceptible characteristics, however complex. McDougall insisted that the releasing "key" hypothesized above is "no magic formula, no mere 'stimulus,' that needs only to be presented in order that the door may swing open." He meant that the releasing stimulus or "key" is commonly a complex pattern of behavior emitted over a length of time, and that the motor response (the "lock") may itself be complex and delicately phased in relation to the developing stimulus situation. Indeed, he compared the instinctive motor response to "one of those vastly complicated locks we sometimes glimpse in a banking house."[55] But no matter how complex the perceptual patterns involved, they could not specify those abstract "classes of objects" which can only be defined linguistically, such as "the performing of any action witnessed by the imitator." This provides a further reason that the preservation of mankind is a goal which can be conceptualized and aimed at by adult men, but which cannot be represented in a newborn baby.

It may be objected that McDougall himself transgressed this principle in characterizing the instincts of anger (combativeness) and curiosity:

> Combative behavior is, then, the expression of an instinct which is peculiar in that it has no specific object; the key that opens its door is not a sense-impression or a sensory pattern of any kind, but rather any obstruction to the smooth progress toward its natural goal of any other instinctive striving. The natural goal of the combative impulse, toward which it tends and the attainment of which alone allays it, may be adequately defined as the getting rid of the obstruction which evoked it . . .
>
> Curiosity, like the combative instinct, has no specific object, is not called into activity by objects of any one type only, but rather by any object or situation which involves a certain feature, namely, imperfect apprehension or perception insufficiently clear to invoke any other instinct.
>
> The goal towards which this instinct strives is fuller apprehension or clearer perception, perception definite enough to determine some other instinctive reaction.[56]

His appreciation of the nature of purposive behavior in general perhaps accounts for McDougall's inclusion of these two "instincts," for a goal-seeking organism might be expected to have some nonlinguistic way of representing (internally modeling) the fact that there is an obstruction to its ongoing activity, and perhaps to have some special mechanism or behavioral routine available for coping with such obstructions. Combative behavior, or anger, is not appropriate to all obstructions, but its effect in many cases will be to remove the obstruction and so to allow the original goal-seeking to continue. One might also expect that an evolutionarily successful purposive organism might have a general tendency to maximize its learning with respect to relevant objects in the environment, at least within the limits set by the satisfaction of its other instincts, such as food-seeking, fear, and sex. Modern research has suggested that, at least in the case of the higher animals, situations of high informational redundancy are a *dis*incentive, and that the organism tends actively to prefer situations of a certain degree of informational novelty.[57]

Instincts, Ethology, and Behavioral Genetics

The extent to which McDougall's account of combativeness and curiosity—and his other listed "instincts"—is acceptable in light of later motivational research need not be discussed here, where the concern is with the conceptual nature of teleological classifications of instinct, rather than the empirical evidence for any particular list of basic "instincts," "motives," or "drives." However, something must be said about the general criticisms of McDougall's approach implicit in subsequent behavioral research.

McDougall's analogy of an innate lock and key is suggestive of the ethological concepts of *fixed action pattern* and *releasing stimulus,* and even his earliest discussions of instinct implied the presence of complex innate releaser mechanisms of some sort, but he never undertook the painstaking experimentation required to show the precise nature of these releasing stimuli. Such experiments were to be carried out by the ethologists, the early work of Konrad Lorenz being a pioneeering effort in the field.[58] Moreover, in a critique of McDougall's classification of instinct, Lorenz himself pointed out that McDougall was anthropomorphic and overly hasty in many of his remarks about instinctive behavior. For instance, in positing a parental instinct in most animals, McDougall implied that all units of "parental" activity in a given animal are controlled by one and the same integrative mechanism—much as human parental behavior is governed largely by the integrative role-concepts of "mother" and "father" current in the particular culture concerned, as well as by the corresponding concept of the goal of "the good of the child." But as Lorenz pointed out: "To assume a 'whole-producing,' directive instinct superior to all part reactions could evidently be justified only if the effects of a regulative factor, exceeding

189

the experimentally demonstrable regulative faculty of the single reactions, could be observed."[59] That such an assumption may be unjustified is shown by the fact that the ethologist can sometimes identify independently controlled units of behavior, which in normal circumstances combine to give the appearance of activity that is planned as a whole and dependent on a recognition of complex means-end relationships. Behavior of this type may appear to be goal-directed, but is not really so. There is no genuine "variation of means." Obstructions are not overcome: the behavioral sequence is either simply arrested by them, or it continues unchanged in what is now an inappropriate environmental context. It is evident that there is no overall "regulative factor" (such as a cognitive representation of the goal and of a relevant means-end nexus) in terms of which the detailed activity can be directed. What may seem, in normal circumstances, to be genuine means-end behavior is rather a number of functionally independent motor units, each one dependent on a specific stimulus situation (or hormonal condition). Since *ex hypothesi* such behavior appears purposive under normal conditions, it requires extremely careful observation—and probably experimentation— to show the true nature of the case. D. S. Lehrman's studies of parental behavior in ring doves provide an excellent example of this type of behavioral analysis.[60] Various hormonal factors and a number of "social" releasing stimuli interact, so that the behavior of the birds and squabs is reciprocally determined in an appropriate manner. The squabs get hatched, reared, and fed, whereby "the parental function" is fulfilled, but *not* by means of truly purposive activity. A purely functional classification of instincts tends to obscure such differences between "the same" instinct at work in different species. The "same" function, such as care of the young, may be achieved consciously and purposively in man, and quite mindlessly in other creatures.

Perhaps one should rather say *relatively* mindlessly, for slight marks of purposiveness are rarely absent from the behavior of animals above the lowest levels of the phylogenetic scale. Indeed, Lehrman's work itself showed the delicate balance of innate and experiential factors in the parental behavior concerned. The concept of instinct has been strongly criticized—both in McDougall's time and in recent years—for exaggerating the rigidity and nonvariability of behavior.[61] But this particular criticism cannot be directed against McDougall, who always insisted that experience and circumstances could modify "instinctive" behavior at all phylogenetic levels: "Instinctive action everywhere displays that adaptability to special circumstances which is the mark of intelligence; instinct is everywhere shot through with intelligence, no matter how constantly, in how routine a fashion, a particular mode of instinctive behaviour may be repeated."[62] Clearly, a teleological definition of instincts (as opposed to one in terms of specific motor mechanisms) can very well allow that instinctive behavior may be flexible rather than rigid.

But such a definition of instincts has another drawback. It is likely to exaggerate the innate-environmental dichotomy, a dichotomy that may sometimes be thoroughly misleading. A teleological classification of natural goals (that is, stopping points in purposive explanation) is not necessarily open to the complaint that it implies too clear-cut a distinction between "nature" and "nurture," for it is possible to accept certain stopping-points on the ground that animals *just do* behave in such and such a way. That is, as Harré's analysis of "powers" might suggest, all detailed questions of heredity can be left aside, even though purposive behavior is held to be somehow based in the organism's "inherited nature." Naturally, such detailed questions can be investigated, but their answers cannot be expected a priori to conform in any simple way with the classification of natural goals accepted by the psychologist. The psychologist himself might be interested in these detailed investigations, but without prejudging them in any way on the basis of his list of natural goals. However, if the concept of natural goal is closely associated with the concept of instinct (rather than with an inheritance-neutral concept, such as propensity or behavior trait), then the resulting classification of instincts may lead to oversimplification of the relations between "hereditary" and "acquired" components of behavior. This is primarily because many traditional uses of the term "instinct" have oversimplified this distinction, and the conceptual associations thereby set up are not easily eliminated in later usage of the term.[63] But it also results from the fact that a teleologically identified behavior trait cannot be attributed to any simple hereditary mechanism. In this sense, natural goals and behavior directed

191

toward them are not usefully defined as "inherited," particularly where the higher animals are concerned. That the infelicity of defining natural goals as "inherited" may be compounded by associating them with the concept of instinct can be seen from McDougall's use of these terms.

McDougall preferred the term "instinct" to the less controversial "propensity," and he defined an instinct as "an inherited disposition."[64] But strictly speaking, all that can be inherited are the genes. The "laws of inheritance," or genetic laws, apply to gene populations, not to individual organisms or individual traits. Behavior traits in the adult individual organism are always a complex resultant of his sample of genes and the whole course of his development from the moment of conception. In general, the genetic endowment (the genotype) determines the *limits* within which the various observable features (the phenotype) will lie. Environmental conditions determine the specific points within those limits which will characterize the individual animal. Sometimes one and the same phenotypic character in two individual creatures may have unlike genetic bases, because differing environmental conditions have compensated for the underlying genetic difference; conversely, identical genotypes may produce obviously different phenotypes in two individuals, again because of the influence of varied environmental histories. G. E. McClearn has pointed out some of "the subtle ways in which genotypic differences may interact with environmental variables" in determining behavior:

> In [the remarkable investigation of A. K. Myers], which dealt with shock-avoidance learning, there were five variables: type of stimulus (CS) (buzzer vs. tone); type of response (pressing a bar vs. rotating a wheel); time of testing (day vs. night); shock condition (floor and three walls shocked vs. floor and all four walls including manipulandum [bar or wheel] shocked); strain of animal (Sprague-Dawley vs. Wistar rats). When the data were analysed . . . a bewildering array of interactions emerged.[65]

In sum, the two strains tended to react differently under any given combination of the other four variables; no simple summary of the results could be given, such as "Wistar rats learn faster," or even "Wistar rats learn faster than Sprague-Dawley in daytime." Clearly, any attempt to ascribe their learning behavior to heredity *or* to environment would be a gross oversimplification. In some cases, of course, one or the other influence may safely be ignored in practice. But even so, it cannot sensibly be asked whether a phenotypic character is due to environment or to heredity; it can only be asked if one of these cooperating influences is relatively strong. To define a purposive behavior trait (which according to McDougall's "sixth mark of purpose" must *essentially* be molded by experience) as an inherited disposition is, therefore, an unfortunate choice of terminology.

Indeed, McDougall himself was seemingly misled by his choice of words here, for he attempted to specify the genetic base of "instincts" in a very simple way. That is, he ascribed instincts to the influence of single genes: "Some simple instincts seem to be transmitted according to the Mendelian laws; and it seems highly probable that, as these studies are carried further, we shall find that 'an instinct' is a Mendelian unit-factor in the make-up of the individual."[66] To ascribe a genetic influence on behavior to a single gene is very often to oversimplify. Occasionally a behavior trait can be shown to be primarily dependent on a single gene, but such single-gene effects, in the higher animals at least, are more likely to be behavioral abnormalities than functional units within normal behavior. For instance, "waltzing" and other muscular and postural abnormalities in mice, and some types of mental deficiency in men, are dependent on a single gene. Those *normal* behavior traits that are carried by a single gene tend to be simple motor mechanisms, and are more important in the relatively rigid behavior of insects than in the purposive activity of the higher mammals. Though such traits may have wider behavioral effects, they are very different from the general teleological "dispositions" referred to as instincts by McDougall. For example, a single gene determines the duration of wing vibration in male *Drosophila*, and this in turn influences the effectiveness of the courtship, because the female fruit fly responds most readily to a particular duration of vibration.[67] But it is a priori more likely, and also borne out by the empirical evidence, that very general purposive traits such as "intelligence" or "food-seeking" in the higher animals are *poly*genically determined.

McDougall's hope that his classification of instincts might be justified by ascribing each "instinct" to a single unit-gene is, therefore, illusory. Whereas this might sometimes be possible for a "reflex" classification of instincts, it is in principle highly improbable where a teleological classification is concerned. While McDougall's teleological definition of instinct allowed him to say that instinctive behavior was not necessarily rigid, the traditional connotations of the term doubtless influenced him in his unacceptable genetic hypotheses about purposive behavior. That is, his use of the concept of instinct and his definition of the problem as the distinction between inherited and noninherited purposive dispositions are not particularly felicitous in the light of modern behavioral genetics.

Instincts and Plans

G. A. Miller, Eugene Galanter, and Karl Pribram recently gave an account of instinct that is logically quite similar to McDougall's, though using the terminology of innate plans and TOTE units to build up the theoretical hierarchy. These two concepts are defined as follows:

> A Plan is any hierarchical process in the organism that can control the order in which a sequence of operations is to be performed . . . We shall also use the term "Plan" to designate a rough sketch of some course of action, just the major topic headings in the outline, as well as the completely detailed specification of every detailed operation . . .
> The reflex is not the unit we should use as the element of behavior: the unit should be the feedback loop itself. [We may generalize this loop as] the Test-Operate-Test-Exit unit—for convenience, we shall call it the TOTE unit.[68]

The language of "feedback loops" and "control of operations" suggests a cybernetic context, and the authors explicitly acknowledge their debt to such contexts: "A Plan is, for an organism, essentially the same as a program for a computer, especially if the program has [a] hierarchical structure [like Allen Newell, H. A. Simon, and J. C. Shaw's GPS simulation of human thought processes] . . . We are reasonably confident that "program" could be substituted everywhere for "Plan.""[69]

194

In thus endorsing the reductionist hypothesis and appealing to machine analogies in support of it, the authors are radically opposed to McDougall's position on the hormic basis of purposive behavior. But it is interesting to compare the following remark with McDougall's characterization of a hormic theory: "Plans are executed because people are alive. This is not a facetious statement, for so long as people are behaving, *some* Plan or other must be executed. The question thus moves from *why* Plans are executed to a concern for *which* Plans are executed."[70] Plans are executed by machines because of the plans of their designers. But the question as to why living organisms execute plans can be given no answer within the terminology of plans, granted that one does not appeal to what McDougall called "the *external* teleology of the theologians," who are wont to refer to the purposes (plans) of God.[71] Living organisms show *internal* teleology in that their own purposes or innate plans provide the stopping points in purposive explanation. Unlike McDougall, Miller and his coauthors accept that these plans function purely by means of causal processes of a mechanistic type. One can say, in principle, *how* plans are executed, even if there can be no answer to the question *why* the most basic plans are executed. The representation of the goal-directedness of behavior by hierarchies of plans of various sorts is logically similar to McDougall's representation of behavior as a purposive hierarchy. With such a logical structure, there remains room for disagreement over the list of basic plans or instincts. Miller et al. allow that some disagreements as to the nature and number of instincts may be resolved by closer observation of behavior or by new information about neurophysiological mechanisms. But some disagreements are conceptual, and these may be more satisfactorily solved by reference to the established usage of purposive concepts than by simple fiat associated with a new technical term. For example, one cannot attribute an instinct of species survival to animals, because of the close logical connection of purpose and cognitive concepts. In discussing a similar example. Miller et al. decide on a similar result, but give no really convincing reason for their decision:

It is almost as if the Plan were not in the organism alone, but

195

in the total constellation of organism and environment together. How far one is willing to extend the concept of a Plan beyond the boundaries of an organism seems to be a matter of meta-physical predilections. We shall try to confine our use of the term to Plans that either are, have been, or could be *known* to the organism, so that we shall not speak of concatenated behavior as part of a Plan even when it is highly adaptive.[72]

Miller et al. stress the hierarchical nature of plans and the functional interdependency of goals and subgoals in behavior. They also remark that human beings have a varied cognitive repertoire as well as a large motor repertoire. Roughly speaking, one may say that the cognitive repertoire is applied in the test phase itself as well as in the preliminary strategic planning, and the motor repertoire carries out the operation phase. Choice of alternative means to a given end is influenced by cognitions (beliefs) about the particular situation involved; it is also affected by individual preferences for certain strategies, given the logic of the problem and "external" factors (such as time constraints) limiting the possible methods of action. Strategies used in the execution of plans may be inferred by the psychologist from the structure of behavior observed, and may also be suggested a priori by the logical structure of the problem facing the organism. In the experimental investigation of "strategies" directing human behavior, both these sources of hypotheses have been tapped.[73] The larger the motor and cognitive repertoires, the more complex and varied may be the behavior directed toward any given goal. A plan may be an element in several higher-level plans; thus, economy of effort is possible, since several purposes that are not in the same means-end series may be pursued together. (John's learning to dance may both impress his girl friend and fulfill the physical education requirements of his college.) Several unrelated plans may be executed simultaneously over a given stretch of time, provided that the organism has available information about the current stage of development of each plan. Differential priori-ties of goals are allowed for, which will be reflected in different plan-hierarchies directing behavior.

The varying degrees of rigidity and flexibility of instinctive behavior which were remarked by McDougall are referred by

196

Miller et al. to the influence of plans of differing types. Some of these are innate, of which some are fixed in their motor aspects and may involve highly specific perceptual releasing mechanisms, while others are more flexible and general in application. The temporal ordering of behavioral units identifiable as consummatory acts is of various types: the flexible integration of human purposive behavior is contrasted with the *chaining* or *concatenation* typical of animal behavior. Miller et al. do not attempt to list the innate plans for any species but refer to the ethological evidence for examples of various types. Their interest is not to draw up a specific list of instincts but to express the hierarchical and integrative nature of instinctive activity by assimilating the concept of "instinct" to that of "plan." Basic plans, inexplicable in terms of other plans, are essential to their conceptual scheme; similarly, instincts provided McDougall with stopping points in purposive explanation by referring to natural goals. In either case, the immediate explanation of goal-directed behavior may be far removed from the base of the theoretical hierarchy. But even so, there must always be some explanation in terms of the basic theoretical units of conation or control (instincts or plans).

According to McDougall, then, one must ascribe *all* purposive activity to an instinct or a natural goal. No such activity is an end in itself, free from direction by one or more of these goals. Indeed, all purposive psychologies must make this claim, although they may recommend different lists of natural goals. But among the explanations of behavior that would typically be accepted without question in everyday life are many which do *not* refer immediately to any end that could plausibly be regarded as a natural goal. Thus, it may satisfy one to be told that a man did something "for the glory of God," "to help his country," or even "to get chosen for the Olympics team," but none of these mentions a natural goal or appeals directly to an instinct. McDougall would not fault them on this account or refuse to acknowledge them as explanations, despite his insistence that his "main thesis ... is that in every case the motive, when truly assigned, will be found to be some instinctive impulse, or some conjunction of two or more such impulses."[74] For he did not regard every action as the direct or immediate expression of an instinct. On the contrary, he regarded very few human actions as being of this type:

197

[One] misinterpretation of my view . . . consists in asserting that I ascribe every human action to some instinct, or regard it as the direct expression of some instinct. This is to ignore the whole scheme of sentiment and character for which my sketch of the instinctive nature of man furnishes merely the foundation . . . In the man of developed character very few actions proceed directly from his instinctive foundations: perhaps an occasional start of fear or sudden gesture of anger; but all others proceed from his sentiments.[75]

McDougall's personality theory, his "scheme of sentiment and character," provides an example showing how a purposive psychologist can reasonably insist that all behavior must ultimately be explained in terms of natural goals, while nevertheless allowing that most human actions cannot be referred to the direct influence of the instincts.

VI Sentiments and Simulation

Looking back over his life's work, McDougall wrote: "An important part of my whole scheme of mental structure is the theory of the sentiments and of character as formed by the hierarchic organization of the sentiments in one integrated system . . . It remains, and, I believe, will remain, as my most original and solid contribution to psychology." This theory extended the scope of McDougall's system to cover all the "likings and dislikings, sympathies and antipathies, respects and contempts, admirations and scorns, friendships and enmities, loves and hates" of mankind.[1]

It also reflected rather more abstract features that are essential to the purposive behavior of human beings. McDougall's theory of the sentiments provided the base for his discussions of the structure of the mind, as reflected in both normal and abnormal behavior. Mental structure was represented by him as a purposive hierarchy, various aspects of which correspond to his concepts of sentiment, emotion, disposition, temper, temperament, and taste. These aspects include the direction of most human behavior to particular foci or goals quite different from "natural goals"; the control of conflicts between two or more instincts; the tactical control of ongoing activity, involving judgments as to its likelihood of success; an individual's characteristic way of goal-seeking in general; and the effect of success in particular activities on the overall development of goal-seeking. These general features of purposiveness would have to be taken into account in any comprehensive explanation (or simulation) of behavior, whether the theoretical vocabulary employed were McDougall's or not.

Much of McDougall's systematic vocabulary was initially drawn from everyday language. Writing before the development of behaviorism and the operationalist philosophy of science, McDougall saw no need to offer a methodological rationale for his terminological borrowings, as Fritz Heider found it necessary to do in defending "naive psychology" half a century after the publication of *An Introduction to Social Psychology*. McDougall unself-consciously drew on the psychological distinctions implicit in daily conversation. His theoretical discussion

199

consisted largely of analytic propositions exhibiting conceptual relationships latent in everyday speech. This is why, despite McDougall's belief that he was doing empirical psychology, his theory was not justified by or related to any detailed experimental program of research. But he did attempt to tighten up the definitions of the terms he took over, so as to fit them consistently into his own theoretical scheme. Consequently, his technical application of terms like "admiration," "reverence," "hope," "anxiety," and "reproach" relied heavily on everyday usage but did not correspond to it precisely. He redefined these words on the basis of his own key systematic concepts, and I shall not ask how far his use of them as technical terms parallels their use in ordinary language. The important point is that McDougall's methodological habit of borrowing terminology from the layman's language provided him with a rich conceptual base on which to draw in expressing the psychological subtleties of human purposiveness, for many complex intensional features of man's behavior are implicit in the conceptual schemes of everyday speech.

Much of our familiar psychological vocabulary does not seem obviously compatible with a mechanistic interpretation. This is particularly true of those concepts that mark specifically human mental phenomena. This has led Charles Taylor, for instance, to argue that everyday purposive terms include a basically non-mechanistic element within their meaning, so that they could no longer be properly employed if the empirical reduction of psychology were ever effected. No doubt McDougall would have agreed. Moreover, he was prepared to welcome such terms as "monad," "telepathy," and "soul" into his systematic psychology. The reductionist must either show that these terms are psychologically useless, or he must show that they may be interpreted in a basically mechanistic fashion. Similarly, he should suggest, if only in a schematic way, how it can be that the vocabulary of ordinary discourse about human psychology may properly be applied to basically mechanistic phenomena. In other words, he must try to show how purposive features of at least the degree of subtlety expressed by McDougall's theoretical psychology could, in principle, be generated by a mechanistic system.

200

The Formation of Sentiments

McDougall allowed that the immediate explanation of human actions would for the most part not include any reference to the natural goals of man. The justification for his claim that these natural goals are, nevertheless, the ultimate ends of all human behavior lies in his account of the complications that gradually modify the "pure" instincts, and which lead to the formation of sentiments.

Although originally—and theoretically—independent, soon after birth the instincts come to be interrelated in various ways. McDougall regarded instincts as only relatively independent functional units, associated with relatively specific ends, for he recognized four principal kinds of complication of instinctive processes:

(1) The instinctive reactions become capable of being initiated, not only by the perception of objects of the kind which directly excite the innate disposition . . . but also by ideas of such objects, and by perceptions and by ideas of objects of other kinds.

(2) The bodily movements in which the instinct finds expression may be modified and complicated to an indefinitely great degree.

(3) Owing to the complexity of the ideas which can bring the human instincts into play, it frequently happens that several instincts are simultaneously excited; when the several processes blend with various degrees of intimacy.

(4) The instinctive tendencies become more or less systematically organized about certain objects or ideas.[2]

The detailed nature of these "complications" is influenced by language, the laws of association or conditioning, feelings of pleasure and pain, the formation of habits, cultural conditions, and the nature of the instinctual hierarchy already built up in the individual. These complications lead to the formation of sentiments, and it is to a sentiment (rather than to an instinct) that most human action must be immediately or directly referred. A man's sudden start of fear on first hearing a burglar downstairs is a purely instinctive response. And his instinctive fear may affect his behavior so that he decides not to face the burglar himself. But his decision to phone the police, or to scare the burglar away by stamping on the stairs, will depend directly on some sentiment, such as his pride in his material possessions or his self-respect.

"Sentiment" was the crucial concept of McDougall's personality theory. His theory of sentiments was stated at length in *An Introduction to Social Psychology* in 1908, and thereafter was modified only in detail. It is characteristic of human behavior that particular objects come to have special importance for each individual. Such objects function not as mere Pavlovian conditioned stimuli but rather as foci with reference to which the various instincts interact and the natural goals are regularly pursued. They form the cognitive core of sentiments of many different kinds. A man's sentiments may range from disgust, gratitude, or suspicion toward the various members of his acquaintance to generalized sentiments for mankind, such as misanthropy or philanthropy. His personal behavior may be determined by sentiments of, for example, scholarship, statesmanship, or megalomania.

McDougall's original definition of a sentiment was: "an organized system of emotional tendencies centered about some object."[3] The concept was borrowed from A. F. Shand, a fact that, together with the definition just quoted, was to lead to a common misunderstanding, for Shand had conceived of sentiments as consisting of emotional dispositions only, whereas McDougall did not.[4] Therefore, McDougall later suggested a more cumbrous definition: "A sentiment is a system in which a cognitive disposition is linked with one or more emotional or affective conative dispositions to form a structural unit that functions as one whole system."[5]

This later definition was intended to stress the cognitive core of a sentiment, its reference to a specific (intensional) object. The "objects" in question may be of very different types: "The sentiments may . . . be classified according to the nature of their objects; they then fall into three main classes, the concrete particular, the concrete general, and the abstract sentiment—*e.g.*, the sentiment of love for a child, of love for children in general, of love for justice or virtue." The cognitive core may become very complex indeed, largely owing to the rich linguistic representations available to the adult man: "The centre . . . of any sentiment is the cognitive ability or disposition corresponding to the object of the sentiment; and this may (and in the case of any strong and enduring sentiment is likely to) grow into an extensive system of abilities (a system of knowledge or "ideas" concerning that object)."[6]

Like instincts, sentiments have the tripartite nature of mental being: they are at once conative, cognitive, and affective. In other words, the full characterization of a sentiment (as of an instinct) must mention the action tendencies or basic motives involved, the intensional object to which these are directed, and the accompanying emotional tone. Whereas the instinctive tendencies are innate, however, the sentiments are individually acquired tendencies. They are thought of in developmental, dynamic terms:

> Each sentiment has a life-history, like every other vital organization. It is gradually built up, increasing in complexity and strength, and may continue to grow indefinitely, or may enter upon a period of decline, and may decay slowly or rapidly, partially or completely. *When any one of the emotions is repeatedly excited by a particular object,* there is formed the rudiment of a sentiment . . . which is liable to die away for lack of stimulus, or, if further relations are maintained with its object, to develop into a more complex organization . . . by the incorporation of other emotional dispositions.[7]

Thus a sentiment can be formed around an object only if that object initially excites, or is associated with the excitation of, one of the instincts with its characteristic emotion. For instance, if a man repeatedly disgusts a woman by his coarseness, continually exciting her instinctive tendency of repulsion, she develops a sentiment of disgust for him. Alternatively, if his kindness constantly arouses her emotions of tenderness and subjection, which correspond respectively to her native tendencies toward parental and self-abasing behavior, then she comes to have a sentiment of gratitude for him. Disgust is a simple sentiment, being based on only one instinct, whereas gratitude is binary. There is no theoretical limit to the number of instincts that may be simultaneously excited by one intensional object, so sentiments of extreme conative complexity can develop. Great conative complexity is more likely if the core object is itself multifaceted, particularly if it is central to a large and varied cognitive system of associations and beliefs. The earliest and most rudimentary sentiments are typically appropriate, or realistic, since the relevant environmental core objects can excite the instincts only by virtue of their intrinsic properties. However, highly inappropriate sentiments may develop if false beliefs associated with the core object mediate the arousal of instincts that would not have been aroused by the object itself. For example, Othello's jealous suspicion of Desdemona was mediated by the cognitive associations in his mind, and it could never have developed if Iago's malicious whisperings had not occurred.

The instincts supply the energy or drive of the sentiment, no matter how complex the cognitive core may become: "The relation between the cognitive disposition and the emotional dispositions comprised within a sentiment is that the latter remain the conative–affective root of the whole system, no matter how large its cognitive division may become, furnishing to it the energy, 'drive,' conative force or interest by which all thinking of the object is sustained, and yielding the wide range of primary, blended, and derived emotions that colour all such thinking."[8]

However, most human behavior does not seem to be directly motivated by instincts, and children seem to become gradually more free of their instinctual urges as they mature. This is because of the growth in complexity of the sentiments during socialization. Socialization does not add new sources of motivation; even the most idealistic actions, directed by highly abstract sentiments, are basically motivated by the instincts. But socialization does add new objects of motivation as nuclei of sentiments, and facilitates the cognitive, largely linguistic representation of such intensional objects: "Social man . . . builds up many sentiments which are traditional in his society, enduring attitudes toward a multitude of objects, both the concrete objects which the natural man knows, and the abstract objects which only the use of language enables the social man to think of or conceive."[9]
A sentiment may be transferred, or widened, to include new

objects because of associations in space-time linking them with the original core-object, as when a man's fondness for a town is determined by some romantic association in his past life, or because of application of the same name.

Sentiments centered around different intensional objects may therefore be hierarchically linked via the linguistic categorizations of their cognitive cores. Linguistic extension of the core is crucial, for instance, to the growth of sentiments centered on various social groups and to the development of motives such as patriotism or the desire for the preservation of mankind. Although furthering the interests of one's country is not a natural goal, it is natural for a man to want to further the interests of his country. Patriotism is not an instinct, but it is a very common sentiment. And as sentiments are defined partly in motivational (instinctive, conative) terms, one may speak of the "motive" of patriotism. Of course, this is not a "motive" identifiable purely by reference to a single instinct, like the basic motives previously discussed. McDougall identified patriotism and similar motives as "quasi-altruistic" extensions of the sentiment of self-regard. The powerful egoistic sentiment becomes transferred to one's family, countrymen, and fellow-men in general by means of the linguistic concepts classifying these disparate individuals together.

Because of the development of a complex system of sentiments, human motivation seems to become largely independent of natural goals as socialization proceeds. McDougall agreed that hardly any human behavior is explicable by immediate reference to an instinct, except "perhaps an occasional start of fear, or sudden gesture of anger." On the contrary, the immediate motivational reference is usually to a sentiment. But only instincts can provide the ultimate explanation, and sentiments were accordingly defined in conative terms.

McDougall thus denied the possibility of any absolute discontinuity between instinctive motivations and purposive activity— even the emergence and pursuit of the primary values of the self. He saw that if a new goal is to be accepted as a purpose of an individual, it must be linked with the goals, natural or "sentimental," already directing the person's behavior. The linkage may be purely cognitive. To cite an earlier example, John believes that the girl he finds so attractive would appreciate his

205

learning to dance. But she may turn out to be a Jehovah's Witness or have some other reason for disapproving of dancing, in which case the sexual purposes directing John's behavior would be directly frustrated by his new skill.

Irrespective of its immediate effect, John's dancing may come to play such a part in his life that it appears to be what G. W. Allport has termed "functionally autonomous."[10] Allport sees this theoretical concept as contrasting with instinct psychologies. But his humanist emphasis on "contemporary" rather than "historical" motivations is compatible with an instinct-based psychology, provided that theoretical allowance is made for the genesis of new motivational complexes that are more complicated than are the instincts, in all three aspects of mental life. Once a form of behavior has been adopted in the service of a single instinct, the goals and motivational tensions involved may come to differ importantly from those that directed the original behavior. In particular, the self-image may influence "mature" behavior to a large degree. For example, once the goal of learning to dance has been accepted by the self, its achievement may be encouraged by the egoistic sentiment, in which case the instincts comprising that sentiment will come into play. John's original decision to learn to dance was taken for exclusively sexual reasons. But he may come to take a pride in dancing and become an international performer, sacrificing all other pleasures for the sake of his career and scorning the ignorant adulation of his female fans. In such a case the initial sexual motivation would be of etiological interest only. For all practical purposes, John's motives in this area of his life would have been essentially transformed. His dancing would now be independent of such simple instinctual needs and might even appear to be done "for its own sake." What determines whether or not this will happen must await consideration of the concepts of taste and self-regard. The point is that the apparently autonomous nature of the complex motivational behavior that typifies adult human life is misleading if it is taken to imply that its instinctive base and etiology are irrelevant in theory as well as in practice. The instincts contributing to John's sentiments related to dancing supply the ultimate teleological explanation for all his actions connected with his dancing, no matter how varied and complicated these

actions may be. McDougall's way of expressing this was to say
that the instincts provide the basic motive power for all human
behavior, even behavior characterizing maturity of a high degree.

Sentiment is a dispositional concept, rather than one marking
any particular mental occurrence. McDougall emphasized that
a sentiment is not a fact or mode of experience, nor is it open to
introspection. It is a "feature of the complexly organized structure of the mind that underlies all our mental activity."[11] Its
presence must be inferred from the emotions and activities associated with the object identified as its core. Thus, one may
properly be said to hate a man even while not thinking of him;
but one is justified in regarding a sentiment as hate only because
of the nature of the emotions it elicits and the actions to which
it impels one at thought or sight of the person. The origin of
sentiments dictates that each one will be associated with one or
more primary emotions. However, while the sentiment is *associated* with emotions, it *consists* of emotional tendencies; that is,
dispositions to experience certain emotions in connection with a
particular object. The distinction between sentiments and emotions parallels that between mental structure and mental process:

> [A] sentiment never displays its nature completely in any one
> emotional event; only by observing the various emotional
> reactions to the loved or hated object on many successive
> occasions and under diverse circumstances are we able to infer
> the structure of the sentiment. The sentiment and the emotion
> . . . illustrate the validity and necessity of the distinction
> between mental structure and mental process or activity . . .
> A sentiment is an enduring structure within the total structure
> of the mind or mental organization, while emotion is a passing
> phase.[12]

The concept of sentiment bears an obvious relation to that of
attitude, which is widely employed in social psychology, but
sentiments differ from attitudes in various respects. They pre-
suppose specific, underlying, innate propensities, whereas attitudes do not; thus, information about a man's attitudes provides
no clue to the basic motivations involved in those cases where
the attitude in question is not "motivationally transparent." Senti-

ments are the more specific in object-reference, though they may
be centered on an abstract object such as justice or power. Sentiments are more lasting and hierarchical than are attitudes, their
interrelations forming the structure of personality, and they are
conceived in more developmental, dynamic terms. Sentiments
are typically conscious and benign as contrasted with Freudian
"complexes," whereas attitudes may be either. McDougall himself objected to the assimilation of "sentiments" to "attitudes":

> American social psychologists and sociologists have recently
> produced a voluminous literature concerning what they call
> "social attitudes"; the term is used to cover a multitude of facts
> of many kinds, including almost every variety of opinion and
> belief and all the abstract qualities of personality . . . as well
> as the units of affective organization which are here called
> "sentiments."
>
> Since a sentiment, such as strong love for a person, may
> engender not only the tender impulse and emotion, but also
> anger, fear, curiosity, and almost every other kind of affective
> response, simple or complex, including the whole range of
> complex feelings from joy and hope to sorrow and despair, how
> inappropriate would be the designation "social attitude"! For
> the word attitude literally means some particular expressive
> position of body and limbs; and, when used metaphorically of
> the mind, it can only mean some particular actual, incipient,
> or potential reaction.[13]

Being at once cognitive, conative, and affective, sentiments
can be characterized or named in terms of their core objects,
their instincts, or their emotions. Since McDougall associated
each primary emotion with one of the instincts, the last two
methods are in a sense equivalent. But the affective (emotional)
characterization stresses the subjective feeling-tone of the sentiment, while the conative (instinctive) description stresses the
ultimate motives and observable goal-seeking activity typical of
the sentiment.[14]

Emotions, Temper, Temperament, and Tastes

A list of someone's sentiments would provide information about

208

the intensional objects that are most important in his life, the natural goals that in his case are related to these intensional objects, and the emotions that typically occur when he thinks about these objects. However, it would not elucidate the teleological function of those affective aspects of mental process that McDougall termed "emotions." It would not specify the strategies usually employed by the man in the service of his sentiments, the means behavior most likely to be chosen by him in his striving to fulfill his varied "sentimental" goals. Nor would it characterize in any way the detailed structure typical of his purposive behavior; it would not distinguish between the optimist and the pessimist or between the fickle and the steadfast individual. In McDougall's theoretical terminology, these features of human purposive behavior are marked by the concepts of emotion (primary, complex, and derived), temper, temperament, and taste.

In 1908 McDougall distinguished between "primary" and "complex" emotions. He had already suggested in the *Physiological Psychology* (1905) that to each instinct there corresponds a specific affective tone or primary emotion. In *An Introduction to Social Psychology* he listed seven instincts corresponding to the primary emotions of fear, anger, tender emotion, disgust, positive and negative self-feeling, and wonder. Though he listed other instincts as well, their corresponding primary emotions were said to be introspectively obscure and so were not specifically named. These instincts and emotions were identifiable as relatively independent functional units in the behavior of the higher animals, and in certain cases of human psychopathology any of them might be morbidly exaggerated. Later, he was to repeat his claim that these instincts are accompanied by subjective feelings of the same order as the named primary emotions.

McDougall held that the primary emotions are commonly experienced in their pure forms only by animals. Although he gave observable criteria of the behavioral expression of emotion in animals, he also consistently spoke of their experienced tone— as in his theoretical analysis of play, where he appealed to the felt emotions of dogs chasing each other in play. Man more commonly experiences complex emotions, in which more than one primary emotion is aroused in a given situation. Most of the complex emotions are related to sentiments:

> The compounding of the primary emotions is largely, though not wholly, due to the existence of sentiments, and some of the complex emotional processes can only be generated from sentiments.

> In very many instances our emotion is an event in the life-history of a sentiment; that is to say, the nature of the emotion is conditioned by the nature of the sentiment from which it springs.[15]

On those occasions when the complex emotion is thus dependent on a sentiment, the emotion may be described as being directed to, or excited by, the intensional object which is the cognitive core of the sentiment concerned.

McDougall claimed that some complex emotions may be excited both by an object that is not the core of any sentiment, and by an object that is the core of a sentiment; his examples include admiration, reverence, scorn, contempt, loathing, fascination, and envy. Similarly, everyday usage of these terms reflects the fact that *many* objects can arouse a man's instinctive tendencies "at first sight" so as to produce these emotions in him. But other complex emotions can arise only when the object exciting them is already the core of a particular sentiment and thus is associated with certain emotional expectations. For instance, only an object that is already the core of a sentiment of love can arouse the complex emotions of reproach, jealousy, solicitude, resentment, or shame. In other words, such "complex emotions" are defined (both by McDougall and in common usage) with reference to a term such as "love," which connotes what McDougall would call a "sentiment" and which itself must be intensionally directed to the intensional object of the emotion.

The distinction between an emotion's being aroused by an object which is, or by one which is not, the core of a sentiment underlies the fact that some emotions are sometimes or always experienced as clearly directed to a particular intensional object, whereas others are not. In other words, although all emotions are in fact directed toward intensional objects, the identification of this object is easier in those cases where a sentiment is involved. This explains Anthony Kenny's remarks about the everyday concept of emotion:

It is not in general possible to [identify] a particular emotional state without at the same time ascribing an object to the emotion . . . No flutterings of the heart or meltings of the bowels could tell me I was in love without telling me with whom.

But are there not objectless emotions, such as pointless depression and undirected fears? . . . We are often unaccountably depressed, on days when for no reason everything seems black; but pointless depression is not objectless depression, and the objects of depression are the things which seem black . . . Still, there are cases where we are afraid, but afraid of nothing, or of something, but we know not what. Perhaps we awake in the morning with a sinking feeling, and a loose and general sense of dread; only later do we remember a dangerous task to be performed . . . The emotional terms derive their appropriateness from [this later anticipation of the task].[16]

Because the emotion of love depends on the sentiment of love, one could not know one was in love without knowing whom one loved. By contrast, because the emotion of depression can arise independently of any sentiment, it may be unclear just what is its intensional object. Moreover, in some cases the intensional object is represented in the mind unconsciously rather than consciously, though it may later "come to mind."

McDougall allowed that the complex emotions are not readily analyzable into their primaries by introspection, and he normally analyzed them via their motor, instinctive aspects. They may be classified as binary, tertiary, or more complex compounds, according to the primary emotions or instincts involved. When two instincts are associated with one object, they give rise to a binary emotion, and when they are repeatedly aroused by an object, they generate a binary sentiment having that object as its cognitive core. Since any number of instincts (emotions) may be associated together, each in varying strength, the complex emotions and the sentiments connected with them may be of extreme complexity. In general, a sentiment and its corresponding emotion are often named by the same word, such as "love." Admiration is a binary emotion, a compound of wonder and negative self-feeling; but since the instincts of curiosity and submission may both be excited by an object on first acquaintance, admiration does not necessarily imply the existence of a sentiment.

211

The action tendencies defining these two instincts are: the impulse to approach and to continue contemplating the object, and the impulse to shrink together, to be still, and to avoid attracting the attention of the object (thus, admiration is primarily directed to animate objects). If these two action tendencies are complicated further by that associated with the emotion of fear (withdrawal or running away), they constitute the tertiary compound of awe. Gratitude is a binary compound of tender emotion and negative self-feeling. When combined with awe it gives the highly complex emotion of reverence, which if constantly elicited by certain intensional objects constitutes the emotion of the religious sentiment.

This last example shows that the more complex emotions and sentiments cannot be distinguished purely by enumerating their instinctual bases. There are only four instincts associated with reverence—curiosity, submission, flight, and the parental instinct—which would suggest that it is a quadruple compound. But this type of reverence can also be represented as a compound of a tertiary and a binary emotion (awe and gratitude), in which the emotion of negative self-feeling (the instinct of submission) enters twice, so that perhaps it is a quintuple emotion. McDougall distinguished another type of reverence, which is made up of the same four primary emotions, being a blend of tender emotion, fear, and admiration (the binary of wonder and negative self-feeling). However, tender emotion enters into it directly, not as an element of gratitude. This kind of reverence has less of a personal note, because it has less negative self-feeling, than does the reverence of which gratitude is a component; it is directed toward impersonal objects, such as great cathedrals, toward the works of man or God rather than to those personal beings themselves. McDougall suggests that the conative structure of the sentiments and the complex emotions may be represented by hierarchical diagrams (such as the one shown here). The two types of reverence can then be shown as distinct hierarchies: each has only four nodes at the highest level (only four primary emotions), but the interconnections between nodes at the lower levels differ. Both types of reverence include somewhat different complexes, since the strength of the component instincts is independently variable. These differences in strength can be represented

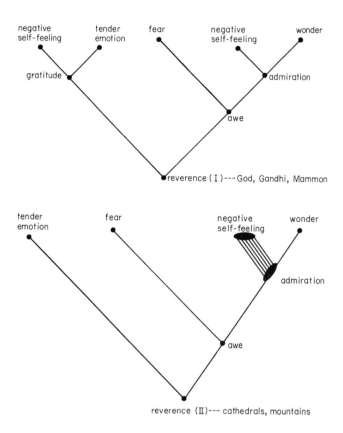

diagrammatically by the number or thickness of the lines linking various points. Many different religious sentiments can thus be represented, by means of diagrams in which a core object (God or Mammon) is connected with these four instincts, themselves hierarchically blended in different fashions.

Since the native intensity and excitability of each primary emotion (instinct) varies independently of the rest, there are an indefinite number of complex emotions, shading into one another by insensible degrees. If one instinct is relatively strong, one natural goal having marked priority over others, then the man (or animal) will have an "emotional disposition" of a characteristic type that can be recognized and named. For instance, if the instinct of pugnacity or of flight is preponderant, then the orga-

213

nism will have an irascible or a timid disposition respectively, its outstanding emotion being anger or fear.

McDougall always insisted on a one:one relationship between instincts and primary emotions, although he admitted that he could not justify this claim introspectively. In 1908 he named only seven "well-defined" emotional qualities as primaries. In *An Outline of Psychology* he listed emotional qualities corresponding to fourteen separate instincts, but acknowledged that some of these were named only by attaching the expression "feeling of" to the name of the instinct. In the early editions of *An Introduction to Social Psychology* the reason for his insistence on this point is obscure, but it may be inferred from his view of the function of the emotions, first clearly stated in the fourteenth edition (1919), and stressed in *An Outline of Psychology* in 1923: "The essential function of the emotional qualities in our mental life [is that] they enable us to recognize our own state, and to regulate, direct, and in some degree control the impulses by which we are moved . . . If the emotional excitements accompanying all instinctive reactions were alike in quality, we should make little progress in self-control."[17]

The emotions (primary and complex) thus act as signs or indicators of the instincts aroused. The emotional feeling qualities are indicators for the organism itself, while their bodily expressions are indicators for his fellows, enabling them to anticipate his actions in some degree. The foresighted control and adjustment of action depend on this information provided by the emotions. For instance, if one feels an impulse to strike a colleague in anger, one may moderate the accompanying tendency to action, either because of a simultaneous emotion of fear or because of the negative self-feeling aroused by one's intention to contravene a moral rule. In the latter case, the sentiment of self-regard is associated with a sentiment of hatred, or aversion, directed to the cognitive object "striking one's colleagues"; and this sentiment itself is linked with a positive sentiment directed toward the cognitive object (moral rule), "One should not do violence to other human beings." In this way the complex emotions and their underlying sentiments free man from the tyranny of direct control by his instincts and allow for the rule-governed conduct of the mature personality. Animals may develop rudi-

214

mentary sentiments, such as a dog's "love" for his master. These do not attain a high degree of complexity, since animals cannot form linguistically-coded abstract concepts, nor do they develop a master sentiment of self-regard. But a dog may be able to inhibit an impulse of attack directed toward its master, if it experiences anger when the impulse is aroused. This type of control of instinctive action clearly requires that a record of the arousal of each instinct be available to the organism. McDougall's view of the teleological function of the emotions thus led him to postulate a specific emotional quality to act as a subjective record for each instinct.

McDougall often implied that this internal, or subjective, indication has to be consciously experienced to be of any use in controlling instinctive behavior (although he did admit that many of the primary emotions are not clearly accessible to introspection and that complex emotions cannot normally be analyzed introspectively). But if "conscious" is understood in its usual, strong sense, this is not so. The minimal functional requirement is that the indication be available to the organism at some level of its mind, but this level need not be a fully conscious one. However, it is true that only "conscious" affect can contribute to genuine self-control. This is because the strong sense of "conscious" can be defined only by reference to the "self." McDougall's interest in the function of the emotions within self-disciplined and moral behavior therefore led him to overemphasize the "consciousness" of emotions in general. But the important point here is that affective states, whether fully conscious or not, function in the control of instinctive activity. This is not to deny that "very strong" emotions are typically associated with uncontrollable behavior, for they may be regarded as signs of a degree of instinctive arousal so extreme as to overpower all potentially regulatory influences. Unconscious emotions, and even unconscious sentiments, can be accounted for in terms of McDougall's concept of "dissociation."

Whereas the primary and complex emotions indicate which natural goals are presently directing behavior, other feeling states were regarded by McDougall as indicating the stage and probable success of ongoing activity, irrespective of which goal is currently being sought. These feeling states therefore accompany and qualify the true emotions, and they too have a characteristic feeling quality and behavioral expression. In 1919 McDougall called these states "derived emotions"; but he later repeated his original claim that they are not properly termed "emotions" and should rather be called "complex feelings."[18] Examples include joy, surprise, sorrow, confidence, hope, anxiety, despondency, and despair. Each of these involves intellectual judgments of the likelihood or nearness of success and the number or nature of obstructions to the goal-seeking activity, and they may be concerned primarily with the means or the end. For instance, in hope one concentrates on the end, even though consciously aware of the means; whereas in anxiety one concentrates on the means, and thus may get bogged down in the details of immediate effort while losing sight of the overall goal that should be directing the activity. McDougall insisted that hope, confidence, and anxiety are not special forces or powers that push one toward a solution of problems, but signs of one's estimate of the likelihood of success: being primarily cognitive rather than conative, they guide activity but do not energize it.[19]

A man's "temper" reflects his characteristic way of goal-seeking in general. Men of well-balanced innate dispositions, with no one instinct or emotion being disproportionately strong, may differ widely in temper:

> The principal factors of temper seem to be of three kinds. First, the conative tendencies, though well balanced, may be all strong or all weak . . . Secondly, independently of their intensity, they may be either extremely persistent or but little persistent . . . Thirdly . . . also independently variable, is the native susceptibility of conation to the influences of pleasure and pain . . . We can explain all the varieties of temper as being conjunctions of these three attributes [intensity, persistence, affectability]. There will be eight well-marked types, corresponding to the eight possible combinations.[20]

These types are defined as steadfast and confident, fickle and shallow, violent and unstable, despondent, anxious, hopeful, placid, and sluggish. The similarity of the concept of temper to that of derived emotion is apparent—but, of course, it is possible for a man of hopeful temper to despair on occasion, or one of despondent temper to be hopeful in a particular case.

McDougall's concept of "temperament" also denotes general behavioral features, but it includes a causal reference: "We may define temperament as the personal qualities that are determined by the chemical influences of the bodily metabolism exerted upon the general working of the brain or nervous system."[21] Examples are fatigability, the level of activity or excitability in general (controlled largely by thyroxin level), bodily growth under the influence of the pituitary, energy of emotional excitement regulated by the adrenals, and the low and high expressiveness of introversion and extroversion (which McDougall assumed to be controlled hormonally). Chemicals that sensitize one propensity selectively (such as the sex instinct) are not sufficiently general in effect to be regarded as bases of temperament, but are rather associated with emotional disposition.

McDougall's early rejection of hedonism was later supported by his concept of "tastes." These were first mentioned in *Character and the Conduct of Life* (1927), but were more fully discussed in *Energies of Men* (1932) and the twenty-third edition of *An Introduction to Social Psychology* (1936). Tastes and distastes are likes and dislikes, as are some sentiments. But tastes are directed toward activities, not objects: "Broadly, we may say that sentiments are likings and dislikings for objects, while tastes are likings and dislikings for particular modes of activity . . . While our sentiments determine the major goals towards which we strive, our tastes determine our choice of means, the kinds of activities and instruments we use, the roads we prefer to follow, in pursuing those goals."[22]

Tastes (and distastes) are acquired and perpetuated solely in the service of the sentiments, which alone determine the goal and motivation of all activity not directly controlled by the instincts. No activity can be truly done for its own sake or for the sake of a new goal completely independent of all natural goals. A man who digs, wanting to dig and not wanting to do anything else instead, is not really treating digging as an end in itself. A taste or distaste for an activity is acquired according to initial success: activity that is successful tends to be pursued at the expense of activity which is not. For instance, a man may take up gardening because of his sentiment for health, or food, or the respect of his neighbors, but only if he turns out to be relatively successful will he develop a taste for gardening rather than turning to athletics, carpentry, or dancing instead. Successful activity is repeated with consequent increase of skill, and one continually tries to increase one's skill until the activity may seem to be performed for its own sake (such as a hobby). McDougall explains this genesis of tastes by saying that skill is rewarding because of its connection with the sentiment of self-regard. Certain skills, or even skill as such, may come to be positively valued because of the social or self-approval involved, and criteria of success determine the frequency with which instrumental activities are repeated—though this effect may be complicated by other factors, for if a child is compelled to acquire the skill of piano-playing, it may well develop a *dis*taste for the activity. Nevertheless, this is the psychological process that would underlie the transformation of John's dancing in the earlier example from a means to a specific sexual end, to an all-absorbing professional activity to which sexual satisfaction is only secondarily relevant. Considering activities that seem to be done for their own sake or, hedonistically, for the sake of the pleasure involved, McDougall admitted to some doubt as to whether tastes could be said to have independent or autonomous motivation. He might have postulated a natural goal and an instinct analogous to *competence*, regarding skillfulness as instinctually rewarding, but he did not.[23] He finally decided that all tastes have an external source of motivation, even if it is only by way of the sentiment of self-regard.

The strategies in terms of which a man expresses and fulfills any sentiment are largely determined by his tastes. The importance of criteria of success, or skillfulness, distinguishes tastes from mere "habits," which may depend purely on chance associations or processes of conditioning. Broadly speaking, tastes are for *actions* or strategies, whereas habits concern *movements* or very low-level actions not liable to the complex development typical of human tastes for gardening, dancing, or surgery. Tastes such as these are relatively enduring features of a man's mind and may color a large proportion of his total activity.

McDougall believed that the confusion of tastes and distastes with sentiments of liking and aversion (attributable to the fact that the familiar concepts of "likes" and "dislikes" do not express these distinctions) is a prime source of hedonism, for it obscures the motivational sources involved.

McDougall's characterological concepts are essentially purposive, for they each mark some feature of the organism's goal-seeking behavior. Because the emotions (whether primary, complex, or derived) reflect relatively short-term features of purposive action, they are aspects of mental process rather than mental structure. But the other concepts mark relatively enduring features of behavior—disposition, temper, and temperament being predominantly innate, whereas sentiments and tastes are acquired. These five concepts, of which the sentiments are particularly important, form the basis of McDougall's notion of the structure of the mind:

> We may define the mind of any organism as the sum of the enduring conditions of its purposive activities. And, in order to mark our recognition of the fact that these conditions are not a mere aggregation, but form rather an organized system of which each part is functionally related to the rest in definite fashion, we may usefully speak of the "structure" of the mind.
>
> [Mental structure is formed by] the hierarchic organization of the sentiments in one organized system.
>
> Each sentiment is a unique formation, which, whether it be relatively simple or highly complex, is a structural and functional unit of the total organization we call the mind.[24]

The sentiments are the basic units of the purposive hierarchy of the mind, for to identify a sentiment is to mark out an intensional object with reference to which one or more natural goals are consistently pursued. The total system of sentiments may be very complex, for the conative-affective aspect of each sentiment is an associative or hierarchical blend of several instincts, and the sentiments may be interlinked both associatively and hierarchically *via* their cognitive cores.

219

Outlines of a Simulation of McDougall's Personality Theory

Since purposive explanation is concerned with intensional functional relationships rather than with material mechanisms, it is not surprising that McDougall criticized material analogies of mental structure as inappropriate: "We speak of the structure of a poem or of a musical composition, meaning a whole consisting of parts in orderly functional relations with one another; and, though the structure of the mind is not of the same order as these structures, yet these, rather than the material structure of a machine, should be thought of as offering the closer analogy."[25] The abstract or logical relationships between the parts of a poem or sonata do not reflect the functional relationships of goals and subgoals that are the concern of purposive explanation. But such means-end relationships could be represented in a computer program designed to simulate purposive behavior, as could the various cognitive linkages and operations involved. It may therefore be asked to what extent McDougall's characterological concepts might be simulated, and to what extent they mark features that would have to be considered in a simulation of complex purposive behavior.

McDougall's systematic vocabulary drew not only on everyday speech but also on more "metaphysical" contexts. His theoretical apparatus included such terms as "monads," "telepathy," "subordinate selves," and "freedom," as well as less arresting items such as "sentiment," "hope," and "despair." In view of the presence of such terms, it is not immediately obvious that McDougall's psychology is suited to the techniques of simulation. Nor would McDougall himself have been sympathetic to such an enterprise. But he did give observable criteria for purpose and regarded his theoretical concepts in general as similarly grounded in empirical fact. Insofar as his concepts mark objectively defined features of purposive behavior, they may be simulable. In other words, the simulator may be able to represent some aspects of his theoretical system, but not others. Insofar as a concept has antimechanistic or "realist" mentalistic overtones largely independent of behavioral criteria, it is not simulable. McDougall's concepts did have such overtones. He hypothesized hormic energy underlying every behavioral phenomenon, believing this to be causally active in states of consciousness existing over and above observable behavior and bodily states. And he emphasized what he believed to be the essentially private, subjective accompaniments of behavior (or "raw feels") in animals and men—an emphasis that drew criticism even from the sympathetically inclined Tolman. It is therefore not to be expected that all aspects of McDougall's theoretical concepts could be represented in a mechanistic simulation.

The purely behavioral aspects of his concepts should, however, be simulable, since it is not a priori impossible that the processes underlying purposive behavior should be mechanistic in form. Moreover, if introspection is not *essentially* private and incommunicable, certain aspects of introspective experience might also be illuminated by means of a cybernetic analogy. One has introspective knowledge of many of one's conative states (such as conscious intentions), of some of the processes involved in the cognitive representation of one's intensional objects or ideas, and of one's affective feelings or emotions. If such knowledge is to qualify as contributing to the "objective data of psychology," then some behavioral, or publicly communicable internal, expressions of introspective experiences must be in principle available. In other words, the criteria of psychological terms, even when used in an introspective way, must be essentially public rather than logically private. Assuming this to be the case, it does not follow that introspective knowledge is not "private" in some sense. Intentions, for instance, are often private in the sense that they are not clear to observers of one's nonverbal behavior; if one chooses not to give any verbal expression of intention, then one's fellows are often at a loss in elucidating one's purposes. In general, if psychological vocabulary is properly applicable to *some* basically mechanistic systems, namely animals and men, there is no reason in principle why functional equivalents of psychological phenomena should not be provided in a computer simulation. This is not to say that current cybernetic concepts and techniques are adequate to provide such equivalents. Indeed, the common "property-list" approach to the programming of cognitive representations is basically incapable of simulating certain everyday psychological processes. Therefore, since McDougall's sentiments are cognitively defined, the simulability of

221

sentiments by means of this approach is limited. But current techniques may suggest initial provisions for simulation that could be improved on later. Specifically, if purpose is basically mechanistic, simulation of concepts such as sentiments, hope, and despair should in principle be possible, though it does not follow that these terms could properly be applied to the computer itself, however successful the simulation.

Such concepts may, however, be difficult to simulate in practice, if they cannot be clearly and unambiguously defined, for programs must be expressed in a precisely definable programming language. Moreover, every theoretical step—every "explanatory" or "predictive" inference—must be precisely specified in order for the step to be taken at all. As one of the GPS programmers has remarked: "In many forms of theorizing, not including mathematics usually, you can get by with hand waving at the appropriate moment. In my constitutional law days, for example, I observed that whenever Chief Justice Marshall got to a delicate point in an opinion he said "Obviously," and went on. If you write a computer program and say "Obviously," and go on, nothing happens."[26] By contrast, the amount of hand-waving in everyday psychologizing is enormous. And McDougall's theoretical terms, being borrowed from everyday contexts, retained much of their conceptual vagueness despite his attempts at redefinition. Their testability and explanatory power were thereby weakened, for the inferences they were supposed to justify depended largely on extra suppositions or "intuitive" interpretations that were not expressly stated, and whose role in lending plausibility to the inferences concerned was unperceived. This means that McDougall's use of his concepts could not be simulated unless all his interpretations and suppositions were rigorously expressed, and all the implications of his system were clearly evident. His "hand-waving" would have to be made explicit for any completely satisfactory simulation.

It might be argued that this clarification of McDougall's concepts, or of the everyday concepts from which they are derived, is not only difficult but impossible in principle. H. L. Dreyfus appealed to "intuition" and "judgment" in the solution of unformalizable problems, and he concluded that digital techniques must be inadequate to the simulation of such human thinking.

The problems of psychological explanation and prediction in personalistic contexts, particularly in the clinical situations of therapy and counseling, certainly cannot be regarded as readily formalizable. Dreyfus would regard them as not formalizable at all: if formal techniques were to be helpful in their solution, the psychologist's "insight" would be crucially involved in the initial structuring of the problem. Similarly, the proponents of *clinical* as opposed to *statistical* prediction in psychology, with their preference for idiographic rather than nomothetic approaches to human personality, would insist that the concepts employed by the sensitive observer of human life, be he clinician or layman, are not analyzable in a precisely formalizable way.[27] But even if some mysterious form of "insight" is said to be involved in the layman's psychological understanding or in original scientific thought, a scientific theory's explanatory power is a function of its clarity. If one cannot be sure what the theory is stating and what its implications are, one cannot know how to test it nor what to count as confirmatory evidence for it. Since simulations necessitate absolute precision of expression, they may function as useful tools in the clarification of psychological theories. This is true irrespective of whether nomothetic theories (general laws) are considered adequate to the explanation of personal behavior, and irrespective of whether everyday psychological concepts are believed to be analyzable in a precise and unambiguous way.

An attempt at an outline simulation of McDougall's psychology could therefore be a useful exercise, because it could help to show just when McDougall's hand was waving, and in which direction it was pointing. It could perhaps suggest objectively definable functional equivalents of some of McDougall's more "high-flown" vocabulary, such as "monads" and "freedom," which might otherwise appear to be mere empty metaphor or superfluous metaphysics. And it could help to show whether McDougall's concepts actually do mark out structural features essential to purposive behavior. If they do, then programmed equivalents of such features would have to be provided in simulations of purposiveness—even though McDougall's system might not be the most suitable theoretical model for representing them in detail. Moreover, insofar as McDougall's theory is simulable, the psychological phenomena concerned must be possible in mechanistic systems. To this extent, then, successful simulation would show that a basically reductionist approach to human psychology is not unreasonable in principle. In view of these points, there may be something to be gained by thinking of McDougall's system in cybernetic terms, despite his own lack of sympathy with mechanistic interpretations of psychology.

In a simulation of McDougall's theory, the instincts would be represented by "basic goals" in the program. Each of these would be associated with a certain class of "motor" subroutines tending toward achievement of the relevant class of goal states. Each would be activated by inputs of a certain type, while also showing a degree of spontaneous activity in the absence of appropriate input. At least one of these basic goals would be involved in the direction of each unit of performance equivalent to a behavioral (conative) unit. Performance controlled directly by one of these goals would show a specific action tendency; in a motor simulation this might be mimicked, but it could be modeled purely symbolically and represented in the print-out. If any performance were allowed for that was not equivalent to a conative behavioral unit, such performance would not be under the control of these basic goals. Thus, the simulation of "pure" reflexes would not require reference to basic goals, since such responses—even if innate—do not qualify as instincts on a teleological basis of classification. And the simulation of play would trigger many of the action tendencies (motor mechanisms) normally directed by basic goals, but the "direction" in this case would be either random or by association with certain sensory inputs: there would be no *integration* of motor performance, for such integration would depend on some basic goal being involved in the overall control.

In any purposive hierarchy with more than one basic goal, competing demands on the system's resources may arise. In other words, there may be conflicts of instincts or of basic goals. An action likely to further one goal might be inimical to the achievement of another goal. Or, two different actions might each tend to increase the probability of achieving two different goals, but one action might increase the probability of goal A more than that of goal B, while the other action might tend in the converse direction. The resolution of such conflicts could be achieved by programming performance to represent a working toward several goals simultaneously, thus "killing two birds with one stone," or by providing for a performance in which one activated goal has priority over all simultaneously activated (potentially inimical) goals. These types of performance are already allowed for by some programs: the basic logical requirement is that potential actions be evaluated with respect to each goal currently active in the direction of performance. The act is then selected that has the highest overall weighted value. This selection is effected by a centralized decision-maker or executive control, functioning as the master program. One such program is the "chess player" written by the GPS programmers Newell, Simon, and Shaw. This program includes the goals of "king safety," "material balance," "center control," "development," "king-side attack," and "promotion." These goals (like instincts) are theoretically independent, in that one or more can be brought into play at any point in time. "Moves" are selected by the program according to the computed probability of their achieving these goals, and the goals may each be treated as equally important, or they may be differentially weighted. Thus, a moderate probability of achieving a heavily weighted goal will select a move in preference to a high probability of achieving a minimally weighted goal. In the chess program the weighting is typically different at different points in the game, just as one's strategical aims in the end-game differ from one's aims in the opening moves.[28] Similarly, instincts are variously pressing at different times, depending partly on immediate environmental circumstances, and partly on the state of satiation of the other instincts. Using this chess program as a model for representing instincts, one could represent the simultaneous satisfaction of two instincts as well as the overriding of one instinct by another more pressing one.

So far it has been assumed that only one action is performed at a time, and that this action is determined by a centralized decision process which has overall control of performance. The chess program makes only one move at a time. Moreover, its overall goal is always one and the same: to win the game. The subgoals, such as king safety, are all related as means to this end and totally subordinated to it: they have no power to initiate

225

activity unrelated to victory. But in instinctive behavior the situation is rather different, for the natural goals can be independently and spontaneously activated and, in the absence of any *master sentiment*, there need not be one overall goal controlling behavior. Furthermore, much normal—and still more abnormal—human behavior shows several functionally independent streams of activity running concurrently. One typically interprets an interlocutor's speech by means of sight and hearing simultaneously, and one can hold a conversation while "absent-mindedly" playing the piano. Such activity suggests that a form of parallel information-processing is going on.

In *parallel* processing, several independent units of information may be processed concurrently and several decisions taken simultaneously. In *serial (sequential)* processing, items of information are handled and decisions are made one by one, with the outcome of each step determining the next step. Computer programs are *realized* serially: they consist of series of instructions that are executed one by one by the machine. In this sense, then, current computers can do only one thing at a time. What is called "simultaneous processing" of independent programs on one computer is really achieved by subtle queuing techniques that enable the component steps of the various programs to be executed in the most economical order, given the data-processing and storage features of the computer concerned.[29] Many programs are also *conceptualized* serially: thus, the chess program was written to produce perfectly integrated and strictly ordered performance directed to one end, winning. Although the serial conceptualizing of programs does not prevent the programming of performance describable as "pursuing two goals simultaneously," it is not well suited to the representation of systems that can do several unrelated things at once. Still less is it suited to the malintegrated or *dissociated* behavior typical of psychopathology. As Newell himself has stated: "Sequential processing . . . encourages us to envision isolated processes devoted to specific functions, each passively waiting in turn to operate when its time comes. It permits us to think of the total program in terms of only one thing going on at a time."[30] The notion that pressing instinctual needs can be simulated by processes that "passively wait in turn to operate when their time comes" is not very plausible, nor is the

226

picture of the human organism as a system in whose behavior there is "only one thing going on at a time." Some form of parallel processing (or an approximation to it) would seem to be indicated for the simulation of instinctive behavior.

Parallel processing may be approximated by systems whose operation is basically sequential in form. Newell points out that sequential processing "encourages" one to think in the way he describes. Sequential processing does not necessitate this way of thinking, however, for some programs (though *realized* serially) are *conceptualized* as simulations of parallel-processing systems.[31] Examples are Pandemonium and Argus.[32] Pandemonium is a pattern-recognition program in which, as in the Newell chess program, "simultaneous" computation of several parameters is essential to centralized decision-making. But the several parameters have a greater degree of theoretical independence than the subgoals in the chess program. Pandemonium is so named because its authors describe its action in terms of the simultaneous shouting of several information-processing demons, each making its decisions independently of the others. Their shouts may vary in loudness according to each demon's judgment of the degree of probability of his message and his opinion of its importance. (If a man shouts "Fire!" at all, he is likely to shout it loudly, whether he is sure that there is a fire or not.) The central master demon makes his decision in the light of the combined shouting of his subordinates, and his decisions determine the performance of the system as a whole. Performance guided by programs of this type is potentially more variable than in the chess-playing case, for the goals, evaluations, and inputs of the various demons may differ greatly; and the master demon need have no *one* method of weighting their messages at all times, nor need his overall goal be closely related to the goal of every subordinate demon. There may be several types as well as layers of demons subordinate to the master. In a simulation of instinctive behavior (uncomplicated by sentiments) based on this type of program, each instinct would be represented primarily by one demon, and these "instinctive" demons would all be on the same level, immediately below the master demon, with lesser, sensory demons subordinated to them. Sometimes several instinctive demons could be satisfied by one and the same decision of the master, thus paralleling the "overdetermination" of behavior: for instance, if the hunger demon and the sex demon each recommended approaching a blonde who had been observed by the sensory demons to be picking apples. But if any two recommended decisions were in conflict, the louder of the two would be preferred by the master.

The possibility of spontaneous and "parallel" activity on the part of the demons, unrelated to any goal of the master demon, makes this type of program rather more suited to the simulation of instincts than is the "single-minded" chess-player (or GPS) of Newell, Simon, and Shaw. Sentiments could also be simulated on this basis, but the discussion so far has shown how instinctual conflicts may be resolved independently of the action of sentiments. The psychological processes involved are fairly primitive in type: McDougall called such cases "brute conflicts." If any one basic goal regularly has priority over the others in instinctual conflicts (being correspondingly weighted in the simulation) or if it is more easily brought into play in the first place, then the system will show an emotional disposition of a characteristic type.

To each instinct there must correspond, in McDougall's system, a primary emotion. In a simulation each primary emotion would be represented by an external sign as well as by an internal sign available to the master program or executive control. These would record the particular basic goal currently directing performance. The external sign would allow for anticipation of the machine's performance by an observer. Many of the characteristic expressions of emotion that have evolved in living animals are preparatory to the instinctive actions likely to follow, but in a simulation arbitrary signs or verbal symbols could perform the equivalent function. Clearly, the information provided by the internal sign would be necessary if the master program were to control the basic action-tendencies in any degree. For instance, if one of the action tendencies were to be inhibited or modified in certain circumstances, then the master program would need the information that the subprogram controlling that tendency was in action, or about to be. These signs would be similarly needed in the overall integration of performance. For instance, if several basic goals can be pursued at once, or if one goal-directed routine can be temporarily interrupted by another, then the master program may adjust ongoing performance in the light of various goal priorities, while keeping the overall goal-seeking pattern reasonably consistent. The record of the arousal of a certain tendency would be required if anticipatory action were needed to assist its operation: for example, if appropriate subprograms were to be prepared or selected in anticipation of possible clashes. The simulator could not decide to ignore McDougall's affective concepts without jeopardizing the attempt to achieve complex teleological control within the cybernetic system.

The derived emotions (such as confidence, hope, anxiety, and despair) also provide information about ongoing goal-seeking. However, they are concerned with the stage and estimated probability of success at a given moment, irrespective of the nature of the particular goal or subgoal involved. They are based on judgments of the nearness of success and the nature and number of obstacles. They influence behavior insofar as these judgments determine the redirection or abandonment of the problem. A simulation could make equivalent assessments, with consequent changes in overall problem-solving performance. For instance, the master program might predict that routine subprograms would be adequate to solve a particular problem and so pass direct control over to them; since none of the working memory would have to be devoted to the development of a new method of solution, a large part of it would be available for the simultaneous solution of other problems. Second, the master program might direct performance itself, continually referring to features of the final goal and adjusting performance accordingly, and predicting a high probability of success. Third, if a subproblem in the overall plan for solution proved difficult, the master program might direct all performance toward it; consequently, the overall solution might be blocked, owing to continual failure in the subsection. Last, failure to achieve a certain subgoal might lead to abandonment of the larger problem, with no attempt made to reach an alternative solution. Simulations with features such as these could represent the cognitive aspects of McDougall's concepts of confidence, hope, anxiety, and despair, respectively. These cognitive judgments influence the conative nature of activity, in that they direct attention, for instance, to the final goal or to more immediate subgoals; thus, the derived emotions, though primarily cognitive, have a conative aspect also. Further, they have a characteristic affective tone by virtue of the internal signs of ongoing activity that are utilized in the feedback necessary to efficient control. In sum, such concepts are essentially purposive, since they mark detailed structural features of ongoing goal-seeking.

The organism's characteristic way of goal-seeking in general is marked by the concept of temper, which has three independent dimensions: intensity, persistence, and affectability. The intensity of temper is the strength or urgency of the instincts, and all the instincts may be strong or all weak. Once an instinct of high intensity has been aroused, immediate satisfaction is attempted, and behavior is forceful and energetic. In a simulation of high intensity, problems could not readily be put into a queue nor could problem-solving be long delayed. The successive solution of two problems would be more common than their solution over the same period of time. In these respects the urgency of high intensity would be represented; and its forcefulness might be partly reflected by a high speed of operation and the availability of the "reserve" resources for relatively many problems. High intensity may or may not be coupled with high persistence; simulation of degrees of persistence would involve differential availability of stop rules, given difficulties in goal achievement, and a varying degree of return to unsolved problems in the light of new information. Affectability is described by McDougall in largely subjective terms, as the effect of pleasure and pain on the derived emotions. In behavioral terms, it is the extent to which success or failure in achieving subgoals affects the predictions of final goal-achievement. A man of high affectability is greatly encouraged or discouraged by trivial successes or failures, so that his predictions of overall success are excessively dependent on the outcome of the current subproblem, as opposed to the overall nature of the problem. He may abandon a problem soon if initial failures cause the predicted probability of success to be so low as to make further effort seem pointless; or he may continue his efforts for a long time if he achieves subgoals fairly regularly. Thus, affectability is independent of persistence, which relates the abandonment of a problem to the time already spent

230

on it and to a particular level of estimated probability of success. In a simulation, the availability of stop rules governed by these two criteria could be independent of the effect of current success or failure on the prediction of overall success. The similarity of the concepts of temper and derived emotions is based predominantly in the dimension of affectability.

The behavioral aspect of temperamental features, such as fatigability or expressiveness, might be reflected by limitations on power supply or memory, and by the extent to which internal symbolic activity was indicated by observable features of performance. But McDougall's concept of temperament also included a causal (hormonal) aspect. Clearly, the causal factors underlying "temperamental" performance in an electronic simulation would be very different in kind, and only their general (behavioral) effects would be closely comparable.

In a simulation of tastes, operations that successfully achieve a basic goal would tend to be repeated. This general principle has already been incorporated into many "learning" programs, such as the Uhr & Vossler program. But in order to distinguish the development of tastes from all other learning dependent on success, the simulation would have to include some parallel of the sentiment of self-regard. Exercises in this type of successful activity or problem-solving would often be carried out not under the direct control of any basic goal, but under the direction of the equivalent of the self-regarding sentiment. A high success rate, or increase in skill—regardless of whether the specific problems dealt with were directly relevant to the satisfaction of a basic goal—would in itself be reinforcing, through the mediation of this sentiment.

The simulation of sentiments would require that, out of all those objects (inputs) which are capable in principle of triggering action directed by the basic goals, a few were in fact more regularly and more strongly associated with such actions than others. Moreover, the fact of this greater association would have to be represented somehow in the simulation. These objects would form a subclass of the class of objects initially capable of triggering action, and the subclass would develop according to the input history. The members of this subclass would comprise the core objects of the developing sentiments. In order that the senti-

231

ments should be able to control performance related to instinc-tively "neutral" objects (which would otherwise elicit no response at all), the core objects must become cognitively linked with others in the memory store. Some of these linkages would be purely associative; others would depend on linguistic categoriza-tion. By virtue of these linkages, the action tendencies of the sentiments concerning the core object in question could be gen-eralized to the linked objects also.

For example, in a simulation of love (the component action-tendencies having become strongly attached to a particular per-son), the "loving" action tendencies may be transferred to that person's dog. This could be based on a mere associative link between the core object Mary and the object Fido; but the trans-ference would be encouraged if there were also some representa-tion of the positive affective relation between Mary and Fido, such as "Mary is fond of Fido," or "Mary/ + + /Fido." The "bal-ance theorists," working in the general area of cognitive disso-nance, investigate behavioral changes that may often be of this nature, involving the transference of attitudes from one object to another.[33] Supposing the system to have been initially neutral toward dogs, it would now have developed a specific action ten-dency in relation to at least one dog. Furthermore, if the input dog were one of those that initially would have triggered "with-drawal" and "fear," then these reactions could be inhibited or overcome by the strong approach-tendency involved in the senti-ment of love. Thus, the simulation's reaction to Fido would be controlled by this sentiment rather than by any basic goal directly. This system provides for a more subtle resolution (and generation) of purposive conflicts than a system that depends on the weighting of each given instinct in general. A man may stroke a dog because he is always—or temporarily—disposed to do so; he may have a kindly disposition toward living creatures, or he may be in a generally benevolent mood at the time. Both of these cases could be represented in the more primitive simulation that relies on the differential weighting of instincts. But the simulation of sentiments would also allow for the representation of a man's stroking Fido, and no other dog, on the basis of his love for Fido's owner, Mary. In this case, the man's "natural" instinctive reactions to dogs are less important than the instincts comprising the sentiment with whose core object Fido happens to be linked.

Most sentiments involve several action tendencies (and emotions) blended together in varying ways. McDougall regarded love and hate as typical sentiments, remarking: "the sentiments of love and hate comprise many of the same emotional dispositions; but the situations of the object of the sentiment that evoke the same emotions are very different and in the main of oppositive character in the two cases."[34] Thus, a simulation of a man's sentiment for a friend or an enemy would require a cognitive representation of their situation: if either were to slip on a banana skin, the component action tendencies would be differentially elicited as a result of that information. In general, the cognitive representations at the core of the sentiment will crucially affect the operation of the component action tendencies. These representations will develop according to input history, and varying associative contexts or linguistic categorizations of the core objects will affect performance connected with other related objects. Relabeling of subroutines will make them available at different points in the master program, or even withdraw them from its control entirely. Such shifting relations between the objects represented in the machine could be quite readily simulated by means of a list-processing language. In spite of the limitations of "property-list" approaches to the simulation of cognitive modeling, the techniques of simulation are relatively well suited to represent the complex cognitive aspects of the sentiments.

The noncognitive aspects of the sentiments (the blended action tendencies and complex emotions) would themselves be most conveniently modeled "cognitively" with the help of verbal expressions typical of the conative and affective features concerned. This is because much human thought, experience, and behavior is linguistic in form, and could only be nonverbally expressed (if at all) by a supreme master of the art of mime. Consequently, although the basic action tendencies such as "approach" and "avoidance" would be involved in the simulation, though not necessarily mimicked by it, a mere listing of the action tendencies contributing to a particular sentiment would not serve to distinguish it from other sentiments of a similar conative nature. For instance, the two types of reverence discussed above involve the same four action tendencies and primary emotions; each is the complex emotional aspect of an underlying religious sentiment. But only one is built up by means of the binary component of gratitude. This is the personal form of reverence, the form that is especially appropriate to the worship of personal beings and less appropriate to the contemplation of impersonal objects. In a simulation, given that an object excited "negative self-feeling" and "tender emotion" simultaneously, verbal expressions typical of gratitude would result if, and only if, the object were classified as personal, or animate. But the simultaneous excitement of negative self-feeling and wonder would give rise to verbal expressions of "admiration" in either case, for admiration is a component of both types of reverence. The strength of the various primaries could be reflected by somewhat different expressions, for instance: "I am wary of it," "I fear it," "I am terrified of it." By these means the simulator could distinguish between the emotion of reverence into which negative self-feeling enters twice, from awe and from gratitude, and reverence into which it enters once but very strongly, as in the impersonal type of reverence that is very close to humility. Some complex emotions can arise only in connection with an object that is already the core of a sentiment. Analogously, in a simulation certain expressions could only occur when others had previously been elicited by the same object. For instance, the reproach "Oh! How could you!"—in contrast with the expletive "Damn you!"—would require that the object concerned had previously elicited "I love you."

Of course, any such simulation, limited to the use of predetermined verbal strings, would appear extremely crude in comparison with the wealth of expressions used spontaneously in everyday life to express the subtle distinctions between the various sentiments and emotions. It could not generate Newton's reputed reproach to his pet dog, who had destroyed some of his working papers, "Oh! Diamond, Diamond, thou little knowest the damage thou hast done!" And it could certainly be no more refined than the most satisfactory psychological or philosophical analyses of the concepts entering into the familiar verbal expressions borrowed by it, and of their logical and psychological interrelations. Reliance on McDougall's comments on such matters could provide some useful leads, for many of his remarks reflected an illuminating psychological understanding. But his understanding was largely "intuitive," and his reasoning implicit. He did not provide, nor did he attempt, a systematic and detailed analysis of all the concepts of everyday psychological language. However, a simulation—or a psychological theory—may indicate the general structure of behavior, even if it is inadequate to represent it in every detail.

McDougall claimed that his theory of sentiments and character "made possible the first intelligible account of the process of volition and moral choice and of its relation to the lower forms of action, and brought into the field of psychology a host of profoundly interesting problems which the traditional division of labour had up to that time left to the tender mercies of the moral philosophers."[35] So far, the concepts of "volition," "morals," and "character" have not entered the discussion. On the basis of the purposive concepts we have already considered, we can explain why a frightened man gets rid of a burglar so as to protect his material possessions. But we cannot explain why he freely chooses to risk fighting the intruder, even though he values no material object in his house and is sorely tempted to remain cringing upstairs. These matters can only be understood in the context of "the hierarchic organization of the sentiments in one integrated system," which completed McDougall's analysis of the structure of the mind. According to his view of mental structure, all behavior that is specifically human is influenced by the integrative master sentiment of self-regard.

VII Purpose and Self

An organism exhibiting purposive activities of various sorts at different times may appear to live from moment to moment, to be constantly at the mercy of the world. In other words, the selection of the goal that is to direct its behavior may always be primarily dependent on the particular environmental situation in which it finds itself at the time. But a creature capable of varied purposive activities may show a degree of overall teleological consistency, in that much of its behavior appears to depend on enduring purposes of its own that are largely independent of environmental changes. Such a creature requires mechanisms for the integration of its activities and the allocation of priorities to its various purposes. The sentiments themselves are such mechanisms, but conflicts are possible between sentiments. If these conflicts are to be fruitfully overcome, there must be a higher-level integrative mechanism at work. This integrative mechanism will affect the behavior of the organism as a whole and partially determine its most comprehensive psychological characteristics, the general structure of its mind.

The degree of teleological consistency achieved in human behavior is normally very great. Admittedly, changing environments, fleeting moods, and alterations in a man's values or beliefs do impair the overall purposive uniformity of his behavior. In rare cases such impairment is so extreme as to suggest that different personalities alternate in commanding one physical body, like "Dr. Jekyll" and "Mr. Hyde." But a normal human individual behaves in so teleologically consistent a fashion that a powerful integrative mechanism must be postulated to explain this overall psychological unity.

McDougall represented the human mind as the organization of the sentiments, which are interrelated and hierarchically integrated by way of a master sentiment, typically the sentiment of self-regard. The account of the growth and function of the self-regarding sentiment forms the focus of McDougall's personality theory. In particular, he held it (and its metaphysical equivalent, the doctrine of monads) to encompass two "opposing" views of the personality, neither of which seems to be expendable: the

236

personality acts as a unitary agent, yet is built up by a gradual integrative process. It is by virtue of this sentiment that the normal personality may be called a "unity," and that purpose, direction, freedom, and moral control may be ascribed to the "self." Abnormal functioning of the sentiment of self-regard, associated with abnormalities in the hierarchical structure of the mind, is characteristic of many of the phenomena encountered by psychiatrists, such as split personality, dissociations, automatisms, and fugues.

This theoretical construct representing the structure of the human mind was assumed by McDougall to be totally incompatible with any mechanistic explanation of personality. However, it may be interpreted by the reductionist as a self-regulatory system guided by an internal model of itself. Even the doctrine of monads, metaphysical though it appears, may usefully be interpreted in cybernetic terms as referring to multifarious purposive units within one integrated teleological system. The unity of personal behavior and of consciousness that typify human individuals can thus be given a basically mechanistic explanation.

The Sentiment of Self-Regard

The integration of the sentiments develops gradually, and it may be more or less complete. The higher animals are capable of developing rudimentary sentiments, units of organization of their behavior that reflect a certain consistency in the goals they follow, such as a dog's "love" for his master. But their behavior often exhibits a "brute conflict" of the sentiments owing to the lack of any further integration of their activities. McDougall pointed out that these units must be organized at a higher level if the behavior is to be of the complexity and steadfastness of purpose typical of human behavior, and if personality concepts, such as character, freedom, and morality, are to be applied in their fullest sense:

> The mere possession of an array of sentiments and tastes, though it gives a certain consistency to conduct, does not constitute character. Character is achieved by a further step of organization, organization of a higher level which integrates

237

the sentiments and tastes into one system. So long as this higher level of organization is not achieved, the various sentiments may enter into brute conflict with one another, with resulting inefficiency of action, waste of energy, confusion of methods and wavering of purposes. It is only the attainment of such higher level of organization that renders a man capable of volition or exercise of willpower in the full sense of the words.[1]

The simplest form of integration involves the development of one sentiment to such a strength and range of influence that it easily overrules the promptings of all other sentiments and all momentary impulses. One example of such a master sentiment would be a widow's single-minded love for her only child; others include an overpowering love of money or country, political obsessions for causes such as "prohibition," and the collector's passion for first editions or beetles. But the most powerful example is the master sentiment of self-regard.

McDougall regarded this master sentiment as the most powerful one because it is centered on the idea of the self, that is, on "an object perpetually present, one from which it is impossible to be separated, one which is inevitably brought to mind in all situations, especially all situations that call for choice of goals and decision as regards means to the chosen goal."[2] The directive power of this "self-as-object" in the activity of the individual is so great that it gives to conduct a consistency greater than any other sentiment can ensure, and McDougall saw it as an essential reference-point in all specifically human behavior.

The sentiment of self-regard is centered about, and develops in conjunction with, the idea of the self. McDougall first described this development, and the normal functioning of the self-regarding sentiment, in 1908 in *An Introduction to Social Psychology*. There he wrote that the child's first idea of the self is of a bodily self, distinguished from external objects, based on the criterion of whether or not things resist his efforts at movement. At first, all inanimate objects are conceived on the pattern of persons, being perceived in physiognomic terms and experienced as potential centers of action. It is only later that the child learns to distinguish animate objects, including other selves, from

238

physical things. The constant interaction between him and these other selves suggests to him the limits of his capacities and of his autonomy, and the full development of self-consciousness is essentially a social process: "The child's idea of his self early comes to be the idea, not merely of his body and of certain bodily and mental capacities, but also of a system of relations between his self and other selves."[3] The cognitive core of the sentiment of self-regard is the idea of the self conceived of as a center of effort, as a purposive system capable of pursuing certain ends. It is essential to the normal self-regulatory function of the sentiment that the self be conceived of in this way, rather than as a passive object having no teleological potential nor any purposive autonomy.

Conatively, the master sentiment draws mainly on two instincts, self-display and self-subjection, and it may involve both positive and negative self-feeling. Its two chief varieties are pride and self-respect, but other distinctive types of self-regard include self-esteem, self-love, vanity, and ambition. The conative composition and mode of working of the self-regarding sentiment is the prime determinant of personal qualities such as selfishness, egotism, conceit, humility, megalomania, bumptiousness, pushfulness, masterfulness, and aggressiveness. Vivid emotional experiences associated with the working of the sentiment act for the agent as reminders or anticipatory signals of the conative impulses excited, or likely to be excited, in him. These affective indicators of the instinctive impulses involved come to be cognitively associated with differential probabilities that a given instinct will be encouraged, tolerated, or discouraged by the particular social community that the man has experienced. Praise and blame can therefore act as effective social sanctions by way of the self-regarding sentiment, and such sanctions may be internalized as moral conscience.

The conceptual structure of McDougall's account of the development of conscience is similar to that of comparable accounts in seventeenth and eighteenth century moral philosophy. These accounts distinguished the motives of "approbativeness," "self-esteem," and "emulation," and compared their relevance to the growth of specifically moral conduct.[4] McDougall expressed these "common sense" insights into the nature of man in terms of his own theoretical vocabulary. He saw the growth of morality in the child as a gradual progress, in which he distinguished four successive stages. At first, the infant's instinctive behavior is modified only by the pains and pleasures that happen to result from his activities. Next, the rewards and punishments systematically administered according to the conventions of his social environment come to have importance in shaping the child's behavior. Later, the child's anticipation of praise and blame from his fellows assumes the main regulatory role. And finally, his behavior comes to be governed by a self-regulatory ideal of conduct, which he pursues irrespective of the sanctions meted out by his immediate social environment.

Such a psychological genealogy of conscience provides a rationale for distinguishing truly "moral" behavior from socially convenient but basically amoral action. A burnt child may shun the fire, but this is a pragmatic rather than a moral rule. Actions of cautious arson on the child's part can only be prevented by providing the information that other selves will tend to frustrate the instinct of self-display if the child starts a fire that actually causes no physical harm to his own person. In special circumstances (such as riots) these social sanctions may be lifted; arson may then proceed unchecked, if the arsonist is not himself harmed by the fire and has not progressed beyond the third stage of morality. Eventually the child comes to apply moral sanctions to his own behavior, regulating his actions by means of his self-respect independently of other people's opinions. For this highest stage of morality it is essential that there be a strong self-regarding sentiment, for the type of conation (volition) characteristic of this stage can only be effective by drawing upon the strong impulses associated with the man's idea (or ideal) of his self. McDougall saw that a moral rule (as opposed to a superstition, a pragmatic rule, or a habit) is a general principle essentially concerned with abstract qualities of conduct. Examples of such qualities include bravery, patience, honesty, and justice; cowardice, meanness, ruthlessness, and fickleness; frankness, impulsiveness, boisterousness, and caution. It is probably fair to say that McDougall typified his sociocultural group in regarding these three lists of personal qualities as respectively morally commendable, morally undesirable, and morally neutral. Clearly,

240

other individuals and other societies may regard these specific qualities of conduct in different ways, either holding moral views opposed to McDougall's or seeing what he would have called "morally relevant" as morally neutral and vice versa. It is important to stress the point that potentially moral qualities must be abstract in character, that (as McDougall claimed) the specifically moral sentiments include such items as the love for justice—but not the concrete sentiment of love for a particular individual. In other words, moral rules are in principle universalizable to all men in comparable circumstances, although sentiments for concrete objects (such as home or family) may sometimes override morality and lead one to make exceptions in particular cases.[5] A frightened man may decide to leave his bed and confront the burglar because of his internalized contempt for cowardice, or because he does not wish to be thought a coward by his wife. In each case his decision is mediated by the self-regarding sentiment, but only the former involves a truly moral element.

Insofar as existentialism recommends action that is independent of universally (and thus impersonally) applied rules, it is antithetical to morality in this sense. But existentialist psychiatrists can and do distinguish between behavior which is self-directed and that which is not. Moreover, they emphasize the difference between principles of action that are internalized with or without serious examination, with or without conscious reference to the primary purposes of the particular individual concerned. If a man's moral attitude toward cowardice was uncritically accepted from his social group, and is never examined by him in light of the specific circumstances of action, his wife may be irritated by his unself-conscious "role-playing" in relation to the burglar even if she is totally ignorant of existentialist philosophy.

The internalization of moral rules is only one mechanism of socialization. Another is the establishment of what McDougall called "quasi-altruistic extensions" of the egoistic sentiment, whereby "the growing child is led on ... to identify himself with, and to extend his self-regarding sentiment to, his school, his college, his town, his profession as a class or collective unit, and finally to his country or his nation as a whole."[6] These extensions can only take place provided that the object in question has relations to other, similar objects, which are analogous to the

241

relations between persons, so that the specifically personal emotions are excited in connection with it and the appropriate
instincts can be fulfilled by way of it. Or more accurately, the
intensional object must be thought of by the man himself as
having such relations. Groups of various sorts are commonly
thought of in this way, and group sentiments are readily developed by extension of the self-regarding sentiment. In this
fashion, purposes such as patriotism or philanthropy, which are
not directed toward natural goals, can become purposes that it is
natural for many men to pursue. These quasi-altruistic purposes
may even come to take precedence over goals more directly
linked with the instincts, such as avoiding danger or finding a
suitable mate.

Many extensions of the sentiment of self-regard do not involve
altruistic purposes and are not even centered on persons or
social institutions. Thus, the mere association of an object with
another already connected with the sentiment of self-regard may
affect the behavior concerned with it. Many men take pride in
their clothes, house, garden, or car much as they take pride in
their own personal qualities, and a man may nostalgically preserve a disused shed because of its associations with the past
activities of his childhood gang. Further extensions may be
brought about by the simple means of naming, whereby several
objects are categorized by a man under one and the same concept, one which is already associated with the self-regarding sentiment. Thereafter, the man's behavior with reference to these
objects will be different—and since the sentiments are seen as
continually developing, varying categorization may include an
object at one time and not at another. Extensions mediated by
naming may or may not involve the development of altruistic
modes of behavior.

McDougall's theory provides for the important distinction
between self-image and ideal self-image, a distinction that is
centrally involved in the autonomous direction of much of
human behavior.[7] The incorporation of moral rules in the self-
regarding sentiment establishes a quasi-altruistic extension of
this sentiment to qualities of conduct that are ideals governing
a man's behavior, ideals which are not necessarily (or usually)
achieved in every particular. The self typically develops toward

242

those ideals, but falls short of them to some extent since perfect integration is never achieved—thus, McDougall was led to the statement, "What is called a self is always an ideal rather than an accomplished fact, an ideal that is in various degrees approximated but never attained."[8]

McDougall always insisted that conscious purposes must be allowed for in the explanation of behavior, even though the basic motivation is instinctive. The more closely involved with the self the goal is, the more absurd he felt it to be to try to explain behavior in mechanistic terms making no reference to any psychological subject. Moreover, conscious purposes often involve risk and difficulty; homeostatic ("equilibrium" and "drive-reduction") explanations are inadequate to explain behavior such as Amundsen's, whom McDougall quoted in illustration: "I irretrievably decided to be an arctic explorer . . . My career has been a steady progress toward a definite goal since I was fifteen years old. Whatever I have accomplished in exploration has been the result of lifelong planning, painstaking preparation, and the hardest kind of conscientious work."[9] Consciousness is important in that it fixates goals for the organism, establishing clear and stable representations for use as standards in problem-solving; and an individual's actions are largely dependent on his ideas and ideals of himself and the world. McDougall held conscious purposes to be crucial to moral action or volition: "The essential and immediate effect of all volition is the maintenance of a presentation at the focus of consciousness."[10]

McDougall's fullest discussion of volition occupied an entire chapter of *An Introduction to Social Psychology*. His views on the nature and development of volition, and its importance for moral control and for character, were to remain basically unaltered thereafter. He tried to find a psychological account of volition that would explain "action against the strongest desire" (in which a weaker, more ideal motive prevails over a coarser, more primitive one) without appealing to any special force or faculty, such as "the will."

Volition was not to be regarded as *sui generis* but as a specially complex case of conation, made possible by the systematic organization of the innate and acquired dispositions; no sharp line can be drawn between volitions and conations of other types.

243

After discussing various types of conation, McDougall continued:

> The essential mark of volition—that which distinguishes it from
> simple desire, or simple conflict of desires—is that the person-
> ality as a whole, or the central feature or nucleus of the
> personality, the man himself ... is thrown upon the side of the
> weaker motive ... In the typical case of volition a man's self,
> in some peculiarly intimate sense of the word "self," is thrown
> upon the side of the motive that is made to prevail. The
> empirical self, the idea of his self that each man entertains,
> plays an essential part in volition.[11]

This passage shows the centrality of the self-image in the exercise of volition. But it is the instincts (primarily those of display
and submission) associated with the idea of the self that basically
energize conduct:

> No mere idea has a motive power that can for a moment with-
> stand the force of strong desire ... and the idea of the self is
> no exception to this rule. The idea of the self, or self-conscious-
> ness, is able to play its great role in volition only in virtue of
> the self-regarding sentiment, the system of emotional and con-
> ative dispositions that is organized about the idea of the self
> and is always brought into play to some extent when the idea
> of the self rises to the focus of consciousness ... We may, then,
> define volition as *the supporting or reinforcing of a desire or
> conation by the co-operation of an impulse excited within the
> system of the self-regarding sentiment.*[12]

Because the growth of the self-regarding sentiment is a gradual
process, there is no sharp line between volitions and other complex conations, and McDougall described various stages in the
development of self-control and morality that follow on the
growth of this sentiment. Volition allows for a high degree of
behavioral autonomy: "The development of self-consciousness
and of the self-regarding sentiment renders the behavior of the
individual progressively less dependent upon his environment; it
involves ... an approximation towards complete self-determination, towards conduct that is the issue of conditions wholly comprised within the constitution of the mind. [It] involves also a

244

progress from predominantly mechanical to predominantly tele-ological determination."[13]

McDougall regarded volition as the expression of a man's freedom, but it has already been noted that he rejected extreme (indeterministic) libertarianism as being neither scientifically nor morally acceptable. He described free action not as *un*determined action, but as action which is *self*-determined. And according to him, horme has the creative power of setting goals independently of past conditions. Thus, even though hormic action is never random, it is impossible *in principle* to predict it in all its details; the unpredictable—and yet also unrandom—action of horme underlies all self-determined behavior, and accounts for its autonomy.

If one rejects McDougall's hormic hypothesis and its associated limitation on predictability in principle, there may nonetheless be a use for his criterion of self-determination as the basis of "freedom" and moral responsibility. It is characteristic of "voluntary" behavior in McDougall's theory that it is not only relatively free from control by the immediate environment, but is closely dependent on the factors of self and of moral self-ideal. Since the precise nature of the self-regarding sentiment is unique to each individual, actions referred to it are predictable only from a knowledge of that individual, in particular from a knowledge of his idea and ideal of his self, not from knowledge of universal generalizations alone. In this sense, specifically human behavior is *idiographic* rather than *nomothetic*, even though there is no assumption of a basic indeterminacy.[14] Behavior under the direct control of the instincts is nomothetic, since it is predictable in terms of general laws, quite independently of any reference to the particular self or self-ideal of the person. But self-determined behavior is idiographic, since its prediction requires detailed knowledge of the given individual, in particular of his specific unifying vision of his self as he is and as he aspires to be. In this sense idiographic prediction concerns "the whole individual person," while nomothetic prediction does not.

The idiographic-nomothetic distinction is related to, but by no means parallel with, McDougall's distinction between those purposes of which a man is conscious and those of which he is not. For he held that while all behavior which is self-governed (idiographic) involves conscious purpose, not all purposes of which a man is conscious can be properly termed purposes of the self. Goal-seeking that is independent of the self (whether conscious or not) differs from behavior that is directed by the self, for only the latter may be influenced by all the complex cognitive and conative systems comprising the self-regarding sentiment. "One and the same" conscious purpose may therefore determine behavior in a very different manner according to whether it is or is not truly a purpose of the self. One's attempt to win a tennis match or to secure the offer of a particular job may be markedly different if one's self-respect requires that the goal in question be achieved.

The distinction between behavior that is, and behavior that is not, under the control of the self—and the relative autonomy or "freedom" of the former—would require a parallel in any program designed to represent McDougall's personality theory. His conceptualization of these specifically human features stressed the sentiment of self-regard. The core of the self-regarding sentiment is the idea, or internal representation, of the self as a purposive system capable of pursuing certain ends. Any simulation of this sentiment must have a master program that constantly refers to such an overall plan of the total activity of the simulation. Indeed, two such plans are required, to represent "actual self-image" and "self-ideal" respectively. At this point, M. L. Minsky's discussion of the importance of "models" within information-processing systems is relevant. Minsky points out that within the internal model of the world which an information-processing system (machine or man) may possess, there may be included a representation of the system itself. And this model of itself may include a representation of the fact that it has a representation of itself. Minsky regards this level of representation as necessary if the system is to answer general questions about itself.[15] Such questions include, "What sort of thing am I?" and "What sort of thing am I aiming to become?" Questions such as these are intimately connected with the "idea" and "ideals" of the "self," as described by McDougall. Less general questions are also closely connected with the idea of the self, such as, "Am I unselfish?" and "Am I intelligent?" Such inquiries can be dealt with at the first level of self-representation. Minsky does not claim that there is a clear distinction between questions answerable at the first level, and questions answerable only at the second; nor is it necessary to do so. The important point is that the over-all plan of a cybernetic system's activity available to the master program (or the self-idea available to the man) may be complex enough to be useful for very sophisticated self-evaluatory and self-regulatory behavior. The purposes or goals most intimately connected with this plan (particularly those crucial to the self-ideal) will be especially influential in performance.

According to McDougall, these purposes draw basically on the energy associated with the two self-regarding instincts. Goals associated with a strong self-system take precedence over other goals, even over instinctive (natural) goals, provided these are not represented in the idea of the self—as sexual behavior was for Don Juan. In a simulation, the basic goals corresponding to "display" and "submission" could be achieved in varying degrees by implementation of the overall plan of activity supposed available to the master program; and they could overrule other basic action tendencies momentarily excited by the environmental input. In general, subprograms could be controlled by the master program according to their representation in the central plan. Various sentiments would be modeled in this plan, but all subordinated in some degree to the self-regarding sentiment.

If the development of the master sentiment were to be simulated, provision would have to be made for this internal model of the activity-as-a-whole to be altered in the light of environmental influences (and ideally, to be built up by the simulation itself rather than initially written into its master program by the simulator). A simulation of social (rather than natural) sanctions would require that a specific input consequent upon activity would not inhibit future activity of that type directly (that is, at the level of the subprogram specifying the activity), but would lead to the inclusion of a new rule in the master program, deleting that activity from the general purposes to be pursued by the simulation. This rule could itself be deleted at a later date, and the activity could then take place, and might even come to be "preferred" owing to a later internalization of opposite sense. A simulation of moral control would require that the initial priorities of basic goals or operations be altered. For instance, the

247

master program could come to include the rule: do not use operation X until all other operations have been tried. But for this to represent a moral rule rather than a superstition, it would have to be rationally linked with other elements in the program in certain ways, with different sorts of linkage representing different sorts (or stages) of morality. For instance, it should be directed toward abstract qualities of performance rather than to specific individuals, and so would be general in its application; it should be scaled for priority relative to other similar rules; it should eventually be linked with the idea of the self and draw on the instincts contributing to the self-regarding sentiment; and it should be based on social or conventional, rather than natural, sanctions.

The Dissociation of Personality

The class of simulations just outlined could include particular instances differing in many ways. One important aspect that could vary is the degree of integration (conversely, of dissociation) of the purposes represented in the system. An organism capable of purposive activities of several sorts is in principle open to conflicts between purposes, for action that is a means to one end may be incompatible with action that is a means to another end, even though both ends may be goals of the organism concerned. The extent to which such conflicts are fruitfully overcome is a measure of the integrative power of the dominant purposive unit (or units) in the system. McDougall pointed out that integration is a matter of degree; ideally, "all the principal sentiments support one another in a succession of actions all of which tend towards the same or closely allied and harmonious ends."[16] Such harmony he regarded as typical of the firm, strong character, one which is well-knit by means of the one master sentiment of self-regard. There may, however, be two master sentiments of divergent tendencies (such as love of learning and love of wealth); and if the inevitable conflict is not resolved at a higher level, the resultant malintegrated behavior may be described in terms of the division of the purposive hierarchy, or the dissociation of personality.

The concept of dissociation (and the associated metaphysical concepts of monad and soul) played a crucial role in McDougall's account of pathological behavior. Such behavior was only briefly touched on in the early statements of his personality theory, and the monadic theory of dissociation did not appear in *An Intro- duction to Social Psychology*. But in 1926 McDougall discussed these matters at length in *An Outline of Abnormal Psychology*. This book was based largely on his experiences as a medical officer in the Great War, and it offered explanations in mental (purposive) rather than physical terms. For instance, manic depression was attributed not to physiological causes but to alternate domination of the sentiment of self-regard by the self-assertive and submissive instincts respectively. The initial upsetting of the normal balance of these two impulses may be attributable to unusual external circumstances, to hormonic imbalance, or to dissociation; but McDougall held that in every case the syndrome is more fruitfully thought of in functional than in physiological terms.[17] This psychosomatic approach in- formed McDougall's treatment of the clinical cases he met dur- ing the war. Thus, most of the paralyses, anesthesias, and amne- sias of "shell-shock" were described as functional disorders similar to the "hysterical" phenomena investigated by Charcot in the nineteenth century. Functional paralyses do not follow genuine anatomical boundaries, but rather the layman patient's ideas of such boundaries; they therefore require psychological explana- tion, in terms of the patient's concepts or beliefs. McDougall regarded them as based in a dissociation of the personality whereby the patient defends himself against trauma. In the final chapters McDougall developed his personality theory, endorsing the Leibnizian approach at which he had hinted in *Body and Mind* and which he had outlined in his presidential address to the Society for Psychical Research in 1920.

McDougall defined the personality (or soul) as a community of monads, linked together in a hierarchical organization, whose disruption accounts for pathological phenomena of various sorts. Each monad is a dynamic conative unit, and may be regarded as a psychic individual: "A monad is an ultimate reality, a being that exists and is active in its own right...potentially at least, a thinking striving self, endowed with the faculty or power of true memory; different monads are of very different degrees of development: some, being relatively undeveloped, exercise the powers common to all in a relatively simple and rudimentary fashion; others, being highly developed, exercise the same powers in a developed fashion." The normal human personality is an integrated system of monads, in the form of a converging hierarchy, and "at the head of the hierarchy is the supreme monad which each of us calls 'myself.' "[18] The uniqueness of personality results from the infinite possibilities of organization among the monads, and its unity (which may develop only gradually) results from the subordination of all other monads to the chief monad. McDougall regarded the *general* purposes of the personality as the purposes of the chief monad; the details of action are determined by the subordinate monads, whose *specific* purposes are not necessarily, or usually, represented in the chief monad.

Division or dissociation of the personality will result to the extent that the monads act independently of one another, and since integration admits of degrees, so also does dissociation. Even under normal conditions, different purposes may be pursued simultaneously and relatively independently: one may be wholly occupied with other thoughts while walking to work, or one may converse while playing the piano. McDougall regarded such activity as produced by the simultaneous influence of several monads, and as incapable of explanation by wholly mechanical principles.[19] Every case of purposive activity not consciously willed by the self was seen by McDougall as directed by a subordinate personality and as evidence of a certain degree of dissociation. The dissociation is least in cases such as these, where the self would immediately acknowledge the actions as intended, and would be capable of consciously directing them (though the detailed movements could not usually be consciously willed). It is greater in dreaming, which seems to be independent of will, and greater still in simple anesthesias, functional paralyses, hypnosis, and those cases described by Freud where purposive tendencies may express themselves for years without ever being acknowledged by the conscious mind or deliberately accepted by the self. Still greater dissociation is evidenced by the phenomena of multiple personality, with alternating—and sometimes coconscious—personalities directing the body's activities. But even the normal personality was represented by McDougall as a colony of monads:

> I who consciously address you am only one among several selves or Egos which my organism, my person, comprises. I am only the dominant member of a society, an association, of similar members. There are many purposive activities within my organism of which I am not aware, which are not my activities but those of my associates. I am conscious at any moment only of those processes within the organism, and of those impressions from without, which it is most necessary that I should take cognizance of ... My subordinates serve me faithfully in the main, provided always that I continue to be resolute and strong ... But, if I am weak and irresolute, if I do not face the problems of life and take the necessary decisions for dealing with them, then conflict arises within the system, one or more of my subordinates gets out of hand, I lose my control, and division of the personality into conflicting systems replaces the normal and harmonious cooperation of all members in one system. And in extreme cases such a revolted subordinate, escaped from the control of the dominant member or monad, may continue his career of insubordination indefinitely, acquiring increased influence over other members of the society and becoming a serious rival to the normal ruler or dominant.[20]

In choosing to mark his theoretical concepts by terms taken from Leibniz's metaphysics, McDougall characteristically invited resistance from those more tough-minded than himself. His picture of the personality as a colony formed of many psychological individuals or selves could hardly be taken literally, and it retained a paradoxical air even when regarded as mere metaphor. But McDougall's monadology was not completely fanciful, for it marked structural features of the complex purposive hierarchies evident in normal and abnormal human behavior. These features would require representation in the simulation of personality, and the monadic theory may be restated in programming terms.

The monads are the conative or purposive units that make up the overall purposive hierarchy of the personality, and their interrelationships are comparable with the relations of those units. Some monads correspond to transitory purposes, such as brushing a fly from one's nose, others to the recurring and long-term purposes of the sentiments; some correspond to the unconscious purposes described by Freud, others to purposes under the conscious control of the self. They are dynamic organizing principles (subprograms, plans), subordinated in various degrees to the chief monad, which corresponds to the master sentiment of self-regard (master program, metaplan). The chief monad may be ignorant of the detailed purposes of his subordinates; similarly, a master program may merely name subroutines under its direction, the details being independently programmed and inaccessible to alteration by the master program, and failure of a given subroutine may or may not divert the overall process to a detailed examination of that routine. Malintegration of subroutines may lead to "loops" pursuing goals other than the final goal of the master program, which would be equivalent to a dissociation of personality, and the various degrees of dissociation might be represented in different simulations.

Parallel processing would be particularly appropriate if two or more purposes were to be pursued independently, as when one does mental arithmetic while walking to work. The simultaneous execution of several subroutines would require that the problem-solving and motor capacities of the simulation not be monopolized by any one subroutine. One sense in which two purposes may be pursued at once ("killing two birds with one stone") depends on the partial identity of means relevant to two ends. This could be simulated by Newell's "chess-player," a program that is purely serial in conception. But computer models that are both realized *and* conceptualized serially conflict with the organizational assumptions of most personality theories, for these models are of systems with a total unity of purpose. Though there may be goals and subgoals, and alternative subroutines possible, yet the control is entirely in terms of one goal; and the subroutines are passively selected as means toward this end, having no intrinsic power to initiate activity. A simulation of instinctive goals would be one in which certain subroutines do initiate activity, granted certain inputs, unless specifically overruled by the master program. Some approximation to parallel processing would allow several instinctive goals to be pursued at

252

once, not all of them being in the focus of consciousness. But high-level control by a master program would be necessary to resolve conflicts and so integrate performance.

The nature of this integration would vary according to the structure of the hierarchy of sentiments available to the master program. Hierarchical structure may be regular and symmetrical (such as a tree generated by the successive dyadic branching of one basic node), or irregular and asymmetrical (such as a tree with some polyadic nodes, or one branching preponderantly on one side). It may be simple, in that from any given node there is only one path connecting with the most basic level; or complex, in that a crisscrossing of interrelations at various levels allows for alternative paths to the base from some of the nonbasic nodes. It may be single, in that it has only one node at the basic level; or divided, in that there are several nodes at the basic level, these being interrelated only via higher levels. Freud's insistence on the primacy of the sex instinct suggests a hierarchical structure that is, in effect, single, whereas McDougall's view that several instincts may be roughly equivalent in power suggests a divided hierarchy. If a hierarchy is divided, the division may be shallow or deep; that is, the interrelations of the basic nodes may proliferate at all levels of the structure, or only at very deep levels of the hierarchy, close to the base. In the latter case, different parts of the hierarchy will be relatively separated or dissociated, for only a very long and complex path will interconnect superficial nodes on either side of the division. The equivalents of some of these types of malintegration were distinguished by McDougall in his theoretical writings on personality, and various types of simulation may be suggested that parallel the phenomena he described.

The most striking examples of malintegration, or dissociation, are the clinical instances of "multiple personality." R. L. Stevenson's fictional account of Dr. Jekyll and Mr. Hyde is no more strange than the history of "Spanish Maria," and much less complex than that of "Sally Beauchamp." Both these clinical cases were much discussed in the early decades of the century, as "Eve White" and "Eve Black" have been in recent years. Such cases apparently demonstrate the influence of more than one personality on one and the same human body. The

253

body's behavior is markedly different at different times, and actions performed on Monday may be systematically undone on Tuesday. Monday's personality may be timid and shrinking, while Tuesday's personality may be bold and self-assertive. Spanish Maria, for instance, showed a regular alternation of these two types of personal behavior. Sally Beauchamp evidenced a bewildering complexity of psychological phenomena. Five or six significantly different streams of personal activity could be distinguished at various times. Some of these apparently had non-reciprocal access to the memories and experience of others, and even took delight in deliberately thwarting the will of the weaker personalities so as continually to frustrate their purposes in life. Insulting letters written by one personality to another were common. But of course, the same bodily hand held the pen as later opened the envelope and tore the insulting missive to shreds. In all such cases of multiple personality, each individual stream of personal behavior is reasonably well integrated, even though it is continually interrupted for varying lengths of time. Were it not so, the clinicians involved could not identify different "personalities" in the first place. However, psychological integration, whether of action or consciousness, is absent as between the several "selves."[21]

In discussing the faulty integration thus typical of multiple personality, McDougall attributed it to the sentiments' having been organized not in one fairly close-knit hierarchy, as is usual, but in two or more interlocking groups with two or more master sentiments. The deeper the split in the hierarchy (the nearer to the instinctive level itself), the more powerful the dissociation and the more distinct the personalities; he suggested that in the case of Spanish Maria, the developing sentiment of self-regard split into two with the separation of the instincts of self-assertion and submission. In simulation terms, two basic goals that in other cases are typically pursued together, neither having absolute priority over the other, would only be pursued independently of one another (the alternation of control between the two goals could be triggered by specific inputs or directed by a time switch). Since the two goals could never simultaneously direct behavior associated with any object, no equivalent of a sentiment comprising the two corresponding action-tendencies could

254

develop—although sentiments involving any other combination of basic goals could arise. The faulty integration of a Spanish Maria or a Sally Beauchamp is obvious. But McDougall pointed out that an apparently unitary personality may be malintegrated in the sense that the master sentiment is associated with potentially conflicting purposes. This conflict may result in more serious dissociation unless one purpose can be clearly subordinated to the other by way of a higher-level master-sentiment. The "cure" of pathological dissociation lies in the effecting of such a subordination, but the clinician may have some difficulty in deciding which personality (purpose) to encourage at the expense of others. Published case histories show that his decision may be influenced not only by the motivational and moral character of the competing "personalities" but also by the direction and extent of reciprocal or nonreciprocal control and coconsciousness.[22]

Dissociation and Conscious Unity

McDougall attempted to explain coconsciousness within cases of multiple personality in terms of direct telepathic communication between the rival monads; and he claimed that the monads within a normal personality communicate telepathically, both in waking life and dreaming.[23] This suggestion was not totally arbitrary. McDougall's study of parapsychology, which led to the founding of the well-known series of ESP experiments at Duke University, where J. B. Rhine was originally McDougall's assistant, had already persuaded him to accept the case for telepathy between distinct organisms. And the monads were supposed by him to be psychic individuals or potential selves. But his suggestion's being nonarbitrary did not prevent its being obscure. It illuminated neither the unity of consciousness of the normal mind nor the coconsciousness of multiple personality. Nor did it satisfactorily answer McDougall's question: "What is the nature of the process of communication between the members of the society, those communications by means of which the chief monad receives his information and those by means of which he directs the operations of his subordinates?"[24]

However, this question of intrapsychic communication can

perhaps only be satisfactorily answered with the help of the concepts of cybernetics and information theory. These concepts mark features of information usage and control that are not easily distinguished by means of familiar psychological terms. When a certain intrapsychic transfer is specified—for example, retrieving a unit of information stored in one subsystem and passing it on as a datum to another subsystem, it is not clear just what psychological process is represented. Is this "unconscious memory"? Psychological concepts based on the gross behavior of organisms cannot readily specify the various types of intra-psychic process that must be severally represented in a computer program. For instance, one must distinguish between the request for, the search for, the retrieval, transfer, and association of stored units, in subsystems that are more or less closely linked with or subordinated to one another, and more or less crucial for or obstructive of the attainment of the overall goal. Thus, the problem underlying McDougall's question faces the simulator of today, who must specify "the manner and form in which information, commands and requests at one level in the system are transmitted elsewhere." The simulator's difficulties are increased if he has to consider "a system in which subsystems are able to do such things as induce concealment or refuse access to information which other systems require to achieve their aims."[25] But such a system would be required in order to represent the limitations on integrative unity or coconsciousness typical of the split personality. It would even be required to represent the self-deception and unconscious intentions that occur in the normal personality.

Many years before the publication of *An Outline of Abnormal Psychology*, McDougall had discussed the unity of consciousness in connection with the mind-body problem. In *Body and Mind* he had argued that the unity of consciousness of the normal personality is incompatible with parallelism, the view that every psychical process has its physical aspect or counterpart. This unity, he asserted, can only be based in the control of the body by a single and indivisible psychic being.

Parallelists such as G. T. Fechner and Eduard von Hartmann had claimed that "the condition or ground of the unity of personal consciousness is the material and functional connection between the cells of which the brain is composed."[26] In support of this claim, Fechner had hypothesized that if the human cerebrum could be divided by section of the *corpus callosum,* the nervous activities of each part would be accompanied by its own stream of consciousness. Fechner's hypothesis has recently been revived by research on "split brains," notably the work described by R. W. Sperry and M. S. Gazzaniga. The cutting of the great cerebral commissure in effect provides the organism with two independent brains, which can learn different responses to equivalent stimuli and which can compete for control of the organism:

> The split-brain monkey learns, remembers and performs as if it were two different individuals, its identity depending on which hemisphere it happens to be using at the moment . . . When the brain is bisected, we see two separate "selves"— essentially a divided organism with two mental units, each with its own memories and its own will—competing for control over the organism. One is tempted to speculate on whether or not the normally intact brain is sometimes subject to conflicts that are attributable to the brain's double structure.
>
> Each hemisphere seems to have its own separate and private sensations; its own perceptions; its own concepts; and its own impulses to act, with related volitional, cognitive, and learning experiences.
>
> All the evidence indicates that separation of the hemispheres [in man] creates two independent spheres of consciousness within a single organism . . . It is entirely possible that if a human brain were divided in a very young person, both hemispheres could as a result separately and independently develop mental functions of a high order at the level attained only in the left hemisphere of normal individuals.[27]

McDougall, however, would not have been converted to the parallelist position by such evidence. He admitted that in pathological dissociation there may be a conflict of wills for the control of the motor mechanisms and sense organs of the body, and that certain dissociated conditions do lend support to Fechner's doctrine. But he nonetheless decided to reject this doctrine.

257

He specifically anticipated findings such as those of Sperry and Gazzaniga, asserting that regardless of such findings, the doctrine that the condition for the unity of consciousness is the material continuity of brain matter "would not render in the least degree intelligible the fact that a unitary consciousness is correlated with a multitude of discrete brain-processes. The doctrine, if empirically established, would remain the statement of an absolutely unintelligible fact." A single and indivisible psychic being must control the body in the normal case, and purposive bodily activity in general shows "that subordination of the parts to the whole which is the essence of organic unity and which is incapable of being accounted for on purely mechanical principles."[28]

In this matter McDougall relied on the faulty assumption that since purposive phenomena cannot be described in mechanistic terms, they therefore cannot be dependent on purely mechanistic processes. But a coherent master-program will result in unity of performance, despite the complexity of its mechanical embodiment. As K. J. W. Craik has pointed out:

> Those who assert that physiological theories of the nervous system could explain only complexity and not such supposedly "simple" things as consciousness, thought, colours and images seem to forget that there are several ways of putting the parts of an engine together. You can drop them all into a bucket, in which case the complexity is fairly high but the simplicity of performance nil; or you can put them together correctly and let the engine start, in which case the complexity is in a sense greater because now there is relational as well as atomic complexity and the possibility of performance is increased, yet at the same time there has entered a new simplicity and co-ordination very like that of a living organism.[29]

The performance of information-processing systems in general may show differing degrees of integration. If overall "unity" is to result, the same system that *receives* the environmental input must *process* it and *control* the final performance in the light of criteria of various types. But the degree of this "unity" will depend on the extent and nature of interdependence between the various subsystems. If coconsciousness is thought of as the reciprocal availability of information between the subsystems of

258

the mind, and unity of consciousness is thought of as the integration controlled by the master system, it becomes clear how an
organism (or simulation) can have differing degrees of unity of
purpose and consciousness even though it is a mechanistic
physical system.

In almost his first published article, McDougall had claimed
that if there were no frustration of purpose in action, there
would be no consciousness.[30] Later he wrote in the concluding
passage of *Body and Mind*:

> So long as the psycho-physical processes . . . proceed smoothly
> in the routine fashion proper to the species, they go on
> unconsciously or subconsciously. But whenever the circum-
> stances of the organism demand new and more specialised
> adjustment of response, their smooth automatic working is
> disturbed, the corresponding meanings are brought to con-
> sciousness and by conscious perception and thinking and
> striving the required adjustment is effected.[31]

Similarly, a subprogram could be executed without continual
reference to the master program and without use of the working
memory reserved for tasks controlled by the master program,
until a signal of failure were communicated to the master program. In this case the subprogram might be modified in detail by
the master program, which process might be printed out by the
machine if a record of "present activity" were called for. But as
long as the subprogram was working efficiently, it might not be
possible for the machine to print it out, or even for it to be
represented within the master program so as to be available for
the information of the system as a whole. A relevant analogy
has been suggested by Minsky, based on the distinction between
interpreted and compiled programs. Suppose that the simulation
executes compiled programs until failure triggers a switch to an
interpreted program: this would correspond to the occurrence
of conscious discriminations at points of difficulty, allowing for
examination of the next step in the process before its actual
execution. Some very basic operations might never be available
in detail to the master program and might never be printed out;
such operations could be under the control of a compiled program only, no interpreted program being available for their step-

by-step analysis by any higher level of control. This would parallel the apparent simplicity of thought and action as viewed by introspection, which does not reflect the many operations underlying what is called simply "perception," "memory," "insight," or "will."[32]

It might be asked at this point why anyone should want to simulate the "conscious perception, thinking and striving" which McDougall held to accompany frustration of purpose. Are they not better ignored in the interests of scientific objectivity? The answer is that if one attempts to simulate a complex purposive system in which such behavioral frustrations may occur, one is forced to simulate these processes in some form. They cannot simply be ignored, because conscious perception, thinking, and striving are necessarily involved in the overcoming of frustration of purpose. In other words, they are conceptually connected with such activity, not merely contingently connected with it. This can be seen by examining the logical role of the vocabulary of consciousness in the description and explanation of purposive behavior.

VIII   Purpose, Consciousness, and Intensionality

The general vocabulary of consciousness is typical of purposive accounts of behavior, although systematic psychologies vary in the extent to which they employ neologistic equivalents of familiar psychological terms. The terms involved may be roughly classified as expressing conative, cognitive, or affective concepts. These three classes respectively cover the broad categories of desire, knowledge, and feeling. Many psychological terms cannot be assigned straightforwardly to one and only one of these classes. This can be seen from the everyday examples of "hope," "confidence," and "anxiety." These terms are affective in marking feeling states that accompany and signify three different manners of goal-seeking; they are cognitive in expressing different intellectual judgments of the likelihood or nearness of success; and they are conative in distinguishing activity that primarily attempts to reach the final goal from activity which concentrates effort on the subgoals involved in means behavior. This psychological complexity underlay McDougall's doubts as to whether hope, confidence, and anxiety should be termed "derived emotions" or "complex feelings." Nevertheless, the threefold classification of the vocabulary of consciousness is useful.

Purely affective terms are less prominent in theoretical psychologies, particularly animal psychologies, than are cognitive and conative terms. This is explicable on the assumption that the teleological function of affective states is to signify (subjectively to the agent and, secondarily, objectively to other organisms) the conative impulses currently excited or incipiently aroused by an intensional object. The psychologist as observer often utilizes behavioral expressions of affect as clues to the conative characterization of the behavior he is observing, but his theoretical terms may not clearly distinguish the affective from the motivational aspect of behavior since he is not primarily interested in the affect itself. The psychologist as empathizer, by contrast, is interested in subjective affect for its own sake. However, theoreticians of the post-Watson era do not see the aim of animal psychology as being to empathize with one's experimental subjects, and even human psychology is not typically thought of in this way except by some Third Force workers in counseling and therapeutic contexts. The exception occurs because psychologists who try to help another person to develop greater control over his own motivational life may reasonably concern themselves with the subjective indications of his basic conative processes that are available to the man, although they clearly have to rely on his verbal behavior for much of their information. Analogously, a programmer attempting to simulate a complex purposive system would have to ensure that internal signs of the activation of various subprograms were available to the master program, if efficient teleological control were to be achieved. Subjective affect therefore cannot be ignored if one's primary aim is to increase the subtlety of autonomous control in a particular teleological system, whether the system in question be oneself, one's patient, or one's computer. But a psychologist without this practical aim may choose to neglect affective phenomena, or to assimilate the emotional and motivational aspects in his conceptualization of behavior, and many theoretical psychologists have done so.[1]

Cognitive and conative terms, by contrast, are crucial to the theoretical systems of many behaviorists, of Freud and neo-Freudians, of the Third Force in general, and also of McDougall. No teleological explanation, however crude, can be expressed without reference to conation and cognition. However, agreement on their necessity for purposive explanation does not exclude disagreement over their detailed philosophical analysis. In other words, the logical function of conative and cognitive terms is controversial, and their explanatory role is disputed.

McDougall's analysis of consciousness may be termed "mentalist" on two counts. First, he denied that the concepts of consciousness are based primarily on behavioral criteria, believing consciousness to be contingently rather than conceptually connected with observable features of behavior. Second, he claimed that some conscious states are causally active in the production of behavior. Only conative states were said by him to be truly causal, their activity being attributable to hormic energy inherently directed toward specific ends (the organism's instinctive goals). In contrast, cognitive states serve merely to guide behavior, without energizing it in any way. He held that both cognitive and conative states can be attributed only to a psychological subject, and that no mechanistic system powered purely by physical energy can be such a subject.

This analysis is unacceptable. McDougall was mistaken both in his belief that the criteria of consciousness cannot be behavioral and in his insistence on the causal efficacy of consciousness. His postulation of horme was grounded in a misinterpretation of of the logical function of conative concepts in teleological explanation and in a misunderstanding of the conceptual distinction between a plan and the mechanism required to execute a plan. Only if one can link "plans," "purposes," and "ideas" with causal mechanisms of a specific sort can one understand how it is possible for purposes to influence the bodily behavior of a psychological subject. Intensionality can be a feature of mechanistic systems, provided that their behavior is controlled largely by idiosyncratic mediating mechanisms that function as models representing the environment in certain respects. Only such systems may properly be regarded as psychological subjects. In them *final causes* may be said to influence *efficient causes,* and the mind may be said to direct the purposive actions of the body.

Cause, Contingency, and Consciousness

McDougall insisted that all purpose involves consciousness. But in formulating his concept of *dissociation,* he showed that he did not believe all behavior to be self-conscious, or to be constantly attended to, or to be open to introspection and description by the agent. Indeed, he agreed with Freud that quite complex or sophisticated human purposes may be unconscious, in the sense that the man, or self, is incapable of recognizing them as his own purposes. Moreover, he acknowledged that the terms "conscious" and "purpose" are most commonly ascribed (to adult human beings) in a sense that is never appropriate to animals. Accordingly, he postulated various levels of consciousness, both within human behavior and throughout the phylogenetic scale. When McDougall (or Perry, or Tolman) argued that purposiveness necessarily involves striving, desire, foresight, or belief, there was no assumption that these terms must be applicable in the same degree to all human and animal behavior.

In considering McDougall's views on such matters, and in

263

relating them to the general connection of purpose with the predicates of consciousness; I shall therefore not use "consciousness" in its strongest sense. Thought or motor behavior that is "conscious" in the strongest sense is under the direct control of the self; it is being actively attended to; it is guided by precise foresight of the goal; and it is open to introspection in the sense that its component features are discriminable (and verbally describable) by the psychological subject. Behavior that is variously deficient in these respects may nevertheless be termed "conscious" in the wide sense that is relevant here. McDougall did not offer a detailed analysis of the various "levels" of consciousness ascribed by him to men and animals, nor is such an analysis needed for my argument.[2] But it is necessary to understand why McDougall insisted that, in some sense, animals are "conscious"—in other words, why he, (like the purposive behaviorists), felt himself bound to use at least some of the recognized predicates of consciousness in explaining the behavior of lower animals. The term "purpose" itself presents no difficulty, for *ex hypothesi* the behavior in question is describable as "purposive" to some degree on the basis of McDougall's objective (behavioral) criteria. But it needs to be made clear why purposive behavior must always be explained in terms of the general categories of consciousness.

Before this can be clarified, one must realize that the logical nature of the connection between purpose and consciousness determines the general type of explanation that may be involved. McDougall claimed that there is an "intimate relation" between conscious activity and goal-seeking.[3] But the crucial problem is how to characterize the logical nature of this relation. It may be a contingent connection, a matter of hypothesis or empirical fact that might conceivably have been different. Alternatively, it may be a conceptual connection, one that follows logically from the criteria of the concepts involved and so could not conceivably have been different. The question whether consciousness and purposive action are contingently associated or conceptually linked is "crucial" because the answer will determine the possibility or impossibility of ascribing causal efficacy to consciousness. For, as the term is used here, the "cause" of bodily change is not just any factor that might be mentioned in answering the question "Why did that happen?" Nor is it even any factor that might unexceptionably be termed a "cause" in everyday explanations of behavior. Rather, the causes of bodily change are the efficient causes of it, the antecedent conditions or underlying energy mechanisms that somehow effect the change. If "consciousness" and "purposive action" are contingently related, the relationship need not be a causal one—it might, for example, be a mere correlation in time. But if they are conceptually connected, their relationship cannot be a causal one.

This is because the fact that there is a causal connection between the members of any two specific classes of condition or event is a contingent matter, even though the concepts of "cause" and "effect" are themselves conceptually linked. It is logically necessary that any cause must have some effect, just as any father must have a child. But it is contingently true that a certain movement is caused by a particular neuromuscular unit, as it is contingently true that a certain boy is the child of a particular man, or that a certain man happens to be a father. This follows from the logical requirement that conditions or events picked out as "cause" and "effect" be separately identifiable. In this sense cause and effect are atomistic concepts, and therefore in this sense Hume's analysis of causation is correct.[4]

This is not to deny that the cause and the effect might be said to be "conceptually linked" in some senses. For instance, the cause may sometimes be referred to or individuated by way of referring to its effect: thus, it can be described as "that event or condition which is the cause of effect *E*." This point has been stressed in a recent discussion intended to show that conceptual connection is not inimical to causal relation, a discussion conducted within the specific context of the mind-body problem.[5] Were any atomistic analysis of causation so extreme in its atomism as to deny the possibility of ever individuating a cause by way of referring to its effect, that analysis would be unacceptable. It could not provide a methodological rationale for such scientific activities as the original postulation of the tubercle bacillus, wherein the bacillus was conceived as "that (unknown) agent, *X*, which is causally responsible for tuberculosis." However, this postulation depended on the tacit understanding that *X* was of such a logical type that it could, in principle, be identified inde-

265

pendently of any such reference. Hume himself did not deny that one can hypothesize and search for causal regularities where only one term of the relation is known at the beginning of the search. He would have denied, however, that one may sensibly speak of a causal relation between two terms if all the possible individuating references to the "cause" are (implicitly or explicitly) of this nonatomistic type, or are such that they simultaneously guarantee the presence of the "effect" as a matter of logical necessity.

There is a second, rather stronger sense in which cause and effect might be said to be "conceptually linked." Our (empirical) knowledge of causal relations often becomes incorporated into the meaning of the terms most commonly used to refer to some cause or effect, with the consequence that cause and effect may appear to be linked logically rather than contingently. That is, the substantive term referring to an object, condition, or event is often "theory-laden" in such a way that particular causal hypotheses are implicit in its meaning.[6] For instance, to call an object a "billiard ball" is to imply that—unlike the hedgehog "balls" in Alice's croquet game—its behavior accords with the laws of mechanics; and the "tubercle bacillus" is obviously conceptually connected with the symptoms of tuberculosis. Indeed, both these examples could contribute to what would very naturally be termed "observation" statements. One would normally allow that everyone can observe an object to be a billiard ball, and that a competent pathologist could observe the tubercle bacillus by means of a microscope. This is to suggest that Hume's associationist and atomistic analysis of observation statements is incorrect, as McDougall himself insisted. Hume's epistemology was faulty in that he underestimated the role of background knowledge, or theory, in observation and perception. He also underestimated the extent to which observed correlations are only termed "causal" if there is a certain theoretical background explaining the correlations. That is, causal correlations are those that can be deduced from a theory. Given the theory, statements predicting the occurrence of the effect follow necessarily from statements specifying the cause as initial condition. This deductive relation between theoretical and observation statements is responsible for what Hume called the "feeling of necessity" link-

266

ing cause and effect. Hume's analysis was concentrated on the level of the basic observational evidence for causal claims, and he consequently assimilated the notions of causal connection and mere temporal correlation that were contrasted earlier in the discussion.

Nevertheless, Hume's insight about the discovery of causes was well-grounded. He realized that in order to discover that a given object in fact behaves in a Newtonian fashion, or causes the symptoms of tuberculosis, one must be able to identify the object independently of its Newtonian behavior or its connection with the tubercular syndrome. Causal explanation involves the assertion of functional dependence between two independently identifiable variables, whatever else it may involve. Accordingly, the claim that purposive action is caused by consciousness requires that the two be separately identifiable and, in this sense, be connected contingently rather than conceptually. Causal relationships must be established by empirical discovery, not by conceptual analysis. If conscious processes are said to cause purposive behavior, then the criteria for identifying those processes must be independent of the criteria of purposive behavior.

McDougall evidently assumed that the relation between conscious activity and goal-seeking is contingent. This might be inferred from his constant assertion of a causal connection between the two, but there is other evidence as well. For instance, he characterized the relationship as "a very close correlation in time." He believed that the conscious activity correlated with goal-seeking includes both perception and foresight, together with the thinking out of suitable means to the desired end: "Knowing or cognition is always a becoming aware of something, or of some state of affairs, as given or present, together with an anticipation of some change ... [Mental life] consists always in an activity of a subject in respect of an object apprehended, an activity which constantly changes or modifies the relation between subject and object." Further evidence that McDougall assumed a contingent connection is provided by his claim that it is possible (though not likely) that purposive activity in other men and animals may not be accompanied by consciousness: "We are thus led to *suspect* that goal-seeking behaviour, whenever and wherever it occurs, is accompanied by, or is a

267

manifestation of, conscious activity: and, *though we cannot hope to establish the generalization beyond all possibility of doubt,* it becomes a *fair working assumption* that conscious activity (allied in nature to our experience of desireful foresight) and goal-seeking behaviour are always but two partial aspects of one total system of activity, a psychophysical activity." This passage from *Energies of Men* reiterates McDougall's early view that it is impossible to attain "absolute proof of the existence of any consciousness other than one's own."[7]

Such skeptical conclusions are an inevitable result of the assumption that behavior and consciousness are contingently correlated. Underlying this assumption is the view that all the criteria for the ascription of consciousness to an organism are essentially private, so that one is logically unassailable only when ascribing consciousness to oneself (such self-ascription depending not at all on behavioral criteria). On this view, the ascription of consciousness to psychological subjects other than oneself must depend on analogical inference based on the similarity between their behavior and one's own. One's knowledge of others' consciousness must be wholly inferential, rather than in any sense direct.

Recent philosophical discussions of this position have shown that the inferences supposedly involved are very shaky.[8] Normally, the conclusion of an analogical inference is one that could, logically, be checked in a more direct manner. Thus, one may infer the presence of the tubercle bacillus on the basis of bodily symptoms, without checking the inference by means of the microscope. This requires that the symptoms be analogous to those found in many other cases where the tubercle bacillus was known to be present. But, if desired, one can stain the bacillus whose existence has been inferred so that it becomes observable to the microscopist. Sometimes one cannot, in practice, carry out a more direct check, as when the past existence of a dinosaur is inferred on the basis of the analogy between its present fossil-ized footprint and the footprints of numerous extant animals. Nevertheless, more direct ways of knowing of the dinosaur's existence were, in principle, available during its lifetime. The inferences supposedly involved when one makes third-person psychological statements are, however, very different. The "corre-

lation" between behavior and consciousness appealed to in justification of these inferences can be directly checked in one case
only—one's own. It is logically impossible that the truth of any
third-person psychological statement could be known directly to
the speaker in the way in which it is (typically) known to the
person being spoken about. John cannot know that Joan has a
headache in the way that Joan does, for any headache which
John knows in that way must, necessarily, be his own. Thus, not
only is there no direct check of third-person psychological statements, but there can be no such check. The "argument from
analogy," therefore, cannot avoid McDougall's philosophical conclusion that it is impossible to attain absolute proof of the
existence of any consciousness other than one's own. Moreover,
it cannot even justify claims as to the *probability* of the existence
of other minds, since the "analogical" inferences involved are so
radically different from normal cases of analogical argument.
This extreme solipsistic conclusion—that one cannot even attain
probable opinion, let alone indubitable knowledge, of other
minds—is highly paradoxical. Since it follows from the claim that
behavior and consciousness are contingently correlated, this claim
itself has been increasingly questioned in philosophical discussions of recent date.

The alternative to viewing consciousness and behavior as contingently correlated is to view them as somehow conceptually
connected. In other words, it is to regard the criteria of consciousness as in some degree behavioral rather than purely introspective. Since behavior is publicly observable, the proper ascription
of consciousness does not then depend purely on logically private, and thus incommunicable, criteria. A number of writers
have defended some form of this alternative position regarding
the meaning of psychological language.[9] Though their detailed
analyses vary, they are in general strongly influenced by the
later philosophy of Ludwig Wittgenstein.

Wittgenstein insisted that "an 'inner process' stands in need of
outer criteria."[10] As well as stressing the publicly available nature
of the criteria actually underlying our use of psychological language in everyday contexts, Wittgenstein intended this remark to
imply that no logically private language is in principle possible.
A logically private language would be a language referring to

269

one's "inner" mental processes quite independently of any behavioral criteria, and so intelligible only to oneself. If a private language is indeed impossible, then the solipsistic position mentioned above must be not merely incredible, but senseless and void: the "problem" of proving other men and animals to be conscious like oneself disappears, since it cannot even be coherently stated. This denial of the coherence (as opposed to the credibility) of solipsism has been widely—though not universally—accepted.[11] However, since one might concede that our everyday use of psychological language in fact involves (and must involve) behavioral criteria, without subscribing to the stronger thesis that no essentially private language is possible, a defense of this strong thesis is not strictly necessary here. Unless one is willing to accept the highly paradoxical solipsism discussed above, one must allow that the meaning of psychological terms is at least largely behavioral. It is because publicly observable features are intrinsic to (criterial of) psychological concepts that communication on psychological matters—and the learning of psychological language in the social context—is possible.

Insofar as the use of psychological terms depends on behavioral criteria, knowledge of the minds of others may be regarded as direct rather than wholly inferential (although "direct" here clearly has a different force from its use in expressions such as "direct access to the mind of another"). It does not follow that the meaning of psychological terms is "wholly behavioral," in the sense that they may be said to refer to observable behavior and nothing more. Nor does it follow that one always appeals directly to behavioral criteria in every case where one ascribes a mental state to a psychological, or intensional, subject. The normal introspective use of such terms does not require the observation of one's own current behavior, and nor does it refer to one's own behavior. To say "I see the diagram as a sail" or "I see it as a stingray," is neither to observe nor to refer to one's behavior. One may truly say "I feel angry" or "I'm afraid" without actually attacking or fleeing from the object of one's anger or fear. Nor is the truth of "My nose itches" dependent on one's actually scratching one's nose.[12] The point, rather, is that the introspective self-ascription of psychological terms is a secondary use, which is intelligible only because of its background of behavioral criteria, and which one learns only after being taught the primary use by means of such criteria. Thus, although an introspected state may be "private" in the sense that only verbal behavior on the part of the subject can reliably inform observers of its nature, it is not essentially private since it is always publicly communicable if the subject chooses to communicate it.

According to this view, publicly observable behavior is not merely a contingent symptom of some underlying and utterly private mental event. On the contrary, behavior can provide logically adequate criteria justifying ascriptions of psychological predicates, as mere contingent symptoms could never do. Of course, behavior can mislead a man in his hypotheses about an organism's mental states or psychological characteristics. The confidence trickster makes his living by capitalizing on this fact. It may therefore be objected that behavior cannot be criterial of mental states but is merely symptomatic of them. Mere symptoms often do mislead: the patient's "consumptive complexion" may turn out not to have been caused by a tubercle bacillus after all. Moreover, it is conceivable that a whole set of symptoms might be systematically misleading. It is always logically possible to question the underlying condition that has been inferred, even though all the acknowledged symptoms are present. By contrast, if all the criteria of a concept are satisfied, then no possibility remains that the condition connoted by that concept may not be correctly ascribable in the case being considered. One can, of course, still pronounce the interrogative form of words: "Yes, but is it really X?" But this does not now express any answerable question. Thus, the fact that behavior sometimes misleads one in ascribing psychological terms might understandably suggest that behavior is symptomatic of psychological states, rather than criterial of them.

However, if the behavioral features involved are largely structural or dispositional rather than episodic, involving behavior patterns spreading over time, it follows that psychological predicates cannot be infallibly applied to any organism merely on grounds relating to its momentary bodily state. It is always possible in principle reasonably to apply a psychological predicate at one moment, nonetheless being forced later to withdraw it on the grounds of subsequent behavior. For example, McDougall

271

himself pointed out that one cannot normally be absolutely certain what purpose an animal is following at any instant—particularly if only a small temporal section of its behavior has been observed. Unless the animal is actually engaged in consummatory activity, its behavior may in principle be directed to more than one goal: a bird's flight may be migratory or food-seeking, aggressive or defensive. But familiarity with the species concerned will show what behavioral patterns are in fact typical, and so will aid the psychologist in his attribution of goal-seeking to the organism at any given instant. In general, the more the various behavioral criteria of a psychological term can be spread out over time, the more difficulty there may be in correctly ascribing that term on the basis of the sample of behavioral evidence actually available. This difficulty is particularly great in the ascription of psychological states to human beings, where anticipation, contingency planning, and even intentional deception on the part of the agent can complicate matters greatly. A further complication arises from the fact that the detailed purposes and beliefs of human individuals differ considerably. Consequently, even if it is granted that a particular behavioral sequence is complete, that there is no more behavioral evidence to come in, it is always theoretically (if implausibly) possible to question the ascribed purpose because it is always theoretically possible to ascribe a different system of background beliefs. For example, many of the purposes unhesitatingly ascribed to the spy Philby by his closest colleagues in MI5, purposes "obviously" apparent in his behavior, were in fact not Philby's purposes at all. Since his colleagues were mistaken about his background political beliefs, they were often mistaken about his purposes.

The example of Philby is a complex illustration of what Wittgenstein called "the fluctuation in grammar between criteria and symptoms [which] makes it look as if there were nothing at all but symptoms."[13] This fluctuation is an important source of difficulty in regarding behavior as providing logically adequate criteria for psychological predicates. Pleading with someone that they should not throw one into the briar-bush is a criterion (and a very important one) of the speaker's wish to avoid such a fate. Nevertheless, Brer Rabbit's piteous pleas to Brer Fox were symptomatic of his hidden purpose to secure that very end. The

272

satisfaction of even the most central criterion of a psychological characteristic is neither necessary nor sufficient to guarantee the presence of that characteristic. Other criteria (such as Brer Rabbit's effortless escape and his triumphant cry that he was "born and bred in the briar-bush") may override the criterion in question in a particular case. This undoubtedly shows that the sense in which certain behavioral features are "criteria" of mental states is less straightforward than the sense in which being male and unmarried are "criteria" of being a bachelor.[14] And it probably shows that by "logically adequate criteria of X," in this context, one should not understand "criteria which logically *entail* X." However, it does not show that behavior is "nothing at all but symptoms." Nor does it show that one can reasonably question the ascription of purpose or consciousness to an organism in those cases where all the paradigmatic behavioral criteria are satisfied and no conflicting evidence is available. In particular, it does not destroy the logical adequacy of behavioral criteria for the ascription of generic, as opposed to specific, psychological predicates. From the fact that, as it happens, it would have been reasonable to question virtually any specific purpose of any interest attributed to Philby, it does not follow that it would have been reasonable to doubt his status as a purposive creature.

McDougall's solipsistic doubts concerning the concept of consciousness did not prevent his confident ascription of purposiveness to other organisms, for McDougall did not subscribe to the "contingency" view of the connection between purpose and behavior. To be sure, he postulated hormic energy as underlying and causing purposive behavior. But he explicitly stated the concept of purpose itself to be objectively applicable without recourse to any such hypothesis. Nor did he claim that one needs direct access to the consciousness of other organisms in order properly to ascribe purposiveness to their behavior. He wished to define the subject matter of psychological science while avoiding questionable and speculative hypotheses not open to observational check. Recognizing that the data of any science must be publicly observable, he was therefore careful to provide "objective marks" of purpose that were criterial of his use of the term. These observable behavioral features were thus treated by McDougall as merely symptomatic of horme, but as criterial of purpose. If all these features are actually observed, it would make sense to question the underlying existence of horme—but it would be logically absurd to question the purposiveness of behavior.

If the behavioral features that are criterial of purposiveness are also criterial of the vocabulary of consciousness in general, then McDougall's residual doubt over the universal correlation of consciousness and goal-seeking can be allayed. In such a case, purpose and consciousness must be conceptually related rather than contingently correlated. McDougall provided objective criteria for his characterological concepts, by means of which even terms such as "hope," "anxiety," "persistence," and "despair" were based in the observable structure of purposive behavior. If there is an essential connection between terms such as "perception," "idea," "instrumental activity," "voluntary action," "intention," "desire," "psychological subject," and "purpose," then purposive behavior must in principle be open to description and (intensional) explanation in these terms also. More generally, cognitive and conative terms must be somehow logically essential to purposive accounts of behavior. We must therefore ask whether purposive behavior, identifiable by McDougall's "objective marks of purpose," does indeed provide the criteria for the application of such terms.

What is it, for example, to perceive an object? What are the criteria of perception? Discrimination is a necessary part of percipient behavior, and is shown by the attachment of different responses (or frequencies of response) to particular configurations of stimuli. That is, differential response is a central behavioral criterion of discrimination. Discriminatory behavior normally involves some form of stimulus generalization, since different encounters with the same environmental feature (except in highly artificial situations) present somewhat differing stimuli to the creature. A blind man cannot discriminate between certain sorts of stimulus situation, so one is justified in saying he can perceive nothing of these special sorts of situation. In calling him "blind" or "lacking in visual perception," one is not suggesting a hypothesis that might conceivably be false; one is not inferring a particular defect in his consciousness, as one might infer a specific lesion in the anatomical visual system. One is describing his

274

behavior insofar as it is not discriminatory, and explaining some of his subsequent behavior as being attributable to his not having made the appropriate discriminations in the first place.

Differences in the blind man's behavior can thus be explained, since "perception" typically involves more than mere arbitrary discrimination: it involves the use of discrimination in the guidance of motor and instrumental activity. The performance of complex tasks necessarily involves the adjustment of behavior to the detailed features of the task environment. In another terminology, the type of information-processing labeled "perceptual" is required for the type of problem-solving labeled "complex motor activity." Differential responses to particular environmental features are required to guide the choice and application of means to a given end, and to direct the overall strategy by picking out feasible subgoals and rejecting inappropriate ones. To adjust behavior in this way is to make the sorts of discrimination between different aspects of the environment that are termed "perceptual" discrimination. To attain certain goals, certain procedures are appropriate; but a man who cannot tell the difference between a hawk and a handsaw is likely to find some difficulty in fitting these procedures to reality. His failure can then be explained in terms of his mistaken (or nonexistent) perception, and the nature of this misperception may be inferred from the detailed structure of the fruitless behavior itself. This is a conceptual matter: I am claiming that what is called "perceptual discrimination" is necessarily involved in those cases where an organism is said to be learning new skills, or to be adjusting his behavior in conditions of difficulty in reaching the goal pursued. I am not claiming that all motor activity under the control of the organism is directed merely by a continuous series of perceptual or kinesthetic sensations: indeed, there is good experimental evidence against such a view.[15]

Instrumental or motor behavior can be identified as purposive by McDougall's objective criteria only if it shows appropriate, nice adjustments to environmental obstacles. And these adjustments are themselves sufficient criteria for the ascription of a range of perceptual and other cognitive terms to the organism. The degree of nicety of adustment will logically determine the degree of precision ascribed to the cognitive operations and representations involved. Similarly, to use M. L. Minsky's terminology, the range and precision of the "questions" answered by an organism must reflect the range and precision of its "models," and so will unavoidably influence one in attributing models to it. The reason for this is that the "models" are defined in terms of the questions with which the organism can cope. The models present must be at least powerful enough to generate the "answers" apparent in the organism's behavior.

Thus, a conceptual truth underlies McDougall's remark about the cognitive guidance of behavior: "Where the anticipatory representation of the end is vague and sketchy and general, there the action will be general, vague, imperfectly directed in detail; where it is more detailed and full, there action is more specialized, more nicely adjusted to the achievement of its end."[16] Purposive behavior, by McDougall's definition, is observed to "tend towards a change of situation of a particular kind" and then to "cease." This differential response shows that the organism can discriminate between presence and absence of the goal state. *Ex hypothesi* the regulation of behavior is autonomous rather than dependent on any external force. Therefore, this discrimination must depend on an internal condition.

Where the unsophisticated direction of behavior by natural goals is concerned, it is often found that many differing environmental situations may be correlated with the cessation of behavior on achievement of the end state. In such cases there is no reason to speak of any internal condition that closely reflects specific environmental features. It may in fact be discovered that the behavior ceases simply on the achievement of a diffuse bodily condition, such as a particular blood-sugar or hormonal level. Here one may speak of "satisfaction" of the organism's striving, but hardly of "ideas" or "recognition of the goal." But when the goal state involves a specific state of affairs external to the organism, the internal condition must necessarily be one which reflects that external situation to some extent, one which "represents" that situation in some degree. Even nonpurposive responses may involve such representations. For example, a passerine chick will crouch the first time it sees a hawk flying, and a female stickleback will respond in a species-characteristic fashion to her mate's "dance." These fixed responses require the discrimination of one

276

particular stimulus-class from others, and so must depend upon an innate representation of this stimulus-class—what McDougall called an innate "key." It is perfectly clear from the structure of purposive behavior that some such representations are functioning between the presentation of the environmental stimulus and the organism's response, although it is an empirical question which specific ones are involved in a particular case. There is always a large range of possible representations, of varying levels of abstractness and focusing on varying aspects of the stimulus-class, that might be involved in a particular case of perceptual discrimination. It may be a difficult matter to find out precisely which features of hawks are the discriminanda for grouse chicks, as it may be difficult to discover the relative importance, for rats, of olfactory, visual, and enactive or "spatial" representations of mazes. But that discriminatory response to the goal state must be explained by some representation or other is clear, and such representations are commonly termed "ideas." Thus, the description of behavior in terms of a conceptual scheme centered on purpose necessitates the use of cognitive concepts such as perception and idea. This is why all those behaviorist writers who recommend the term "purpose" in animal psychology also approve the use of cognitive terms such as "belief," "expectancy," "foresight," "hypothesis," "insight," and "idea."

It does not follow that it is always a simple matter to decide whether generic concepts such as perception and idea are properly applicable in a particular case, and still less does it follow that the ascription of a specific perception or idea is always clearly right or clearly wrong. If a creature reacts differentially to different environments, then one may say that it is "sensitive" to changes in the environmental features involved. A limpet on a rock, or a sea urchin, may be sensitive to sunrise and sunset, or even to the shadow of a boat passing through the water, and this sensitivity may be shown by changes in the muscular tonus of the organism.[17] But to speak of "perception" here would be out of place, for this would require a more complex background of behavior. The concept of perception is particularly appropriate where behavior is of such flexibility that obstacles and difficulties are likely to be overcome, and overcome with a certain economy of effort so that the goal is reached as efficiently as possible, granted the motor abilities of the organism. This is the basis of McDougall's view that "whenever the circumstances of the organism demand new and more specialized adjustment of response . . . by conscious perception and thinking and striving the required adjustment is effected."[18] This may be seen by considering examples of behavior that may mislead one, to the extent that perceptions are ascribed inappropriately and the wrong sort of explanation is implied.

Suppose, for instance, that one sees a squirrel digging a hole in the ground and burying a nut in it, replacing the soil over the nut and patting it down until it is flat. One might well be tempted to explain the squirrel's behavior in terms of its guiding perceptions, discriminations used in the service of the overall purpose of finding a safe, well-camouflaged hiding-place for next autumn's food. One may then discover that a squirrel raised from birth in a cage with a concrete floor and no nuts will go through exactly the same motions, even to the extent of "tamping" the concrete ground with its nose at the end of the operation.[19] One should now feel a good deal less happy about explaining the movements as being guided throughout by a series of accurate perceptual discriminations of the environment. Similarly, a robin defending his territory in spring will behave in exactly the same aggressive fashion whether he is confronted with a male robin or a bundle of red feathers waggling on a stick. The bird's behavior is fixed. It is determined by this particular stimulus-sign, by a small part of the total stimulus-array that happens— in normal circumstances —to form part of a second, and possibly rival, robin. The bird's behavior is not to be explained in terms of its perceptual judgments about the relevance or threatening character of environmental intruders. The robin's sensitivity to, or discrimination of, a specific feature of the environment is responsible for the occurrence of the behavior in these conditions rather than others. But it does not go on to make the further discriminations that would be involved in a cessation or modification of the activity so as to fit it more appropriately to the environment.

I do not wish to suggest that there is a clear dividing line between what may properly be called "perception" and what is called "sensitivity." It may be that, in view of the flexible motor abilities of the robin in other circumstances, one is justified in saying that it "perceives" a red patch in this case. However, to say that it perceives or "has an idea of" a rival robin and reacts accordingly does not seem to be in order. Nor can one say that the passerine chick "has an idea of hawks" upon discovering that it will crouch when *any* cross-shaped stimulus—within certain definable limits—is moved short-end (head-end) forward.[20] Stereotyped and rigid behavior may be triggered by a series, or concatenation, of discriminations related to a number of releasing stimuli in the environment. But it is unresponsive to unusual features of the environment, and so the organism may easily be cheated of its "goal." This type of behavior may be quite complex —as in the courtship and nest-building behavior of some fish and birds, such as the ringdoves in D. S. Lehrmann's studies. Its structure is, however, clearly different from the structure of behavior which—being closely guided by perception—varies continuously so as to maximize the probability of reaching the goal.

Just as stereotyped inflexible behavior, no matter how well adapted to normal environmental circumstances, logically cannot be explained by reference to a continuous series of nice perceptual discriminations, neither can it be explained in terms of the goals or intentions of the organism concerned. Where there is no variation of means nor margin of modifiability in behavior, there is—strictly speaking—no purpose. Though such behavior may sometimes be said to "serve a purpose," such as species survival, the purpose concerned cannot be attributed to the individual organism. But the greater the flexibility and idiosyncracy of behavior, the more its explanation may involve reference to the purposes of the organism considered as an individual, rather than as a member of a class—for example, the class of robins. Thus, the robin's behavior so far discussed is predictable from a knowledge of environmental conditions (the season and the presence of a particular releasing-stimulus) and, possibly, of a constitutional factor such as a hormonal level of a particular nature. Successful prediction does not require reference to the ongoing behavior of the bird; it does not require one to ascribe particular purposes or intentions to this individual robin. Often one cannot predict or explain behavior from a knowledge of the environmental situation alone, nor even from a knowledge of the instincts proper to the given species. One must rather explain the occurrence of this

279

particular goal-seeking behavior rather than any other that lies within the organism's repertoire by referring to behavioral patterns which are not closely dependent on specific stimuli from outside, and which may differ in different individuals. The autonomous selection or spontaneity evident in such cases varies in different instances, and is a matter of degree rather than an all-or-none phenomenon. McDougall viewed conative behavior as showing various degrees of autonomy, and he distinguished "voluntary" behavior as being particularly influenced by the conscious purposes of the human individual and the self-ideal associated with them. It is only because the concept of voluntary action requires that the organism be regarded as an individual, as a unique psychological subject, that the ascription of individual responsibility can be conceptually linked with voluntariness. And the more "self-conscious" the behavior—the more it is governed by ideal goals associated with the individual's concept of himself —the more ready one may be to call it "voluntary."

In general, the greater the flexibility of behavior, the greater its autonomy vis-à-vis specific environmental features, and the more the organization of behavior varies across individuals, the more logically justified one will be in speaking of the goals or purposes of the organism itself and of its voluntary or perceptual activity in seeking those goals. Since the purposive hierarchies involved may be of very different degrees of complexity, one should not expect any clear dividing line between those types of behavior that are quite readily described as conscious, perceptual, or voluntary, and those where one hesitates to use such terms. Moreover, there may be many different levels, or degrees, of "consciousness." But the crucial point is that all these concepts hang together, all being logically based in the objective criteria of purposiveness listed by McDougall.

Therefore, contrary to McDougall's view, it is not in fact possible that other men and the higher animals are not in some sense conscious. It does not follow that one must necessarily ascribe consciousness to some conceivable machine artifact, given that it solves problems by means of instrumental motor behavior, and so on. The behavioral criteria considered so far are normally associated with many other features; for instance, they are assumed to be ascribed to soft-bodied living organisms. Were

280

one required to decide to apply or to refuse to apply psychological predicates to machines, the differences between organisms and artifacts might possibly be regarded as more important than their similarities, no matter how impressive the similarities. However, whether or not one may properly regard some hypothetical machine as genuinely conscious is not the point at issue. The point is rather the inadmissibility of McDougall's doubts as to whether other men and animals may be said to be conscious. This antiskeptical conclusion is important because it implies that the general vocabulary of consciousness is logically essential for describing the psychological structure of behavior, and for explaining that structure in terms of the intensional dependencies between psychological variables.

Conation and Causation

In mistakenly assuming a contingent connection between consciousness and behavior, McDougall shared one of the basic tenets of epiphenomenalism, as expressed by T. H. Huxley: "What *proof* is there that brutes are other than a superior race of marionettes, which eat without pleasure, cry without pain, desire nothing, know nothing, and only simulate intelligence as a bee simulates a mathematician . . . It must be premised, that it is *wholly impossible absolutely to prove* the presence or absence of consciousness in anything but one's own brain, though by analogy, we are justified in assuming its existence in other men."[21] However, in many of his works McDougall took pains to deny the second basic tenet of epiphenomenalism, namely, that consciousness has no causal function. McDougall labeled himself an "interactionist" because he was convinced that mental process, far from being an idle epiphenomenon, had a function:

I assume that psychic activity is no less real than physical process and *no less causally efficacious*, a part of nature, neither a supernatural influx nor an unintelligible and otiose by-product.

Conation is fundamentally the direction of the mechanical processes of the body *by the purposive activity* of mind.

Excessive and prolonged activity, maintained . . . by mental impressions, may produce visible changes in the neurones concerned, due to excess of metabolism. That is a clear case of structural change *functionally induced by mental impressions and mental activity.*

To accept the teleological causation of human agents is to believe in the *causal efficacy* of mental events.

Clear consciousness and conation play some real part in bringing about the organization of nervous elements . . . the relation between conation or conscious mental activity and nervous organization is the *causal* relation.[22]

But just what sort of causal relation this can be is difficult to understand. It is not clear how states of consciousness can possibly operate as causes of bodily action or neuronal change. Huxley had expressed the difficulty thus: "How is it possible to imagine that volition, which is a state of consciousness, and, as such, has not the slightest community of nature with matter in motion, can act on the moving matter of which the body is composed, as it is assumed to do in voluntary acts?" Regarding neurophysiology as basically an investigation into physical energy mechanisms, and assuming bodily processes to be "purely mechanical" (basically mechanistic), Huxley was led to the epiphenomenalist conclusion that: "Volitions do not enter into the chain of causation of actions at all . . . The consciousness of brutes [and men] would appear to be related to the mechanism of their body simply as a collateral product of its working, and to be as completely without any power of modifying that working as the steam-whistle which accompanies the work of a locomotive engine is without influence upon its machinery."[23]

McDougall rejected this conclusion. He insisted on the causal efficacy of consciousness because his reliance on purposive explanation committed him to the view that final causes have some function. By "function" in this context we may understand "effect," for McDougall was misled into assimilating final causes to efficient causes. He did not make this assimilation in the sense of regarding final causes, or purposes, as backward-working efficient causes, and he even admitted that "an idea of the goal . . . is not easily conceived as a causal agent."[24] But he believed

282

he could answer Huxley's difficulty in conceiving conscious states as causes of material change, for he believed he could give an acceptable analysis of how final causes operate.

McDougall countered Huxley's objection to interactionism by postulating a special kind of energy, which he termed variously "neurin," "neurokyme," and "horme." Reference to the causal action of horme was one of McDougall's four criteria of teleological explanation—the only one which in fact is not acceptable. In identifying the point at which this hormic energy supposedly exercised its function, McDougall relied on the neo-Kantian distinction between cognitive and conative concepts. These cover the general categories of knowledge and desire, respectively. He insisted that the intellect cannot determine a man's goals but can reconcile and adjust them when they conflict; knowing is for the sake of action; knowing is the process by which the will works toward its end; volition is essentially attentional, and attention is to be understood as conation revealing itself in cognition. These few notions reflect McDougall's recognition of the relationship between cognitive and conative concepts, a relationship that has been well expressed by C. I. Lewis:

> Knowledge, action, and evaluation are *essentially* connected. The primary and pervasive significance of knowledge lies in its guidance of action: knowing is for the sake of doing. And action, obviously, is rooted in evaluation. For a being which did not assign comparative values, deliberate action would be pointless; and for one which did not know, it would be impossible.
>
> Conversely, only an active being could have knowledge, and only such a being could assign values to anything beyond his own feelings. A creature which did not enter into the process of reality to alter in some part the future content of it, could apprehend a world only in the sense of intuitive or esthetic contemplation; and such contemplation would not possess the significance of knowledge but only that of enjoying and suffering.[25]

Thus, although it is often convenient to speak of conative and cognitive concepts as though they were completely distinct, they are in fact essentially connected, for a man's wants and knowl-

283

edge (whether long-standing beliefs or momentary perceptions) must co-operate in his purposive action. McDougall himself remarked that one should not exaggerate the independence of conative, cognitive, and affective factors in psychological phenomena:

> We cannot speak of knowing, striving, feeling as three phases of mental activity, but only as three distinguishable and insep-arable parts of one activity; for they occur together in intimate interplay with one another.
>
> If every mental process is at once a knowing, an affection, and a striving, it must be recognized that one or other of these aspects is commonly dominant; so that we are led to speak of each kind of mental process by the name of the dominant aspect; thus we speak of acts of perception, recognition, recollec-tion, reasoning, when we are predominantly cognitive; of states of emotion, or feeling, when affection is dominant; of volition, resolution, deciding, desiring, when we are vividly conscious of striving towards an end. It is this way of speaking which has led to the common error of regarding these aspects of all mental process as separable functions; an error of which the commonest and most serious form has been to regard intellec-tual processes as capable of being purely cognitive or com-pletely freed from the influence of the emotions and the will.[26]

However, McDougall distinguished sharply between cognition and conation when discussing the incidence of psychophysical interaction: "Just as cognition is fundamentally a reaction of the mind of the subject upon impressions made by objects on its body . . . so conation is fundamentally the direction of the mechanical processes of the body by the purposive activity of mind."[27] He believed cognitive phenomena to be specifically psychic, and impossible in any purely material system. Not only is a man's knowledge influenced by his interests and desires, but cognitive representations (including the agent's "idea" of the goal state that he desires) have a generality of application that he believed to be inexplicable mechanistically. Nevertheless, the causal action of mind on body was said by McDougall to be grounded in the conative aspect of thinking alone.

Given McDougall's belief that both cognition and conation are nonmechanistic, the fact that he associated his hypothesis of hormic energy or psychic causation only with the latter requires explanation. Everyday usage is not so selective, for in daily life we often speak of knowledge and beliefs as "causing" actions, besides speaking of purposes and wants in this way. And the ideomotor theory is a sophisticated version of the everyday assumption that a man's ideas may sometimes "cause" him to behave in a particular way. Even the behaviorist R. B. Perry called belief a "condition of action," and E. C. Tolman classified cognition as a "determiner" of behavior. McDougall's insistence that the causal action of mind on body is grounded in conation alone was attributable to a confused recognition on his part of the general conceptual character of conative terms. Conative concepts are concerned with active striving toward valued ends, in that they denote the organism's intentions, motives, instincts, and desires. In general, they specify the various purposes truly ascribable to the organism, the goals toward which it actually strives. Conative concepts thus emphasize the purposive striving and active changes in behavior, since they mark out the specific "changes of situation" that the organism desires. By contrast, cognitive concepts mark mental states which, although functioning in the selection of appropriate means behavior, are relevant to the whole class of hypothetical goal states that the organism may possibly have in mind rather than to the smaller subclass of end states that it actually tries to achieve. To understand the world is not to change it, even though to change the world one must understand it. Consequently, conative concepts are rather more likely than are cognitive concepts to be regarded as the active principles of behavioral change, by writers who misguidedly interpret the "causal" relation between mental and physical phenomena as a subclass of efficient causation.

McDougall's assimilation of final causes to efficient causes led him thus to misrepresent conative phenomena as "active principles" in two senses. First, he saw conative states as the only conscious states to be truly causal:

> "An idea of the goal" (since we cannot conceive "an idea" in any clear fashion) is not easily conceived as a causal agent. But thinking is an activity with which we all have intimate and

immediate acquaintance; and that such activity should have causal efficacy seems so natural and inevitable that it can be doubted or denied only by those who have undergone a long course of perverting sophistication. But it is said: How can mere thinking, even thinking of a goal, make a difference to the course of physical events? We answer: It is not mere thinking that makes the difference; it is rather thinking in that peculiar way we call desiring, or being averse from, that of which we think . . . It is thinking of this sort for which we claim causal efficacy upon the course of events.[28]

Second, identifying instincts as the basic conative concepts of his system presented in *An Introduction to Social Psychology*, he associated them with notions such as impulse and hormic energy:

We may say, then, that directly or indirectly the instincts are the *prime movers* of all human activity; by the *conative or impulsive force* of some instinct (or of some habit derived from an instinct), every train of thought, however cold and passionless it may seem, is borne along towards its end, and every bodily activity is initiated and sustained. The instinctive *impulses* determine the ends of all activities and *supply the driving power* by which all mental activities are sustained; and all the complex intellectual apparatus of the most highly developed mind is but a means towards these ends . . . Take away these instinctive dispositions with their *powerful impulses*, and the organism would become *incapable of activity of any kind;* it would *lie inert and motionless* like a wonderful clockwork whose mainspring had been removed or a steam-engine whose fires had been drawn. *These impulses are the mental forces* that maintain and shape all the life of individuals and societies, and in them we are confronted with the central mystery of life and mind and will.[29]

The energy McDougall said was involved presented a "mystery" indeed, and over thirty years later McDougall still had some difficulty in explaining what he meant by "instinctive energy":

We must postulate some energy which conforms to laws not wholly identical with the laws of energy stated by the physical sciences. We have at present no sufficient ground for postulating more than one such form of energy . . . We may call it *hormic energy . . .*

[The typically instinctive action expresses] a propensity which, on being roused from its dormant state, generates an active tendency: and the tendency is, in some cases, an energy; and not merely energy in general or a special kind of energy, but an energy which is directed to a goal, which works towards that goal and is brought to rest only on the attainment of it; an energy which activates the [cognitive or executive] ability and brings it into the service of the tendency as a means towards its end or goal . . .

The electrical energy of the factory is mere energy, indifferent as regards its application. The energy that activates the instinctive abilities is energy *towards;* directed energy; energy directed to a goal. Here we confront a very obscure problem; one which at present we cannot solve.[30]

Now, however, it is possible to solve this "obscure problem," for it has been shown that the identification of an instinct rests on the identification of some natural goal, that all living animals necessarily pursue goals, and that an instinct may be thought of as a plan for achieving a particular goal, a plan in the service of which other—cognitive or executive—plans will be brought into play. McDougall's remark that the organism without its instinctive dispositions would "lie inert and motionless" and become "incapable of activity of any kind" may be compared with the observation of G. A. Miller, Eugene Galanter, and K. H. Pribram: "Plans are executed because people are alive. This is not a facetious statement, for so long as people are behaving, *some* Plan or other must be executed."[31] The "must" in the latter quotation is logical: it is conceptually true that a behaving organism follows some purpose or plan. Purposive explanation of any aspect of behavior involves its reference to a goal of the organism concerned; thus, within a purposive psychology all behavior must be referred to some conative concept or other. And since ultimate explanation in purposive terms requires reference to a fundamental or natural goal, the basic conative concepts are the instincts, the action tendencies associated with such goals.

The notion of energy is related to the concept of instinct in that instincts, being action tendencies, mark certain changes in the animal's own body and in its relations with the material environment, and energy is required for any change to take place in the material world. But this is the familiar energy of the physical world, whether it be drawn from the impact of one inanimate mass upon another or from the phosphates and other molecules within a living body. In *Body and Mind* McDougall spoke approvingly of the Cartesian notion of "guidance without work,"[32] which was supposed to characterize an influence of mind on body consistent with the conservation of energy. Descartes had used the analogy of a rudder guiding a ship; but since a rudder is a material thing subject to and transmitting physical forces, this analogy was not very helpful. Nor was McDougall able to offer a more convincing one. But one may offer the analogy of a program, which is neither matter nor force, and which may be said to *guide* the performance of the machine in which it is "embodied," although it injects no energy into the system. Before the development of cybernetics, the early ethologist Jacob von Uexkull suggested that the concept of instinct be replaced by that of plan, and he remarked: "It is hard to conceive the nature of a *plan*, since it assuredly is *neither matter nor force*. Yet it is not so difficult to gain an idea of the plan, if one bears a concrete example in mind. The most beautiful plan will not drive a nail into the wall, if you have no hammer. But the finest hammer is not enough either, if you have no plan and rely on chance. Then you hit your fingers."[33] Miller et al. illustrate their cybernetic concept of plan by a similar example. Their plans also are "neither matter nor force" but concepts marking certain structural and functional relationships essential to purposive behavior. The energy required to push a nail into a wall cannot be provided by any plan as such, but only by the actual impact of a real hammer on a real nail; but only if such impact is guided in accordance with the appropriate plan will the nail be successfully driven home. Like programs, all plans—whether cognitive or conative—require real physical energy driving specific causal mechanisms for their actualization. Since the conative plans are, by definition, those specifying the purposeful changes in behavior, the actions of the organism, it is understandable that many writers have associated the concept of "energy" more closely with conative concepts than with cognitive categories. For instance, Perry described belief as establishing connecting channels "by which the currents of purposive energy are distributed and directed"; McDougall actually identified conative concepts with hormic energy mechanisms; Charles Taylor, like Perry, does not go this far, but he writes about natural tendencies as involving some "pressure of events . . . which can only be checked by some countervailing force."[34]

When inquiring into the sources of energy, one may ask whether each basic type of goal-seeking activity is dependent on a specific and limited supply of energy, or whether there is a general pool of energy from which all activities can draw indifferently. Both alternatives seem to be supported to some extent by the behavioral phenomena of *satiation* and *displacement activity*, respectively, and further study in the physiology of motivation will be required to unravel the complexities of this question. McDougall was content to raise the problem, and left it as admittedly unsolved: "Shall we assume that each of the several instincts is activated by energy liberated within its own system? Or do all the instincts of the organism draw upon a common source of energy? Does each propensity generate its own current? Or is there a central powerhouse, the propensities serving merely as distributors of the common energy? There is something to be said in favour of both possibilities." This accounts for his remark that there is "no sufficient ground for postulating more than one form of [hormic] energy."[35]

However, there is not sufficient ground for postulating even one such form of energy. Conative concepts such as "instinct" and "intention" may be correlated with underlying energy mechanisms, but cannot be identified with them. Since one cannot expect that the correlation will necessarily turn out to be a simple one, conative concepts may be more of a hindrance than a help in the detailed investigation of energy mechanisms. Thus, R. A. Hinde has warned of the dangers in assimilating the notion of motivation to that of energy, and has criticized the ethologists for their tendency to hypostatize instincts, to think of an instinct as a sort of "thing" inside the animal pushing it in a certain direction.[36] He has also remarked that theories of drives may tempt one to oversimplify the physiological mechanisms of motivation: "Concepts useful at one stage in the analysis [of

289

behavior] may be misleading at another. A classic example . . . is the concept of 'drive,' 'urge' or 'tendency,' which is useful at an initial behavioral level of analysis but can become a handicap at a physiological one."[37] But even if the relations between conative concepts and underlying energy mechanisms were found to be very simple correlations, the two conceptual levels would remain distinct.

The instinct of food-seeking, the motive of hunger, the intention to eat—all these are conceptually connected with the action of eating. By contrast, a particular energy-exchange within the brain may be correlated with eating, but this correlation is for the physiologist to discover, not for the conceptual analyst to uncover. Conative concepts are all teleologically defined, in terms of the behavior toward which they (necessarily) tend. Being thus essentially linked with purposive action, neither instincts, drives, motives, intentions, nor purposes can be called the "causes" of action, if by this term is understood efficient, rather than final, causation.[38] Of course, it does not follow that wants, purposes, and intentions cannot properly be said to "cause" actions in some sense of the term. One can even allow that it is a conceptual, not a contingent, truth that a conative state somehow causes the bodily action toward which it tends. But what has to be stressed is that the sense in which behavior may be said to be caused by, or dependent on, various psychological states is different from the sense in which eating is caused by movements of the jaw musculature and by electrophysiological activity within the brain.

The Cognitive Guidance of Behavior

It is noteworthy that when discussing cognitive, as opposed to conative, concepts, McDougall did not ascribe causal activity to the conscious states ("ideas") involved. Perception, imagination, memory, intellectual thought, insight, knowledge, and belief—none of these were said by him to involve the causal activity of mind on body. McDougall rejected the ideomotor theory, insisting that no idea (not even the idea of the self) can impel one to action.[39] The internal representations or ideas associated with cognitive categories, he claimed, are not properly causally active and do not give any impetus to behavior. But these cognitive states nonetheless influence behavior, for they guide behavior toward the desired goal:

> The representation or idea of the end is not truly the cause or determining condition of the purposive activity . . . the anticipatory representation of the end of action merely serves to guide the course of action in detail . . . Where the anticipatory representation of the end is vague and sketchy and general, there the action will be general, vague, imperfectly directed in detail; where it is more detailed and full, there action is more specialized, more nicely adjusted to the achievement of its end.
>
> Foresight of the goal and of the attainment of it, governs or guides or steers the selective activity which pick out the relevant relations.[40]

Thus, intelligent behavior cannot be explained without reference to cognitive representations, or ideas, but these do not impart any extra energy, hormic or otherwise, into the system. Knowledge serves a guiding function alone.

McDougall preferred not to describe knowledge atomistically, as a mass of "ideas" lying latent in the mind:

> We have rejected the use of the word "idea" because (among other reasons) it confuses the act of thinking of an object with the enduring conditions which render possible the thinking of that object. And we prefer to call that which endures in the mind, as the condition of our thinking of any object, not "an idea," but a *cognitive disposition* . . . If the word idea is to be retained in the scientific vocabulary, it would be best used as the most general name for enduring cognitive dispositions and systems of dispositions, rather than to denote acts of thinking.[41]

In thus suggesting the substitution of the term "disposition" for "idea," McDougall meant by it "the enduring conditions which render possible the thinking of an object."

This sense of "disposition" resembles Rom Harré's use of "power." It should not be confused with Gilbert Ryle's sense of the term "disposition," which is more common in recent discussions of the philosophy of mind. For Ryle, a disposition is an

291

observed tendency to behave in a certain manner, rather than any underlying state of affairs in the organism that causes the observed behavior.[42] Indeed, to ascribe Ryle's type of disposition to a system may be to make a merely hypothetical statement about its behavior in other, unrealized circumstances. According to Ryle, to say that a pane of glass is brittle, or that a sleeping man is a coward or has a knowledge of French, is to make a hypothetical statement based on past observations of actual behavior. The central criteria and primary reference of such dispositional terms are behavioral, and whatever hidden causes there may be, underlying dispositional behavior, do not contribute to the meaning of dispositional terms. McDougall would have insisted that the ascription of a psychological disposition in Ryle's sense implies the ascription of a psychological disposition in his own sense. Whether he was considering cognitive or conative dispositions, McDougall was concerned to explain the organism's behavior by referring to its underlying causes. Accordingly, he appealed to "dispositions" as the enduring, causal conditions within the organism that underlie the behavior and "render it possible." To say of two sleeping men that one is a coward while the other is not would therefore imply an actual (not merely a hypothetical) difference between them, namely, the presence of a particular state of affairs or set of causal conditions in the one case but not in the other. It is these conditions, rather than any cowardly behavior determined by them, to which McDougall's term refers. According to McDougall, the "enduring conditions" constituting conative dispositions involve a supply of hormic energy, whereas those constituting cognitive disposition do not.

A man's cognitive dispositions together make up his knowledge. Knowledge, as McDougall saw, is not a mere aggregation, or mass, of dispositions or "ideas," but rather an organized system of them: "The total system formed by all the cognitive dispositions of the mind constitutes what is commonly called the knowledge possessed by that mind." Knowledge, then, is a system of mental dispositions that enables the organism to exercise its cognitive and conative faculties on objects within its environment. It forms what McDougall termed "the cognitive structure of the mind." It is a system of internal representations of the world that determines the limits of the organism's psychological

292

(intensional) environment, for every object of which the mind can think must have its corresponding disposition or representation. "The mind of a man is, in fact, a microcosm in which the world, insofar as he can be said to know it, is represented in detail, a disposition for every kind of object and every kind of relation of which he can think."[43] Some of the "objects" in question are external states of affairs; others are aspects of the organism's own possible future behavior. Once a disposition has been built up (usually through commerce with the environment, although some dispositions may be inherited), it can then be referred to in the production of behavior. In this way knowledge of past events is used in the anticipation and direction of future events. Cognitive representations or "ideas" thus provide for what McDougall termed "the essential function of mental process," namely, the bringing of past experience to bear in the regulation of present behavior.[44]

The animal's behavioral repertoire and the purposive criterion of "variation of means" are essentially connected with "the cognitive structure of the mind," for the greater the behavioral repertoire, the more motor operations are in principle available to the organism in its means behavior. It follows that a more detailed task-representation is needed to specify the particularity of the required "change of situation." Thus, increased motor complexity must necessarily involve increased cognitive capacity in purposive organisms. An animal with little discriminatory behavior requires only a limited set of sensory ideas or perceptual dispositions.

The cognitive structure of the mind includes what might be termed "techniques of information storage" as well as the "stored information" itself. McDougall cited the Hanna case history of general amnesia as showing the retention of complex "psychic dispositions" to organize knowledge and memory, even though the specific content had apparently been lost. Cerebral concussion had reduced Mr. Hanna to a state in which he could neither speak, read, walk, nor respond appropriately to familiar sensory stimulation. However, he seemed to have retained the ability to categorize his experience in certain sophisticated ways, so that he was able to assimilate new memory content "miraculously" quickly. McDougall concluded that only the content of his knowledge had been lost, while its organizational structure had remained. The distinction between knowledge and its organization cannot always be clearly made; nor can the distinction between information-processing techniques and the information actually processed. For some knowledge is very likely to be used in the actual encoding and interpreting processes, whether in natural or in artificial intelligent systems.[45]

Moreover, both the content and the organization of a man's knowledge are greatly influenced by his interests. Conation affects cognition not only by selecting some of the things to be known, but also by influencing the systematic relationships between them that are to be represented in the mind, for besides having knowledge of particular objects or events "in isolation," one knows many things about their various interrelations. Thus, the internal cognitive models, or dispositions, must be interlinked in ways representing such relations as spatiotemporal association, causality, means-end linkage, class inclusion, and social "norm" relationships of many different kinds. As McDougall put it:

> The many dispositions of any mind do not merely exist side by side; rather they must be conceived as functionally connected to form a vast and elaborately organized system; and this system is the structure of the mind. The more perfectly organized the mind, the more fully are the objects which compose the world and the relations between them represented in the mind by the dispositions and their functional relations . . .
>
> We have to conceive the cognitive dispositions as linked together in minor systems, and those minor systems as linked in larger mental systems, and those again in still larger systems . . . I cannot think of a horse without thinking of it also as a mammal, as a vertebrate, and as an animal, and as a solid material object. [This] is shown by the fact that, if the horse exhibited properties other than those implied by those general terms, if I saw it fly up in the air, or swim under water . . . I should be thrown into a state of confusion and astonishment: I should hesitate to regard the object as a horse.[46]

This last quotation indicates how McDougall believed knowledge to be involved in perception, or observation. He insisted that "perceiving a horse" involves the activation of all those cognitive dispositions that are linked with the sense impressions

294

received from the horse: "How very inadequately so simple a process as perceiving a horse is described by saying that there is evoked in my consciousness a certain field of sensations of particular qualities and spatial arrangement. The sense-impression merely initiates the thinking process." Consequently, an organism with different background knowledge, or dispositions, cannot perceive the horse in the same way: "A young child on seeing a horse for the first time might receive a sense-impression very similar to mine; but his perceiving would be a vastly simpler process than mine, and the difference between the two is quite incapable of being described in terms of sensations. Yet even his perceiving would be much more than the mere reception of the sense-impression; he would perceive it as a moving solid thing out there."[47] The question of whether a very young child (a newborn baby or a year-old infant) would perceive a horse as "a moving solid thing out there" has been investigated in the developmental psychology of Jean Piaget.[48] It is not necessary to examine here to what extent man's spatial perception is based on innate powers of organization, except to note McDougall's insistence that nativistic theories of spatial perception are required, and his claim that a high degree of organization is hereditarily given in the perceptual-sensory system of many lower animals, which accounts for their "instinctive" responses to particular classes of stimuli.[49]

What is important is the general point: that what is called "perception" is an activity of the knowing mind, incapable of being described in passive associationist terms. It involves the operation of cognitive dispositions in the interpretation of the sensory material, the latter acting as the occasion for perception rather than constituting the perception itself. As McDougall expressed it, the "meaning" implicit in perceptual discrimination cannot be furnished by the "sensations" involved. The act of perception is extremely complex: a vast amount of knowledge is implicit in one's recognition of everyday objects, and guides one's behavior in relation to those objects. That the interpretative processes involved in perceptual recognition are not open to introspection does not show that they are mere "mythology": "The fact that 'I am conscious of no machine-shop in my mind' [as William James had objected], that I do not become aware by direct introspection of the complexity of the processes involved in spatial perception, is no guarantee of their simplicity. In this respect spatial perception is not peculiar, but merely conforms to the general rule that our experience is very far from adequately expressing the complexity of the mental processes which issue in acts of knowing and in behavior."[50]

It is crucial to this philosophical position that mental processes "issue in behavior." Perception is essential to what McDougall regarded as "the most fundamental function of mind," namely, "the guidance of bodily movement so as to effect changes in our relations to the objects about us—changes of a kind that will promote our own welfare and that of the race." Being thus involved in the guidance of bodily action, perception is affected by one's interests and goals: attention to one aspect of the perceptual field rather than another is crucial to concentrated effort and is a function of one's purposes. Perception is selective, and is actively controlled by inherited and acquired central regulatory factors. It is not a mere automatic or passive reception of sensory material. Only anoetic sentience would be totally free from such active construction and control. Perception is an anticipatory adjunct to action: it can serve to guide behavior by activating organized knowledge already present in the mind, and it does not depend on the continuous monitoring of isolated sense impressions. As McDougall remarked, the sensory qualities normally "serve merely as signs of objects, guiding us in our discriminations and recognitions."[51]

This essential link between perception and skilled action (which can be discovered by conceptual analysis of these terms) underlies the fact that, as McDougall pointed out, we are normally said to perceive *objects*, not *visual images*. Similarly, although it is sometimes true to say that we perceive external *patterns*— for instance, optical or auditory patterns—this is not a correct characterization of typical cases of perception. Objects are more than patterns, and are categorized (modeled) by percipient organisms largely according to the uses to which the organism can put them, given its particular repertoire of behavioral skills. Visual perception is typically more than mere pattern-recognition, for it involves inferences to nonvisual object characteristics, such as edibility, aggressiveness, texture, and weight. Visual images and

296

optical patterns are not biologically important in themselves, but only insofar as they can provide the percipient organism with information about object characteristics that are important to its activity and survival. They can provide this information if they can selectively activate internal models or "cognitive dispositions" that include parameters representing the nonvisual object properties concerned.[52] In McDougall's words: "the cognitive disposition is a lock which can be turned by a key of appropriate pattern, and the key which is operative in perception is the qualitative, the temporal, or the spatial pattern of the complex sense-impression."[53]

The cognitive dispositions or "locks" involved in most adult human thinking are largely linguistic in form. Whether considering perception, imagination, or the formation and operation of sentiments, McDougall's account stresses the importance of linguistic factors in man's behavior and experience. McDougall regarded cognitive linkage by means of verbal symbolism as a great advance over prelinguistic linkages. It is particularly useful in facilitating the type of abstract thinking based on what McDougall called *apperceptive synthesis*—that is, the perception of similarity between objects that had previously been regarded as quite different: "As an example . . . we may take the young student of physics who, having learnt to think of gases and of liquids as very different states of matter, suddenly becomes aware of those points of similarity in virtue of which they are classed together as fluid matter." Although language is not necessary to the initial process of apperceptive synthesis, it aids enormously in its clarification and communication: "In the mind of him who first discovers the similarity between classes of objects previously thought of separately, and who thus first thinks of the more general object, the apperceptive synthesis of systems must take place without the aid of a name for the more general object. By afterwards giving the object a name, he fixes it for his mind, and achieves a much greater power of thinking of it at will; and, further, he becomes able to communicate his new way of thinking to others." McDougall saw verbal symbolism as "fixing" ideas for the thinker, since its generality frees the subject from attending merely to the sensory properties of the objects of thought, and since language can be used in the self-regulation of behavior. He remarked that stability of free ideas in the mind allows for greater steadiness of behavior: "In the infant, as his powers of representation develop, as he becomes capable of free ideas, the end towards which any instinct impels him becomes more or less clearly represented in his mind as an object of desire. [This leads to] greater continuity of effort; for, when the power of representation of the object has been attained, the attention is not so readily drawn off from it by irrelevant sensory impressions of all sorts."[54]

Recent psychological research on iconic and linguistic representation has endorsed McDougall's view of the importance of stable imagery and of language in the regulation of behavior. For example, visual imagery seems to contribute to efficiency in the motor task of tracing a finger maze through an array of switches on a response board.[55] Language appears to be crucial to the development of planned, consistent, self-regulatory, and "imaginative" play in very young children.[56] And linguistic representation helps older children to resist the misleading evidence of their senses in volume-conservation experiments of the type initiated by Piaget.[57] Such studies indicate the importance of representation by "free ideas," that is, ideas largely independent of current sensory input.

Models and Mechanisms

McDougall remarked that a "principal task of psychology is, then, to provide a general description of these [conative and cognitive] dispositions and their functional relations, and to give some general acount of their development and organization."[58] According to him, no account of the development and organization of the cerebral equivalents of conative dispositions or "ideas" could be adequate if it did not postulate neurin, neurokyme, or horme acting within the nervous system. And cognitive representations should be referred to a physiological base involving specifically psychic laws, not to the principles of physics. He would have explained the power of cognitive representation in terms of "free ideas" of an irreducibly psychic, or basically non-material, nature.

298

The reductionist approach is quite different, for reductionists attribute the power of representation to the presence of stable neural models underlying the "free ideas" of the mind. For instance, in 1943 K. J. W. Craik discussed the problem of how internal models of the environment may be built up in the nervous system, and how they may be organized so as to influence bodily action. Craik saw complex behavior as being largely determined by reference to such models, but insisted that they be thought of as physical mechanisms:

By a model we thus mean any physical or chemical system which has a similar relation-structure to that of the process it imitates. By "relation-structure" I do not mean some obscure non-physical entity which attends the model, but the fact that it is a physical working model which works in the same way as the process it parallels in the aspects under consideration at any moment . . .

Our question . . . is not to ask what kind of thing a number is, but to think what kind of mechanism could represent so many physically possible or impossible, and yet self-consistent, processes as number does . . .

It is likely then that the nervous system is in a fortunate position, as far as modelling physical processes is concerned, in that it has only to produce combinations of excited arcs, not physical objects; its "answer" need only be a combination of consistent patterns of excitation—not a new object which is physically and chemically stable . . .

I can see no great difficulty in understanding how anything so "different" from physical objects and concepts and reasoning can tell us more about those physical objects; for I see no reason to suppose that the processes of reasoning *are* fundamentally different from the mechanism of physical nature. On our model theory neural or other mechanisms can imitate or parallel the behaviour and interaction of physical objects and so supply us with information on physical processes which are not directly observable to us. Our thought, then, has objective validity because it is not fundamentally different from objective reality but is specially suited for imitating it—that is our suggested answer.[59]

Craik discussed these matters in very general terms. He offered little physiological detail as to the neural parameters involved in cerebral representations, and they still remain to be identified by neurophysiologists. The importance of his contribution was to suggest a way of asking questions about psychological and cerebral function so as to illuminate the control of behavior. Craik's point was that the brain may model environmental or abstract features that cannot properly be predicated of the models themselves. A cerebral model of a red-hot poker need be neither red nor hot. But there must be *some* regularities in terms of which these features of the poker can be "mapped" onto certain features of the model, thereby enabling the organism to behave appropriately toward ("answer questions about") red-hot pokers. The hunter who goes out to catch a rabbit skin must have a cerebral model of rabbits: this model (or system of models) will represent his overall purpose, function in his perceptual recognition of rabbits, and guide his means behavior in various ways. In many cases of human behavior, the representation required to generate the behavior may be nothing short of an internalized language: a human hunter may be told where the rabbits are to be found before leaving his fireside.

McDougall remarked that the dispositions or representative structures underlying specifically human behavior are largely linguistic in form. He did speak of "physiological dispositions" generating behavior, but unlike Craik, he did not believe that these "physiological" structures could be realized mechanistically; he regarded it as "incredible" that "purely mechanical determination runs parallel with logical processes and issues in the same results."[60]

It is now known that it is not impossible for mechanistic systems to reflect highly abstract features of this sort, since computers have already been realized that parallel logical thought processes to some extent. Indeed, the more "logical" (formalizable) the thought process, the more readily it lends itself to simulation by current programming techniques. What has turned out to be much more difficult is the simulation of the stimulus generalization involved in commonplace discriminatory behavior, and the creative generalizing behavior that McDougall termed "apperceptive synthesis." No computer can reliably discriminate between rabbits (or even pictures of rabbits) and other objects, if the rabbits are presented to it in differing shapes, sizes, and situations. Nor can any computer (not trivially programmed to do so) "apperceptively" label a man as a rabbit on account of his facial or behavioral characteristics. And no robot or motor automaton, presented with a two-dimensional picture of a scene showing rabbits sitting on rocks, can immediately anticipate its best path to the biggest rabbit—as man, who lives and moves in the three-dimensional spatial world, can do. Further, no machine can use language creatively in the communication of information about the whereabouts of rabbits, nor reliably translate such information from one natural language into another.

New programming techniques may be required to simulate such behavior. Successful simulation should help to elucidate the concept of "model" involved by showing how one thing can model another thing apparently radically different from it. In fact, a start has already been made in this direction. Some current work in artificial intelligence is directed to specifying precise ways in which various attributes of things in the world may be mapped onto representations available to the machine, which in turn determine machine performance. The attributes are not predicable of the representations themselves. But the representations are interpretable by the machine in such a way that it may function efficiently on the attributes of the real world. Of course, it has long been possible for a computer to "model" or "represent" temperature and color so as to monitor chemical processes, such as the smelting of metals; and no part of the computer needs to be red-hot when the metal is. But the discrimination of one or two simple physical properties of a thing, such as the temperature and color of a poker, is very different from the recognition of indefinitely many members of a given class of material objects, presented from infinitely many viewpoints and in very different contexts.

The "classificatory" or "property-list" approach in pattern-recognition programs (one of the most powerful examples of which is the Uhr and Vossler program) was criticized by Minsky in 1961. He complained that: "Because of its fixed size, the property-list scheme is limited (for any given set of properties) in the detail of the distinctions it can make. Its ability to deal with a compound scene containing several objects is critically weak, and its direct extensions [to generate new useful properties] are unwieldy and unnatural. If a machine can recognize a chair and a table, it surely should be able to tell us that 'there is a chair and a table.' " Minsky recommended the development of formal notations descriptive of the input patterns, which would list the primitive objects in the scene and state the relations among them: "such a description entails an ability to separate or 'articulate' the scene into parts." Being based on list structures, the articulations involved would be essentially recursive, and thus could overcome the information limit inherent in the "property-list" approach: "The important thing about such 'articulate' descriptions is that they can be obtained by *repeated application of a fixed set of pattern-recognition techniques*. Thus we can obtain *arbitrarily complex* descriptions from a fixed complexity classification mechanism." Obviously, the use of any such notation involves the ability to segment (or "articulate") the input pattern into parts. This articulation will be implicit in the programmer's choice of definitions of "primitive objects" and the possible "relations" between them. But the segmentation may be carried out on a number of different hierarchical levels, allowing for what McDougall would have termed differential "attention" to particular parts of the input array:

> The new element required in the mechanism (beside the capacity to manipulate the list structures) is the ability to articulate—to "attend fully" to a selected part of the picture and bring all one's resources to bear on that part. In efficient problem-solving programs, we will not usually complete such a description in one single operation. Instead, the depth or detail of description will be under the control of other processes. These will reach deeper, or look more carefully, only when they have to, *e.g.*, when the presently available description is inadequate for a current goal.[61]

The articulation of pictures of physically continuous objects (such as rabbits, chairs, and tables) into parts (such as lines, corners, and curves) requires that the machine be able to recognize the geometrical predicate of connectedness. More recently, Minsky has shown that this ability is in principle denied to a particular class of information-processing system, which he calls "perceptrons."[62] Perceptrons are parallel-processing systems, having no loops or feedback paths, whose computations depend on weighing the evidence afforded by many independent assessments of the members of a set of values, and which are initially random systems having no prior significant structure. A purely random nervous net would be a physiological embodiment of a perceptron; some current ("self-organizing") pattern-recognition programs are specifications of perceptrons; but serial and hierarchically structured programs such as GPS are not. According to Minsky, any "pattern-recognition" program worthy of the name requires some reliance on serial techniques of heuristic programming as well as a rejection of the property-list approach, in order to generate the necessary recursive (hierarchical) descriptions of the input pattern. No merely "classificatory" program, and no pure perceptron, could reliably report that "there is one rabbit on the chair and another under the table."

Partly owing to the influence of Minsky's critique—and partly, also, to the impetus of Noam Chomsky's representation of "surface" linguistic grammar by a "deep" generative grammar of different syntactic form—the property-list approach has been abandoned by many of those currently working on the mechanization of pattern-recognition.[63] Instead, they try to develop recursive languages (formal notations) describing the structure—or "grammar"—of the input picture. And they attempt to specify the ways in which this structure may be interpreted as representing some other, pictured domain.

For example, M. B. Clowes has asked how the spatial characteristics of scenes containing solid three-dimensional bodies may be "mapped onto" two-dimensional line drawings in a precisely formalizable way.[64] So far, he has limited himself to *scenes* in which all bodies are opaque, all surfaces are plane, and all corners are three-surface corners; and all the junctions in his *pictures* are either two-line or three-line junctions. No shading or cross-hatching is allowed for in the pictures; and no rounded bodies or multisurface polyhedral corners are allowed for in the scenes. Clowes has developed a formal notation that describes the structural features of scenes, describes the structural features of pictures, and states the systematic representative relations between the two. These relationships are far from being simple one:one correspondences. Their complexity can be indicated merely by pointing out that certain junctions of lines in the picture will "represent" corners with an *invisible* edge hidden from view. And the formalism must be able to state precisely which junctions these will be, in terms of the rules for mapping scene descriptions onto picture descriptions. Clowes's formalism allows the articulation of *any* line drawing of one or more solid bodies in varying positions relative to one another, given the limitations cited. This "articulation" is a description of the (segments of the) picture. Together with the interpretative mapping rules, it can be used to generate inferences to all the invisible edges, surfaces, and corners. It also shows precisely which bodies are behind other bodies, and what parts of them are hidden by the body in front. And it enables one to discriminate genuine pictures of solid objects from line patterns that are not pictures of solid objects, such as "meaningless" doodles and pictures of "impossible objects." It allows one to say precisely why a given "picture" is not, in fact, a well-formed picture depicting a possible object. The number of pictures the formalism can deal with is infinite, for pictures of any number of objects, of any size, seen from any angle, can be articulated in a precise manner and interpreted as pictures of solid objects.

McDougall believed that such a general interpretative (discriminatory) ability could not be grounded in any merely material mechanism:

> Any familiar object, such as my dog, may be seen in many positions and from many angles and distances, and in each of an indefinite multitude of such cases the visual impression may evoke from me the same reaction (e.g., the calling of his name), though in each case the sum of physical stimuli constituting the impression on the sense-organ is unique. [As Hans Driesch has said] the object "is always recognized as 'the same,' though the actual retinal image differs in every case. It is absolutely impossible to understand this fact on the assumption of any kind of preformed material recipient in the brain, corresponding to the stimulus in question."[65]

According to McDougall, then, no mechanistic neurophysiology could possibly explain man's everyday perceptual discriminations.

If Clowes's formalism were merely one that was usable by human beings, that enabled men to interpret drawings in particular ways, one might say that only the human mind is able to exploit the representational potential of his language. One might say this, too, of Saul Amarel's discussion of "representations" at various levels of abstraction, for his several formalisms are exploitable by the human problem-solver faced with an indefinite number of puzzles of the missionary-and-cannibal type, but have not yet been applied in a programmed form. However, programs in Computer Graphics, such as Sketchpad, have for some years enabled machines to handle lines as units in various ways.[66] And Clowes has recently outlined an algorithm for the application of his notation.[67] This algorithm both articulates the two-dimensional input and then uses the mapping rules to make interpretative inferences to the three-dimensional domain depicted by it. Machines programmed with this algorithm are able to articulate and so to recognize a picture as depicting solid bodies in various positions relative to one another. "Recognition" here involves not merely the ability to label pictures correctly (as depicting solid objects or not), but also the ability to infer the existence of hidden corners, edges, and surfaces of the real objects, given line drawings in which such invisible features are not explicitly depicted. In this way "an indefinite multitude" of pictures can be handled by the machine. It is reasonable to suppose that a motor automaton might use an extension of Clowes's present program to infer its shortest pathway to any object, given the obstacles shown in the picture to be in front of it.

Clearly, the ability to recognize that a line drawing "represents" one solid object placed on top of another, or even that it represents several such pairs of objects placed at different distances from the notional observer, is only a very small part of the total competence involved in interpreting a picture of rabbits sitting on rocks and accordingly walking over to the furriest rabbit. And the representations or models that must be supposed to be functioning within living organisms are not, in any clear sense, programmed into their brains. But the important point here is that a promising start has been made on describing the basic competence involved in visual perception in such a way that it might be realized on a computer, for computers are known to be purely material (mechanistic) systems. This work provides examples of ways in which the structure of representations may be exploited to generate inferences that are crucial for appropriate motor behavior with relation to the objects represented. The "primitive objects" and "relations" underlying human visual perception, of course, may be different from those chosen for any particular "pattern-recognition" program, although there are methodological reasons for doubting that they could be very different.[68] And the causal mechanisms involved are clearly different in type. But there is now a preliminary notion of how it is possible for a material mechanism of finite complexity to represent an infinite number of actual and possible objects varying in indefinitely many details, even though the representation itself differs from those objects in many ways. Psychologists are therefore rather more justified today than were McDougall's reductionist contemporaries in suggesting that the brain is a mechanistic system which models or codes all the varied environmental features to which man responds. Admittedly, very little is still known in detail of the neural parameters involved in such representations, and the physiological processes by which they are built up. Psychologists who now employ the concept of cerebral model in explaining sensory processes have the advantage of recent neuroanatomical and neurophysiological work as well as of purely behavioral data, but their hypotheses about the nature of the cerebral models involved are still highly schematic. Indeed, after outlining a theory concerning the "stored descriptive rules" generating visual recognition of simple patterns, N. S. Sutherland states: "It is possible that we shall find a way of tackling the workings of the [cerebral model] from a neurophysiological standpoint, though at the moment it is difficult to see any way into this problem. The logic of the whole system appears to be so complex that to test and refine our own theories we shall be driven to computer simulation. It may be that we shall have to put up with having only a general understanding of the system."[69] This remark, in effect, reiterates the argument that the detailed empirical reduction of psychology to physiology may never be achieved in practice, even though it is not unreasonable to regard all psychological phenomena as basically mechanistic.

306

It is now clearer how a system may be said to have internal "models" of red-hot pokers and rabbits, even though nothing inside it is either red, hot, or furry. When all the inner workings of an intensional system are known, one can characterize the model precisely in terms of the way it is (or can be) used. For instance, one can show how the articulated description of the picture structure is used by Clowes's machine to "map" input features onto output features. The input is the picture received by the machine (this information might be fed in on punched cards or magnetic tape, or it might be presented as an actual picture "visually" scanned by a photosensitive receptor mechanism); the output is the scene description offered by the machine after the interpretative process is completed. This output could itself be used by the machine in pursuing certain goals within its (pictured) three-dimensional environment. Were one to build a motor robot using this type of model of space, one could show how its motor subroutines were linked up with (mapped onto) its sensory information, given the mediation of its model.

To show how the model is used by the machine is to know what interpretation the model has for the machine. Or rather, it is to show what model it is that the machine has, for the concept of model is itself intensional. It cannot be defined without reference to the way it is used by the system under consideration. There is thus no genuine distinction between a particular system's model of X, and that system's interpretation of its model of X. One could implant a plastic scale-model of the Pentagon into a dog's brain, or a man's, but this would not enable him to find his way around the building. He could not interpret the model in any way. In other words, he really has no model at all: to "have" a cerebral model of something is not to have an (extensionally defined) copy of it within one's brain. Rather, it is to have an (extensionally describable) causal mechanism within one's brain such that representational relationships of the type so far considered can be set up between input and output. In extensional terms, this model may be very "unlike" the object or feature modeled. But whether it is "like" or "unlike" the object modeled, even assuming that there is something in the actual world that can be reasonably identified as such, no purely extensional description of the modeling mechanism can exhibit it as a

307

modeling mechanism. A description of the electronic changes or causal relationships within Clowes' machine would help one to understand *how* it is that a system may have a model of space, but it would not help one to understand *what* it is to have such a model. This can only be exhibited by showing how the model is used by the system, how it is (intensionally) interpreted by that system.

Even if nothing is known about the inner workings of an organism or machine, prolonged observation of its performance may make it apparent that it is an intensional system. Appropriate response to the environment—or in Minsky's terminology, being able to answer questions about the environment—is a criterion of having a "model" in the required sense. That is, appropriate response is a sufficient condition of having a model. Whether it is also a necessary condition is perhaps arguable. That a system may have highly inappropriate models is clear: "crazy" people do. But the question remains whether a system could have totally inappropriate models, models so divorced from reality that they were not even systematically misleading, and if so, whether such a system could be recognized by observers as an intensional system.[70] The difficulty of distinguishing a system with totally inappropriate models from one with no models at all rests on the basic necessity to ascribe certain goals or interests to the system if it is to be regarded as showing "appropriate" response. However, for present purposes this difficulty may be ignored, since the behavior of men and animals (as well as the performance of some man-designed artifacts, such as Clowes's machine) clearly show certain purposes or "questions" and appropriate responses with regard to them. "Appropriate response" to the spatial features of the environment may (though it need not) include the ability to describe the spatial scene correctly. Basically, what is regarded by an observer as a "correct" description of a scene—whether spoken by another man or printed out by a machine—rests on what the observer can do with the description, given that he finds (or imagines) himself in the scene. In general, an "appropriate" response is one that enables the organism to pursue its various purposes with some success.

The models underlying an appropriate response must be reasonably stable, whether they are temporarily "fixed" in attention, or whether they are conceived as the "enduring conditions" of the organism's preferences and cognitive capacities. And a usable model, as Craik realized, must involve physical regularities enabling input and response to be reciprocally mapped so as to achieve the animal's survival in its environment. However, these regularities may be of various degrees of extensional similarity to physical regularities in the environment, and may involve many different types of physical parameter. They may also function at varying levels of abstraction, given physical differences between the members of the stimulus-classes modeled by them. If R. L. Gregory's argument is correct, then some cerebral representations must be analog rather than finite-state in their physical nature. But whatever the physical parameters involved, the crucial point is that the intensional system (organism or machine) is organized so as to function successfully by way of them. Thus, the concept of "model" cannot be defined independently of the way the model is used in the interests of an information-processing system.

Since the concept of cerebral "model" cannot be defined extensionally, accounts that explain behavior by reference to such models are intensional. Yet language referring to "cerebral" or "neural" models might be thought to be physiological *par excellence*, and thus to suggest that psychology may be strictly reducible to physiology after all. Discussion of cerebral models is very likely to be associated with the view that the modeling functions involved in purposive behavior are based in a mechanistic neural embodiment, so that it is naturally termed "physiological." Nevertheless, McDougall referred to cerebral representations or "physiological dispositions" without conceiving them mechanistically. Indeed, he explicitly rejected the view that the word "physiological" should be applied only to mechanistic features of the organism: "The adjective 'physiological' is applicable to any process or structure in the organism that is concerned in the functioning of the organism. But Perry, like so many others, uses the term 'physiological' in a question begging manner; namely, he implies that a 'physiological' disposition is wholly and purely a material structure and must therefore operate according to the laws of mechanism. But that, of course, is exactly the question in dispute."[71] According to McDougall's

309

usage, hormic energy would be classified as a "physiological" factor, whether or not it could be included within the concepts of physics. However, McDougall admitted that many—perhaps most—people assume the term "physiological" to include the meaning "mechanistic."

In the sense in which I have been using the term, only detailed description of the mechanistic elements (such as excitation levels and neurons) causally responsible for the modeling functions would count as "physiological." If one restricts the term to the neuronal level in this way, one can explain but not express the intensional modeling relationships involved. That is, one allows for the empirical reduction of psychology to "physiology," but not for the strict reduction of these two disciplines. Alternatively, one might decide, for instance, to call Craik's language "physiological," in which case intensional features would be included within the meaning of the term. And should one ever discover the detailed neuronal mechanisms involved in the functioning of different models, it would then be possible to establish detailed fiat conventions, in terms of which "neural process X" would be taken to mean "functioning of cerebral model involved in psychological process Y." There is much empirical evidence suggesting that this is a practical impossibility, even though it may be possible in principle. Cerebral equipotentiality and the differences between natural languages and cultures cast doubt on the feasibility of discovering the mechanistic details of human cerebral models. Even such a simple mechanism as Clowes's machine may "recognize a cube" in an infinite number of mechanistically described ways: one could not necessarily state the sufficient mechanistic conditions of cube recognition, even though one knew how a given machine executing Clowes's program was constructed by the engineer. With the caveat that language referring to neural or cerebral models may naturally be termed "physiological," since they are usually conceived of in mechanistic terms, I shall continue to use the term "physiological" in its restrictive extensional sense.

Intensionality in Behavior and Consciousness

Neural models (or in McDougall's terms, conative and cognitive dispositions within the brain) are thus involved in the mediate

310

processes interpolated between stimulus and response. Behavior that is determined by them will naturally reflect their features. Such models therefore provide a mechanistic basis for the ascription of intensionality to behavior. For instance, neural models of the environment will be in some respects inadequate, leading to errors of omission or of commission. Thus, performance may fail, owing to various forms of "blindness," "ignorance," or "mistake"—all typically intensional terms. Blindness results when for some reason, particular to the individual or common to the species, the internal models do not have parameters capable of reflecting a certain environmental feature: for example, there is no neural property that can have a range of values dependent on different values of the environmental feature, light. Ignorance occurs when the feature in question could be reflected in an internal model but—through absence of informational input—is not yet so reflected. Mistake occurs, for instance, when an environmental feature is of a type which can be represented in the model, but the actual values of the relevant parameters do not reflect the detailed nature of that feature to the usual degree of accuracy. If information presented at the periphery cannot be represented in these intermediary models, then it cannot be used in the behavior of the animal as a whole, even though the peripheral receptors might be capable of accepting it. For instance, the retinas of cats seem to be adequately equipped for color vision, but the cats themselves are colorblind. In general, the information available must be economically coded if it is to be represented in the nervous system.[72] And this code must be deciphered if one is to understand the basic detailed discriminations and recognition involved in such general mental functions as "perception" and "memory."

McDougall held that these general psychological functions are built up from the faculties of *simple apprehension or awareness of objects, affirming, denying* and *comparing.* He defined a "faculty" as "a capacity for an ultimate, irreducible or unanalysable mode of thinking of, or being conscious of, objects; a capacity which we have to accept as a fact, and which we cannot hope to explain as a conjunction of more fundamental capacities."[73] Such "faculties" may be compared with the basic coding operations involved in perception or memory, or with the logi-

311

cally basic operations built into computer programs, out of which general functions such as "searching" or "pattern-recognition" may be built. The equivalents of these "faculties" would have to be mentioned in an account of those detailed intensional features that are determined by the microgenesis of perception.

Just what those equivalents are is an empirical question. The detailed basic operations underlying what seems introspectively to be "simple apprehension or awareness of objects" are largely unknown, whether one wishes to describe them in physiological or psychological terms. To put it another way, the "primitive objects" and "relations" basic to human perception are not known. Consequently, it cannot be explained *why* we interpret particular sensory patterns as we do. For instance, it is often introspectively obvious that a visual "shift" or interpretative reorganization has occurred, as when one views ambiguous figures and pictures of "impossible objects," or experiences figure-ground illusions. But describing and explaining the perceptual shift is no simple matter. Typically, as William James pointed out, introspection gives one no inkling of any "machine-shop" functioning in one's mind. The higher-level representations in the brain do not have access to the details of the lower-level representations involved.

When viewing the familiar sail/sting-ray diagram of the Gestalt psychologists a man knows introspectively that he sometimes sees it in one way and sometimes in the other. That is, he sometimes produces the description he has learned to be appropriate to physical sails, while at other times he gives the description he normally applies to a stingray. Although he does not produce the overt behavior appropriate to either of these physical objects (or even if he does, does not need to observe his behavior in order to say, "I see it as a sail"), he is aware of his perceptual readiness to behave in the appropriate way. But the precise nature of this "readiness" is not introspectively available. Even when introspection appears to give information about this "readiness," it may be misleading, for a man's task-performance may show that he is not, in fact, able to use his "visual image" for his behaviorial guidance in quite the way he says he is using it. For instance, in a discussion of the diagnosis of mental imagery, M. R. Fernald quoted subects who were able to give the contents of an array of letters formerly presented to them visually. These subjects claimed to have visual images of the array, from which they "read off" the letters. But they could give the letters only in the familiar order, not from bottom to top or diagonally.[74] Clearly, the spatial relationships of the letters were somehow represented (modeled) so that the order was preserved; but the information about diagonal relationships had either not been stored at all, or was not retrievable by the subject. Thus, the introspective claim to be "reading off" one's visual image much as one "reads off" a physical array cannot necessarily be accepted without qualification. An observer of the sail/stingray diagram is indeed introspectively aware that his perceptual response to the diagram shifts, that sometimes one perceptual model is activated, sometimes the other. But introspection does not explain why this shift occurs, nor how it is mediated, nor why he cannot "see" the stimulus in certain other ways. The Gestalt psychologists tried to characterize the shift rather more precisely than can be done in the terms of everyday phenomenological description. They appealed to concepts such as *recentering* and the like. But the Gestalt concepts are still too vague: a full understanding of these perceptual phenomena would require more precise terminology.

In a discussion of human vision, Clowes has pointed out the need for a metalanguage precisely characterizing all the many distinct relationships that we can readily identify and name in pictures, and formally defining just those relationships which *in fact* mediate our visual grasp of the structure of the picture concerned.[75] Clowes refers to pictures as "pictorial expressions" and calls his task a search for "picture-grammars," for he sees a close parallel between Chomsky's attempt to describe our grammatical competence in interpreting linguistic expressions, and his own approach to the interpretations implicit in visual perception. Like Chomsky, Clowes believes that the system of attainable concepts (the "cognitive dispositions" of the mind) may be limited by a priori features, whether perceptual or linguistic. He suggests a skeleton formal metalanguage, and tries to state human intuitions of spatial form and position in terms of it. He also uses it to express certain deeper intuitions which he believes—on empirical grounds—to be involved in man's visual perception, such as the use of implicit axes, or the implicit assignment of an interval scale with a small and relatively fixed number of units. These basic relationships, he claims, we expect a priori to find in visual patterns; and they determine our perceptual interpretations of form and objects on the basis of visual patterns taken in at the periphery. According to this view—and also to McDougall's—the functioning of man's visual representations is largely inherent in his constitution, as well as being unavailable to direct introspection. With reference to the perceptual shift involved when one views the sail/stingray diagram, Clowes is able to express precise hypotheses as to the basic structuring operations involved in this shift, as well as suggesting why these two seem to be the only possible visual interpretations of the stimulus figure. His detailed hypotheses may be wrong, but the general approach is potentially fruitful. The detailed description of man's perceptual competence in terms of its most basic operations (representative functions) is likely to prove a highly complex task. For instance, it may be necessary to assume several distinct *levels* of representation in the introspectively "simple" recognition of an isolated character or digit.[76] And the number of levels on which we implicitly structure perceptual data that is highly complex and context-dependent may be accordingly greater. These matters are still highly obscure. But if they can be clarified, it should be possible to explain many intensional features of human experience and behavior that McDougall would perhaps have regarded as "ultimate, irreducible or unanalysable modes of thinking of objects."

Of course, to use the general term "perception," and to speak of its role in behavior, one does not need to know the details—whether psychological or physiological—of its microgenesis. It is conceptually true that the psychological functions termed "perceiving," "imagining," and "remembering" are involved in complex purposive behavior. These general functions also contribute to the intensionality of behavior, in a more obvious way than do the details of the underlying "machine-shop." It has long been recognized that intensional behavior reflects these specifically psychological characteristics of the organism and cannot be explained without reference to the purposes, perceptions, beliefs, and ideas of a psychological subject.

314

In his discussions of consciousness McDougall stressed the intensionality of conation and cognition:

> For over and above all the features that are capable of being introspectively seized and described in general terms as sensations or other feelings of specific qualities, the consciousness of any moment involves something more subtle which eludes all attempts to describe it in this way. And this residue, though it is so subtle and elusive, is nevertheless *the most important part of consciousness.* It is the essential thought-activity: it is *the reference of consciousness to an object*: and it can only be defined or described by naming the *object* of which the *subject* is thinking at the moment.[77]

This essential reference of the predicates of consciousness to a psychological subject, with corresponding objects forming its phenomenal (intensional) world, has the result that their logic differs from that of nonpsychological predicates. Indeed, the term "intensionality" is sometimes defined in a purely logical way, in terms of the implicative relations between propositions. Accordingly, "thought" and "knowledge" are said to be essentially propositional.[78] But a dog's understanding of space—like man's introspectively "simple" interpretations of visual patterns —is not verbalizable by the animal. This does not mean that it could not be verbally described in some natural (or more probably, formal) language, but it does mean that not all knowledge, not all thought, is propositional. This is why I earlier defined "intensionality" in the seemingly vague terms of "the direction of the mind on an object," instead of in the more precise, logical terms used by some philosophers. The "mind," as McDougall stated, should be thought of as a system of cognitive and conative representations of the world, which guides the organism's bodily behavior in accordance with his purposes and with actual environmental conditions. These representations, or models, may or may not be verbal. One can thus accommodate both the linguistically influenced and verbally expressible thought of human beings, and the unverbalized knowledge of animals and men, as truly "intensional." And one can also, of course, allow for the truth conditions of an intensional proposition and of its derivatives to depend primarily on psychological propositions about the subject, rather than on nonintensional truths about the object—even assuming that there is something in the physical world that one can sensibly identify as "the object" in the particular case. Not how the world is, but rather how the subject conceives it to be (represents it as being), is crucial, for this is what determines the truth or falsity of intensional propositions. And this too determines the validity of purposive explanations.

For example, in his abnormal psychology, McDougall recognized that the hysterical paralyses have to be explained psychologically, by reference to the patient's concepts or ideas of anatomical boundaries. This in part accounts for his ascription of them to the activity of a secondary *personality*. Since these paralyses do not follow the objective anatomical boundaries determined by segmental neuromuscular distribution, they cannot be explained in terms of the injury or inhibition of gross nerve-trunks. Naturally, there must be some physiological mechanism causally responsible for the pathological behavior. This mechanism will involve a neural model in the brain, which functions as the patient's concept of *arm*. But what this is is not yet known (and may never be known) in physiological terms. It is clear from the behavioral evidence, however, that it must be one which represents the arm as a unit bounded roughly by the line of the armhole of a sleeveless shirt, rather than by the actual limits of neuromuscular distribution.

It is conceivable that a competent anatomist might develop a "hysterical" paralysis of his arm so nicely adjusted to the objective neuromuscular boundaries, by virtue of his professional subjective knowledge of these boundaries, that he would never be sent to a psychiatrist. Instead, he would offer an intractable problem to the "straight" neurologists. Possibly, they might inject some miracle drug into the brachial nerve-trunks in question so as to counteract the inhibitory messages originating in the patient's brain. Whereupon the specific group of muscles supplied by the sciatic or the femoral nerve might suddenly become paralyzed (assuming that the anatomist's unconscious purposes could be equally well served by a paralysis of his leg as of his

316

arm). The neurologists might be able to counteract the inhibition of these muscles too, thereby "curing" the leg paralysis, but this would not show the patient to be psychologically normal. It would not show that psychological explanations (and ideally, psychological treatment) of the bodily behavior are not required. It would merely show that the functioning of ideas in the guidance of behavior may be upset in various ways by tinkering with the causal mechanisms involved. Patients with hemiplegia caused by lesions in the parietal lobes sometimes systematically ignore one half of their body. For example, they only dress on one side, wash on one side, and put facial make-up on one side.[79] A man's everyday notion of what constitutes "one-half" of his body corresponds closely to objective anatomical criteria (at least if one ignores the asymmetrical internal organs and considers only the body surface and those parts of the body under voluntary control). Consequently, "hemiplegic" behavorial effects could doubtless be fairly readily induced under hypnosis. But the explanation in either case would be totally different. In one case the physiological conditions necessary for normal body awareness and body control would be present, whereas in the other they would not. These examples show in what sense one may agree with those who, like McDougall and Charles Taylor, claim that physiological causes are *necessary but not sufficient* for the explanation of intensional behavior.[80]

With regard to the application of psychological predicates to machines, the mediation of an internal informational store or "model" between input and output provides a basis for the use of intensional terms. Similarly, it provides a basis for regarding different machines (with differing internal models) as analogs of unique psychological individuals. For, insofar as the internal models differ, the machine's performance cannot be explained in terms of laws about machines in general, but must be referred to the details of information storage within each individual machine. These details may differ even in machines directed by the same basic program, if the informational inputs have been different. One could build a group of robots in which the arrangement of gross physical components, such as "limbs" and the wires and levers controlling them, paralleled the gross anatomy of man. If one wished to simulate a hysterical paralysis of the arm in such a robot, it could not be done by simple switching-off of gross "neuromuscular" units corresponding to the various brachial nerves. It would be necessary to supply the central control of the robot with a model or "concept" of arm, in which the sleevehole boundary would be treated as a defining characteristic. For instance, the robot's articulation of pictures of its body would be such that it would mention this feature in the structural description of the picture. It would be interpreted by the robot as the boundary of the physical object (its arm), so that action referred to its arm would be limited by this intensional boundary. Should the robot be instructed to wash its arm, and only its arm, its self-ablutions would be correspondingly limited. And if one arranged for the immediate inhibition of any incipient movement of the arm, the resultant performance would be analogous to that observed in the human patient. Any robot without such an internal model representing its arm simply could not show the "paralytic" performance required.

By virtue of its internal models, many sentences describing the robot's performance would share the characteristic logical features of intensionality. For instance, the sentence "The robot is avoiding moving (inhibiting movement of) its left hand" is referentially opaque. One cannot infer from it "The robot is avoiding moving that part of its body which is made up of such-and-such metals in such-and-such a combination," for this information is nowhere stored (represented) inside the robot. Even if it were, one still could not infer such a thing if this feature were not specifically connected to the inhibitory mechanism by the program, so that it acted as one of the criteria governing inhibition of movement. Similarly, the logical characteristics of indeterminacy, failure of existential generalization, nonextensional occurrence, and nonimplication of embedded clauses (as well as the more complex characteristics recently suggested by R. M. Chisholm) are all applicable to some sentences describing the robot's performance.[81] For present purposes, the main point is that the robot's behavior (its simulated paralysis) would be dependent on its representative models of itself and its environment. Consequently, some descriptions and

318

explanations of the "paralytic" behavior would be intensional in form.

Descriptions of the movements occurring—and of movements *not* observed to occur—in terms of changes in the spatiotemporal co-ordinates of the parts of the robot's body would be extensional, not intensional. And explanations citing the electronic mechanism involved (in terms of the concepts of physics) would be formally mechanistic, not intensional. But the intensional dependencies in the machine's behavior could not be exhibited at this level, for intensional ("psychological") explanation would require an understanding of how the inner representation or model (the robot's "concept") directs the performance of this individual robot. Such explanations, however, would be *basically* mechanistic. They could be underwritten at the causal level by the electronic engineer. Thus, although the distinction between psychological subject and object can be made only within the terms of a psychological vocabulary, nonetheless we can understand how it is possible that this intensional distinction may be based in a purely mechanistic system. The system must be organized in such a way that much of its behavior is directed by reference to internal models representing the actual and possible environment. Since some of these will be so usable as to correspond more closely to actual environmental features than others, the behavior of the system as a whole may show varying degrees of correlation with the facts of the external world. We can thus understand how it is that cognitive representations or ideas can function in the guidance of behavior, and how it is that behavior can seem to be dependent on specific purposes and beliefs, even on false beliefs and unrealizable purposes.

One may think of an animal's purpose as being the goal state toward which it is set to strive, which state is represented inside the organism "with extremely different degrees of clearness and fullness." Test criteria of various types of match-mismatch between this representation and others (perceptual or imaginal) will be used in guiding the behavior to the desired end. So long as these criteria provide information on nearness-of-match, the organism may strive consistently toward a goal it never reaches, or even one that is impossible of achievement. The clearer the representation of the goal state, and the clearer the perceptual representation of present conditions, the more sensible, consistent, and nicely adjusted the behavior may be. A representation that generates recognition in an indefinite number of cases allows for the selection of appropriate response in an "infinite" class of situations, thus mediating the teleological flexibility stressed by Charles Taylor. Some problem-solving programs in which the desired outcome can be clearly stated employ the heuristic of "working backward" from the goal, and use various criteria of comparison in the matching of *present* with *required* state. For this they clearly require some representation of the goal that can function in the direction of behavior before the goal is actually reached. To this extent, programs such as H. L. Gelernter's geometrician and Allen Newell's chess player have organizational features analogous to those found in more complex intensional systems.[82] But the goal representations involved in such programs are less complex (less generalizable) than those that could be represented by some version of Clowes's picture-interpreting program. And this program, in turn, relies on modeling relationships that are rudimentary and crude in comparison with those that must be assumed to underlie the "simple" perceptual recognition and "infinitely" flexible purposive behavior of everyday human life.

These representations or models may be thought of in purely functional terms, neglecting all reference to their material embodiment, but their actual functioning requires a concrete mechanism or substratum. In computers this mechanism is electronic, and the details of the causal processes involved are known. In living organisms the modeling mechanisms must be dependent on neural properties that can be used to represent environmental features, and the physical embodiment of what are abstractly termed "test criteria" must be a set of adjustable relationships between basic neural parameters. If one wishes to formulate hypotheses about the mechanisms of purposive bodily change, there is no reason to postulate any form of energy other than physical energy. There is no reason to insist that the basis of purposiveness cannot be mechanistic.

In sum, to ascribe purpose to an organism is to ascribe consciousness to that organism in some degree. The general categories

of conation and cognition are conceptually related to that of purpose, being based in common criteria. The observable features of
behavior that McDougall recognized as criterial of purposiveness
are also those that logically justify the ascription of other psychological predicates. There can thus be no doubt that clearly
purposive behavior involves *consciousness, beliefs, desires, perception,* and *ideas.* If such terms are interpreted intensionally (not
causally), they can play a part in purposive explanation, for such
explanation requires both cognitive and conative variables. Which
specific purposive variables are most helpful must be decided on
the basis of theoretical and empirical inquiry. Even the terms
"stimulus" and "response" have commonly been interpreted intensionally, and the variety of terms that may be classed under the
general psychological categories of conation and cognition is very
great. But whichever theoretical terminology is preferred, the
intensional relationships of purposive behavior can only be
expressed by psychological concepts that mark the behavioral
distinctions underlying the everyday vocabulary of consciousness.[83] The term "idea" is central, in that it may be interpreted
psychologically or physiologically. This dual interpretation underlies both the common wish to ascribe a function to consciousness,
and the common reluctance to postulate a causal connection
between mind and matter. Interpreted psychologically, "ideas"
cannot be said to cause any bodily action (if by "cause" is understood the efficient cause of change), although they may be said
to function in its guidance. But interpreted as physiological
mechanisms which are used to represent the external world
within the brain of the organism, "ideas" can be seen to play their
part in the causal determination of behavior. Psychology is, in
principle, empirically reducible to physiology. Indeed, "final
causes" require "efficient causes" to affect behavior in any way.
It is a particular type of physical organization—one involving
models representing the world—that allows one to speak of behavior as being directed by thoughts of nonexistent objects and by
purposes impossible of achievement. Only if the predicates of
consciousness are ascribed to mechanistic systems of this sort can
one understand how it is possible for the mind to influence the
body, how it is that a man's purposes may be said to direct his
bodily efforts in the material world.

IX Purpose and Mind

No theoretical analysis of teleological explanation in psychology can be properly understood unless its wider philosophical implications are clear. At an earlier point I claimed that the issues of purpose and mechanism are inextricably linked with the perennial philosophical problem of mind and body, and that an adequate account of them should answer questions like these: is there any real distinction between mental and nonmental aspects of the organism? What is the mind, and does it have a structure? Are there group minds? What is the self, and what is meant by the "unity" or "integration" of the personality? Is each human personality unique? What is human freedom, and is it essential to morality? Are men's actions unpredictable? What is a psychological being, or "subject?" What is the role of ideas mediating between stimulus and response? Are conscious purposes important? Does the mind determine the body?

This claim was, in effect, a promissory note that must now be redeemed. In developing my analysis of the logical nature of purposive explanation and of its relation to mechanistic accounts of behavior, I have offered a rationale for approaching the mind-body problem in a particular way. Indeed, most of the questions listed above have already entered the discussion. A summary statement of my answers to them will indicate how my position compares with behaviorist or Third Force approaches to philosophical psychology. In particular, it will show how my conclusions differ from McDougall's, for a recapitulation of the ways in which his conclusions are or are not acceptable will assist the formulation of my own solutions to some familiar puzzles in the philosophy of mind.

The Distinction Between Mind and Body

McDougall distinguished between mental and nonmental aspects of the organism in terms of the appropriateness of purposive and mechanistic explanations respectively: "Physical processes seem to conform to the laws of strict determination or mechanistic causation; psychical processes conform to the laws of purposive

322

striving, the seeking of goals or ends."[1] Provided that "mechanistic" is understood in McDougall's second sense, the formal
sense, this distinction is acceptable. Mental aspects of the organism are explicable in terms that make reference to purposes or
goals, while nonmental aspects are not. But this distinction is not
acceptable if "mechanistic" is understood in McDougall's third
sense, for explanations that are formally teleological may nevertheless be basically mechanistic. In other words, purposive explanations are, in principle, reducible to formally mechanistic ones.

It does not follow that the reduction, if effected, would involve
one:one, necessary and sufficient correlations between physiological and psychological phenomena, nor that it will ever in fact
be achieved in any but highly schematic terms. Still less does it
follow that mental and nonmental aspects of the organism are
identical, having no real distinction between them. Even if the
reduction were effected in detail, this would not be so. "Reducibility" is a relation holding between sets of statements, not
between properties or entities. Provided that one is not dealing
with a case of strict reducibility, the two sets of statements—the
two theoretical languages—are each required to describe the
properties of the world. In this instance, the case is not one of
strict reducibility, for intensional psychological statements cannot be translated into extensional physiological terms. If the
success of some future empirical reduction were to lead us to
establish fiat conventions in terms of which the meaning of today's
physiological language was changed, then "physiological" language would thereafter qualify as intensional and the present
point would still stand. In McDougall's words: "The mind has a
nature and a structure and a function of its own which cannot be
fully and adequately described in terms of structure of the brain
and its physical processes."[2] Though I accept McDougall's words
here, I do not agree with him that the mechanist must take
teleological language to be merely a convenient shorthand for
causal language, for these two explanatory languages are not
strictly reducible one to another. Explanations in formally
mechanistic terms, making no distinction between psychological
subject and object, are inadequate to express the purposive characteristics of behavior, even though causal explanations of intensional phenomena are always in principle available.

323

While one may, like A. H. Maslow, express this idea as the need to keep sight of "both kinds of world," such expressions may be misleading. The empirical reducibility of psychology to physiology does not imply that there is no real distinction between the mental and physical properties of organisms. But it does imply that there is no need to posit a special ontological realm of substances or forces radically different from material substance or physical forces. To explain psychological phenomena, there is no need to postulate horme.

The mind was said by McDougall to be "the sum of the enduring conditions of [the organism's] purposive activities, [forming] an organized system of which each part is functionally related to the rest in definite fashion."[3] McDougall sometimes referred to the mind as "an immaterial thing." If this expression is taken to mean that mental and physical (material) aspects of the organism are different from one another and cannot be described in the same terms, it is unexceptionable. But the same may be said about the physical and the information-processing aspects of computers. There is no more reason to interpret the "thing" which is the mind in a strong ontological sense, than there is so to interpret the "thing" which is the program. By interpreting "in a strong ontological sense," I mean assimilating the term in question to the category of substance or to the category of energy. McDougall himself resisted the notion that the mind is a special sort of substance. But he succumbed to the temptation to describe the mind in terms of psychic energy.

Because of the organization within the mind, McDougall saw that "we may usefully speak of the 'structure' of the mind," and the structure of the mind was characterized by him as a hierarchy of purposes and goals: "I have sketched the hierarchy of sentiments which we call character in terms of mental structure, of the organization of affective dispositions. The same development may be stated in terms of goals and purposes, the goals towards which the sentiments or their impulses are directed, the purposes that spring from them."[4] As used in this passage, "goals" are cognitive variables and "purposes" are conative ones. But the near synonymy of these terms as commonly used reflects the fact that the explanation of any purposive action must employ both cognitive and conative terms.

324

Cognitive terms define the organism's knowledge and thereby set general limits to the goal states that the creature is capable of having in mind. Conative terms, by contrast, mark out those goal states toward which the organism actually strives. Since the organism's purposes may affect both the content and the general principles of organization of its knowledge, no absolute distinction can be drawn between its conative and cognitive dispositions. Its "mental structure" will involve both these types of disposition, interrelated in many different ways. McDougall gave an account of the many objects and relations that may be represented on the various levels of a man's knowledge. He also gave an account of their connections to conative dispositions by way of innate instinctual bonds or acquired sentiments. These accounts together indicate the general form of the structure of the mind. Whether or not one prefers to use McDougall's terminology, the conceptual outlines of any description of the structure of the mind must be logically equivalent to those of his theory. The potentiality of affect, which functions so as to indicate the specific conative dispositions aroused at a given moment, may be said to be an aspect of mental structure; but the occurrence of affect is more properly regarded as mental process. In view of behavioral properties such as hope and fickleness, mental structure includes also the characteristic ways in which the organism follows its goals, both in the short and the long run. If particular strategies are typically employed in the service of various goals, these too form part of mental structure. An organism's intensional world is determined by the detailed nature of the structure of the mind: the objects and relations of which it can think, and the desires and intentions that it can connect with those objects.

Mental structure is largely hidden to introspection, as is much mental process. Whether consisting of cognitive or conative dispositions, knowledge or intentions, mental activity is largely unconscious and implicit in behavior, rather than being explicitly expressed or open to conscious inspection and control. That is, the detailed operations involved in the mind's overall information-processing are neither clearly evident in behavior nor introspectively available at the higher levels of the mind in question.

A purposive creature is a sensor-effector system as well as a locus for internal informational control. If a creature is striving toward a certain goal state—some "change in situation" in its environment—whether or not it actually achieves that state will depend largely on its motor abilities. This does not preclude the occurrence of "purely intellectual" purposive activity that is not directly expressed in motor behavior, such as the thinking out of means to a chosen end, or the silent solving of a problem in mental arithmetic. Increase of behavioral repertoire necessarily involves increase in cognitive complexity, which in turn sets limits to the conative aspect (the possible ambitions) of the mind. It follows that a complete description of mental structure must include reference to the executive capacities of the organism in its environment. In other words, it must include reference to the behavioral embodiment of the mind in question.

McDougall wrote a book called *Group Mind* as a sequel to *An Introduction to Social Psychology,* although later admitting that "the title was unfortunate, for it antagonized many."[5] In view of his definition of mind, McDougall was not wholly unjustified in using this expression, for an organized and enduring group instills in its members certain "group sentiments," such as professionalism and patriotism, class hatred and xenophobia. These sentiments involve specific ways of seeing the world and of striving within it. They cannot be referred to a person regarded merely as an isolated individual, but must rather be referred to a person considered within his social setting. The group as a whole may be said to "make decisions" and "take actions" that would not be possible to an isolated individual. A solitary individual could not declare war on Germany, for instance, or direct his actions according to any professional etiquette. It may be preferable, however, to say that an individual declares war, or wages it, on behalf of a group, rather than to speak of a "group mind," for all the "behavior" of the group must be effected through the behavior of the group members. The group mind has no embodiment except through its influence on the embodied minds of its members. Nevertheless, there is a distinction between behavior which can be explained without reference to the individual's place in an organized social setting, and that which cannot. Behavior that must be explained by reference to such a setting may be described as influenced by a "group mind." Some of this behavior will be directed by powerful group sentiments, whose power depends on the individual's view of his self as being a member of particular groups.

Self, Individuality, and Freedom

In McDougall's theory, the self is a cognitive representation of the organism contained within the organism. This theoretical analysis is broadly acceptable, and it is useful in showing how the self comes to be a crucial part of the self-conscious organism's mental structure. The idea of the self is associated with particularly strong conative dispositions and thus can play an influential part in guiding any behavior whose goal can be cognitively linked with it. Such behavior forms an important and distinctive subclass of human purposive behavior. McDougall outlined the development from the idea of the self as "a centre of effort" to the idea of the self as "certain bodily and mental capacities, [and] also of a system of relations between [the] self and other selves." He pointed out that the child's idea of his self develops "in large part by accepting the ideas of himself that he finds expressed by those about him."[6] In other words, the idea of the self is a high-level model of the organism: a representation of the fact that it has a representation of itself. Only information-processing systems that have such a model, which is used to answer general questions about themselves, may properly be termed "selves." Such general questions include, "What sort of person am I?" and "What sort of person am I aiming to become?"

Psychologically, each of these questions plays a very important part in normal human life, as McDougall realized. His account of the self anticipated the distinction between self-image and self-ideal, and stressed what were later called ego involvement and propriate striving, for there are at least two "ideas of the self" in the normal man: his model of himself as he believes himself to be, and his model of what he would like to be. Each of these, in the normal personality, represents the self as a purposive system capable of pursuing certain ends and guides the person's behavior accordingly. Each of them (like all cognitive dispositions) may be more or less "realistic," more or less appropriate to his actual capacities and to the environmental constraints on his behavior. Unless there are special reasons to the contrary, a man's idea of

327

what he would like to be strongly influences his idea of what he will try to become.

The Third Force psychologists in general stress "becoming" as the process of growth towards "being."[7] In other words, they are concerned with the changes in a man's life pattern that are directed by the man's striving toward his ideal self-image. One reason they oppose reductionist psychologies is that, like McDougall, they fear that a man's belief in the incompatibility of purpose and mechanism may destroy the possibility of a conative linkage between his self-image and his self-ideal. For such a belief, given the acceptance of reductionism, could provide a "special reason" for seeing the model of what one would like to be as irrelevant to the model of what one is trying to become. Analogously, people who wish they had been born in the eighteenth century, or male instead of female, do not normally try to become so impossibly different from what they are. The "depersonalization" often encountered by psychiatrists rests on a degradation of the self-model, so that the self is no longer seen as a purposive system capable of pursuing certain ends, but rather as a passive object in the world. Clearly, such a model cannot be used to give practical answers to questions such as, "How can I become like this?" or "How can I achieve that?" Such pathological depersonalization may have many degrees, and may spring from many sources. One possible contributory source, given the common antireductionist view of purpose and freedom, is a high-status reductionist psychology. But if the models of purpose and mechanism can be reconciled—if it can be shown how purposive and mechanistic explanation can be applied to the same physical system, each being necessary to the full understanding of that system—then both may be incorporated into one's self-model without any consequent depersonalizing effect. For similar reasons, it is of practical importance to insist that empirical reducibility does not imply that mental properties are "really" physical, that there is no real distinction between them.

The idea of the self forms the cognitive core of the self-regarding sentiment. The integration of the conative dispositions of the mind by means of this master sentiment is the integration of the personality—what McDougall called "character." A high degree of integration results in the purposive unity and consistency

328

typical of the normal personality: "Character is achieved by . . . organization of a higher level which integrates the sentiments and tastes into one system. So long as this higher level of organization is not achieved, the various sentiments may enter into brute conflict with one another, with resulting inefficiency of action, waste of energy, confusion of methods and wavering of purposes."[8]

Despite his insistence that human character cannot be basically mechanistic, McDougall's theoretical psychology is useful in helping to explore the extent of the analogy between mind-and-body and program-and-machine. To claim that there is such an analogy is not to deny that there may also be significant differences. Nor is it merely to make a philosophical point leading to inconclusive debates on what McDougall would have called "questionable and speculative hypotheses." For the analogy may be psychologically useful in directing a general research strategy, and in suggesting questionable empirical hypotheses, with reference to various levels of psychological inquiry. These hypotheses will concern the detailed nature of the information-processing carried out by the organism, whether at the level of perceptual microgenesis or of the purposive integration typical of human personality. For example, McDougall's account of the growth of the hierarchical structure of the mind and his views on "dissociated personalities" are suggestive of problems about the degree of executive control that may be influenced by one level of a complex program (or set of programs) over others. A recent writer has referred to "the question of how organized and integrated identity emerges from, and gives organization to, the antecedent processes that generate it" as the greatest of all the problems that have been abandoned by psychologists because of their complexity and philosophical implications, but as one which might yield to inquiry given some of the insights of cybernetics.[9] McDougall attempted to deal with this problem in terms of monads and the master sentiment of self-regard. These concepts, which may be interpreted cybernetically, can be used by the reductionist to explain two "opposing" truths about personality: though it acts as a unitary agent, it is built up by a gradual integrative process.

Self-directed behavior, then, is not to be referred to any

329

homunculus or "pure ego." Rather, it should be referred to a high-level executive control system, which has access both to sensory input and to stored knowledge in deciding upon and monitoring the action taken. McDougall's term for this integrative mechanism was the master sentiment of self-regard. Ideally, all mental dispositions—conative, cognitive, and executive—should be accessible to some degree of control by the self-regarding sentiment, and conflicts of purpose should never occur. In fact, perfect integration is never achieved, and only relatively extreme cases of behavioral malintegration are classed as psychopathological.

McDougall believed each human personality to be unique: "The structure of the mind seems to be peculiar to each individual."[10] He explained this in terms of the infinitely many possible combinations of the various dispositions contributing to the structure of the mind. His position here is reasonable, for quite apart from any innate differences that there may be between human individuals (and McDougall, with his emphasis on eugenics and racial characteristics,[11] believed there to be many), different people have differing environmental histories. They grow up in different cultures, are reared by different parents, and meet with different accidents and obstacles in life. Their sentiments thus become centered about different core-objects, and the many varying associations thereby encouraged strengthen the differences accordingly. Provided that one does not interpret "mental structure" at an extremely fine-grained level, it is possible in principle that there might be two human persons with identical mental structure.[12] But it is at least as unlikely as that the sand on a beach might be distributed in precisely the same way on two different days. Even two dogs are likely to differ in mental structure, fawning on different masters and exploring different environments.

However, dogs—although perhaps "unique"—cannot be said to be free. To be sure, their behavior does show a certain degree of autonomy with respect to their environment, for they are fairly complex purposive creatures. But they do not qualify for the ascription of freedom, since free action is self-determined action. In other words, a conceptual analysis of the everyday notions of "freedom" or "voluntary action" must involve reference to the

330

action's being somehow determined by the self of the acting individual. It is because dogs have no self-image or self-ideal that their behavior cannot be regarded as truly voluntary, or as the action of morally responsible beings. In McDougall's terminology, volition can achieve "action against the strongest desire" because the conative powers of the self-regarding sentiment come into play as the person strives to live up to his self-ideal.[13]

Within a man's self-ideal, if he is a normal adult rather than one with a highly pathological self-image, there are represented certain very general moral rules of conduct. Action that is guided by these moral aspects of the agent's representation of himself differs from action that is not so guided. And action which—given the agent's mental structure—could have been so guided but was not, is nevertheless action for which the man may be held morally responsible. An act done irresponsibly, without reference to moral considerations or ideals, may thus merit moral praise or blame. Similarly, although free action is typically conscious, a man may be said to have acted freely on an occasion when he did something "automatically" that he could have controlled by conscious deliberation if he had tried. As McDougall pointed out, some of man's actions (some of the subordinate monads) are amenable to conscious self-control, and some are not. One can thus allow that the normal personality shows predominantly self-planned and self-regulated behavior, without accepting either an indeterministic interpretation of freedom or the existentialist interpretation offered by some present-day psychotherapists.

The apparent unpredictability of human behavior rests on three factors. First, prediction based purely on knowledge of the organism's purposes always has "degrees of freedom." The detailed choice of means behavior typically depends on factors other than the conative structure of the mind. Such factors may include the past history of conditioning, current environmental constraints, and physiological causes, such as the hormones regarded by Mc-Dougall as basic to temperament. The type of behavior that is most suited to explanation in terms of simple conditioning is behavior which is conatively undecidable in this way. Once a habit of response has been acquired, it may be made use of in purposive behavior. But it may sometimes prove recalcitrant to control by related purposive dispositions: the habit of smoking may be resistant to moral resolutions, though not to aversive conditioning. The selection of means behavior also depends on the organism's beliefs, giving rise to the second limitation on the predictability of behavior. What R. B. Perry called the "independent variability" of purpose and belief implies that if a man's detailed beliefs are not known, reliable prediction of his behavior is impossible, even though one knows the purposes he has in mind. The variety and complexity of the cognitive and conative structure of the human mind make reliable prediction very difficult. This difficulty is compounded by the third complicating factor: the role played by the self-image in directing human actions. The Third Force emphasis on "idiographic" methods in psychology may be largely justified in these terms, for a man's idiosyncratic concept of himself is often a crucial determinant of his behavior, and the understanding of a man's life as he sees it himself may help the psychologist in his predictions regarding the man.

A traditional argument for freedom claims that a man may always choose not to stamp his foot, whatever predictions an observer may make about the matter. A psychological observer who informs a man of his prediction that the man will now stamp his foot, because a fly has landed on it, may also happen to know that this particular man thinks of himself as a free agent whose actions are unpredictable in scientific terms. Accordingly, he may silently predict that the man will endure the tickling of the fly rather than be seen, by himself or by the psychologist, as a predictable, deterministic creature. The fact that this silent prediction will very likely be verified if kept silent, but may not be verified if communicated to the man by the observing psychologist, in no way weakens the case for predictability. For it is only to be expected that the man's (and also the psychologist's) behavior will be influenced by the receipt of information about what others think of him, as well as by his own thoughts about himself. Examples taken from clinical contexts, instead of from medieval disputation, are likely to be more complex than this one, and to recall more forcefully Maslow's insistence that the psychologist cannot always be a purely neutral, or "objective," observer.[14] But the basic point is that the correct prediction of behavior will often be one which takes into account the individual's particular self-image, rather than one which relies purely on nomothetic generalizations unrelated to the self-image (such as the statistical probability of a man's stamping his foot after a fly alights on it). McDougall expressed this by saying that action is predictable in terms of psychological laws rather than the laws of physics.

McDougall backed up his claim that human action is not predictable by the laws of physics with an appeal to what he saw as the indeterministic implications of quantum mechanics. Physicists are agreed that the prediction of individual quantum jumps is impossible; however, they differ over the philosophical implications of this fact. But the advisability of idiographic methods in certain psychological contexts, and the purposiveness of behavior in general, in no way imply that the causal mechanism involved is not wholly deterministic. It may be, or it may not. Recent neurophysiological research suggests that the response of individual nerve cells to stimulation is stochastic, or indeterminate, in that it requires statistical analysis in terms of probability of firing.[15] Any meaningful statement of the relation between an individual neural response and a particular stimulus is thus impossible. This indeterminacy rests on spontaneous random activity at the synapses: but "random" here means "unpredictable in terms of the incoming stimulus," not "unpredictable in principle." Synaptic activity may or may not involve indeterminacy at the quantal level. Even if it does, the "unpredictability" of human behavior on which some personality psychologists insist would not thereby be vindicated. Indeed, McDougall himself saw that a radical indeterminism at the origin of action would be incompatible with human freedom and responsibility, rather than essential to it. A radical indeterminism in "conatively undecidable" behavior would not threaten human purposiveness. Thus, if alternative means-behaviors to an important end are equally likely to effect it, and are indifferent relative to a man's other goals, he may—and often does—decide between them by tossing a coin. And an intermittent toe-twitch triggered by some cerebral quantum-jump would be purposively irrelevant, unless he happened to want to perfect his powers of dancing, in which case it would be included as one of the many physical constraints imposed by a man's body on his goal-seeking capacities. The issue of indeterminism in physics is therefore totally irrelevant to the psychology of action, unless there are independent reasons for believing that physical indeterminacy may result in the upsetting of specifically purposive behavior. No such reasons were offered by McDougall; indeed, he implicitly discounted them by claiming that purposive behavior *is* predictable, if only by psychological laws.

Subjectivity and Conscious Purposes

It might seem that, if psychology is basically mechanistic, then action must be predictable in terms of physical laws, for certain bodily changes describable in the vocabulary of physics are sufficient conditions of actions and all other psychological phenomena. These changes are, in principle, predictable by the laws of physics.[16] But the crucial point is that these changes are so predictable only as described in physical terms, not as psychological phenomena, for extensional vocabularies making no distinction between subject and object logically cannot express the specifically intensional dependencies between psychological phenomena that are essential to "action" properly so-called.

The intensionality of behavior is grounded in ideas mediating between stimulus and response. McDougall regarded ideas as mental dispositions or enduring conditions contributing to the structure of the mind, rather than as momentary psychic events or "sensations." And they are always to be ascribed to a thinking subject. But, although he maintained that, "so far as we positively know . . . this subject is always a material organism, or is embodied in, and manifests itself to us only in and through the medium of, a material organism," he also stated that an idea could not possibly be "any kind of preformed material recipient in the brain."[17] According to him, the representational power of ideas cannot be based purely in mechanism.

However, some physical systems may be said to use internal subsystems as "models" or "representations" of the outer world. The notion of "model," or the relation of "representation," cannot be defined extensionally, without reference to the system's general interests or to the use to which the "model" may be put by

334

the system concerned. Nevertheless, these basic intensional categories may be ascribed to physical systems, given the fact that
the causal mechanism of the system is organized in the requisite
way. The relation of mind to body is somewhat analogous to the
relation of program to machine. But it is more closely analogous
to the relation between an internal model and the various stimulus patterns and motor sequences that are systematically linked
by way of the model. To express this linkage, intensional vocabulary is required—but only a causal mechanism so organized as to
generate the linkage within the system's overall performance can
function as the material embodiment of the model in question.
In programmed systems of this type the causal mechanism is
known. In nonprogrammed systems, such as living organisms, it
is not, nor are all of the intensionally describable information-
processing operations taking place within these systems. But the
mere fact that a mechanistic explanation is available for all the
physical changes within a physical system does not preclude the
ascription of intensional predicates to it.

Mechanisms whose behavior is determined by models in the
appropriate sense may be regarded as rudimentary or complex
psychological beings. With the possible exception of "anoetic
sentience," all psychological commerce with the environment—
or with the structure of one's own mind—is intensional in nature.
Motor behavior and "idle" thought alike involve a psychological
subject-object distinction that cannot be ignored in the understanding of purposive phenomena. A physical system having some
functioning models or other is, therefore, an intensional system.
And the detailed nature of its models or "ideas" determines the
truth of any detailed intensional or psychological propositions
that may be used in describing it.

Likewise, the validity of any suggested purposive explanation
depends on the nature of the representational models actually
underlying and generating the purposive phenomenon in question. In general, the purpose of any activity is the directive idea,
or representation, of the goal state that the organism has in mind.
If purpose is interpreted in this way, rather than as "the attainment of the goal" considered as some future event, there is no
special difficulty in understanding how behavior may be directed
by unrealized or unrealizable purposes.

335

A purposive pyschology must distinguish between purposes that are conscious and those that are not. McDougall stressed the role of conscious purposes in behavior. While he was sensitive to the influence of unconscious purposes, whether in normal or pathological behavior, he regarded conscious intentions as being particularly important. Like the Third Force, he emphasized the adult man's self-conscious striving toward unrealized goals, rather than the repressed infantile motivations emphasized by Freud. An essential feature of conscious purpose is the selective attention of the mind to a particular part of the actual or intended environment. The direction of one's attention is a function of one's purposes at the time. The effect of attention is not only to select and stabilize a particular focus for thought, but to allow for a more detailed analysis, and therefore a more subtle control, of actions taken with respect to that focus. Analogously, hierarchical programs based on recursive routines may temporarily "focus" on one level or aspect of a problem to the exclusion of others. This exclusion may be total (which in real life would doubtless be highly inefficient, since danger may threaten at any moment) or it may be relative to indefinitely many factors of the problem situation. A subroutine normally executed by a compiled program might, given its failure, be switched to an interpreted program, allowing for step-by-step analysis by a higher level of control. This switch to a different form of information-processing would parallel McDougall's theory that conscious discrimination appears only at points of difficulty. To allow for the introspective simplicity and resistance to conscious control of many psychological processes, one may assume that some subroutines are relatively autonomous, their details not being amenable to high-level direction nor even available as information to higher levels of the system. Although having information about the detailed operations involved in the subroutine does not necessarily ensure the ability to "interfere with" or control it in detail, the converse is not true.

To be conscious of a feature is at least to have some information about it available at one level of the mind. And to be conscious of a feature of one's own mind—such as a purpose or intention—is at least to have some information about it available at a higher level of the mind. But the commonest sense of "conscious" involves more than this, for it involves also the introspectively available knowledge that one has the information in question. A conscious purpose, then, is one of which one is introspectively aware, or which one can recognize introspectively fairly readily, should one be required to do so. To be able to state verbally that one has the relevant information is generally regarded as a sufficient condition of having this self-knowledge, barring special circumstances such as play-acting or posthypnotic suggestion. It is not a necessary condition, however, since some aphasic patients who could not verbalize it could nevertheless show themselves to possess this introspective information in other ways.[18] Since this level of knowledge involves a reflexive reference, it requires a representation of the mind within itself. And full "self-consciousness" requires that there be some representation of that representation. In general, any model or level of representation can have knowledge of itself only by way of a model of itself. Moreover, the relation of representation is essentially recursive, in that any model of a system within the system can, in principle, itself be modeled, and the process repeated indefinitely. This accounts for what some philosophers have called the "systematic elusiveness" of self-consciousness.[19] Reciprocal and nonreciprocal limitations on the availability of information between models on various levels account for the common intensional phenomena of self-deception, unconscious intentions, and "compartmentalized" knowledge, as well as for the uncommon phenomena of multiple personality.

McDougall's claim that all the self's purposes are conscious rests partly on the fact that self-directed behavior necessarily involves reflexive reference and information; otherwise, it would not qualify as *self*-directed behavior.[20] McDougall's claim rests also on the fact that, in his terms, purposes of the self are under the conative control of the powerful self-regarding sentiment. Many conscious purposes are not purposes of the self in this sense. For instance, a man may consciously strive to reach an apple on a tree, and devise various cunning stratagems in the process; but unless his self-image is such that he cannot bear to fail at any task, however trivial, his action will be directed by instincts or sentiments other than those directly connected with the self. His attention is selectively directed to the apple, but his self-image

337

is not involved in any way. To describe the self-regarding senti-ment as "powerful" is to say that, on the whole, its purposes have priority over others. Being thus important, these purposes are especially likely to receive the attention of the mind, particularly if they run into difficulties. This, then, is a further reason why McDougall regarded all the purposes of the self as conscious purposes. It does not follow that the most detailed operations involved in the self's activities are ever available to introspection or self-control. Nor does it follow that the higher-level operations involved are continuously so available, or always being attended to.

How the Mind Determines the Body

McDougall was in no doubt that the mind does, indeed, deter-mine the body. "In some sense," he wrote, "the goal plays a part in determining the action."[21] According to him, thinking plays a causal role in behavior, though not all thinking is capable of doing so:

> The representation or idea of the end is not truly the cause or determining condition of the purposive activity.
> It is not mere thinking that makes the difference; it is rather thinking in that peculiar way we call desiring . . . It is thinking of this sort for which we claim causal efficacy upon the course of events.[22]

McDougall's attribution of hormic powers to "thinking in that peculiar way we call desiring" rested on a misinterpretation of the logic of conative terms. It rested also on his joint beliefs that all explanation should ultimately refer to energy mechanisms, and that physical, mechanistic energy mechanisms are incapable of generating purposive phenomena. I have argued that purposive explanation does not, in and of itself, refer to energy mecha-nisms. It exhibits the functional relationships between behavioral and cerebral variables defined in intensional terms; in other words, it analyzes the structure of the mind.

Nevertheless, mechanistic systems of a certain sort can generate purposive phenomena. Indeed, only by thinking of purposive explanation in the light of its applicability to such systems can

338

one understand how it is possible for the mind to influence the body. The inner organization of these mechanistic systems involves representational models of the world (and of possible worlds) that mediate between stimulus and response. For any given behavioral unit, the model currently functioning as the purpose of the activity in question is particularly important. But no explanation of its function can be complete without reference to the other models that are brought into play in concert with it. These include representations of current perceptual information, of various values and moral attitudes, and of differentially realistic background beliefs. All these models must be attributed to one and the same intensional subject. The most general subject-term is mind; and one of the most important object-terms is body. For behaving organisms are able to pursue most of their purposes by bodily actions affecting the environment in various ways. This bodily action is mapped onto their inner representations in such a way as to be guided by them. Thus, only explanations of motor action that refer to the conative and cognitive representations determining it can exhibit its place in the life of the purposive organism. Despite the empirical reducibility of psychology, no formally mechanistic physiological explanation of bodily movement is logically capable of doing this.

We may, then, agree with McDougall that in some sense the goal plays a part in determining the action. Moreover, we can understand and accept the confession of William James—whose "disciple and humble pupil" McDougall felt himself to be,[23]

Let one try as one will to represent the cerebral activity in exclusively mechanical terms, I, for one, find it quite impossible to enumerate what seem to be the facts and yet to make no mention of the psychic side which they possess . . . The psychic side . . . seems, somewhat like the applause or hissing at a spectacle, to be an encouraging or adverse *comment* on what the machinery brings forth. The soul *presents* nothing herself, *creates* nothing, is at the mercy of the material forces for all *possibilities*, but amongst these possibilities she *selects*, and by reinforcing one and checking others, she figures not as an "epiphenomenon," but as something from which the play gets moral support.[24]

339

The emphases in this passage, provided by James himself, could not have been better placed for the present discussion. The purposes of the mind may be thought of as guiding what the bodily machinery brings forth, and as selecting from all the material possibilities just those bodily changes that will tend toward the goals they represent. But one must always be prepared for the question how a particular purposive phenomenon is actually generated by being embodied in some physical mechanism. Analogously, a computer program is thought of as guiding or directing the machine that executes its instructions; but the program is totally dependent on the material forces of the physical mechanism, and in this sense can create nothing itself.

The representational models within an intensional system (whether the system is programmed or not) may reasonably be said to "determine" its behavior. In addition, if one wishes to influence or predict the purposive behavior of such a system, it is crucial to have some information about its models. In view of these points, the everyday usage of "cause," in which purposes are said to "cause" bodily actions, may be defended. We may allow that the purpose of alarming a burglar can cause a man to stamp his feet on the stairs. We may even allow that cognitive factors such as beliefs and ideas can cause bodily actions. More generally, the mind may understandably be said to cause changes in the body. But the distinction between final causes and efficient causes must not be forgotten. If it is, we are liable to fall into ways of speaking no less misguided than the Mock Turtle's assurance to Alice that, "No wise fish would go anywhere without a porpoise . . . Why, if a fish came to me, and told me he was going a journey, I should say 'With what porpoise?' "

Though the Mock Turtle was misguided, he was not misleading: Alice realized that, despite his protestation to the contrary, he really meant "purpose." The same cannot be said for philosophical interpretations of purpose that represent it as totally incompatible with mechanism, or for claims that purposiveness involves a special psychic energizing factor. Their plausibility rests on their recognition that teleological explanation cannot be strictly reduced to formally mechanistic terms. Their mistake lies in assuming that empirical reducibility entails strict reducibility, so that if psychology is reducible to physiology, then we

340

are not what we thought we were: we are not "really" purposive, thinking creatures. Rather than accept the latter conclusion, many people—professional psychologists among them—have resisted the general reductionist influence of those psychological traditions that assume behavior to be basically mechanistic. But such resistance is misdirected.

Specific mechanistic theories may, of course, be questioned. There may be differences of opinion over how much animal or human behavior can be fruitfully studied in the terms of conditioning or simple stimulus-response connections. Even if it is agreed that stimulus and response should be interpreted intensionally, and that a strictly peripheralist behaviorism is unacceptable, there is room for disagreement over the precise nature of the centralist theoretical concepts to be employed in behavioral research. There is also room for debate over the question whether relatively molecular terms such as "stimulus" and "response" are practically or theoretically useful in all areas of psychological inquiry. Some personality theorists have based their conceptual systems on these terms, whereas others theorize on a relatively molar level. The research strategies associated with different psychological theories may be differentially suited to various interests. And as the background knowledge alters, the fruitfulness of a given strategy of research or a particular level of theorizing may alter also. These disagreements cannot be settled in the abstract. They require close attention to specific psychological theories, and careful reference to the type of psychological problem that a given theoretician hopes to solve.

A particular "mechanistic" psychology may be faulted for asserting the strict reducibility of purpose. Or it may be rejected as unsuited to the problems that interest the particular psychologist attacking it. But mechanistic psychologies in general cannot be dismissed merely on the ground that they assume the empirical reducibility of purpose, and so supposedly deny us our humanity. Purposive psychologies may properly be regarded as basically mechanistic, no matter how "molar" or "humanist" their theoretical terms may be. To regard all purposive creatures as, basically, physical mechanisms is not to deny the reality of mind, nor to assert the inhumanity of man.

341

Bibliography   Notes   Index

Bibliography

Abelson, R. P. "Computer Simulation of 'Hot' Cognition," in *Computer Simulation of Personality,* ed. S. S. Tomkins and Samuel Messick, pp. 277–298. New York: Wiley, 1963.

Albritton, Rogers. "On Wittgenstein's Use of the Term 'Criterion,'" *Journal of Philosophy,* 56 (1959), 845–857.

Allport, G. W. *The Use of Personal Documents in Psychological Science.* Social Science Research Council Bulletin 49. New York, 1942.

————. "Effect: A Secondary Principle of Learning," *Psychological Review,* 53 (1946), 335–347.

————. "Personalistic Psychology as Science: A Reply," *Psychological Review,* 53 (1946), 132–135.

————. *Becoming: Basic Considerations for a Psychology of Personality.* New Haven: Yale University Press, 1955.

————. "The Open System in Personality Theory," *Journal of Abnormal and Social Psychology,* 61 (1960), 301–310.

————. *Pattern and Growth in Personality.* Rev. ed. New York: Holt, Rinehart, and Winston, 1961.

————. "The Historical Background of Modern Social Psychology," in *The Handbook of Social Psychology,* ed. Gardner Lindzey and Elliot Aronson, 2nd ed., I, 1–80. Reading, Mass.: Addison-Wesley, 1968.

Amacher, Peter. "Freud's Neurological Education and Its Influence on Psychoanalytic Theory," in *Psychological Issues,* ed. G. S. Klein, IV, no. 4, Monograph 16. New York: International Universities Press, 1965.

Amarel, Saul. "On Representations of Problems of Reasoning About Actions," in *Machine Intelligence,* ed. Donald Michie, III, 131–172. Edinburgh: Edinburgh University Press, 1968.

Anscombe, G. E. M. *Intention.* Oxford: Blackwell, 1957.

————. "The Intentionality of Sensation: A Grammatical Feature," in *Analytical Philosophy: Second Series,* ed. R. J. Butler, pp. 158–180. Oxford: Blackwell, 1965.

Attneave, Fred. "Some Informational Aspects of Visual Perception," *Psychological Review,* 61 (1954), 183–193.

Austin, J. L. "Other Minds," *Proceedings of the Aristotelian Society,* supplementary 20 (1946), 148–187.

Ayer, A. J. "One's Knowledge of Other Minds," *Theoria,* 19 (1954), 1–20.

345

————, ed. *Logical Positivism*. The Library of Philosophical Movements. Glencoe, Ill.: Free Press, 1959.

Baldwin, A. L. *Theories of Child Development*. New York: Wiley, 1967.

Barlow, H. B. "The Coding of Sensory Messages," in *Current Problems in Animal Behaviour*, ed. W. H. Thorpe and O. L. Zangwill, pp. 331–360. Cambridge: Cambridge University Press, 1961.

Beach, F. A. "The Descent of Instinct," *Psychological Review*, 62 (1955), 401–410.

————, D. O. Hebb, C. T. Morgan, and H. W. Nissen, eds. *The Neuropsychology of Lashley: Selected Papers of K. S. Lashley*. McGraw-Hill Series in Psychology. New York: McGraw-Hill, 1960.

Berlyne, D. E. *Conflict, Arousal, and Curiosity*. McGraw-Hill Series in Psychology. New York: McGraw-Hill, 1960.

Bernard, L. L. *Instinct: A Study of Social Psychology*. New York: Holt, 1924.

Bishop, M. P., S. T. Elder, and R. G. Heath. "Intracranial Self-Stimulation in Man," *Science*, 140 (1963), 394–396.

Boden, M. A. "Brain and Consciousness: A Reply to Professor Burt," *Bulletin of the British Psychological Society*, 22 (1969), 47–49.

————. "Intentionality and Physical Systems," *Philosophy of Science*, 37 (1970), 200–214.

Boring, E. G. "Mind and Mechanism," *American Journal of Psychology*, 59 (1946), 173–192.

————. *A History of Experimental Psychology*. 2nd ed. The Century Psychology Series. New York: Appleton-Century-Crofts, 1957.

Bridgman, P. W. *The Logic of Modern Physics*. New York: Macmillan, 1927.

Brown, Roger. *Social Psychology*. New York: Free Press, 1965.

Brown, S. C. "Intentionality Without Grammar," *Proceedings of the Aristotelian Society*, 65 (1965), 123–146.

Bruner, J. S. "Preface to the Beacon Press Edition," in William McDougall, *Body and Mind: A History and a Defense of Animism*, pp. vii-xvii. Boston: Beacon Press, 1961.

————, Jacqueline Goodnow, and George Austin. *A Study of Thinking*. New York: Wiley, 1956.

————, Rose Olver, and P. M. Greenfield. *Studies in Cognitive Growth*. New York: Wiley, 1966.

Brunswik, Egon. "Probability as a Determiner of Rat Behavior," *Journal of Experimental Psychology*, 25 (1939), 175–197.

————. *Perception and the Representative Design of Psychological Experiments*. Berkeley: University of California Press, 1956.

Buck, R. C. "Non-other Minds," in *Analytical Philosophy*, ed. R. J.

Butler, pp. 187–210. Oxford: Blackwell, 1962.

Burns, B. D. *The Uncertain Nervous System.* London: Edward Arnold, 1968.

Burt, Cyril. "Brain and Consciousness," *British Journal of Psychology,* 59 (1968), 55–69.

Butler, R. J., ed. *Analytical Philosophy.* Oxford: Blackwell, 1962.

Carnap, Rudolf. "Testability and Meaning," *Philosophy of Science,* 3 (1936), 419–471; 4 (1937), 1–40.

Chihara, C. S., and J. A. Fodor. "Operationalism and Ordinary Language: A Critique of Wittgenstein," *American Philosophical Quarterly,* 2 (1965), 281–295.

Chisholm, R. M. *Perceiving: A Philosophical Study.* Ithaca, N.Y.: Cornell University Press, 1957.

————. "Intentionality," in *The Encyclopedia of Philosophy,* ed. Paul Edwards, IV, 201–204. New York: Macmillan, 1967.

Chomsky, Noam. "Review of Skinner's *Verbal Behavior,*" *Language,* 35 (1959), 26–58.

————. *Aspects of the Theory of Syntax.* Cambridge, Mass.: MIT Press, 1965.

Clowes, M. B. "Pictorial Relationships—A Syntactic Approach," in *Machine Intelligence,* ed. Bernard Meltzer and Donald Michie, IV, 361–383. Edinburgh: Edinburgh University Press, 1969.

————. "On Seeing Things," *Journal of Artificial Intelligence,* 1 (1971), forthcoming.

Craik, K. J. W. *The Nature of Explanation.* Cambridge: Cambridge University Press, 1943.

Critchley, Macdonald. *The Parietal Lobes.* London: Edward Arnold, 1953.

Danto, A. C. "On Consciousness in Machines," in *Dimensions of Mind: A Symposium,* ed. Sidney Hook, pp. 180–187. New York: New York University Press, 1960.

Darwin, Charles. *The Descent of Man, and Selection in Relation to Sex.* 2nd ed. London: John Murray, 1874.

Davidson, Donald. "Actions, Reasons, and Causes," *Journal of Philosophy,* 60 (1963), 685–700.

Day, J. P. "Hope," *American Philosophical Quarterly,* 6 (1969), 89–102.

————. "The Anatomy of Hope and Fear," *Mind,* n.s. 79 (1970), 369–384.

Dennis, Wayne, ed. *Readings in the History of Psychology.* The Century Psychology Series. New York: Appleton-Century-Crofts, 1948.

Descartes, René. *Les passions de l'ame.* Amsterdam, 1650.

Deutsch, J. A. *The Structural Basis of Behavior.* Cambridge: Cambridge University Press, 1964.

Dewey, John. "The Reflex Arc Concept in Psychology," *Psychological Review*, 3 (1896), 357–370.

Doran, J. E. "Experiments with a Pleasure-Seeking Automaton," in *Machine Intelligence*, ed. Donald Michie, III, 195–216. Edinburgh: Edinburgh University Press, 1968.

————. "Planning and Generalization in an Automaton/Environment System," in *Machine Intelligence*, ed. Bernard Meltzer and Donald Michie, IV, 433–454. Edinburgh: Edinburgh University Press, 1969.

————. "Planning and Robots," in *Machine Intelligence*, ed. Bernard Meltzer and Donald Michie, V, 519–532. Edinburgh: Edinburgh University Press, 1969.

Dreyfus, H. L. *Alchemy and Artificial Intelligence*. Rand Corporation P-3244. Santa Monica, Calif., December 1965.

————. "Why Computers Must Have Bodies in Order To Be Intelligent," *Review of Metaphysics*, 21 (1967), 13–32.

————. "Mechanism and Phenomenology," *Noûs*, 5 (1971), 81–96.

Eccles, J. C. *The Neurophysiological Basis of Mind: The Principles of Neurophysiology*. Oxford: Clarendon Press, 1953.

————. *The Brain and The Unity of Conscious Experience*. Arthur Stanley Eddington Memorial Lecture 19. Cambridge: Cambridge University Press, 1965.

————, ed. *Brain and Conscious Experience: Study Week, September 28 to October 4, 1964, of the Pontificia Academia Scientiarum*. Berlin: Springer-Verlag, 1966.

Edwards, Paul, ed. *The Encyclopedia of Philosophy*. 8 vols. New York: Macmillan, 1967.

Elliot, H. S. "Modern Vitalism," *Bedrock: A Quarterly Review of Scientific Thought*, 1 (1912), 312–332.

Eysenck, H. J. *The Biological Basis of Personality*. American Lecture Series 689. Springfield: Thomas, 1967.

Fechner, G. T. *Elements of Psychophysics*. 2 vols. Leipzig: 1860.

Feigenbaum, E. A., and Julian Feldman, eds. *Computers and Thought*. New York: McGraw-Hill, 1963.

Fernald, M. R. "The Diagnosis of Mental Imagery," *Psychological Monographs*, 14, no. 58 (February 1912), pp. 1–169.

Ferster, C. B., and B. F. Skinner. *Schedules of Reinforcement*. The Century Psychology Series. New York: Appleton-Century-Crofts, 1957.

Flavell, J. H. *The Developmental Psychology of Jean Piaget*. New York: Van Nostrand, 1963.

Flugel, J. C. *A Hundred Years of Psychology, 1833–1933: With Additional Part on Developments 1933–1947*. London: Duckworth, 1951.

348

_____, and William McDougall. "Further Observations on the Variation of the Intensity of Visual Sensation with the Duration of the Stimulus," *British Journal of Psychology*, 3 (1909), 178–207.

Fodor, J. A. *Psychological Explanation: An Introduction to the Philosophy of Psychology*. Random House Studies in Philosophy. New York: Random House, 1968.

Gauld, Alan. "Could a Machine Perceive?" *British Journal for the Philosophy of Science*, 17 (1966), 44–58.

Gazzaniga, M. S. "The Split Brain in Man," *Scientific American*, 217, no. 2 (1967), 24–29.

Gelernter, H. L. "Realization of a Geometry-Theorem Proving Machine," *Proceedings of the International Conference on Information Processing* (Paris, 1959), pp. 273–282.

Gosling, J. C. B. *Pleasure and Desire: The Case for Hedonism Reviewed*. Oxford: Clarendon Press, 1969.

Gough, H. G. "Clinical Versus Statistical Prediction in Psychology," in *Psychology in the Making: Histories of Selected Research Problems*, ed. Leo Postman, pp. 526–584. Knopf Publications in Psychology: The Core Series. New York: Alfred A. Knopf, 1963.

Gregory, R. L. "On Physical Model Explanations in Psychology," *British Journal for the Philosophy of Science*, 4 (1953), 192–197.

_____. *On How So Little Information Controls So Much Behaviour*. Bionics Research Reports No. 1. Edinburgh: Edinburgh University Press, April 1968.

Green, B. F. *Digital Computers in Research: An Introduction for Behavioral and Social Scientists*. Lincoln Laboratory Publications. New York: McGraw-Hill, 1963.

Groos, Carl. *The Play of Animals: A Study of Animal Life and Instinct*. Trans. E. L. Baldwin. London: Chapman and Hall, 1898.

_____. *The Play of Man*. Trans. E. L. Baldwin. New York: Appleton, 1901.

Gunderson, Keith. "Robots, Consciousness, and Programmed Behaviour," *British Journal for the Philosophy of Science*, 19 (1968), 109–122.

Guthrie, E. R. *The Psychology of Learning*. Rev. ed. New York: Harper and Row, 1952.

Hampshire, Stuart. "The Analogy of Feeling," *Mind*, n.s. 61 (1952), 1–12.

Hanson, N. R. *Patterns of Discovery: An Inquiry into the Conceptual Foundations of Science*. Cambridge: Cambridge University Press, 1958.

Hare, R. M. "Universalisability," *Proceedings of the Aristotelian Society*, 55 (1955), 295–312.

————. *Freedom and Reason.* Oxford: Clarendon Press, 1963.

Harlow, H. F. "Learning and Satiation of Response in Intrinsically Motivated Complex Puzzle Performance by Monkeys," *Journal of Comparative Physiology and Psychology,* 43 (1950), 289–294.

Harré, Rom. "Powers," *British Journal for the Philosophy of Science,* 21 (1970), 81–101.

Hearnshaw, L. S. *A Short History of British Psychology, 1840–1940.* Methuen's Manuals of Modern Psychology. London: Methuen, 1964.

Hebb, D. O. *The Organization of Behavior: A Neuropsychological Theory.* New York: Wiley, 1949.

Heider, Fritz. *The Psychology of Interpersonal Relations.* New York: Wiley, 1958.

Helmholtz, H. L. F. von. *Popular Lectures on Scientific Subjects.* London: Longmans, Green, 1881.

Hempel, C. G. *Aspects of Scientific Explanation, and Other Essays in the Philosophy of Science.* New York: Free Press, 1965.

————, and Paul Oppenheim. "Studies in the Logic of Explanation," *Philosophy of Science,* 15 (1948), 135–178.

Hinde, R. A. "Unitary Drives," *Animal Behaviour,* 7 (1959), 130–141.

————. "Energy Models of Motivation," *Symposium of the Society for Experimental Biology,* 14 (1960), 199–213.

————. *Animal Behavior: A Synthesis of Ethological and Comparative Psychology.* New York: McGraw-Hill, 1966.

Hobart, R. E. "Free-Will as Involving Determination and Inconceivable Without it," *Mind,* n.s. 43 (1934), 1–27.

Holt, E. B. *The Concept of Consciousness.* New York: Macmillan, 1914.

————. *The Freudian Wish and Its Place in Ethics.* New York: Holt, Rinehart, and Winston, 1915.

————. "Response and Cognition," *Journal of Philosophy,* 12 (1915), 365–373, 393–409.

————. *Animal Drive and the Learning Process: An Essay Toward Radical Empiricism.* New York: Holt, Rinehart, and Winston, 1931.

————. "Materialism and the Criterion of the Psychic," *Psychological Review,* 44 (1937), 33–53.

————, W. T. Marvin, W. P. Montague, R. B. Perry, W. B. Pitkin, and E. G. Spaulding. "The Program and First Platform of Six Realists," *Journal of Philosophy and Psychology,* 7 (1910), 393.

————. *The New Realism: Cooperative Studies in Philosophy.* New York: Macmillan, 1912.

Hubel, D. H., and T. N. Wiesel. "Receptive Fields of Single Neurones in the Cat's Striate Cortex," *Journal of Physiology,* 148 (1959), 579–591.

_____. "Receptive Fields, Binocular Interaction and Functional Architecture in the Cat's Visual Cortex," *Journal of Physiology*, 160 (1962), 106–154.

_____. "Receptive Fields and Functional Architecture of Monkey Striate Cortex," *Journal of Physiology*, 195 (1968), 215–243.

Hull, C. L. "Knowledge and Purpose as Habit Mechanisms," *Psychological Review*, 37 (1930), 511–525.

_____. "The Concept of the Habit-Family-Hierarchy and Maze-Learning," *Psychological Review*, 41 (1934), 33–54, 134–152.

_____. "Mind, Mechanism and Adaptive Behavior," *Psychological Review*, 44 (1937), 1–32.

_____. *Principles of Behavior: An Introduction to Behavior Theory.* The Century Psychology Series. New York: Appleton-Century-Crofts, 1943.

Hume, David. *A Treatise on Human Nature: Being an Attempt To Introduce the Experimental Method of Reasoning into Moral Subjects*, vol. I. London: 1739.

_____. *An Enquiry Concerning the Human Understanding.* London: 1748.

Humphrey, George. *Thinking: An Introduction to Its Experimental Psychology.* London: Methuen, 1951.

Huxley, T. H. "On the Hypothesis That Animals Are Automata, and Its History," in T. H. Huxley, *Method and Results: Essays*, pp. 199–250. London: Macmillan, 1893.

James, William. *The Principles of Psychology.* 2 vols. New York: Holt, 1890.

_____. *Pragmatism: A New Name for Some Old Ways of Thinking.* London: Longman, 1907.

_____. *A Pluralistic Universe: Hibbert Lectures at Manchester College on the Present Situation in Philosophy.* London: Longmans, Green, 1909.

Jasper, H. H. "Brain Mechanisms and States of Consciousness," in *Brain and Conscious Experience*, ed. J. C. Eccles, pp. 256–282. Berlin: Springer-Verlag, 1966.

Jones, O. R., ed. *The Private Language Argument.* Controversies in Philosophy. London: Macmillan, 1971.

Kenny, Anthony. *Action, Emotion and Will.* Studies in Philosophical Psychology. London: Routledge and Kegan Paul, 1963.

Kneale, William, and A. N. Prior. "Intentionality and Intensionality," *Proceedings of the Aristotelian Society*, supplementary 42 (1968), 73–106.

Koch, Sigmund, ed. *Psychology: A Study of a Science.* Study 1: Conceptual and Systematic. Vol. II, *General Systematic Formulations,*

351

Learning, and Special Processes. New York: McGraw-Hill, 1959.

Kohler, Wolfgang. *The Mentality of Apes.* 2nd rev. ed. Trans. Ella Winter. London: Routledge and Kegan Paul, 1927.

Kuhn, T. S. *The Structure of Scientific Revolutions.* The International Encyclopedia of Unified Science, vol. II, no. 2. Chicago: University of Chicago Press, 1962.

Laing, R. D. *The Divided Self: A Study of Sanity and Madness.* Studies in Existential Analysis and Phenomenology. London: Tavistock Press, 1960.

Lashley, K. S. "The Behavioristic Interpretation of Consciousness," *Psychological Review,* 30 (1923), 237–272, 329–353.

————. *Brain Mechanisms and Intelligence: A Quantitative Study of Injuries to the Brain.* Chicago: University of Chicago Press, 1929.

————. "Functional Determinants of Cerebral Localization," *Archives of Neurology and Psychiatry,* 38 (1937), 371–387.

————. "In Search of the Engram," *Symposium of the Society of Experimental Biology,* no. 4, 454–482. Cambridge: Cambridge University Press, 1950.

————. "The Problem of Serial Order in Behavior," in *Cerebral Mechanisms in Behavior: The Hixon Symposium,* ed. L. A. Jeffress, pp. 112–135. New York: Wiley, 1951.

Lehrman, D. S. "The Physiological Basis of Parental Feeding Behavior in the Ring Dove (*Streptopelia Risoria*)," *Behaviour,* 7 (1955), 241–286.

————. "Effect of Female Sex Hormones on Incubation Behavior in the Ring Dove (*Streptopelia Risoria*)," *Journal of Comparative and Physiological Psychology,* 51 (1958), 142–145.

————. "Induction of Broodiness by Participation in Courtship and Nest-Building in the Ring Dove (*Streptopelia Risoria*)," *Journal of Comparative and Physiological Psychology,* 51 (1958), 32–36.

Leibniz, G. W. *Monadology.* 1714.

Leipold, Karl, and W. E. Rekowski. "A Method for the Simultaneous Processing of Several Programs," in *Proceedings of the International Federation of Information Processing Congress,* II, 320–321. Washington, D.C.: Spartan, 1965.

Lettvin, J. Y., H. R. Maturana, Walter Pitts, and W. S. McCulloch. "What the Frog's Eye Tells the Frog's Brain," *Proceedings of the Institute of Radio Engineers,* 47 (1959), 1940–1959.

————. "Two Remarks on the Visual System of the Frog," in *Sensory Communication: Contributions to the Symposium on Principles of Sensory Communication, July 19-August 1, 1959, Endicott House, M.I.T.,* ed. W. A. Rosenblith, pp. 757–776. M.I.T. Books in the Communications Sciences. Cambridge, Mass.: MIT Press, 1961.

Lewis, C. I. *An Analysis of Knowledge and Valuation.* Paul Carus Lectures, 7th Series, 1945. La Salle, Ill.: Open Court, 1946.

Lloyd Morgan, Conwy. *An Introduction to Comparative Psychology.* 2nd ed. The Contemporary Science Series. London: Walter Scott Publishing Co., 1903.

Locke, John. *An Essay Concerning Human Understanding.* London: 1690.

Lorenz, Konrad. "Companionship in Bird Life: Fellow Members of the Species as Releasers of Social Behavior," and "The Nature of Instinct: The Conception of Instinctive Behavior," in *Instinctive Behavior,* ed. C. H. Schiller, pp. 83–175. New York: International Universities Press, 1957.

Lovejoy, A. O. *Reflections on Human Nature.* Baltimore: Johns Hopkins, 1961.

Luria, A. R., and F. Ia. Yudovich. *Speech and the Development of Mental Processes in the Child.* Trans. Joan Simon. London: Staples Press, 1959.

McClearn, G. E. "The Inheritance of Behavior," in *Psychology in the Making: Histories of Selected Research Problems,* ed. Leo Postman, pp. 144–254. Knopf Publications in Psychology: The Core Series. New York: Alfred A. Knopf, 1963.

McCulloch, W. S. *Embodiments of Mind.* Cambridge, Mass.: MIT Press, 1965.

————, and W. H. Pitts. "A Logical Calculus of the Ideas Immanent in Nervous Activity," *Bulletin of Mathematical Biophysics,* 5 (1943), 115–133.

McDougall, William. "On the Structure of Cross-Striated Muscle, and a Suggestion as to the Nature of Its Contraction," *Journal of Anatomy and Physiology,* 31 (1897), 410–441, 539–585.

————. "A Contribution Towards an Improvement in Psychological Method," *Mind,* n.s. 7 (1898), 15–33, 159–178, 364–387.

————. "On the Seat of the Psycho-Physical Processes," *Brain,* 24 (1901), 577–630.

————. "Some New Observations in Support of Thomas Young's Theory of Light and Colour Vision," *Mind,* n.s. 10 (1901), 52–97, 210–245, 347–382.

————. "The Physiological Factors of the Attention-Process," *Mind,* n.s. 11 (1902), 316–351; *Mind,* n.s. 12 (1903), 289–302, 473–488; *Mind,* n.s. 15 (1906), 329–359.

————. "The Sensations Excited by a Single Momentary Stimulation of the Eye," *British Journal of Psychology,* 1 (1904), 78–113.

————. *Physiological Psychology.* The Temple Primers. London: Dent, 1905.

_____. *An Introduction to Social Psychology*. London: Methuen, 1908. Enlarged editions. published in 1912 (5th ed.), 1914 (8th ed.), 1919 (14th ed.), 1925 (20th ed.), 1928 (21st ed.), 1931 (22nd ed.), and 1936 (23rd ed.).

_____. *Body and Mind: A History and a Defense of Animism*. London: Methuen, 1911.

_____. *Psychology: The Study of Behaviour*. Home University Library of Modern Knowledge. London: Williams and Norgate, 1912.

_____. "Modern Materialism," *Bedrock: A Quarterly Review of Scientific Thought*, 2 (1913), 24–41.

_____. *The Group Mind: A Sketch of the Principles of Collective Psychology with Some Attempt To Apply Them to the Interpretation of National Life and Character*. Cambridge Psychological Library. Cambridge: University Press, 1920.

_____. "Motives in the Light of Recent Discussion," *Mind*, n.s. 29 (1920), 277–293.

_____. "Presidential Address," *Proceedings of the Society for Psychical Research*, 30 (1920), 105–123.

_____. *National Welfare and National Decay*. London: Methuen, 1921. Also published as *Is America Safe for Democracy?* New York: Scribner, 1921.

_____. "The Use and Abuse of Instinct in Social Psychology," *Journal of Abnormal and Social Psychology*, 16 (1922), 285–333.

_____. "The Need for Psychic Research," *Journal of the American Society for Psychical Research*, 17 (1923), 4–14.

_____. *An Outline of Psychology*. London: Methuen, 1923.

_____. "Purposive or Mechanical Psychology?" *Psychological Review*, 30 (1923), 273–288.

_____. "Can Sociology and Social Psychology Dispense with Instincts?" *Journal of Abnormal and Social Psychology*, 19 (1924), 13–41.

_____. "Men or Robots?" *Pedagogical Seminary and Journal of Genetic Psychology*, 33 (1926), 71–102. Also in *Psychologies of 1925: Powell Lectures in Psychological Theory*, ed. Clark Murchison, pp. 273–305. Worcester, Mass.: Clark University Press, 1926.

_____. *An Outline of Abnormal Psychology*. London: Methuen, 1926.

_____. *Character and the Conduct of Life: Practical Psychology for Everyman*. London: Methuen, 1927.

_____. "An Experiment for the Testing of the Hypothesis of Lamarck," *British Journal of Psychology*, 17 (1927), 267–304.

_____. *Modern Materialism and Emergent Evolution*. London:

Methuen, 1929.

————. "Autobiography," in *A History of Psychology in Autobiography*, ed. Clark Murchison, 1, 191–223. Worcester, Mass.: Clark University Press, 1930.

————. "The Hormic Psychology," in *Psychologies of 1930*, ed. Clark Murchison, pp. 3–36. International University Series in Psychology. Worcester, Mass.: Clark University Press, 1930. Also in his *An Introduction to Social Psychology*, 22nd and later eds.

————. "Second Report on a Lamarckian Experiment," *British Journal of Psychology*, 20 (1930), 201–218.

————. *The Energies of Men: A Study of the Fundamentals of Dynamic Psychology*. London: Methuen, 1932. 2nd ed., 1934.

————. *The Frontiers of Psychology*. Contemporary Library of Psychology. London: Nisbet, and Cambridge University Press, 1934.

————. "Fourth Report on a Lamarckian Experiment," *British Journal of Psychology*, 28 (1938), 321–345, 365–395.

————. "Tendencies as Indispensable Postulates of All Psychology," *Proceedings of the Eleventh International Congress of Psychology, Paris, July 25-31, 1937*, pp. 157–170. Paris: Felix Alcan, 1938.

Malcolm, Norman. "Wittgenstein's *Philosophical Investigations*," *Philosophical Review*, 63 (1954), 530–559.

————. "Knowledge of Other Minds," *Journal of Philosophy*, 55 (1958), 969–978.

————. "The Conceivability of Mechanism," *Philosophical Review*, 77 (1968), 45–72.

Mandler, George. "Transfer of Training as a Function of Degree of Response Overlearning," *Journal of Experimental Psychology*, 47 (1954), 411–417.

————. "Emotion," in *New Directions in Psychology*, ed. T. M. Newcomb, pp. 267–343. New York: Holt, Rinehart, and Winston, 1962.

————. "From Association to Structure," *Psychological Review*, 69 (1962), 415–427.

————, and C. K. Kuhlmann. "Proactive and Retroactive Effects of Overlearning," *Journal of Experimental Psychology*, 61 (1961), 76–81.

Mandler, J. M., and George Mandler. *Thinking: From Association to Gestalt*. Perspectives in Psychology. New York: Wiley, 1964.

Maslow, A. H. *Toward a Psychology of Being*. Princeton, N.J.: Van Nostrand, 1962.

————. *The Psychology of Science: A Reconnaissance*. New York: Harper and Row, 1966.

May, Rollo, ed. *Existential Psychology*. Random House Studies in

Psychology. New York: Random House, 1961.

Meehl, P. E. "On the Circularity of the Law of Effect," *Psychological Bulletin*, 47 (1950), 52–75.

_____. *Clinical Versus Statistical Prediction: A Theoretical Analysis and a Review of the Evidence*. Minneapolis: University of Minnesota Press, 1954.

Melden, A. I. *Free Action*. Studies in Philosophical Psychology. London: Routledge and Kegan Paul, 1961.

Meltzer, Bernard, and Donald Michie, eds. *Machine Intelligence*, vol. IV. Edinburgh: Edinburgh University Press, 1969.

Michie, Donald, ed. *Machine Intelligence*, vol. III. Edinburgh: Edinburgh University Press, 1968.

Miller, G. A., Eugene Galanter, and K. H. Pribram. *Plans and the Structure of Behavior*. New York: Holt, 1960.

Miller, N. E., and John Dollard. *Social Learning and Imitation*. New Haven: Yale University Press, 1941.

Minsky, M. L. "Steps Toward Artificial Intelligence," *Proceedings of the Institute of Radio Engineers*, 49 (1961), 8–30.

_____. "Matter, Mind, and Models," in *Proceedings of the International Federation of Information Processing Congress*, I, 45–49. Washington, D.C.: Spartan, 1965.

_____, and Seymour Papert. *Perceptrons: An Introduction to Computational Geometry*. Cambridge, Mass.: MIT Press, 1969.

Moruzzi, Giuseppe, Alfred Fessard, and H. H. Jasper, eds. *Brain Mechanisms: Progress in Brain Research*, vol. I. Amsterdam: Elsevier, 1963.

Mowrer, O. H. *Learning Theory and Behavior*. New York: Wiley, 1960.

_____. *Learning Theory and the Symbolic Processes*. New York: Wiley, 1960.

Nagel, Ernest. *The Structure of Science: Problems in the Logic of Scientific Explanation*. New York: Harcourt, Brace and World, 1961.

Neisser, Ulric. "The Imitation of Man by Machine," *Science*, 139 (1963), 193–197.

_____. *Cognitive Psychology*. The Century Psychology Series. New York: Appleton-Century-Crofts, 1967.

Newell, Allen. "Some Problems of Basic Organization in Problem-Solving Programs," in *Self-Organizing Systems, 1962*, ed. M. C. Yovits, G. T. Jacobi, and G. D. Goldstein, pp. 393–423. Washington, D.C.: Spartan, 1962.

_____, J. C. Shaw, and H. A. Simon. "Empirical Explorations with the Logic Theory Machine," *Proceedings of the Western Joint Computer Conference*, 15 (1957), 218–239.

————, J. C. Shaw, and H. A. Simon. "Chess-Playing Programs and the Problem of Complexity," *IBM Journal of Research and Development,* 2 (1958), 320–335.

————, and H. A. Simon. "GPS—A Program That Simulates Human Thought," in *Lernende Automaten,* ed. Heinz Billing, pp. 109–124. Munich: Oldenbourg, 1961.

————, F. M. Tonge, E. A. Feigenbaum, B. F. Green, and G. H. Mealy. *Information Processing Language—V Manual.* 2nd ed., prepared by H. S. Kelly and A. Newell. Englewood Cliffs, N.J.: Prentice-Hall, 1964.

Olds, James, and Peter Milner. "Positive Reinforcement Produced by Electrical Stimulation of Septal Area and Other Regions of Rat Brain," *Journal of Comparative and Physiological Psychology,* 47 (1954), 419–427.

O'Shaughnessy, Brian. "The Powerlessness of Dispositions," *Analysis,* 31 (1970), 1–15.

Pavlov, I. P. *Conditioned Reflexes: An Investigation of the Physiological Activity of the Cerebral Cortex.* Trans. G. V. Anrep. London: Humphrey Milford, 1927.

————. *Lectures on Conditioned Reflexes: Twenty-five Years of Objective Study of the Higher Nervous Activity (Behaviour) of Animals.* Trans. W. H. Gantt. New York: International Publishers, 1928.

Perry, R. B. *Present Philosophical Tendencies: A Critical Survey of Naturalism, Idealism, Pragmatism and Realism, Together with a Synopsis of the Philosophy of William James.* New York: Longman, 1912.

————. "Docility and Purposiveness," *Psychological Review,* 25 (1918), 1–21.

————. "A Behavioristic View of Purpose," *Journal of Philosophy,* 18 (1921), 85–105.

————. "The Cognitive Interest and Its Refinement," *Journal of Philosophy,* 18 (1921), 365–375.

————. "The Independent Variability of Purpose and Belief," *Journal of Philosophy,* 18 (1921), 169–180.

Peters, R. S. *The Concept of Motivation.* Studies in Philosophical Psychology. London: Routledge and Kegan Paul, 1958.

————. "Motivation, Emotion, and the Conceptual Schemes of Common Sense," in *Human Action: Conceptual and Empirical Issues,* ed. Theodore Mischel, pp. 135–166. New York: Academic Press, 1969.

————, and C. A. Mace. "Emotions and the Category of Passivity," *Proceedings of the Aristotelian Society,* 62 (1962), 117–142.

Bibliography

Piaget, Jean. *The Construction of Reality in the Child.* New York: Basic Books, 1954.

Postman, Leo. "The History and Present Status of the Law of Effect," *Psychological Bulletin,* 44 (1947), 489–563.

————, ed. *Psychology in the Making: Histories of Selected Research Problems.* Knopf Publications in Psychology: The Core Series. New York: Alfred A. Knopf, 1963.

Prince, Morton. *The Dissociation of a Personality: A Biographical Study in Abnormal Psychology.* New York: Longman, 1905.

Puccetti, Roland. *Persons: A Study of Possible Moral Agents in the Universe.* London: Macmillan, 1968.

Putnam, Hilary. "Dreaming and 'Depth Grammar,'" in *Analytical Philosophy,* ed. R. J. Butler, pp. 211–235. Oxford, Blackwell, 1962.

Rapoport, David. "The Structure of Psychoanalytic Theory: A Systematizing Attempt," in *Psychology: A Study of a Science,* ed. Sigmund Koch, Vol. III, *Formulations of the Person and the Social Context,* pp. 55–183. New York: McGraw-Hill, 1959.

Reitman, W. R. "Personality as a Problem-Solving Coalition," in *Computer Simulation of Personality,* ed. S. S. Tomkins and Samuel Messick, pp. 69–100. New York: Wiley, 1963.

————. *Cognition and Thought: An Information-Processing Approach.* New York: Wiley, 1965.

————, R. B. Grove, and R. G. Shoup. "Argus: An Information-Processing Model of Thinking," *Behavioral Science,* 9 (1964), 270–281.

Rhine, J. B., and William McDougall. "Third report on a Lamarckian Experiment," *British Journal of Psychology,* 24 (1933), 213–235.

Robinson, A. L. *William McDougall, M.B., D.Sc., F.R.S.: A Bibliography, Together with a Brief Outline of His Life.* Durham, N.C.: Duke University Press, 1943.

Rochester, Nathaniel, J. H. Holland, L. H. Haibt, and W. L. Duda. "Test on a Cell Assembly Theory of the Brain, Using a Large Digital Computer," *Institute of Radio Engineers Transactions in Information Theory,* 2 (1956), 80–93.

Rosenberg, M. J. "Simulated Man and the Humanistic Criticism," in *Computer Simulation of Personality,* ed. S. S. Tomkins and Samuel Messick, pp. 113–126. New York: Wiley, 1963.

Rosenblueth, Arturo, and Norbert Wiener. "Purposeful and Non-Purposeful Behavior," *Philosophy of Science,* 17 (1950), 318–326.

————, and Julian Bigelow. "Behavior, Purpose and Teleology," *Philosophy of Science,* 10 (1943), 18–24.

Rosenthal, Robert. "The Effect of the Experimenter on the Result of Psychological Research," in *Progress in Experimental Personality*

Research, ed. B. A. Maher, pp. 79–114. New York: Academic Press, 1964.

————, and K. L. Fode. "The Effect of Experimenter Bias on the Performance of the Albino Rat," *Behavioral Science,* 8 (1963), 183–189.

Ryle, Gilbert. *The Concept of Mind.* Hutchinson's University Library. London: Hutchinson, 1949.

Sayre, K. M. *Recognition: A Study in the Philosophy of Artificial Intelligence.* Notre Dame, Ind.: University of Notre Dame Press, 1965.

————. "Intelligence, Bodies, and Digital Computers," *Review of Metaphysics,* 21 (1968), 714–723.

————. *Consciousness: A Philosophic Study of Minds and Machines.* Random House Studies in Philosophy. New York: Random House, 1969.

————, and F. J. Crosson. *The Modeling of Mind: Computers and Intelligence.* Notre Dame, Ind.: University of Notre Dame Press, 1963.

Schiller, C. H., ed. *Instinctive Behavior: The Development of a Modern Concept.* New York: International Universities Press, 1957.

Schneider, H. W. "Review of McDougall's *Group Mind,*" *Journal of Philosophy,* 18 (1921), 690–697.

Schneirla, T. C. "The Concept of Development in Comparative Psychology," in *The Concept of Development: An Issue in the Study of Human Behavior,* ed. D. B. Harris. pp. 78–108. Minneapolis: University of Minnesota Press, 1957.

Selfridge, O. G. "Pandemonium: A Paradigm for Learning," in *Proceedings of the Symposium on Mechanisation of Thought Processes,* ed. D. V. Blake and A. M. Uttley, pp. 511–529. London: H. M. Stationery Office, 1959.

Seward, J. P. "Reinforcement and Expectancy: Two Theories in Search of a Controversy," *Psychological Review,* 63 (1956), 105–113.

Shand, A. F. "Character and the Emotions," *Mind, n.s.,* 5 (1896), 203–226.

————. "M. Ribot's Theory of the Passions," *Mind, n.s.* 16 (1907), 477–505.

Sherrington, C. S. *The Integrative Action of the Nervous System.* New Haven: Yale University Press, 1906.

Simon, H. A., and Allen Newell. "Simulation of Human Thinking," in *Computers and the World of the Future,* ed. Martin Greenberger, pp. 94–133. Cambridge, Mass.: MIT Press, 1962.

Skinner, B. F. "The Concept of the Reflex in the Description of

Behavior," *Journal of General Psychology,* 5 (1931), 427–458.

―――――. *The Behavior of Organisms: An Experimental Analysis.* The Century Psychology Series. New York: Appleton-Century-Crofts, 1938.

―――――. *Walden Two.* New York: Macmillan, 1948.

―――――. "Are Theories of Learning Necessary?" *Psychological Review,* 57 (1950), 193–216.

―――――. *Science and Human Behavior.* New York: Free Press, 1953.

―――――. *Verbal Behavior.* The Century Psychology Series. New York: Appleton-Century-Crofts, 1957.

―――――. "A Case History in Scientific Method," in *Psychology: A Study of a Science,* ed. Sigmund Koch, II, 359–379. New York: McGraw-Hill, 1959.

―――――. "Autobiography," in *A History of Psychology in Autobiography,* Vol. V, ed. E. G. Boring and Gardner Lindzey, pp. 385–414. The Century Psychology Series. New York: Appleton-Century-Crofts, 1967.

―――――. *Contingencies of Reinforcement: A Theoretical Analysis.* The Century Psychology Series. New York: Appleton-Century-Crofts, 1969.

Sommerhoff, G. W. C. *Analytical Biology.* London: Oxford University Press, 1950.

Spence, K. W. "The Nature of Theory Construction in Contemporary Psychology," *Psychological Review,* 51 (1944), 47–68.

―――――. "The Postulates and Methods of Behaviorism," *Psychological Review,* 55 (1948), 67–68.

―――――. "Cognitive Versus Stimulus-Response Theories of Learning," *Psychological Review,* 57 (1950), 159–172.

―――――. *Behavior Theory and Conditioning.* New Haven: Yale University Press, 1956.

―――――. "Theoretical Interpretations of Learning," in *Handbook of Experimental Psychology,* ed. S. S. Stevens, pp. 690–729. New York: Wiley, 1961.

Sperry, R. W. "The Great Cerebral Commissure," *Scientific American,* 210, no. 1 (1964), 42–52.

―――――. "Hemisphere Deconnection and Unity in Conscious Awareness," *American Psychologist,* 23 (1968), 723–733.

―――――. "A Modified Concept of Consciousness," *Psychological Review,* 76 (1969), 532–536.

Sprigge, T. L. S. "Teleological Explanation," *Proceedings of the Aristotelian Society,* supplementary 45 (1971), 149–170.

Squires, Roger. "Are Dispositions Lost Causes?" *Analysis,* 31 (1970), 15–18.

Stout, G. F. "Is the Distinction of Feeling, Cognition and Conation Valid as the Ultimate Distinction of Mental Functions?" *Proceedings of the Aristotelian Society,* o.s. 1 (1891), 142–150.

————. *Analytic Psychology.* 2 vols. Muirhead Library of Philosophy. London: Swan Sonnenschein, 1896.

————. *A Manual of Psychology.* The University Tutorial Series. London: University Tutorial Press, 1899.

Strawson, P. F. *Individuals: An Essay in Descriptive Metaphysics.* London: Methuen, 1959.

Sutherland, I. E. *Sketchpad: A Man-Machine Graphical Communication System.* MIT Lincoln Laboratory Technical Report no. 296. Cambridge, Mass.: MIT Press, 1963.

Sutherland, N. S. "Motives as Explanations," *Mind,* n.s. 68 (1959), 145–159.

————. "Review of Taylor's *Explanation of Behaviour,*" *Philosophical Quarterly,* 15 (1965), 379–381.

————. "Outlines of a Theory of Visual Pattern Recognition in Animals and Man," *Proceedings of the Royal Society B,* 171 (1968), 297–317.

Taylor, Charles. *The Explanation of Behaviour.* International Library of Philosophy and Scientific Method. London: Routledge and Kegan Paul, 1964.

————. "The Explanation of Purposive Behaviour," in *Explanation in the Behavioural Sciences,* ed. Robert Borger and Frank Cioffi, pp. 49–79, 89–95. Cambridge: Cambridge University Press, 1970.

Taylor, Richard. *Action and Purpose.* Englewood Cliffs, N.J.: Prentice-Hall, 1966.

————. "Causation," in *The Encyclopedia of Philosophy,* ed. Paul Edwards, II, 56–66. New York: Macmillan, 1967.

Thigpen, C. H., and H. M. Cleckley. *The Three Faces of Eve.* London: Secker and Warburg, 1957.

Thorndike, E. L. "Animal Intelligence: An Experimental Study of the Associative Processes in Animals," *Psychological Review Monograph Supplement,* no. 8, 1898.

————. *Animal Intelligence: Experimental Studies.* New York: Hafner, 1911.

Thorne, J. P., Paul Bratley, and H. M. Dewar. "The Syntactic Analysis of English by Machine," in *Machine Intelligence,* ed. Donald Michie, III, 281–309. Edinburgh: Edinburgh University Press, 1968.

Tinbergen, Nikolaas. *The Study of Instinct.* Oxford: Clarendon Press, 1951.

Tolman, E. C. "Instinct and Purpose," *Psychological Review,* 27

(1920), 217–233.

————. "A New Formula for Behaviorism," *Psychological Review,* 29 (1922), 44–53.

————. "The Nature of Instinct," *Psychological Bulletin,* 20 (1923), 200–216.

————. "Behaviorism and Purpose," *Journal of Philosophy,* 22 (1925), 36–41.

————. "Purpose and Cognition: The Determiners of Animal Learning," *Psychological Review,* 32 (1925), 285–297.

————. *Purposive Behavior in Animals and Men.* The Century Psychology Series. New York: Appleton-Century-Crofts, 1932.

————. "Psychology Versus Immediate Experience," *Philosophy of Science,* 2 (1935), 356–380.

————. "Operational Behaviorism and Current Trends in Psychology," *Proceedings of the XXV Anniversary of the Inauguration of Graduate Studies* (Los Angeles, 1936), 89–103.

————. "Physiology, Psychology and Sociology," *Psychological Review,* 45 (1938), 228–241.

————. "Cognitive Maps in Rats and Men," *Psychological Review,* 55 (1948), 189–208.

————. "A Psychological Model," in *Toward a General Theory of Action,* ed. Talcott Parsons and E. A. Shils, pp. 279–361. Cambridge, Mass.: Harvard University Press, 1951.

————. *Behavior and Psychological Man: Essays in Motivation and Learning.* Berkeley: University of California Press, 1958.

————. "Principles of Purposive Behavior," in *Psychology: A Study of A Science,* ed. Sigmund Koch, II, 92–157. New York: McGraw-Hill, 1959.

Tomkins, S. S., and Samuel Messick, eds. *Computer Simulation of Personality: Frontier of Psychological Theory.* New York: Wiley, 1963.

Troland, L. T. *The Fundamentals of Human Motivation.* New York: Hafner, 1928.

Turing, A. M. "Computing Machinery and Intelligence," *Mind,* n.s. 59 (1950), 439–442.

Uexkull, J. Von. "A Stroll Through the Worlds of Animals and Men," in *Instinctive Behavior,* ed. C. H. Schiller, pp. 5–82. New York: International Universities Press, 1957.

Uhr, Leonard, and Charles Vossler. "A Pattern Recognition Program That Generates, Evaluates, and Adjusts Its Own Operators," in *Computers and Thought,* ed. E. A. Feigenbaum and Julian Feldman, pp. 251–268. New York: McGraw-Hill, 1963.

Urmson, J. O. "Motives and Causes," *Proceedings of the Aristotelian*

Society, supplementary 26 (1952), 179–194.

————, and L. J. Cohen. "Criteria of Intensionality," *Proceedings of the Aristotelian Society,* supplementary 42 (1968), 107–142.

Verplanck, W. S. "Since Learned Behavior Is Innate, and Vice Versa, What Now?" *Psychological Review,* 62 (1955), 139–144.

Ward, James. "Psychology," in *Encyclopaedia Britannica,* 9th ed., vol. XX. London: 1885.

————. *The Realm of Ends, or Pluralism and Theism.* Cambridge: University Press, 1911.

Watson, J. B. "Psychology as the Behaviorist Views It," *Psychological Review,* 20 (1913), 158–177.

————. *Psychology from the Standpoint of a Behaviorist.* 2nd ed. London: J. P. Lippincott, 1924.

————. *Behaviorism.* London: Kegan Paul, Trench, and Trubner, 1925.

————, and William McDougall. *The Battle of Behaviourism: An Exposition and an Exposure.* Psyche Miniatures, General Series. London: Kegan Paul, Trench, and Trubner, 1928.

Wertheimer, Max. *Productive Thinking.* New York: Harper and Row, 1945.

White, R. W. "Motivation Reconsidered: The Concept of Competence," *Psychological Review,* 66 (1959), 297–333.

Wiener, Norbert. *Cybernetics, or Control and Communication in the Animal and the Machine.* New York: Wiley, 1948.

Wisdom, John. "Other Minds," *Proceedings of the Aristotelian Society,* supplementary 20 (1946), 122–147.

Wittgenstein, Ludwig. *Philosophical Investigations.* Trans. G. E. M. Anscombe. Oxford: Blackwell, 1953.

————. *Zettel.* Ed. G. E. M. Anscombe and G. H. von Wright. Trans. G. E. M. Anscombe. Oxford: Blackwell, 1967.

Wundt, Wilhelm. *Principles of Physiological Psychology.* 5th ed. Trans. E. B. Titchener. London: Swan Sonnenschein, 1904.

Wylie, Ruth. *The Self Concept: A Critical Survey of Pertinent Research Literature.* Lincoln, Neb.: University of Nebraska Press, 1961.

Young, J. Z. *A Model of the Brain.* Oxford: Clarendon Press, 1964.

Ziff, Paul. "The Feelings of Robots," *Analysis,* 19 (1959), 64–68.

Notes

Abbreviations of Works by William McDougall

BM   *Body and Mind: A History and a Defense of Animism* (London: Methuen, 1911).

EM   *The Energies of Men: A Study of The Fundamentals of Dynamic Psychology* (London: Methuen, 1932).

ISP   *An Introduction to Social Psychology,* 23rd ed. enlarged (London: Methuen, 1936). The main text of the first edition, published in 1908, remained essentially unchanged in all later editions, except that new prefaces and supplementary chapters were added in the editions of 1912, 1914, 1919, 1925, 1928, and 1931. The 23rd edition, cited here throughout, contains all material included in these earlier editions. It is also readily accessible, having been reprinted with identical pagination in 1960 in Methuen's University Paperbacks series, no. 6.

    Readers wishing to place my citations within the chronological development of McDougall's views should note the following dates and page spans: 1908—pp. 1–302; 1912—pp. 303–330; 1914—pp. 331–363; 1919—pp. 364–385; 1925—pp. 386–430; 1928—pp. 431–443; 1931—pp. 444–494; 1936—pp. 495–512.

MMEE *Modern Materialism and Emergent Evolution* (London: Methuen, 1929).

OAP   *An Outline of Abnormal Psychology* (London: Methuen, 1926).

OP   *An Outline of Psychology* (London: Methuen, 1923).

P   *Psychology: The Study of Behaviour,* Home University Library of Modern Knowledge (London: Williams and Norgate, 1912).

PP   *Physiological Psychology,* The Temple Primers (London: Dent, 1905).

I. Introduction

1. J. A. Deutsch, *The Structural Basis of Behavior* (Cambridge, 1964), p. 1.

2. E. G. Boring, "Mind and Mechanism," *American Journal of Psychology,* 59 (1946), 191.

3. P. E. Meehl, *Clinical Versus Statistical Prediction: A Theoretical Analysis and a Review of the Evidence* (Minneapolis, 1954), p. 4. For a more recent review of this controversy, see H. G. Gough,

"Clinical Versus Statistical Prediction in Psychology," in Leo Postman, ed., *Psychology in the Making: Histories of Selected Research Problems* (New York, 1963), pp. 526–584.

4. William James, *Pragmatism: A New Name for Some Old Ways of Thinking* (London, 1907), p. 13.

5. James established an informal psychophysiological laboratory in 1875, and Wundt instituted the first formal psychological laboratory in 1879. E. G. Boring, *A History of Experimental Psychology,* 2nd ed. (New York, 1957), pp. 323–324, 509.

6. Specifically, McDougall wrote 189 articles and 43 books. A. L. Robinson, *William McDougall, M.B., D.Sc., F.R.S.: A Bibliography, Together with a Brief Outline of His Life* (Durham, 1943).

7. William McDougall, "Autobiography," in Clark Murchison, ed., *A History of Psychology in Autobiography,* vol. I (Worcester, 1930), p. 218.

8. J. C. Flugel, *A Hundred Years of Psychology, 1833–1933: With Additional Part on Developments 1933–1947* (London, 1951), pp. 272, 277.

9. Bruner suggests that there is some analogy between McDougall's psychology and cybernetic concepts. J. S. Bruner, "Preface to the Beacon Press Edition," *BM,* p. xv. I try to explore this analogy in detail.

10. William McDougall, "On the Structure of Cross-Striated Muscle, and a Suggestion as to the Nature of Its Contraction," *Journal of Anatomy and Physiology,* 31 (1897), 410–441, 539–585.

11. L. S. Hearnshaw, *A Short History of British Psychology, 1840–1940* (London, 1964), p. 186.

12. William McDougall, "Some New Observations in Support of Thomas Young's Theory of Light and Colour Vision," *Mind,* n.s. 10 (1901), 52–97, 210–245, 347–382; William McDougall, "The Physiological Factors of the Attention-Process," *Mind,* n.s. 11 (1902), 316–351; 12 (1903), 289–302, 473–488; 15 (1906), 329–359; William McDougall, "The Sensations Excited by a Single Momentary Stimulation of the Eye," *British Journal of Psychology,* 1 (1904), 78–113; J. C. Flugel and William McDougall, "Further Observations on the Variation of the Intensity of Visual Sensation with the Duration of the Stimulus," *British Journal of Psychology,* 3 (1909), 178–207.

13. William McDougall, "An Experiment for the Testing of the Hypothesis of Lamarck," *British Journal of Psychology,* 17 (1927), 267–304; William McDougall, "Second Report on a Lamarckian Experiment," *British Journal of Psychology,* 20 (1930), 201–218; J. B. Rhine and William McDougall, "Third Report on a Lamarckian Experiment," *British Journal of Psychology,* 24 (1933), 213–235;

William McDougall, "Fourth Report on a Lamarckian Experiment," *British Journal of Psychology*, 28 (1938), 321–345, 365–395. McDougall's apparently positive results were probably owing to experimenter bias effects of the type described in Robert Rosenthal and K. L. Fode, "The Effect of Experimenter Bias on the Performance of the Albino Rat," *Behavioral Science*, 8 (1963), 183–189.

14. William McDougall, "Autobiography," p. 204.

15. William McDougall, "A Contribution Towards an Improvement in Psychological Method," *Mind*, n.s. 7 (1898), 15–33, 159–178, 364–387.

16. H. S. Elliot, "Modern Vitalism," *Bedrock: A Quarterly Review of Scientific Thought*, 1 (1912), 312–332. McDougall replied to Elliot's highly critical review in his "Modern Materialism," *Bedrock: A Quarterly Review of Scientific Thought*, 2 (1913), 24–41.

17. William McDougall, "Presidential Address," *Proceedings of the Society for Psychical Research*, 30 (1920), 105–123.

18. Wilhelm Wundt, *Physiologische Psychologie*, 6th ed. (1911), III, 739–754; Wilhelm Wundt, *Logik* (1921), III, 249–257; T. H. Huxley, "On the Hypothesis That Animals Are Automata, and Its History," *Method and Results: Essays* (London, 1893), pp. 199–250, first published in the popular *Fortnightly Review*, 16 (1874), 555–580. McDougall named Jacob Moleschott, Carl Vogt, and Ludwig Buchner as mainly responsible for spreading the dogmatic materialism encouraged by the progress of mechanistic physiology typified by the work of Johannes Muller (himself a vitalist). *BM*, p. 98. Four of Muller's own pupils (H. L. F. von Helmholtz, Emil du Bois-Raymond, Ernst Brucke, and C. F. Ludwig) were particularly influential in their determination to combat vitalism, and Helmholtz's paper on the conservation of energy was written in support of the materialist thesis two years after these four had formed a pact to disseminate their philosophical views. Boring, *History of Psychology*, p. 708.

19. Helmholtz's paper, "Die Erhaltung der Kraft," was first published in 1847. His own popular exposition of it was published in English in 1881 as *Popular Lectures on Scientific Subjects* (London, 1881), First Series, lectures v and vii.

20. G. T. Fechner, *Elements of Psychophysics* (Leipzig, 1860), I, ch. i. For a discussion of Fechner's psychical monism by one of McDougall's contemporaries, see William James, *A Pluralistic Universe: Hibbert Lectures at Manchester College on the Present Situation in Philosophy* (London, 1909), pp. 131–178.

21. *BM*, pp. 192, viii (italics mine), x.

22. *OAP*, p. 519. Italics mine.

23. *EM*, p. 7; *BM*, pp. 365 (italics mine), 349, 365.

24. Boring, *History of Psychology*, p. 331; Wilhelm Wundt, *Principles of Physiological Psychology*, 5th ed., trans. E. B. Titchener (London, 1904), I, 2, 1, 11.

25. William James, *The Principles of Psychology* (New York, 1896), I, 1.

26. *OP*, pp. 16–18.

27. See esp. *BM*, ch. xxiv; *P*, ch. iii. In later works McDougall complained of the "evil influence" of the mosaic tradition (*OP*, p. xi) and welcomed the Gestalt psychologists' attack on atomism (*EM*, pp. 17–18).

28. William McDougall, "A Contribution Towards an Improvement in Psychological Method," and "The Physiological Factors of the Attention-Process."

29. Wundt, *Physiological Psychology*, I, 7. Wundt insisted that psychology involves the use of introspection as a controlled experimental technique rather than as the uncontrolled self-observation of one's everyday "introspective" moments: "It is only with grave reservations that what is called 'pure self-observation' can properly be termed observation at all, and under no circumstances can it lay claim to accuracy" (p. 4).

30. James Ward, "Psychology," in *Encyclopaedia Britannica*, 9th ed. (1885), XX, 37–85; Flugel, *Hundred Years of Psychology*, p. 150.

31. See, e.g., G. F. Stout, "Is the Distinction of Feeling, Cognition and Conation Valid as the Ultimate Distinction of Mental Functions?" *Proceedings of the Aristotelian Society*, o.s. 1 (1891), 142–150; G. F. Stout, *A Manual of Psychology* (London, 1898) I, 56–70. McDougall refers to Stout and James as "the only two men of whom I have felt myself to be in some degree the disciple and humble pupil." McDougall, "Autobiography," p. 209.

32. The traditional "structuralist" psychology was represented by Wundt and his pupil Titchener; they were in conflict with the "Wurzburg School." Boring, *History of Psychology*, ch. xviii, gives a general historical account, while extracts from contemporary papers are given in J. M. Mandler and George Mandler, *Thinking: From Association to Gestalt* (New York, 1964), especially chs. iv and v. See also George Humphrey, *Thinking: An Introduction to Its Experimental Psychology* (London, 1951), chs. i-iv.

33. G. F. Stout, *Analytic Psychology* (London, 1896), I, 12–15.

34. Conwy Lloyd Morgan, *An Introduction to Comparative Psychology*, 2nd ed. (London, 1903), pp. 47, 48–49.

35. Lloyd Morgan, *Comparative Psychology*, p. 53.

36. Stout, *Analytic Psychology*, I, 1.

37. *PP*, p. 1; *ISP*, p. 13.

38. J. B. Watson, "Psychology as the Behaviorist Views It," *Psychological Review*, 20 (1913), 158–177. Reprinted in Wayne Dennis, ed., *Readings in the History of Psychology* (New York, 1948), pp. 457–471.

39. *P*, pp. 31–32, 71, 77–81.

40. *MMEE*, p. vi.

41. *OP*, p. 38.

42. William McDougall, "Men or Robots?" in Clark Murchison, ed., *Psychologies of 1925: Powell Lectures in Psychological Theory* (Worcester, 1926), p. 276.

43. *OP*, p. 35; *ISP*, p. 24; *EM*, p. 3; *OAP*, p. 48; *P*, pp. 69–70 (italics mine).

44. James Ward, *The Realm of Ends, or Pluralism and Theism* (Cambridge, 1911), esp. lectures iii and xii. McDougall did not cite Ward in support of his monadic theory, but it is highly unlikely that he was unaware of Ward's position.

II. The Concept of Purpose

1. *OP*, p. 47.

2. There is an extensive philosophical literature on the various meanings of "cause"; see e.g., Richard Taylor, "Causation," in Paul Edwards, ed., *The Encyclopedia of Philosophy* (New York, 1967), II, 56–66. Taylor remarks that in philosophical and scientific writings the term is commonly assumed to be equivalent to efficient cause. Denials that purposes (or reasons) can truly be said to "cause" actions usually rest on this assumption. Davidson has rebutted such denials, arguing against the view that "reasons do not cause, in any ordinary sense of the word, the actions that they rationalize." Donald Davidson, "Actions, Reasons, and Causes," *Journal of Philosophy*, 60 (1963), 685–700. I agree that purposes and reasons "cause" actions in an ordinary everyday sense of the word, while denying that they do so qua "efficient causes."

3. C. L. Hull, *Principles of Behavior: An Introduction to Behavior Theory* (New York, 1943), p. 26.

4. *OP*, p. 47n.

5. *MMEE*, pp. 61–62, 59.

6. William McDougall, "Men or Robots?" in Clark Murchison, ed., *Psychologies of 1925: Powell Lectures in Psychological Theory* (Worcester, 1926), p. 299.

7. *ISP*, p. 24.

8. *ISP*, pp. 304–305.

9. *P*, pp. 19–20.

10. *ISP*, pp. 411–412.

11. Hull, *Principles of Behavior,* p. 26.

12. *ISP,* p. 416.

13. Some psychologists have deliberately adopted everyday vocabulary in formulating a systematic theory, arguing that the insights implicit in the conceptual schemes of "naive" or "common sense" psychology are often more reliable and subtle than the hypotheses of neologistic psychological theories. Such psychologists are typically prepared to accept "intention" as a key systematic concept. See, e.g., Fritz Heider, *The Psychology of Interpersonal Relations* (New York, 1958). For an operationalist critique of Heider's use of "intention," see A. L. Baldwin, *Theories of Child Development* (New York, 1967), pp. 56–61.

14. For alternative definitions and examples of "scientific explanation," see Ernest Nagel, *The Structure of Science: Problems in the Logic of Scientific Explanation* (New York, 1961), chs. i-iii; C. G. Hempel, *Aspects of Scientific Explanation, and Other Essays in the Philosophy of Science* (New York, 1965), esp. pp. 333–496.

15. For a brief statement of the hypothetico-deductive model of scientific explanation, see C. G. Hempel and Paul Oppenheim, "Studies in the Logic of Explanation," *Philosophy of Science,* 15 (1948), 135–178.

16. *EM,* p. 5; *ISP,* p. 422.

17. William McDougall, *The Frontiers of Psychology* (London, 1934), pp. 13–14.

18. *MMEE,* p. 163.

19. *MMEE,* p. 3.

20. Nagel, *Structure of Science,* p. 170.

21. Nagel, *Structure of Science,* pp. 172–173.

22. *MMEE,* pp. 163–164.

23. *BM,* p. xi.

24. C. I. Lewis, *An Analysis of Knowledge and Valuation* (La Salle, 1946), p. 367.

25. This point is discussed in Charles Taylor, *The Explanation of Behaviour* (London, 1964), ch. iv.

26. Hull, *Principles of Behavior,* p. 25.

27. Among the philosophical writings cited by behaviorists during the development of behaviorism were P. W. Bridgman, *The Logic of Modern Physics* (New York, 1927); Rudolf Carnap, "Testability and Meaning," *Philosophy of Science,* 3 (1936), 419–471; 4 (1937), 1–40. Further examples of the positivist approach to science and epistemology appear in A. J. Ayer, ed., *Logical Positivism* (Glencoe, 1959).

28. The seminal source of radical attacks on the general epistemo-

logical assumptions of logical positivism is Ludwig Wittgenstein, *Philosophical Investigations* (Oxford, 1953). For the specific application of these attacks to the philosophy of science, see N. R. Hanson, *Patterns of Discovery: An Inquiry into the Conceptual Foundations of Science* (Cambridge, 1958); T. S. Kuhn, *The Structure of Scientific Revolutions* (Chicago, 1962).

29. See Hanson, *Patterns of Discovery,* ch. iii.

30. *ISP,* p. 312.

31. William McDougall, "Tendencies as Indispensable Postulates of All Psychology," *Proceedings of the Eleventh International Congress of Psychology, Paris, July 25–31, 1937* (Paris, 1938), pp. 157–170.

32. In an earlier paper, however, McDougall had welcomed the assimilation of inorganic to organic process suggested by the Gestaltists' description of soap bubbles as "tending" to the spherical. McDougall, "Men or Robots?" pp. 304–305.

33. *EM,* p. 5; *ISP,* pp. 306, 26n.

34. *ISP,* pp. 306–309.

35. *EM,* p. 137.

36. *P,* pp. 59–60.

37. *EM,* p. 136.

38. *OP,* p. 41. Cf. *P,* pp. 58–59.

39. See R. M. Chisholm, *Perceiving: A Philosophical Study* (Ithaca, 1957), ch. xi; R. M. Chisholm, "Intentionality," in Edwards, ed., *Encyclopedia of Philosophy,* IV, 201–204; William Kneale and A. N. Prior, "Intentionality and Intensionality," *Proceedings of the Aristotelian Society,* supplementary 42 (1968), 73–106; J. O. Urmson and L. J. Cohen, "Criteria of Intensionality," *Proceedings of the Aristotelian Society,* supplementary 42 (1968), 107–142; G. E. M. Anscombe, "The Intentionality of Sensation," in R. J. Butler, ed., *Analytical Philosophy,* second series (Oxford, 1965), pp. 158–180; S. C. Brown, "Intentionality Without Grammar," *Proceedings of the Aristotelian Society,* 65 (1965), 123–146.

As these titles show, the crucial word is sometimes spelled with an *s* and sometimes with a *t.* When spelled with an *s,* the word more clearly suggests a contrast to the logician's term "extension" and thus emphasizes the logical peculiarities referred to in the text. When spelled with a *t,* the word more clearly suggests a psychological context and is particularly likely to bring to mind the psychological term "intention." Opinions differ as to the suitability of either form— largely because opinions differ as to the best definition or analysis of the concept in question. I have chosen the *s*-form, even though I define the concept psychologically rather than logically, because to use the *t*-form in the context of a discussion of purposive explanation would probably encourage the mistaken view that I am specifically concerned with intentional (as opposed to "unintentional") phenomena.

40. *P*, p. 37.

41. Taylor, *Explanation of Behaviour*, p. 71.

42. *BM*, p. 235.

43. *BM*, p. 237.

44. See Nagel, *Structure of Science*, ch. xii; G. W. C. Sommerhoff, *Analytical Biology* (London, 1950).

45. See Nagel, *Structure of Science*, pp. 402–403.

46. *ISP*, p. 460.

47. *EM*, p. 10.

48. William McDougall, "A Contribution Towards an Improvement in Psychological Method," *Mind*, n.s. 7 (1898), 15–33, 159–178, 364–387; William McDougall, "On the Seat of the Psycho-Physical Processes," *Brain*, 24 (1901), 577–630; William McDougall, "The Physiological Factors of the Attention-Process," *Mind*, 11 (1902), 316–351; 10 (1901), 52–97, 210–245, 347–382.

49. *PP*, pp. 59–60; *BM*, pp. 278–279.

50. *OAP*, p. 27. McDougall remarked that Jung had used the term "horme" because of its Greek origin and had explicitly related it to Bergson's *elan vital*, conceiving of it as "an energetic expression for psychological values." Jung's usage was not likely to recommend the term to neurophysiologists, and McDougall therefore avoided it when discussing mental life "from the neurological point of view."

51. Nagel, *Structure of Science*, pp. 354–355. Chs. xi and xii of Nagel's book provide a useful discussion of the reduction of scientific theories.

52. For a general discussion of the importance of referring "reduction" to sets of statements rather than to real properties, see Nagel, *Structure of Science*, pp. 364–366.

53. Nagel, *Structure of Science*, pp. 354–358.

54. *P*, pp. 36, 38.

55. *ISP*, pp. 453–454n, 446; *EM*, p. xiii; *OAP*, p. 521.

56. *BM*, pp. 145–146, 170–171; *ISP*, p. 312; *MMEE*, pp. 57–58.

57. For a historical and critical survey of the logical and psychological definitions of intensionality, see Kneale and Prior, "Intentionality and Intensionality," pp. 73–90. For a recent attempt to formulate a logical definition whose denotation coincides with a psychological definition, see Chisholm, *Perceiving*, ch. xi; Chisholm, "Intentionality," p. 203. For the claim that Chisholm's logical definition does not coincide with a psychological definition, see Urmson and Cohen, "Criteria of Intensionality," *passim*.

371

58. *OP*, pp. 36–37.

59. *ISP*, pp. 453, 199, 202. For a fuller discussion of this point, see R. E. Hobart, "Free-Will as Involving Determination and Inconceivable Without It," *Mind*, n.s. 43 (1934), 1–27.

60. *ISP*, p. 460.

61. C. S. Sherrington, *The Integrative Action of the Nervous System* (New Haven, 1906). After his initial investigation of conditioned secretory responses, Pavlov studied the conditioning of different types of response. His collected lectures were first published in English in the 1920s. I. P. Pavlov, *Conditioned Reflexes: An Investigation of the Physiological Activity of the Cerebral Cortex,* trans. G. V. Anrep (London, 1927); I. P. Pavlov, *Lectures on Conditioned Reflexes,* trans. W. G. Gantt (New York, 1928).

62. Dewey analyzed the distinction between stimulus and response as a "teleological distinction of interpretation" with reference to an assumed end, rather than as a "distinction of existence." John Dewey, "The Reflex Arc Concept in Psychology," *Psychological Review*, 3 (1896), 357–370.

63. K. S. Lashley, "The Behavioristic Interpretation of Consciousness," *Psychological Review*, 30 (1923), 237–272, 329–353.

III. Behaviorist Interpretations of Purpose

1. *OP*, p. ix; William McDougall, "Autobiography," in Clark Murchison, ed., *A History of Psychology in Autobiography*, vol I (Worcester, 1930), p. 222.

2. *EM*, p. 16.

3. McDougall, "Autobiography," p. 204.

4. J. B. Watson, "Psychology as the Behaviorist Views It," in Wayne Dennis ed., *Readings in the History of Psychology* (New York, 1948), p. 459; J. B. Watson, *Psychology from the Standpoint of a Behaviorist,* 2nd ed. (London, 1924), p. viii.

5. Watson, *Psychology*, pp. 10–11; J. B. Watson, *Behaviorism* (London, 1925), p. 7.

6. Watson, "Psychology as the Behaviorist Views It," pp. 463, 464.

7. The reviewer of the American edition of William McDougall, *The Group Mind: A Sketch of the Principles of Collective Psychology with Some Attempt To Apply Them to the Interpretation of National Life and Character* (Cambridge, 1920), described the subtitle as "excessively eulogistic" and the book as "a contribution to idealistic philosophy rather than to collective psychology." H. W. Schneider, "Review of McDougall's *Group Mind*," *Journal of Philosophy*, 18 (1921), 692, 697.

8. McDougall, "Autobiography," p. 213.

9. *OP*, p. 38.

10. See, e.g., William McDougall, "Purposive or Mechanical Psychology?" *Psychological Review*, 30 (1923), 273–288; William McDougall, "Men or Robots?" in Clark Murchison, ed., *Psychologies of 1925: Powell Lectures in Psychological Theory* (Worcester, 1926), *passim;* J. B. Watson and William McDougall, *The Battle of Behaviourism: An Exposition and an Exposure* (London, 1928).

11. McDougall, "Men or Robots?" p. 277.

12. McDougall, "Men or Robots?" p. 280.

13. Watson, *Psychology*, pp. 19–21; *ISP*, p. 424.

14. Wolfgang Kohler, *The Mentality of Apes* (London, 1927).

15. McDougall, "Men or Robots?" pp. 287–289.

16. *OP*, p. 69.

17. Watson, *Psychology*, pp. 252, 273.

18. See e.g., L. L. Bernard, *Instinct: A Study of Social Psychology* (New York, 1924).

19. R. B. Perry, "A Behavioristic View of Purpose," *Journal of Philosophy*, 18 (1921), 93. Perry cites as examples Thorstein Veblen, *Instinct of Workmanship* (1914); Ordway Tead, *Instincts in Industry* (1918); C. H. Parker, "Motives in Economic Life," *Proc. Amer. Econ. Assoc.* (1917).

20. R. B. Perry, "Docility and Purposiveness," *Psychological Review*, 25 (1918), 1–21; Perry, "A Behavioristic View of Purpose"; R. B. Perry, "The Independent Variability of Purpose and Belief," *Journal of Philosophy*, 18 (1921), 169–180; R. B. Perry, "The Cognitive Interest and Its Refinement," *Journal of Philosophy*, 18 (1921), 365–375.

21. Perry, "Docility and Purposiveness," pp. 12–14.

22. Perry, "A Behavioristic View of Purpose," p. 102.

23. Perry, "Docility and Purposiveness," p. 7.

24. Perry, "Docility and Purposiveness," pp. 17, 103n, 169, 174, 175.

25. Perry, "Docility and Purposiveness," pp. 2, 3, 20; "A Behavioristic View of Purpose," pp. 95, 100.

26. *MMEE*, pp. 191–196.

27. Perry, "A Behavioristic View of Purpose," pp. 91–92.

28. R. B. Perry, *Present Philosophical Tendencies: A Critical Survey of Naturalism, Idealism, Pragmatism and Realism, Together with a Synopsis of the Philosophy of William James* (New York, 1912), pp. 342, 303–304; Perry, "A Behavioristic View of Purpose," p. 94.

29. *MMEE*, pp. 191, 193–194.

30. E. B. Holt, W. T. Marvin, W. P. Montague, R. B. Perry, W. B.

Pitkin, and E. G. Spaulding, "The Program and First Platform of Six Realists," *Journal of Philosophy and Psychology,* 7 (1910), 393.

31. E. B. Holt, W. T. Marvin, W. P. Montague, R. B. Perry, W. B. Pitkin, and E. G. Spaulding, *The New Realism: Cooperative Studies in Philosophy* (New York, 1912), pp. 303–377.

32. E. B. Holt, "Response and Cognition," *Journal of Philosophy,* 12 (1915), 365–373, 393–409; E. B. Holt, *The Concept of Consciousness* (New York, 1914); E. B. Holt, *The Freudian Wish and Its Place in Ethics* (New York, 1915).

33. Holt, "Response and Cognition," p. 409; E. B. Holt, "Materialism and the Criterion of the Psychic," *Psychological Review,* 44 (1937), 33–53.

34. Holt, "Response and Cognition," Part I.

35. Holt, *The Freudian Wish,* pp. 78, 161.

36. Holt, *The Freudian Wish,* p. 76.

37. Holt, *The Freudian Wish,* pp. 56–57, 59.

38. E. B. Holt, *Animal Drive and the Learning Process: An Essay Toward Radical Empiricism* (New York, 1931), pp. 256, 263.

39. Holt, "Materialism and the Criterion of the Psychic," p. 53.

40. Holt et al., *The New Realism,* pp. 475–476.

41. *OP,* p. 27.

42. *EM,* p. 324n.

43. E. C. Tolman, *Purposive Behavior in Animals and Men* (New York, 1932), pp. 6–7, 12.

44. E. C. Tolman, "A New Formula for Behaviorism," in Tolman, *Behavior and Psychological Man: Essays in Motivation and Learning* (Berkeley, 1958), p. 6.

45. E. C. Tolman, "Behaviorism and Purpose," in Tolman, *Behavior and Psychological Man,* p. 33.

46. E. C. Tolman, "Purpose and Cognition: The Determiners of Animal Learning," in Tolman, *Behavior and Psychological Man,* pp. 38–47.

47. E. C. Tolman, "Cognitive Maps in Rats and Men," in Tolman, *Behavior and Psychological Man,* pp. 241–264.

48. E. C. Tolman, "Psychology vs. Immediate Experience," in Tolman, *Behavior and Psychological Man,* pp. 94–114.

49. E. C. Tolman, "A Psychological Model," in Talcott Parsons and E. A. Shils, eds., *Toward a General Theory of Action* (Cambridge, 1951), pp. 279–361.

50. E. C. Tolman, "Operational Behaviorism and Current Trends in Psychology," in Tolman, *Behavior and Psychological Man,* p. 118.

51. E. C. Tolman, "Principles of Purposive Behavior," in Sigmund Koch, ed., *Psychology: A Study of a Science,* vol. II: *General Sys-*

tematic Formulations, Learning, and Special Processes (New York, 1959), p. 98n.

52. E. C. Tolman, "Physiology, Psychology and Sociology" (1938), in Tolman, *Behavior and Psychological Man,* p. 188.

53. Tolman, "Psychology vs. Immediate Experience," p. 102.

54. Tolman, *Purposive Behavior,* p. 423n.

55. Tolman, "Behaviorism and Purpose," p. 37; Tolman, *Purposive Behavior,* p. 15n.

56. Tolman, "New Formula for Behaviorism," p. 17. See also E. C. Tolman, "Instinct and Purpose," *Psychological Review,* 27 (1920), 217–233.

57. Tolman, "Behaviorism and Purpose," p. 33; Tolman, *Purposive Behavior,* p. 16.

58. McDougall, "Men or Robots?" p. 299.

59. McDougall, "Purposive or Mechanical Psychology?" p. 288.

60. *ISP,* pp. 444–446.

61. See F. A. Beach, D. O. Hebb, C. T. Morgan, and H. W. Nissen, eds., *The Neuropsychology of Lashley: Selected Papers of K. S. Lashley* (New York, 1960); E. R. Guthrie, *The Psychology of Learning,* rev. ed. (New York, 1952); Egon Brunswik, "Probability as a Determiner of Rat Behavior," *Journal of Experimental Psychology,* 25 (1939), 175–197; Egon Brunswik, *Perception and the Representative Design of Psychological Experiments* (Berkeley, 1956); N. E. Miller and John Dollard, *Social Learning and Imitation* (New Haven, 1941).

62. C. L. Hull, *Principles of Behavior: An Introduction to Behavior Theory* (New York, 1943), p. 25.

63. C. L. Hull, "Knowledge and Purpose as Habit Mechanisms," *Psychological Review,* 37 (1930), 511–525.

64. C. L. Hull, "The Concept of the Habit-Family-Hierarchy and Maze-Learning," *Psychological Review,* 41 (1934), 33–54, 134–152.

65. See J. P. Seward, "Reinforcement and Expectancy: Two Theories in Search of a Controversy," *Psychological Review,* 63 (1956), 105–113.

66. C. L. Hull, "Mind, Mechanism and Adaptive Behavior," *Psychological Review,* 44 (1937), 1–32.

67. Hull, *Principles of Behavior,* pp. 25–26.

68. K. W. Spence, *Behavior Theory and Conditioning* (New Haven, 1956); K. W. Spence, "The Nature of Theory Construction in Contemporary Psychology," *Psychological Review,* 51 (1944), 47–68; K. W. Spence, "Theoretical Interpretations of Learning," in S. S. Stevens, ed., *Handbook of Experimental Psychology* (New York, 1951), pp. 690–729; K. W. Spence, "The Postulates and Methods of

Behaviorism," *Psychological Review*, 55 (1948), 67–68; K. W. Spence, "Cognitive vs. Stimulus-Response Theories of Learning," *Psychological Review*, 57 (1950), 159–172.

69. Spence, "Cognitive vs. Stimulus-Response Theories," p. 167; Spence, "Postulates of Behaviorism," p. 75.

70. Tolman, "Principles of Purposive Behavior," p. 97.

71. Spence, "Cognitive vs. Stimulus-Response Theories," p. 171.

72. B. F. Skinner, "Are Theories of Learning Necessary?" *Psychological Review*, 57 (1950), 193–216; B. F. Skinner, "A Case History in Scientific Method," in Koch, ed., *Psychology*, II, 359–379.

73. B. F. Skinner, "The Concept of the Reflex in the Description of Behavior," *Journal of General Psychology*, 5 (1931), 427–458.

74. B. F. Skinner, *Contingencies of Reinforcement: A Theoretical Analysis* (New York, 1969), p. 28. The common practice of referring to Skinner as a "stimulus-response" psychologist is therefore not strictly accurate.

75. C. B. Ferster and B. F. Skinner, *Schedules of Reinforcement* (New York, 1957).

76. B. F. Skinner, *Verbal Behavior* (New York, 1957); Noam Chomsky, "Review of Skinner's *Verbal Behavior*," *Language*, 35 (1959), 26–58.

77. B. F. Skinner, *Walden Two* (New York, 1948).

78. B. F. Skinner, *The Behavior of Organisms: An Experimental Analysis* (New York, 1938), pp. 6–7, 42.

79. B. F. Skinner, *Science and Human Behavior* (New York, 1953), pp. 87, 89–90.

80. B. F. Skinner, "Autobiography," in E. G. Boring and Gardner Lindzey, eds., *A History of Psychology in Autobiography*, Vol. V (New York, 1967), p. 408.

81. Skinner, *Contingencies of Reinforcement*, pp. 159, 162–163.

82. Skinner, *Contingencies of Reinforcement*, p. 126.

83. Skinner, *Contingencies of Reinforcement*, p. 282.

84. Chomsky shows that Skinner's new technical terms, such as "tact" and "mand," are implicitly mentalistic, or purposive; moreover, Skinner's use of terms like "reinforcement" and "deprivation," which can be operationally defined in some strictly controlled experimental situations, is also covertly mentalistic. Chomsky, "Review of *Verbal Behavior*," esp. secs. ii–iv.

85. O. H. Mowrer, *Learning Theory and Behavior* (New York, 1960); O. H. Mowrer, *Learning Theory and the Symbolic Processes* (New York, 1960).

86. Mowrer, *Learning Theory and Behavior*, pp. 6–7.

87. Mowrer, *Learning Theory and Behavior*, p. 7.

88. Mowrer, *Learning Theory and Behavior,* pp. 30, 270.

89. *EM,* p. 9.

90. See H. H. Jasper, "Brain Mechanisms and States of Consciousness," in J. C. Eccles, ed., *Brain and Conscious Experience: Study Week of the Pontificia Academia Scientiarum* (Berlin, 1966), pp. 256–282; Giuseppe Moruzzi, Alfred Fessard, and H. H. Jasper, eds., *Brain Mechanisms: Progress in Brain Research,* vol. I (Amsterdam, 1963). Eysenck has applied the results of such physiological research to problems in personality theory. H. J. Eysenck, *The Biological Basis of Personality* (Springfield, 1967).

91. See D. H. Hubel and T. N. Wiesel, "Receptive Fields of Single Neurones in the Cat's Striate Cortex," *Journal of Physiology,* 148 (1959), 579–591; D. H. Hubel and T. N. Wiesel, "Receptive Fields, Binocular Interaction and Functional Architecture in the Cat's Visual Cortex," *Journal of Physiology,* 160 (1962), 106–154; D. H. Hubel and T. N. Wiesel, "Receptive Fields and Functional Architecture of Monkey Striate Cortex," *Journal of Physiology,* 195 (1968), 215–243; J. Y. Lettvin, H. R. Maturana, Walter Pitts, and W. S. McCulloch, "What the Frog's Eye Tells the Frog's Brain" (1959), in W. S. McCulloch, *Embodiments of Mind* (Cambridge, 1965), pp. 230–255; J. Y. Lettvin, H. R. Maturana, Walter Pitts, and W. S. McCulloch, "Two Remarks on the Visual System of the Frog," in W. A. Rosenblith, ed., *Sensory Communication: Contributions to a Symposium* (Cambridge, 1961), pp. 757–776.

IV. Purpose, Reductionism, and Cybernetics

1. A. H. Maslow, *Toward a Psychology of Being* (New York, 1962), p. vi.

2. A. H. Maslow, *The Psychology of Science* (New York, 1966), p. 4.

3. Maslow, *Psychology of Being,* p. 202.

4. Maslow, *Psychology of Being,* p. 188.

5. Maslow, *Psychology of Science,* p. 18.

6. Maslow, *Psychology of Science,* pp. 55–56.

7. R. D. Laing, *The Divided Self: A Study of Sanity and Madness* (London, 1960), p. 21.

8. Laing, *Divided Self,* p. 20.

9. Allport contrasts *proactive* with *reactive* psychological approaches, the former stressing spontaneous, future-oriented behavior. G. W. Allport, "The Open System in Personality Theory," *Journal of Abnormal and Social Psychology,* 61 (1960), 301–310. Following is an example of the Third Force emphasis on the future: "[The Third Force] have sensitized us to the necessity of grappling with and systematizing the dynamic role of the future in the presently

existing personality, e.g., growth and becoming and possibility necessarily point toward the future; so do the concepts of potentiality and
hoping, and of wishing and imagining; reduction to the concrete is
a loss of future; threat and apprehension point to the future (no
future=no neurosis); self-actualization is meaningless without reference to a currently active future; life can be a gestalt in time, etc.,
etc." Maslow, *Psychology of Being*, p. 14.

10. Laing, *Divided Self*, p. 21.

11. Rollo May, ed., *Existential Psychology* (New York, 1961),
pp. 20, 41, 43.

12. Alan Gauld, "Could a Machine Perceive?" *British Journal for
the Philosophy of Science*, 17 (1966), 58.

13. Norbert Wiener, *Cybernetics, or Control and Communication
in the Animal and the Machine* (New York, 1948), esp. pp. 13–20.

14. Arturo Rosenblueth, Norbert Wiener, and Julian Bigelow,
"Behavior, Purpose, and Teleology," *Philosophy of Science*, 10
(1943), 19. Compare the later, essentially similar discussion in Arturo
Rosenblueth and Norbert Wiener, "Purposeful and Non-Purposeful
Behavior," *Philosophy of Science*, 17 (1950), 318–326.

15. Gilbert Ryle, *The Concept of Mind* (London, 1949), ch. i.

16. B. F. Green, *Digital Computers in Research: An Introduction
for Behavioral and Social Scientists* (New York, 1963), ch. xiv, answers the question "How does the computer execute instructions?"
at the level of logical combinations of circuit components. Green
recommends "electronic" texts for those interested in the electronic
details. It is significant that these engineering details are irrelevant
for Green's purposes.

17. The basic machine operations of copying, adding, shifting,
combining logically, decoding, and counting are described in Green,
Digital Computers, ch. xiv. Chs. i-v provide a useful brief discussion
of machine codes and programming languages.

18. Compilers and interpreters convert the statements of the programming language into machine instructions in two fundamentally
different ways. Green, *Digital Computers*, pp. 77–78. Compilers first
translate them into series of instructions in an intermediate language.
These are then converted into instructions in machine code and stored
on tape. When the compiled program is run, only this tape is fed
into the computer. Thus, the original instructions in the programming
language are no longer available and cannot be referred to by the
computer while executing the compiled program. Interpreters do not
separate the translation and execution phases in this way. They
translate each high-level statement as it comes up to be executed on
the machine. Even if a statement has to be executed repeatedly

within "one" problem, it has to be translated first each time. An interpreted program therefore takes longer to run than its equivalent compiled program. But it has continual step-by-step access to the original form of the program in the high-level language. It has been suggested that the appearance of "conscious deliberation" at points of difficulty in task performance may be analogous to the switch from executing compiled programs to executing interpreted programs.

19. This example is adapted from Green, *Digital Computers*, p. 32.

20. J. A. Deutsch, *The Structural Basis of Behavior* (Cambridge, 1964), p. 13. A corollary is that if one has to reject the neurophysiology of a psychologist speculating on brain mechanisms, it is not necessary to reject his psychological explanation. Deutsch mentions the unjust rejection of Kohler's theory of figural aftereffects following on the justified rejection of its "electrophysiological fancy-dress." Deutsch, *Structural Basis of Behavior*, p. 15. Likewise, rejection of neurin or horme does not entail rejection of McDougall's psychological theory.

21. For a short description of GPS, see Allen Newell and H. A. Simon, "GPS—A Program That Simulates Human Thought," in E. A. Feigenbaum and Julian Feldman, eds., *Computers and Thought* (New York, 1963), pp. 279–296.

22. H. A. Simon and Allen Newell, "Simulation of Human Thinking," in Martin Greenberger, ed., *Computers and the World of the Future* (Cambridge, 1962), p. 101.

23. GPS has been used to prove theorems in the propositional calculus and to solve the missionaries-and-cannibals problem; a version of GPS has been applied to chess; and Simon and Newell suggest, in Greenberger, ed., *Computers and the Future*, pp. 94–133, that it could simulate the child's acquisition of correct pronunciation.

24. Newell and Simon, "GPS," in Feigenbaum and Feldman, eds., *Computers and Thought*, p. 286.

25. Allen Newell, F. M. Tonge, E. A. Feigenbaum, B. F. Green, and G. H. Mealy, *Information Processing Language—V Manual*, 2nd ed. (Englewood Cliffs, 1964), pp. 8–9.

26. M. L. Minsky, "Steps Toward Artificial Intelligence," in Feigenbaum and Feldman, eds., *Computers and Thought*, p. 447.

27. *BM*, p. 260.

28. Allen Newell, J. C. Shaw, and H. A. Simon, "Explorations with the Logic Theorist: A Case Study in Heuristics," in Feigenbaum and Feldman, eds., *Computers and Thought*, pp. 109–133.

29. This overemphasis of the similarities between GPS and human thought is discussed in Allen Newell, "Some Problems of Basic Organization in Problem-Solving Programs," in M. C. Yovits, G. T. Jacobi,

and G. D. Goldstein, eds., *Self-Organizing Systems, 1962* (Washington, D.C., 1962), pp. 393–423; W. R. Reitman, *Cognition and Thought: An Information-Processing Approach* (New York, 1965), esp. ch. vii; Ulric Neisser, "The Imitation of Man by Machine," *Science,* 139 (1963), 193–197; H. L. Dreyfus, *Alchemy and Artificial Intelligence* (Santa Monica, 1965).

30. William McDougall, "Men or Robots?" in Clark Murchison, ed., *Psychologies of 1925: Powell Lectures in Psychological Theory* (Worcester, 1926), p. 283n. See also *ISP*, pp. 447–455.

31. Richard Taylor, *Action and Purpose* (Englewood Cliffs, 1966), pp. 231–233.

32. Charles Taylor, *The Explanation of Behaviour* (London, 1964), p. 20.

33. Taylor, *Explanation of Behavior*, pp. 9–16, Part II *passim.* Taylor restricts himself to peripheralist (as opposed to centralist) theories; cf. pp. 107–108, 272. Taylor's discussion of specific psychological theories is criticized forcefully in a review by N. S. Sutherland, *Philosophical Quarterly,* 15 (1965), 379–381.

34. Taylor, *Explanation of Behaviour*, pp. 12–15, 17, 211. In discussing Taylor's position, Sayre has objected: "Many of the goals normally governing our actions are such that *no* particular form of behavior is necessary or in any sense *required* for their achievement. If I wish to insult a colleague there are many ways in which this might be done." K. M. Sayre, *Consciousness: A Philosophic Study of Minds and Machines* (New York, 1969), p. 69. In fact, the purposive criterion of "variation of means" implies that some details of action must always be "conatively undecidable" in that *any one* of a certain class of responses could function as the means to the purposed end. Consequently, in the explanation of response-selection, one must appeal to *non*teleological factors as well as to the goal or purpose directing the behavior. Though Taylor himself has recently admitted the "possibility" that there may be several occurrences in a given situation which would bring about the goal, he still insists that "with animate beings, it can plausibly be claimed that a unique selection [of the one and only event which would achieve the goal] usually takes place, through limitation of repertoire, or through some norm." Charles Taylor, "The Explanation of Purposive Behaviour," in Robert Borger and Frank Cioffi, eds., *Explanation in the Behavioural Sciences* (Cambridge, 1970), p. 55n. Several of the positions defended or implied in Taylor's book have been qualified in this paper, and reference to "inherent powers" has been dropped. In view of the wider influence of the book, I consider Taylor's original discussion within the text and indicate his later modifications in the notes.

35. Taylor, *Explanation of Behaviour*, pp. 17–18, 21, 22.

36. See T. L. S. Sprigge, "Teleological Explanation," *Proceedings of the Aristotelian Society*, supplementary vol. 45 (1971), pp. 149–170.

37. Taylor, *Explanation of Behaviour*, p. 24.

38. Taylor, *Explanation of Behaviour*, pp. 22, 25n.

39. In a recent paper Taylor explicitly disclaims any such implication. Taylor, "Explanation of Purposive Behaviour," pp. 67–72.

40. Taylor, *Explanation of Behaviour*, p. 21.

41. Taylor, *Explanation of Behaviour*, p. 54. Cf. pp. 33–45.

42. See e.g., Norman Malcolm, "The Conceivability of Mechanism," *Philosophical Review*, 77 (1968), 45–72. For Taylor's rebuttal of Malcolm's argument, see Taylor, "Explanation of Purposive Behaviour," pp. 89–93.

43. Taylor, *Explanation of Behaviour*, pp. 42–53, 98–102, 272. Taylor's position when writing this book was clearly that purposive and mechanistic explanations are incompatible, for admittedly mechanistic systems can not be regarded as truly purposive. In his latest discussion, Taylor does not insist on this point; he even allows that "mechanist and purposive explanations can co-exist to the extent that they are related as more and less basic explanations." Taylor, "Explanation of Purposive Behaviour," p. 94. This is to admit the possibility (conceivability) of the empirical reduction of psychology to physiology. Taylor does not reveal whether he still thinks that such a reduction (if achieved) would lead to a radical undermining of the present image of man, nor does he discuss the appropriateness of purposive concepts in cybernetic contexts.

44. R. M. Chisholm, "Intentionality," in Paul Edwards, ed., *The Encyclopedia of Philosophy* (New York, 1967), IV, 201–204; Chisholm, *Perceiving: A Philosophical Study* (Ithaca, 1957), ch. xi. Chisholm allows for the possibility of what McDougall called "anoetic sentience" in that the sentence, "He is in pain," may not entail any object of awareness. Chisholm, "Intentionality," p. 204. But he believes intensionality to be a sufficient condition of the psychological. Defining intensionality in Chisholm's logical terms, Cohen has argued that some *non*psychological sentences show the implicative peculiarities concerned. J. O. Urmson and L. J. Cohen, "Criteria of Intensionality," *Proceedings of the Aristotelian Society*, supplementary 42 (1968), esp. pp. 123–142.

45. Chisholm, "Intentionality," p. 203.

46. M. L. Minsky, "Matter, Mind, and Models," *Proceedings of the International Federation of Information Processing Congress*, vol. 1 (Washington, D.C., 1965), p. 45.

47. Minsky, "Matter, Mind, and Models," pp. 47, 45.

48. Saul Amarel, "On Representations of Problems of Reasoning about Actions," in Donald Michie, ed., *Machine Intelligence III* (Edinburgh, 1968), pp. 131–172. Amarel's problem is: three missionaries and three cannibals seek to cross a river, say from the left bank to the right bank. A boat is available that will hold two people, and which can be navigated by any combination of missionaries and cannibals involving one or two people. If the missionaries on either bank of the river, or en route across the river, are outnumbered at any time by cannibals, the cannibals will indulge their anthropophagic tendencies and do away with the missionaries. Find the simplest schedule of crossings that will permit all the missionaries and cannibals to cross the river safely. In a more generalized version of this problem, there are N missionaries and N cannibals (where $N \geqslant 3$) and the boat has a capacity k (where $k \geqslant 2$))

49. Amarel, "On Representations," p. 160.

50. Amarel, "On Representations," p. 169.

51. Amarel, "On Representations," p. 131.

52. An expupil of McDougall and C. S. Sherrington has recently written: "If, with most epistemologists, we regard consciousness . . . as essentially a two-term relation, then we must assume . . . something very like a pure ego to serve as the subject—a witness of the field . . . 'an "I" that counts itself a cause.' The same subject not only perceives; it also apparently wills. If so, we must suppose that this 'active factor' interacts with the brain rather like a system of non-physical forces." Cyril Burt, "Brain and Consciousness," *British Journal of Psychology*, 59 (1968), 67.

53. I have discussed this point at greater length in M. A. Boden, "Intentionality and Physical Systems," *Philosophy of Science*, 37 (1970), 200–214.

54. Taylor, *Explanation of Behaviour*, pp. 107–108.

55. In the context of communication engineering, "information" is defined and measured in terms of the statistical probability of the physical signals transmitted by an information channel, such as a telephone system. That a channel "transmits information" in this sense implies neither that the channel understands the signal nor even that the signal is intelligible in the first place. Indeed, "maximum information" would be carried by a completely unpredictable, *random* series of signals. The processing and understanding of information of course requires that the input message be efficiently received and transmitted without gross distortion within the system. It is these aspects only of what is normally termed "the transmission and use of information" that are involved in communication-engineering uses of the

term. This sense is also useful in discussions of the psychology of perception.

56. J. E. Doran, "Planning and Robots," in Bernard Meltzer and Donald Michie, eds., *Machine Intelligence V* (Edinburgh, 1969), p. 528.

57. In an "infinite loop," a rule or series of rules in the program is applied over and over again, endlessly, so that the task performance is blocked in a characteristic fashion. This could happen if, for example, the conditional jump that should end the loop could not occur, owing to incorrect testing of the specific condition concerned. A conditional jump is an instruction of the general form: Do X if variable v has value n; otherwise, do Y. If this instruction were itself expressed wrongly in the program, or if the testing procedure to compute the value of v were faulty, a loop might result.

58. Taylor, *Explanation of Behaviour*, p. 22 (italics mine).

59. In his latest discussion, Taylor admits that every mental event may have a neural expression. However, he still insists that if one assumes psychological processes to be "completely caused" by neural processes, one is legislating a priori about "the type of concepts which will figure in an adequate explanation." Taylor, "Explanation of Purposive Behaviour," p. 73. This remark suggests both that the mechanist must regard causal accounts as fully adequate to the explanation of behavior, and that he must regard the future empirical reduction of psychology to neurophysiology as a practical possibility. These suggestions are mistaken, for the reductionist is not committed to either position.

60. For example, consider the last two sentences of this passage from Taylor's most recent paper, which eschews reference to "powers": "The problem is thus to account for how the appropriate response gets selected . . . We are looking for an antecedent condition of this form: a property of the response which earns its selection. Now a mechanistic solution to this problem must select a [nonteleological] property which . . . makes no mention of that property of the response which is its being appropriate . . . But it is an unjustifiable assumption that the true explanation must be of this form. It may be, that is, that we can only account for the selection of the response in terms of its appropriateness. In other words, it may be that there is no other [intrinsic, mechanistic] property I which determines which behaviour is selected —the antecedent condition of its selection is just that a behaviour is A [appropriate] . . . there is, in other words, no further explanation for A's occurring on the grounds that it is I." Taylor, "Explanation of Purposive Behavior," p. 70.

61. Minsky, "Matter, Mind, and Models," p. 47. Minsky states later (p. 49): "When intelligent machines are constructed, we should not be surprised to find them as confused and stubborn as men in their convictions about mind-matter, consciousness, free will, and the like. For all such questions are pointed at explaining the complicated interactions between parts of the self-model. A man's or a machine's strength of conviction about such things tells us nothing about the man or about the machine except what it tells us about his model of himself."

62. Paul Ziff, "The Feelings of Robots," *Analysis*, 19 (1959), 64–68; Keith Gunderson, "Robots, Consciousness, and Programmed Behaviour," *British Journal for the Philosophy of Science*, 19 (1968), 109–122.

63. Gunderson, "Robots, Consciousness, and Programmed Behaviour," p. 116.

64. Roland Puccetti, *Persons: A Study of Possible Moral Agents in the Universe* (London, 1968), ch. ii.

65. A. C. Danto, "On Consciousness in Machines," in Sidney Hook, ed., *Dimensions of Mind: A Symposium* (New York, 1960), pp. 180–187. Cf. a relevant discussion, though not directed specifically to this point, by Hilary Putnam, "Dreaming and 'Depth Grammar,'" in R. J. Butler, ed., *Analytical Philosophy* (Oxford, 1962), pp. 211–235.

66. Ludwig Wittgenstein, *Zettel* (Oxford, 1967), paras. 528–534.

67. See Puccetti, *Persons*, pp. 51, 53.

68. K. M. Sayre, *Recognition: A Study in the Philosophy of Artificial Intelligence* (Notre Dame, 1965).

69. Leonard Uhr and Charles Vossler, "A Pattern Recognition Program That Generates, Evaluates, and Adjusts Its Own Operators," in Feigenbaum and Feldman, eds., *Computers and Thought*, pp. 251–268.

70. Sayre, *Recognition*, esp. ch. vi.

71. J. E. Doran, "Experiments with a Pleasure-Seeking Automaton," in Michie, ed., *Machine Intelligence III*, pp. 195–216.

72. One development is discussed in J. E. Doran, "Planning and Generalisation in an Automaton/Environment System," in Bernard Meltzer and Donald Michie, eds., *Machine Intelligence IV* (Edinburgh, 1969), pp. 433–454. Doran states (p. 435): "This work is not intended as a model of animal learning or other behaviour, nor as a serious robot simulation." But in the earlier paper he had asked: "[A rat in a cage] perceives its rather simple environment in a variety of ways, it remembers, learns, predicts, and acts towards goals which ultimately derive from basic necessities such as food, sleep, and the avoidance of pain. Can one write a computer program which, how-

ever primitively, simulates the rat and its surroundings and which demonstrates the simulated rat displaying such rudimentary intelligence as it is reasonable to require?" Doran, "Experiments with a Pleasure-Seeking Automaton," pp. 195–196. Evidently, Doran became more sensitive to the differences between rats and "simulated rats" in the interval.

73. Insofar as behavior may be determined by contingent factors not represented within the simulated theory, the details of behavior are not predictable by means of the simulation alone. In an analogous fashion, a theory of "deep structure grammar" can explain certain aspects of linguistic behavior but cannot predict at what times a man will speak nor what he will say. The more that "prediction of behavior" is understood to concern such specific details, the less a general theory, or simulation, is capable of "predicting" behavior as well as explaining its overall structure.

74. This point is elaborated in Reitman, *Cognition and Thought*, chs. i and ii; J. A. Fodor, *Psychological Explanation: An Introduction to the Philosophy of Psychology* (New York, 1968), ch. iv; K. M. Sayre and F. J. Crosson, eds., *The Modeling of Mind: Computers and Intelligence* (Notre Dame, 1963), ch. i.

75. By a "pure" approach I mean one that has not found it convenient to poach on the psychologist's territory by deliberately including features of human cognition because these provide the most efficient way known of getting results. For an example of the "impure" approach, see J. P. Thorne, Paul Bratley, and H. M. Dewar, "The Syntactic Analysis of English by Machine," in Michie, ed., *Machine Intelligence III*, pp. 281–309.

76. See Fodor, *Psychological Explanation*, p. 142.

77. For the original discussion of cell assemblies, see D. O. Hebb, *The Organization of Behavior: A Neuropsychological Theory* (New York, 1949). Hebb's concept has inspired much cybernetic work relating to the problem of neural computation and learning. For an example of a direct application of computer simulation to Hebb's theory, see Nathaniel Rochester, J. H. Holland, L. H. Haibt, and W. L. Duda, "Test on a Cell Assembly Theory of the Brain, Using a Large Digital Computer," *Institute of Radio Engineers Transactions in Information Theory*, 2 (1956), 80–93. This simulation showed up hidden contradictions within Hebb's verbal arguments from his theory.

The classic paper of McCulloch and Pitts was crucial in initiating cybernetic thinking about the activity of neural nets and in proposing symbolic models of the neurophysiological mechanisms underlying purposive behavior and "mind" in general. W. S. McCulloch and W. H. Pitts, "A Logical Calculus of the Ideas Immanent in Nervous

Activity," in W. S. McCulloch, *Embodiments of Mind* (Cambridge, 1965), ch. ii. Two of McCulloch's colleagues have recently shown that certain types of neurophysiological mechanism (completely random neural nets), and machine "perceptrons" with no significant prior structure, could not achieve certain types of pattern recognition or learning which are achieved by some mammalian brains. Anatomical, histological, and physiological evidence has long been available to show that the mammalian brain has a significant prior structure, but this analytical work attempts to show just *why* a random neural net (or a quasi-universal perceptron) could not be a "self-organizing system" competent to carry out certain psychological tasks. M. L. Minsky and Seymour Papert, *Perceptrons: An Introduction to Computational Geometry* (Cambridge, 1969).

78. The degree of optimism is indicated by the quotes appearing in Dreyfus, *Alchemy and Artificial Intelligence*, esp. pp. 2–17.

79. A. M. Turing, "Computing Machinery and Intelligence," *Mind*, n.s. 59 (1950), 439–442.

80. Dreyfus, *Alchemy and Artificial Intelligence*, pp. 59, 85. See also H. L. Dreyfus, "Why Computers Must Have Bodies in Order To Be Intelligent," *Review of Metaphysics*, 21 (1967), 13–32.

81. For a summary of this evidence, see B. D. Burns, *The Uncertain Nervous System* (London, 1968), esp. chs. ii, iv, v. For a discussion of brain activity as digital or analog from an engineering approach, see R. L. Gregory, "On Physical Model Explanations in Psychology," *British Journal for the Philosophy of Science*, 4 (1953), 192–197.

82. Amarel, "On Representations," pp. 166, 170.

83. Newell, "Problems of Basic Organizations," esp. pp. 397–402; Reitman, *Cognition and Thought*, chs. viii, ix; Ulric Neisser, *Cognitive Psychology* (New York, 1967), p. 9; Neisser, "Imitation of Man," *passim*.

84. K. M. Sayre, "Intelligence, Bodies, and Digital Computers," *Review of Metaphysics*, 21 (1968), 722.

85. R. L. Gregory, "On How So Little Information Controls So Much Behaviour," *Bionics Research Reports* (Edinburgh), no. 1 (1968), p. 17.

86. Dreyfus, *Alchemy and Artificial Intelligence*, pp. 59–61; H. L. Dreyfus, "Mechanism and Phenomenology," *Noûs*, 5 (1971), 81–96.

87. Rapaport has stated: "In the first phase of psychoanalytic theory (abreaction theory—up to 1898), psychological energy was equated with affects . . . In the second phase (1900–1926), psychological energy was conceptualized as drive energy, and the methods used in discharging it as the primary process. It was recognized that

other (secondary) processes, using minute quantities of energy, exert a regulative function over those which dispose of drive energies. The relationship between these two kinds of processes was conceived much like that described nowadays as obtaining between power engineering and information engineering . . . These psychological energies are not equated with any known kind of biochemical energy . . . (However, it is neither implied nor ruled out that biochemical energy exchanges may eventually be discovered which correspond to the exchanges of psychological energy inferred from behavior by psychoanalysis)." David Rapaport, "The Structure of Psychoanalytic Theory: A Systematizing Attempt," in Sigmund Koch, ed., *Psychology: A Study of a Science* (New York, 1959), III, 91–93. Freud's psychological theories were greatly influenced by his neurological training under Ernst Brucke (one of the four founders of the "Helmholtz School" of medicine), who, he wrote, "carried more weight with me than anyone else in my whole life." Peter Amacher, "Freud's Neurological Education and Its Influence on Psychoanalytic Theory," *Psychological Issues*, IV, no. 4, Monograph 16 (New York, 1965), p. 9.

88. R. W. Sperry, "A Modified Concept of Consciousness," *Psychological Review*, 76 (1969), 533–534.

89. J. C. Eccles, *The Neurophysiological Basis of Mind: The Principles of Neurophysiology* (Oxford, 1953), ch. viii; J. C. Eccles, ed., *Brain and Conscious Experience: Study Week, September 28 to October 4, 1964, of the Pontificia Academia Scientiarum* (Berlin, 1966), p. 327; J. C. Eccles, *The Brain and the Unity of Conscious Experience* (Cambridge, 1965); Burt, "Brain and Consciousness." See also M. A. Boden, "Brain and Consciousness: A Reply to Professor Burt," *Bulletin of the British Psychological Society*, 22 (1969), 47–49.

90. Eccles, *Neurophysiological Basis of Mind*, pp. 277–278.

91. For the classic experiments supporting the principle of cerebral equipotentiality and casting doubt on the precise cortical localization of function, see K. S. Lashley, *Brain Mechanisms and Intelligence: A Quantitative Study of Injuries to the Brain* (Chicago, 1929); K. S. Lashley, "Functional Determinants of Cerebral Localization," *Archives of Neurology and Psychiatry*, 38 (1937), 371–387; K. S. Lashley, "In Search of the Engram," *Symposium of the Society of Experimental Biology*, no. 4 (Cambridge, 1950), pp. 454–482.

V. Purpose, Instincts, and Natural Goals

1. William McDougall, "The Hormic Psychology," in Clark Murchison, ed., *Psychologies of 1930* (Worcester, 1930), pp. 3–36. Included as supplementary chapter in *ISP* (1931).

2. L. T. Troland, *The Fundamentals of Human Motivation* (New

York, 1928), chs. xvi–xvii, esp. pp. 276–280. For McDougall's comment, see *ISP*, pp. 455–458.

3. *ISP*, p. 456.

4. *ISP*, pp. 456–457

5. *ISP*, p. 457.

6. *ISP*, p. 457.

7. *ISP*, p. 37. A recent discussion of hypnosis has suggested that pain may be a very general "stop-rule" that can be temporarily suspended during hypnosis. G. A. Miller, Eugene Galanter, and K. H. Pribram, *Plans and the Structure of Behavior* (New York, 1960), pp. 109–110.

8. *ISP*, p. 25 (italics mine). See also *BM*, pp. 324–325, where McDougall gives a strange "evolutionary" argument against mind-body parallelism that also rests on the conceptual connection of pleasure with *appetitive* or *purposive* behavior. He imagines all species-beneficial behavior as being *un*pleasurable and continues: "Such a state of things would seem to us *profoundly irrational and absurd.*" This remark can only be justified by pointing out that the connection is conceptual rather than empirical.

9. Gilbert Ryle, *The Concept of Mind* (London, 1949), pp. 108–109.

10. James Olds and Peter Milner, "Positive Reinforcement Produced by Electrical Stimulation of Septal Area and Other Regions of Rat Brain," *Journal of Comparative and Physiological Psychology*, 47 (1954), 419–427; M. P. Bishop, S. T. Elder, and R. G. Heath, "Intracranial Self-Stimulation in Man," *Science*, 140 (1963), 394–396.

11. J. C. B. Gosling, *Pleasure and Desire: The Case For Hedonism Reviewed* (Oxford, 1969), esp. chs. iv–vi. In ch. vii Gosling discusses the view that purposive activity *necessarily* involves pleasure in the prospect of success: he concludes that while a population might possibly pursue ends without experiencing any such pleasure, they would be incapable of entering into an important range of moral-psychological human relationships.

12. Carl Groos, *The Play of Animals: A Study of Animal Life and Instinct* (London, 1898); Carl Groos, *The Play of Man* (New York, 1901); R. W. White, "Motivation Reconsidered: The Concept of Competence," *Psychological Review*, 66 (1959), 297–333. McDougall first accepted and later rebutted Groos's psychological analysis of play. *ISP*, pp. 93–99, 399–401; *OP*, pp. 170–173.

13. *OP*, p. 171.

14. E. L. Thorndike, "Animal Intelligence: An Experimental Study of the Associative Processes in Animals," *Psychological Review Monograph Supplement*, No. 8, 1898, reprinted in E. L. Thorndike, *Animal*

Intelligence: Experimental Studies (New York, 1911), pp. 20–155.

15. See G. W. Allport, "Effect: A Secondary Principle of Learning," *Psychological Review*, 53 (1946), 335–347; Leo Postman, "The History and Present Status of the Law of Effect," *Psychological Bulletin*, 44 (1947), 489–563.

16. P. E. Meehl, "On the Circularity of the Law of Effect," *Psychological Bulletin*, 47 (1950), 52–75.

17. *ISP*, p. 458.

18. *ISP*, p. 416.

19. Meehl, "On the Circularity of the Law of Effect," p. 58.

20. *OP*, p. 122.

21. *OP*, p. 122.

22. *OP*, pp. 124, 125.

23. See Anthony Kenny, *Action, Emotion and Will* (London, 1963), esp. chs. iii–iv; R. S. Peters and C. A. Mace, "Emotions and the Category of Passivity," *Proceedings of the Aristotelian Society*, 62 (1962), 117–142; R. S. Peters, "Motivation, Emotion, and the Conceptual Schemes of Common Sense," in Theodore Mischel, ed., *Human Action: Conceptual and Empirical Issues* (New York, 1969), pp. 135–166, esp. pp. 153–163.

24. *OP*, p. 128.

25. G. E. M. Anscombe, *Intention* (Oxford, 1957), esp. pp. 67–74.

26. Since the patriotic and religious sentiments, like most sentiments, draw on several different instincts, to speak of "the" patriotic or religious motive may be misleading. The religious motive is a compound motive, to which the basic motives involved in the religious sentiment contribute. Moreover, religious sentiments may be of an indefinite variety in different individuals, and the relative importance of the basic instincts involved thus differs from man to man.

27. *ISP*, pp. 311–312.

28. *EM*, p. 9.

29. *ISP*, p. 458.

30. *ISP*, pp. 310–311.

31. *ISP*, p. 449.

32. Rom Harré, "Powers," *British Journal for the Philosophy of Science*, 21 (1970), pp. 85, 91.

33. *ISP*, pp. 25, 29.

34. *ISP*, pp. 77, 42.

35. *ISP*, p. 310.

36. *ISP*, pp. 416 (italics mine), 422.

37. *EM*, p. vi.

38. In 1924 a critic of McDougall offered a statistical analysis of nearly 6,000 different "instincts" listed by over 400 writers. L. L. Ber-

nard, *Instinct: A Study of Social Psychology* (New York, 1924), ch. ix, esp. pp. 182–220.

39. *ISP*, p. 75.

40. *EM*, pp. 97–98.

41. *OP*, chs. ii–v, esp. pp. 103–120; William McDougall, "The Use and Abuse of Instinct in Social Psychology," *Journal of Abnormal and Social Psychology*, 15 (1922), 285–333; William McDougall, "Can Sociology and Social Psychology Dispense with Instincts?" *Journal of Abnormal and Social Psychology*, 19 (1924) 13–41; *ISP*, pp. 405–430.

42. *ISP*, p. 423.

43. *ISP*, pp. 423, 75.

44. *ISP*, pp. 425–426. Despite their differences over the place of specific instincts, and Freud's hedonistic appeal to the "pleasure principle," McDougall welcomed Freud's psychology as supporting his own general position, originally expressed in *ISP* independently of Freud's works. *ISP*, p. 424. Freud, too, stressed inborn dynamic principles and the purposiveness of both conscious and unconscious mental life, as well as regarding the "self" as an organizer of behavior motivated essentially by instinct. McDougall would have approved the development of neo-Freudian ego-psychology, which stresses the role of rationality and cognition in behavior and tempers the pre-eminence of the sex instinct. *OAP*, chs. vi, viii, xxv–xxvi.

45. *OP*, p. 110.

46. *ISP*, p. 416.

47. Tolman refers to three of McDougall's contemporaries as committing this blunder, namely Stewart Paton, S. J. Holmes, and H. C. Warren. E. C. Tolman, "The Nature of Instinct," *Psychological Bulletin*, 20 (1923), p. 208.

48. *OP*, p. 173.

49. Tolman, "The Nature of Instinct," p. 201.

50. Charles Darwin, *The Descent of Man, and Selection in Relation to Sex*, 2nd ed. (London, 1874), p. 145.

51. *OP*, p. 173.

52. *OP*, p. 119.

53. *OP*, pp. 172–173.

54. *ISP*, p. 25.

55. *OP*, pp. 98, 99.

56. *OP*, pp. 140–141, 143.

57. For an early experimental study suggesting the "intrinsic motivation" of informational novelty, see H. F. Harlow, "Learning and Satiation of Response in Intrinsically Motivated Complex Puzzle Per-

formance by Monkeys," *Journal of Comparative Physiology and Psychology,* 43 (1950), 289–294. For a discussion and review of the subsequent research literature, see D. E. Berlyne, *Conflict, Arousal, and Curiosity* (New York, 1960).

58. Konrad Lorenz, "Companionship in Bird Life: Fellow Members of the Species as Releasers of Social Behavior" (1935) and "The Nature of Instinct: The Conception of Instinctive Behavior" (1937), in C. H. Schiller, ed., *Instinctive Behavior: The Development of a Modern Concept* (New York, 1957), pp. 83–175.

59. Lorenz, "The Nature of Instinct," p. 157.

60. D. S. Lehrman, "Induction of Broodiness by Participation in Courtship and Nest-Building in the Ring Dove (*Streptopelia Risoria*)," *Journal of Comparative and Physiological Psychology,* 51 (1958), 32–36; D. S. Lehrman, "Effect of Female Sex Hormones on Incubation Behavior in the Ring Dove (*Streptopelia Risoria*)," *Journal of Comparative and Physiological Psychology,* 51 (1958), 142–145; D. S. Lehrman, "The Physiological Basis of Parental Feeding Behavior in the Ring Dove (*Streptopelia Risoria*)," *Behaviour,* 7 (1955), 241–286.

61. See F. A. Beach, "The Descent of Instinct," *Psychological Review,* 62 (1955), 401–410.

62. *ISP,* p. 421.

63. See, e.g., Beach, "Descent of Instinct"; W. S. Verplanck, "Since Learned Behavior Is Innate, and Vice Versa, What Now?" *Psychological Review,* 62 (1955),139–144.

64. *ISP,* p. 25.

65. G. E. McClearn, "The Inheritance of Behavior," in Leo Postman, ed., *Psychology in the Making: Histories of Selected Research Problems* (New York, 1963), p. 226.

66. *OP,* p. 104.

67. McClearn, "The Inheritance of Behavior," p. 230.

68. Miller et al., *Plans and the Structure of Behavior,* pp. 16–17, 27.

69. Miller et al., *Plans and the Structure of Behavior,* p. 16.

70. Miller et al., *Plans and the Structure of Behavior,* p. 62.

71. *ISP,* p. 449.

72. Miller et al., *Plans and the Structure of Behavior,* p. 78 (italics mine).

73. See J. S. Bruner, Jacqueline Goodnow, and George Austin, *A Study of Thinking* (New York, 1956); Max Wertheimer, *Productive Thinking* (New York, 1945).

74. *OP,* p. 218.

75. *ISP,* p. 438.

VI. Sentiments and Simulation

1. *EM*, 2nd ed. (1934), p. xiv; *EM*, p. 219.
2. *ISP*, pp. 27–28.
3. *ISP*, p. 105.
4. A. F. Shand, "Character and the Emotions," *Mind*, n.s. 5 (1896), 203–226; A. F. Shand, "M. Ribot's Theory of the Passions," *Mind*, n.s. 16 (1907), 477–505. See also *ISP*, pp. vii–viii.
5. *ISP*, p. 437.
6. *ISP*, p. 140; *EM*, p. 223.
7. *ISP*, pp. 140–141 (italics mine).
8. *ISP*, p. 438.
9. *OP*, p. 213.
10. For a discussion of the concept of functional autonomy, see G. W. Allport, *Pattern and Growth in Personality*, rev. ed. (New York, 1961), pp. 229, 244, ch. x *passim*.
11. *ISP*, p. 105.
12. *ISP*, pp. 435–436.
13. *EM*, pp. 219n, 225n. For a comparison of "sentiment" and "attitude," see G. W. Allport, "The Historical Background of Modern Social Psychology," in Gardner Lindzey and Elliot Aronson, eds., *The Handbook of Social Psychology* (Reading, 1968), I, pp. 63–64.
14. In his last revised edition of *ISP* (1936), pp. 495–508, McDougall remarked that he had previously exaggerated the distinction between the conative and affective aspects of instincts.
15. *ISP*, pp. 104, 435.
16. Anthony Kenny, *Action, Emotion and Will* (London, 1963), pp. 60–61.
17. *OP*, p. 326.
18. *ISP*, pp. 128–135; *EM*, p. 156.
19. For a recent discussion of various conceptual analyses of hope, and problems concerning its experimental measurement, see J. P. Day, "Hope," *American Philosophical Quarterly*, 6 (1969), 89–102; J. P. Day, "The Anatomy of Hope and Fear," *Mind*, n.s. 79 (1970), 369–384.
20. *ISP*, pp. 381–382. Cf. *EM*, pp. 172–174.
21. *EM*, p. 177.
22. *EM*, p. 239.
23. See R. W. White, "Motivation Reconsidered: The Concept of Competence," *Psychological Review*, 66 (1959), 297–333.
24. *P*, pp. 69–70; *EM*, 2nd ed. (1934), p. xiv; *EM*, p. 223.
25. *OP*, p. 42.
26. H. A. Simon and Allen Newell, "Simulation of Human Think-

ing," in Martin Greenberger, ed., *Computers and the World of the Future* (Cambridge, 1962), p. 123.

27. See P. E. Meehl, *Clinical Versus Statistical Prediction: A Theoretical Analysis and a Review of the Evidence* (Minneapolis, 1954).

28. Allen Newell, J. C. Shaw, and H. A. Simon, "Chess-Playing Programs and the Problem of Complexity," in E. A. Feigenbaum and Julian Feldman, eds., *Computers and Thought* (New York, 1963), pp. 39–70.

29. Karl Leipold and W. E. Rekowski, "A Method for the Simultaneous Processing of Several Programs," *Proceedings of the International Federation of Information Processing Congress* (Washington, D.C., 1965), II, 320–321.

30. Allen Newell, "Some Problems of Basic Organization in Problem-Solving Programs," in M. C. Yovits, G. T. Jacobi, and G. D. Goldstein, eds., *Self-Organizing Systems, 1962* (Washington, 1962), p. 398.

31. This distinction between the realization and the conceptualization of programs is made in W. R. Reitman, "Personality as a Problem-Solving Coalition," in S. S. Tomkins and Samuel Messick, eds., *Computer Simulation of Personality: Frontier of Psychological Theory* (New York, 1963), pp. 69–100, esp. p. 79.

32. O. G. Selfridge, "Pandemonium: A Paradigm for Learning," in D. V. Blake and A. M. Uttley, eds., *Proceedings of the Symposium on Mechanisation of Thought Processes* (London, 1959), pp. 511–529; W. R. Reitman, R. B. Grove, and R. G. Shoup, "Argus: An Information-Processing Model of Thinking," *Behavioral Science*, 9 (1964), 270–281. This program is discussed further in W. R. Reitman, *Cognition and Thought: An Information-Processing Approach* (New York, 1965), esp. ch. viii.

33. For a discussion of various theoretical models of attitude change employed in recent research, see Roger Brown, *Social Psychology* (New York, 1965), ch. xi. For the pioneering study of such changes, see Fritz Heider, *The Psychology of Interpersonal Relations* (New York, 1958). For an early attempt to simulate them, see R. P. Abelson, "Computer Simulation of 'Hot' Cognition," in Tomkins and Messick, eds., *Computer Simulation of Personality*, pp. 277–298.

34. *ISP*, p. 106.

35. *EM*, p. xiv; Preface to 2nd ed. (1934).

VII. Purpose and Self

1. *EM*, pp. 379–380.
2. *EM*, p. 381.
3. *ISP*, p. 160.

4. A. O. Lovejoy, *Reflections on Human Nature* (Baltimore, 1961), pp. 67–128.

5. Compare Hare's discussion of the importance of universalizability as a criterion of moral rules. R. M. Hare, "Universalisability," *Proceedings of the Aristotelian Society,* 55 (1955), 295–312; R. M. Hare, *Freedom and Reason* (Oxford, 1963).

6. *ISP,* p. 178.

7. See Ruth Wylie, *The Self Concept: A Critical Survey of Pertinent Research Literature* (Lincoln, 1961).

8. *OP,* p. 529.

9. *MMEE,* p. 200.

10. *ISP,* pp. 208–209.

11. *ISP,* p. 207.

12. *ISP,* pp. 213, 214.

13. *ISP,* p. 226.

14. The idiographic-nomothetic distinction (originally proposed by Wilhelm Windelband) has been stressed in the psychological writings of G. W. Allport. Idiographic research aims at knowledge of particular individual facts; nomothetic research aims at knowledge of universal laws or generalizations. Behavior that is predictable in terms of universal generalizations, without the necessity of particular reference to the individual organism concerned, may thus be termed "nomothetic" —although strictly speaking, it is the methodology of explanation and prediction employed that is either idiographic or nomothetic. This methodological distinction is closely similar to Meehl's distinction between "clinical" and "statistical" methods of prediction in psychology. Idiographic or clinical methods are favored by the Third Force psychologists in general. See G. W. Allport, *The Use of Personal Documents in Psychological Science* (New York, 1942); G. W. Allport, "Personalistic Psychology as Science: A Reply," *Psychological Review,* 53 (1946), 132–135; P. E. Meehl, *Clinical Versus Statistical Prediction: A Theoretical Analysis and a Review of the Evidence* (Minneapolis, 1954).

15. M. L. Minsky, "Matter, Mind and Models," in *Proceedings of the International Federation of Information Processing Congress,* I (Washington, D.C., 1965), p. 46.

16. *ISP,* p. 134.

17. *OAP,* pp. 3, 357.

18. *OAP,* p. 546.

19. Even in *BM* (p. 327), McDougall had stressed the fact that an intention once formed may continue to operate when no longer present to consciousness, regarding such a conative process as one "to which no mechanical process is even remotely analogous."

20. *OAP*, pp. 547–548.

21. For the classic account of the case of Sally Beauchamp, see Morton Prince, *The Dissociation of a Personality: A Biographical Study in Abnormal Psychology* (New York, 1905). Similar cases were described by William James, Boris Sidis, Pierre Janet, and J. M. Charcot, some of which were referred to by McDougall in *OAP*, chs. xxx–xxxiv. For a recent example, see C. H. Thigpen and H. M. Cleckley, *The Three Faces of Eve* (London, 1957).

22. For examples of the application of this principle to clinical cases, see Prince, *Dissociation of a Personality*, esp. chs. xxx–xxxii; Thigpen and Cleckley, *The Three Faces of Eve*, esp. chs. xxiii–xxv.

23. See *OAP*, pp. 548–551; William McDougall, "Presidential Address," *Proceedings of the Society for Psychical Research*, 30 (1920), 105–123; William McDougall, "The Need for Psychic Research," *Journal of the American Society for Psychical Research*, 17 (1923), 4–14.

24. *OAP*, p. 548.

25. W. R. Reitman, "Personality as a Problem-Solving Coalition," in S. S. Tomkins and Samuel Messick, eds., *Computer Simulation of Personality: Frontier of Psychological Theory* (New York, 1963), pp. 73, 85.

26. *BM*, p. 117.

27. R. W. Sperry, "The Great Cerebral Commissure," *Scientific American*, 210, no. 1 (1964), 51–52; R. W. Sperry, "Hemisphere Deconnection and Unity in Conscious Awareness," *American Psychologist*, 23 (1968), 724; M. S. Gazzaniga, "The Split Brain in Man," *Scientific American*, 217, no. 2 (1967), 29.

28. *BM*, pp. 296, 326–327.

29. K. J. W. Craik, *The Nature of Explanation* (Cambridge, 1943), pp. 84–85.

30. Though this article, "A Contribution Towards an Improvement in Psychological Method," was read to the Aristotelian Society in November 1897, it was not published in its entirety until 1898. McDougall refers to it in *BM* as "my first published article," but strictly speaking his first published article was "On the Structure of Cross-Striated Muscle."

31. *BM*, p. 379.

32. Minsky, "Matter, Mind and Models," p. 48.

VIII. Purpose, Consciousness, and Intensionality

1. For a review of various psychological approaches to behavioral and subjective affective phenomena, see George Mandler, "Emotion," in T. M. Newcomb, ed., *New Directions in Psychology* (New York,

1962), pp. 267–343. Mandler criticizes existentialist and phenomenologist psychologists for their emphasis on introspectively experienced emotions, referring to them as "knights in nineteenth-century armor" (p. 302). Insofar as these psychologists represent subjective affect as essentially, or logically, private, they may indeed be faulted; but insofar as they emphasize (essentially public or communicable) subjective phenomena within the patient's mind, rather than observable expressions of emotion that are not typically noticed or acted upon by the patient himself, they may be defended both philosophically and psychologically.

2. For a discussion of the emergence of psychological properties at successive levels of development, of releasers as weak or strong influences on behavior, and of the gradual appearance of autonomy or freedom in the phylogenetic scale, see T. C. Schneirla, "The Concept of Development in Comparative Psychology," in D. B. Harris, ed., *The Concept of Development: An Issue in the Study of Human Behavior* (Minneapolis, 1957), pp. 78–108.

3. *EM,* p. 4.

4. See David Hume, *A Treatise on Human Nature: Being an Attempt to Introduce the Experimental Method of Reasoning into Moral Subjects,* I (London, 1739), bk. I, pt. iii. Elsewhere, Hume argued against Locke's view that the causal relation between volition and action is a special case, the only one where it is really possible to see and understand the "necessity" involved. David Hume, *An Enquiry Concerning the Human Understanding* (London, 1748), sec. vii. But both Hume and Locke agreed that a "causal" relation may be posited between volitional ideas and bodily movements. The radical conceptual flaw in this "ideomotor" theory is that the particular "idea" or "act of will" supposed to cause any given movement can be logically identified only by way of referring to that very movement. See A. I. Melden, *Free Action* (London, 1961), chs. iii–v.

5. Donald Davidson, "Actions, Reasons, and Causes," *Journal of Philosophy,* 60 (1963), esp. sec. iv.

6. See N. R. Hanson, *Patterns of Discovery* (Cambridge, 1958), ch. iii.

7. *EM,* p. 4; *ISP,* p. 308, *EM,* p. 4 (italics mine); *BM,* p. 272.

8. For a classic statement of the singular weakness of the argument from analogy, see John Wisdom, "Other Minds," *Proceedings of the Aristotelian Society,* supplementary 20 (1946), 122–147. For a complaint that Wisdom's approach misuses the verb "to know" so that his skeptical doubts are misdirected, see J. L. Austin, "Other Minds," *Proceedings of the Aristotelian Society,* supplementary 20 (1946), 148–187. For attempts to defend the argument from analogy, see Stuart

Hampshire, "The Analogy of Feeling," *Mind*, n.s. 61 (1952), 1–12; A. J. Ayer, "One's Knowledge of Other Minds," *Theoria*, 19 (1954), 1–20.

9. See, e.g., Norman Malcolm, "Wittgenstein's *Philosophical Investigations*," *Philosophical Review*, 63 (1954), 530–559; Norman Malcolm, "Knowledge of Other Minds," *Journal of Philosophy*, 55 (1958), 969–978; P. F. Strawson, *Individuals: An Essay in Descriptive Metaphysics* (London, 1959), ch. iii.

10. Ludwig Wittgenstein, *Philosophical Investigations* (Oxford, 1953), para. 580. Many other sections of *Philosophical Investigations* are relevant to this discussion, esp. paras. 242–316.

11. Many of the influential articles in this debate are collected in O. R. Jones, ed., *The Private Language Argument* (London, 1971).

12. Wittgenstein suggested that the verbal self-ascription of pain, for example, replaces the natural, behavioral expression of pain. Wittgenstein, *Philosophical Investigations*, para. 244. This example has been used by Malcolm as the basis of the claim that psychological self-ascription in general should be thought of as "evincing" one's psychological processes rather than as "reporting" or "describing" them. Malcolm, "Knowledge of Other Minds," esp. p. 978. The implausibility of this claim, and the resultant "overturning" of the original problem so that knowledge of *one's own* mind becomes more philosophically obscure than knowledge of other minds, is discussed in R. C. Buck, "Non-other Minds," in R. J. Butler, ed., *Analytical Philosophy* (Oxford, 1962), pp. 187–210.

13. Wittgenstein, *Philosophical Investigations*, para. 354.

14. The relevant sense of "criterion" is discussed in Malcolm, "Wittgenstein's *Philosophical Investigations*"; Strawson, *Individuals*, ch. iii (esp. sec. iv); Rogers Albritton, "On Wittgenstein's Use of the Term 'Criterion,'" *Journal of Philosophy*, 56 (1959), 845–857; C. S. Chihara and J. A. Fodor, "Operationalism and Ordinary Language: A Critique of Wittgenstein," *American Philosophical Quarterly*, 2 (1965), 281–295.

15. See K. S. Lashley, "The Problem of Serial Order in Behavior," in L. A. Jeffress, ed., *Cerebral Mechanisms in Behavior: The Hixon Symposium* (New York, 1951), pp. 112–135.

16. *ISP*, p. 309.

17. This example is one of a number discussed in an early ethological paper that stresses the subjective (intensional) worlds of different animals. Jacob von Uexkull, "A Stroll Through the Worlds of Animals and Men," in C. H. Schiller, ed., *Instinctive Behavior: The Development of A Modern Concept* (New York, 1957), pp. 5–82.

18. *BM*, p. 379.

397

19. See Roger Brown, *Social Psychology* (New York, 1965), p. 23.

20. These two examples, as well as others, are described in Nikolaas Tinbergen, *The Study of Instinct* (Oxford, 1951), ch. ii, esp. pp. 25–46.

21. T. H. Huxley, "On the Hypothesis That Animals Are Automata, and Its History," in T. H. Huxley, *Method and Results: Essays* (London, 1893), pp. 218–219 (italics mine).

22. *EM* (1934), p. xii; *P*, p. 112; *OAP*, p. 42; *ISP*, p. 450; *BM*, p. 277 (italics mine).

23. Huxley, "Hypothesis That Animals Are Automata," pp. 241, 240.

24. *MMEE*, p. 62.

25. C. I. Lewis, *An Analysis of Knowledge and Valuation* (La Salle, 1946) p. 1 (italics mine).

26. *EM*, p. 147; *P*, pp. 63–64.

27. *P*, pp. 112.

28. *MMEE*, p. 62.

29. *ISP*, p. 38 (italics mine).

30. *EM*, pp. 10, 86–87, 50.

31. G. A. Miller, Eugene Galanter, and K. H. Pribram, *Plans and the Structure of Behavior* (New York, 1960) p. 62.

32. *BM*, p. 211.

33. Von Uexkull, "The Worlds of Animals and Men," pp. 46–47 (italics mine).

34. R. B. Perry, "The Independent Variability of Purpose and Belief," *Journal of Philosophy*, 18 (1921), p. 175; Charles Taylor, *The Explanation of Behaviour* (London, 1964) p. 24.

35. *EM*, p. 50.

36. R. A. Hinde, "Energy Models of Motivation," *Symposium of the Society for Experimental Biology*, 14 (1960), 199–213; R. A. Hinde, "Unitary Drives," *Animal Behaviour*, 7 (1959), 130–141.

37. R. A. Hinde, *Animal Behavior: A Synthesis of Ethological and Comparative Psychology* (New York, 1966), p. 7.

38. For the relation of the concepts of motive and cause, see N. S. Sutherland, "Motives as Explanations," *Mind*, n.s. 68 (1959), 145–159; R. S. Peters, *The Concept of Motivation* (London, 1958); J. O. Urmson, "Motives and Causes," *Proceedings of the Aristotelian Society*, supplementary 26 (1952), 179–194; A. I. Melden, *Free Action* (London, 1961), ch. ix.

39. William James remarked that "the essential achievement of the will is to *attend* to a difficult object and hold it fast before the mind." William James, *The Principles of Psychology* (New York, 1890), II, 561. Although McDougall agreed with this form of words, he criticized the ideomotor theory as propounded by James, for its neglect of the

concept of motivation. William McDougall, "Motives in the Light of Recent Discussion," *Mind*, n.s. 29 (1920), 277–293.

40. *ISP*, p. 309; *EM*, p. 348.

41. *OP*, p. 259 and n.

42. See Gilbert Ryle, *The Concept of Mind* (London, 1949), esp. ch. v. The distinction between Ryle's dispositions and causes, and the logical relationships between such dispositions and the states of affairs constituting their causal basis ("disposition" in McDougall's sense) are discussed in Brian O'Shaughnessy, "The Powerlessness of Dispositions," *Analysis*, 31 (1970), 1–15; Roger Squires, "Are Dispositions Lost Causes?" *Analysis*, 31 (1970), 15–18.

43. *P*, pp. 82–83;

44. *ISP*, p. 330.

45. See M. L. Minsky, "Matter, Mind, and Models," in *Proceedings of the International Federation of Information Processing Congress*, I (Washington, D.C., 1965), p. 45.

46. *P*, pp. 83–85.

47. *P*, pp. 85–86.

48. See, e.g., Jean Piaget, *The Construction of Reality in the Child* (New York, 1954); J. H. Flavell, *The Developmental Psychology of Jean Piaget* (New York, 1963).

49. For example, the homing of wasps is discussed in *OP*, ch. iii.

50. *OP*, p. 248.

51. *OP*, pp. 235–236, 225.

52. This point is discussed by Gregory, with reference to the importance of analog representations working in real time. R. L. Gregory, "On How So Little Information Controls So Much Behaviour," *Bionics Research Reports* (Edinburgh), no. 1 (1968), pp. 14–15.

53. *OP*, p. 247.

54. *P*, pp. 92, 97; *ISP*, p. 151.

55. George Mandler, "Transfer of Training as a Function of Degree of Response Overlearning," *Journal of Experimental Psychology*, 47 (1954), 411–417; George Mandler, "From Association to Structure," *Psychological Review*, 69 (1962), 415–427; George Mandler and C. K. Kuhlmann, "Proactive and Retroactive Effects of Overlearning," *Journal of Experimental Psychology*, 61 (1961), 76–81.

56. J. S. Bruner, Rose Olver, and P. M. Greenfield, *Studies in Cognitive Growth* (New York, 1966), chs. i, ii.

57. A. R. Luria and F. Ia. Yudovich, *Speech and the Development of Mental Processes in the Child* (London, 1959).

58. *P*, p, 83.

59. K. J. W. Craik, *The Nature of Explanation* (Cambridge, 1943), pp. 51, 55, 56, 99.

60. *BM*, p. 174.

61. M. L. Minsky, "Steps Toward Artificial Intelligence," in E. A. Feigenbaum and Julian Feldman, eds., *Computers and Thought* (New York, 1963), pp. 422, 423, 424.

62. M. L. Minsky and Seymour Papert, *Perceptrons: An Introduction to Computational Geometry* (Cambridge, 1969), esp. pp. 12–14, 73–95, 232–239.

63. See esp. Noam Chomsky, *Aspects of the Theory of Syntax* (Cambridge, 1965).

64. M. B. Clowes, "On Seeing Things," *Journal of Artificial Intelligence*, 1, forthcoming.

65. *BM*, pp. 268–269n.

66. I. E. Sutherland, *Sketchpad—A Man-Machine Graphical Communication System* (Cambridge, 1963).

67. Personal communication, M. B. Clowes.

68. In discussing how to find criteria for assessing the adequacy of putative (machine) descriptions of line drawings, Clowes relies on Chomsky's methodology. That is, he tries to select descriptive schemata that accurately convey our own intuitions about structure, and these intuitions are to be exposed by our recognition of visual "paraphrase," "anomaly," and "ambiguity." A radically different approach to the assessment of adequacy would presumably be required if the primitive objects and relations utilized by the program were radically different from man's. See Clowes, "On Seeing Things."

69. N. S. Sutherland, "Outlines of a Theory of Visual Pattern Recognition in Animals and Man," *Proceedings of the Royal Society B.*, 171 (1968), p. 316. For a general discussion of the concept of cerebral models, with an application of the concept to various sensory processes in the octopus, see J. Z. Young, *A Model of the Brain* (Oxford, 1964).

70. If one had designed and manufactured the system oneself, there would be no problem in knowing whether it incorporated anything describable as a "model." But the recognition of a system as truly intensional on the basis of observed behavior alone would require certain hypotheses or assumptions concerning what could count as "appropriate response" on its part.

71. *MMEE*, p. 196.

72. See Fred Attneave, "Some Informational Aspects of Visual Perception," *Psychological Review*, 61 (1954), 183–193; H. B. Barlow, "The Coding of Sensory Messages," in W. H. Thorpe and O. L. Zangwill, eds., *Current Problems in Animal Behaviour* (Cambridge, 1961), pp. 331–360.

73. *P*, p. 78.

74. M. R. Fernald, "The Diagnosis of Mental Imagery," *Psychological Monographs*, 14, no. 58 (February 1912), esp. pp. 70–78.

75. M. B. Clowes, "Pictorial Relationships—A Syntactic Approach," in Bernard Meltzer and Donald Michie, eds., *Machine Intelligence*, vol. IV (Edinburgh, 1969), pp. 361–383.

76. Personal communication, M. B. Clowes.

77. *P*, p. 54. Italics mine.

78. See, e.g., William Kneale and A. N. Prior, "Intentionality and Intensionality," *Proceedings of the Aristotelian Society*, supplementary 42 (1968), p. 73: "The entertainment of propositions is essential to thinking."

79. Various disorders of the body image following disease of the parietal lobes are described in Macdonald Critchley, *The Parietal Lobes* (London, 1953), ch. viii.

80. *OP*, pp. 36–37; Taylor, *Explanation of Behaviour*, p. 25n.

81. R. M. Chisholm, "Intentionality," in Paul Edwards, ed., *The Encyclopedia of Philosophy* (New York, 1967), IV, p. 203; M. A. Boden, "Intentionality and Physical Systems," *Philosophy of Science*, 37 (1970), esp. pp. 209–213.

82. H. L. Gelernter, "Realization of a Geometry-Theorem Proving Machine," in Feigenbaum and Feldman, eds., *Computers and Thought*, pp. 134–152; Allen Newell, J. C. Shaw, and H. A. Simon, "Empirical Explorations with the Logic Theory Machine," *Proceedings of the Western Joint Computer Conference*, 15 (1957), 218–239.

83. It follows that careful attention to everyday psychological concepts is likely to suggest psychological distinctions and hypotheses that may be of value in more theoretical contexts. To this extent, McDougall's unself-conscious use of ordinary language and Fritz Heider's deliberate adoption of "naive" terminology may be defended. Only detailed analysis of specific everyday concepts and their various neologistic "equivalents" in specialist psychologies could decide whether ordinary language is superior in every way. McDougall evidently felt that it is not, since his theoretical use of "motive," for example, corresponds with only one of the senses in common use. Were all the other senses to be similarly distinguished, they could then be accepted as clearly different terms within a superficially neologistic theory. E. C. Tolman's theory provides an example of the systematic definition of new technical terms on the basis of "everyday phenomenology" and familiar psychological vocabulary.

IX. Purpose and Mind

1. *OAP*, p. 519.

2. *OAP*, p. 48.

3. *P*, pp. 69–70.

4. *P*, p. 70; *OAP*, p. 526.

5. William McDougall, "Autobiography," in Clark Murchison, ed., *A History of Psychology in Autobiography*, vol. I (Worcester, 1930), p. 211.

6. *ISP*, pp. 157, 160.

7. See G. W. Allport, *Becoming: Basic Considerations for a Psychology of Personality* (New Haven, 1955); A. H. Maslow, *Toward a Psychology of Being* (Princeton, 1962), p. 188n.

8. *EM*, p. 379.

9. M. J. Rosenberg, "Simulated Man and the Humanistic Criticism," in S. S. Tomkins and Samuel Messick, eds., *Computer Simulation of Personality: Frontier of Psychological Research* (New York, 1963), p. 122.

10. *OP*, p. 36.

11. See, e.g., William McDougall, *National Welfare and National Decay* (London, 1921). McDougall's eugenics were not directed merely to avoiding inherited disease, but also to making America "safe for democracy." According to McDougall, this program involved the recognition that "the social stratification which exists in modern industrial communities is positively correlated with a corresponding stratification of innate moral and intellectual quality"; further, he saw the recent flood of immigration and the colored population as threatening "the deterioration of the innate qualities of the [American] population" (p. v). The contrast between such an attitude and the egalitarian implications of the environmentalist behaviorism of the time is clear, and it doubtless contributed to the rancor of the debate in which McDougall was involved during the 1920s and 1930s. See William McDougall, "Autobiography," p. 213.

12. At the most detailed level, a man's "mental structure" involves all the particular experiences he has had throughout his life. It is logically possible that two men might have "the same" mental structure even when described at this level. This would mean that their spatial paths through life had been identical, that they were temporally separated only very slightly, and that it had never chanced, for example, that a brick fell from a roof hitting the man who happened to be passing through a narrow doorway first, but missing his "mental twin" passing through immediately behind him. After such an experience the two men would no longer be mental twins, in the inordinately strict sense in question here.

13. *ISP*, pp. 204–205.

14. Evidence that the experimenter's expectations may influence the behavior of his subjects—whether animal or human—is reviewed in Robert Rosenthal, "The Effect of the Experimenter on the

Result of Psychological Research," in B. A. Maher, ed., *Progress in Experimental Personality Research*, vol. I (New York, 1964), pp. 79–114.

15. This stochastic model of nervous function replaces the "telephone exchange" model, which was based on C. S. Sherrington's experimental work on the reflex. New experimental techniques (in particular, the use of microelectrodes capable of recording the firing of a single cell in the unanesthetized animal) have shown that the predictability of response of gross nerve trunks in the typical Sherrington experimental situation coexists with an unpredictability at the more detailed neuronal level. See B. D. Burns, *The Uncertain Nervous System* (London, 1968), esp. chs. i–iv.

16. Atomic physics can provide reliable prediction of individual events. Subatomic physics provides only statistical prediction of subatomic events.

17. *OP*, p. 40; *BM*, p. 269n.

18. There are many different types of aphasia, in some of which linguistic comprehension is unaffected, but spoken or written verbal expression is faulty, or even absent. Such patients could answer questions about their introspectively available consciousness by means of an arbitrary sign (such as biting their thumb for Yes), even though they could not formulate sentences expressing their knowledge. Such behavior would, of course, involve the use of language, since the questions answered must themselves be expressed verbally and interpreted as linguistic utterances by the patient.

19. See Gilbert Ryle, *The Concept of Mind* (London, 1949), pp. 195–198. Minsky claims that "there is no paradox even in a machine's having a model of itself complete in all detail. For example, it is possible to construct a Turing machine that can print out an entire description of itself and also execute an arbitrarily complicated computation, so that the machine is not expending all its structure on its description." Marvin Minsky, "Matter, Mind, and Models," in *Proceedings of the International Federation of Information Processing Congress*, I (Washington, D.C., 1965), p. 48.

20. In the terminology of monads, this claim of McDougall's means that the purposes of the dominant monad (the dominant self) are conscious. McDougall's doctrine of monadic dissociation was not developed until the 1920s, well after he wrote *An Introduction to Social Psychology*.

21. *MMEE*, p. 61.

22. *ISP*, p. 309; *MMEE*, p. 62.

23. William McDougall, "Autobiography," p. 209.

24. William James, *The Principles of Psychology* (New York, 1890), II, 583–584.

Index